THE LOCATOR

The Locator

Troy Dunn

and the staff of the International Locator, Inc./BigHugs.com

DOUBLEDAY

New York London Toronto Sydney Auckland

A MAIN STREET BOOK

PUBLISHED BY DOUBLEDAY
a division of Random House, Inc.
1540 Broadway, New York, New York 10036

MAIN STREET BOOKS, DOUBLEDAY, and the portrayal of a building with a tree are trademarks of Doubleday, a division of Random House, Inc.

Book design by Richard Oriolo

LIBRARY OF CONGRESS CATALOGING-IN-PUBLICATION DATA

Dunn, Troy.
The Locator / Troy Dunn and the staff of the International Locator, Inc. / BigHugs.com
p. cm.
1. Missing persons—Investigation—United States.
I. International Locator, Inc. II. Title.
HV6762.U5D86 2000
363.2'336—dc21 99-37144
CIP

ISBN 0-385-49452-1

Printed in the United States of America
February 2000
First Edition

1 2 3 4 5 6 7 8 9 10

To all the people on our staff who
so diligently have dedicated
their lives to helping others.

Thank you!

DID is a word of achievement.
WON'T is a word of retreat.
MIGHT is a word of bereavement.
CAN'T is a word of defeat.
OUGHT is a word of duty.
TRY is a word each hour.
WILL is a word of beauty.
CAN is a word of power.

—ANONYMOUS

C O N T E N T S

Introduction

Congratulations!

The book you are now holding contains the keys you need to find anybody, anywhere. Reading this book marks the beginning of an exciting journey, one that will end at the doorstep of the special someone you've been searching for, or thinking about, or imagining, all these years.

You may be an adoptee seeking your birth parents; a parent looking for children you gave up for adoption; a romantic searching for a lost love; a mother tracking down a deadbeat dad; a veteran locating military buddies. No matter who you are, no matter whom you're looking for, *The Locator* will show you what to do—even if you know *absolutely nothing* about the person you want to find!

How can this be possible? And how can we be so certain the techniques in this book will work?

We at the International Locator, Inc./BigHugs.com have successfully reunited *thousands* of friends and families, using the very techniques described in this book. In these pages we have given you the strategies, the methods, the information, the documents: everything you will need to complete your search, no matter what kind of search it is. We've explored, between the covers of this book, virtually every scenario you could possibly run into—and many you probaby won't. We've even interviewed people just like you, who've searched for and found their missing loved ones, so that you could see firsthand how they did it and how it turned out.

The president of the International Locator, Inc./BigHugs.com, Troy Dunn, comes from a family with adoptees, as do many of the employees here. We personally know how wonderful adoption can be, but we also understand the mysteries it creates. After our own reunions with our lost family members, we dedicated our lives to helping others break down the walls and finally get their own answers to a lifetime of questions. As we continued our work with adoptees and birth parents, we realized that the powerful techniques we had pioneered would also be used to find anyone who is missing! Now we search for anyone anywhere, for any reason. And our successes have been astonishing, even to us!

In a nutshell, we've done everything possible to make your reunion happen as quickly and simply as it can. All you have to do is read this book. The entire package is designed so you shouldn't need any outside help; however, our consultation line is always open, just in case you get stuck or have a question (see Appendix 1 for details on how to reach us).

But before you turn the page and begin your journey, please make note of our one request. When you've gotten to the end of the book, put the strategies in motion, and found whomever you're looking for, please drop us a card and a photo after the reunion. We have walls in our offices dedicated to reunion photos, and we'd love yours to be on it.

Follow your heart, know that this *will* happen for you, and *never* give up. Your reunion day is closer than you think!

O N E

Getting Your Feet Wet

Here is what you need to do in order to search successfully:

Be persistent.

Be patient.

Be creative.

Turn over every stone—no piece of information is too small; nothing is insignificant.

Keep these four things in mind at all times. You have to view your search as a process of elimination. When you acquire an important document only to discover that it contains no new information, you are still one step closer to your reunion: You've eliminated one more possibility and narrowed your search effectively. If you've tracked your subject down, located his or her phone number, and made that final call—only to discover that the name is the same but the person is someone else entirely—you're still a step closer: That's another lead checked off, another avenue exhausted. You have to keep at it and stay positive. With persistence, patience, creativity, and attention to detail, you'll eventually find your person. Trust us, we've done it thousands of times.

Start with a Name

There are two parts to every search. The first part is getting the name of the person you are looking for; the second part is actually looking for (and locating) the person. If you are trying to find a long-lost relative, an old friend, or anyone you have previously known and since lost contact with, you probably already have his or her current or previous name. This means that you've won half the battle before you've even begun!

If you are adopted, you probably do not know the name or names of your birth parents, and your search will have to start at the very beginning. With that difference in mind, this first chapter provides two overviews: first, an overview of the basic approach when looking for someone whose name you already know; second, an overview of the basic approach when looking for an adoptee or birth parents.

Throughout the book, and throughout your entire search, keep these words in mind: The easiest way to move forward in locating people is to go backward in time, tracing them from their beginnings. This is the first principle of locating. As you will see, the fastest way to find people is generally to go back to the family, friends, and places they knew earlier in their life. Of course, it isn't always as easy as it sounds to track down this kind of information, but *The Locator* will help you go backward in time in both the simple cases and the hard cases.

Searches: The General Approach

As mentioned above, some parts of *The Locator* are written from the perspective of the adoptee or birth parent, since those are the worst-case scenarios, where little or no information is available. If you are embarking on a nonadoptive search, you'll have to pick and choose which information applies to your case and which doesn't. As you read this book, however, you'll find that almost all the techniques are the same. We strongly suggest that you read everything in the book, because you can find ideas and techniques from all sorts of searches that will apply to your own unique situation.

Nonadoptive searches usually involve one or more of the following: old friends and relatives, lost loves, deadbeat dads, missing children, and people who are or were in the military. Brief introductions to each situation's specific techniques are covered in chapters four through seven, but the general techniques from all of those chapters apply to your case as well, no matter who you are or whom you're looking for.

It will be hard for you to imagine just how much of a head start you have over adoptees and birth parents, who usually don't even know the names of the people they're looking for. However, there are some cases where you may be looking for an old friend, a family member, or a person important to you, whose name you don't know. Maybe your mother never told you your father's name. Maybe you're working on a family tree and you know you have a second cousin but can't find any references to her in your family's albums or files. Maybe you want to find a doctor or fireman who helped you once but never knew who the person was. There are thousands of possible scenarios where you may not know the person's name; in those cases, you'll want to follow some of the adoption techniques as well.

We also suggest that you look over the "useful terminology" section on page 4. Most of the specialized language refers to adoptions, but some of it will explain things you'll need to know about in a nonadoptive search too. You should at least remember that there's a glossary there so you can refer to it later on if you come across a term you don't understand.

Adoptive Searches: The General Approach

Every search is different. Right now you are in a unique situation, looking for a unique person. However, it is also true that every search is similar to all the searches that have gone before it, and there is much to learn from the experiences of other people. Learning from their achievements is what this book is all about.

There are numerous ways to approach any given search, but in all cases, the first step is to find the birth name of the adoptee and the full names (or partial names if the full names are unavailable) of the birth parents. Later on, we'll go over many of the ways you can track down these names and tell you what to do after you know the names.

But for now, instead of moving forward to tell you what steps you'll be taking in the future, let's move backward to the adoption itself. It's important that you have a real-world framework for locating your child or birth parent, to give a sense of order to something that most people see as a random series of events. We can't stress this enough: You're not alone in your search; many others have made the same journey, and, with persistence, they have succeeded. You will too.

Over the last several years at the International Locator, Inc./BigHugs.com, working daily with literally thousands of birth parents and adoptees, we've learned that almost everyone remembers or views their adoption in the same way.

For a birth parent, this was a very emotional and confusing time. Because of the nature of what was happening (and, unfortunately, because of the stigma attached to the typical pregnancy that results in adoption), many birth parents remember only glimpses of what actually happened. A good percentage was so upset over having to give up their child that they honestly don't remember signing relinquishment papers. If any of this sounds familiar, don't feel bad—it only shows you're human.

However, as a birth parent doing your search, it is important to keep in mind that the strength of these emotions, mixed with the years that have passed, can sometimes hide or distort memories, so it will be important to take some extra time when, under the guidance of the next chapter, you write down your memories of the event.

The vast majority of adoptees look on their adoption as a one-time event they can't possibly remember. What little they do know usually comes from a few brief, scattered conversations with their adoptive parents. For those of you who are adoptees, it is important to get a solid handle on the series of events that resulted in your adoption, so that you can get a clear picture of where the records are—and how to start looking for them.

Useful Terminology

Before you begin your journey toward a happy reunion, you must familiarize yourself with the terms and buzzwords used in these searches. We understand your excitement and your strong desire to jump ahead to the meat and potatoes of the location techniques. If you do, though, you will find yourself feeling like a visitor in a foreign country—unable to speak the language or communicate with the locals to get what you came for. So take a few minutes, read through this list of words and definitions, and refer to this section often. An important part of your search will involve writing letters, and you will need to use this language properly in all your correspondences.

adoptee — a person who has been adopted

adoption decree — the final order from the courts declaring the adoption to be legal; held by the birth parents

adoptive parent — the person(s) who legally assumes parental rights and responsibilities for a child

agency adoption — an adoption coordinated by a licensed state or private adoption agency (usually this type of adoption requires detailed records of everyone involved)

background check — a brief investigation, usually run by professionals, into sensitive areas of a person's life: his or her assets, liens, employment history, licenses, etc.

birth certificate — There is more than one kind of birth certificate:
Original: the legal document issued at birth, identifying the birth family and the adoptee's original name; usually the original birth

certificate is sealed in the court records when the adoption is complete (i.e., finalized)
Amended: An amended birth certificate is issued when the adoption is finalized. It replaces the original birth information with the adoptive information and becomes the adoptee's legal birth certificate

birth family all genetic, or blood, relatives (parents, grandparents, aunts, uncles, siblings, etc.)

birth parents the people who conceived and/or gave birth to a child and later surrendered their parental rights

contact direct communication at the end of a search (written letters, telephone conversations, face-to-face reunions, etc.)

court of jurisdiction the court or legal entity that presided over the adoption; typically the court that presided over the adoption maintains control over all court-related documents (some states have more than one such entity)

decree the court-issued document that finalizes the adoption; it legally transfers parental rights and responsibilities to the adoptive parents and changes the adoptee's birth name to the name of the adoptive parents

documentation material evidence or proof gathered during the search process (names, addresses, phone numbers, official records, correspondence, etc.)

Family History Centers genealogical archives maintained by the Mormon church; these centers are usually the best and most extensive records available

foundling an abandoned child of unknown parents

identifying information any background data (such as a full name, a social security number, an address) that allows a searcher to directly identify or locate the person being sought

independent adoption an adoption arranged by a doctor or a lawyer, or an agreement directly between the birth family and the adoptive parents

interlocutory papers the papers from the temporary decree; these are issued immediately, and are in effect until the relinquishment papers and adoption decree are issued

intermediary — a third party go-between in any phase of a search; often, intermediaries are used when either party needs information and wishes to remain anonymous (some states have court-appointed intermediaries)

legal notice — an announcement of an event or legal action. To meet the requirements of the law in some proceedings, legal notices must be printed in a newspaper

nonidentifying information — any background data (such as height, age, educational background, hair color, religious affiliation) that do not allow a searcher to directly identify or locate the person being sought

open adoption — an adoption in which birth and adoptive families may have varying degrees of contact or ongoing communication

open records — records to which access is not restricted; primarily, records available to both the adoptive and birth families

petition — There are two types of petitions: (1) A formal request by the prospective adoptive parent(s) to the court of jurisdiction for legal custody and full guardianship of a child, and (2) The process of applying to a court or governmental body for access to adoption records

private adoption — see "independent adoption"

probate records — documents kept at the county level that record matters of inheritance and estate settlement

relinquishment — see "surrender"

relinquishment papers — the final order from the courts declaring the adoption to be legal; held by the birth parents

reunion — the bringing together of parties separated by adoption or otherwise

reunion registry — a state or private system through which separated family members may be registered, matched, and reunited

SASE — "Self-Addressed Stamped Envelope." An SASE should accompany all requests for written information

sealed records — documents and files restricted by law or policy from view and/or duplication by the public (see "open records" for comparison)

search the process of investigation and documentation that leads to the location or knowledge of separated family members

significant others siblings, grandparents, aunts, uncles, spouses, and other extended family members

social history often adoption records include "social histories," which describe people in terms of their number of siblings, names of parents and grandparents, occupations, education levels, religions, special interests, and hobbies

surrender the birth parents' signing of documents to terminate their parental rights and responsibilities for the child being given up for adoption (also referred to as relinquishment)

triad The three categories of persons directly involved in an adoption: (1) The adoptee, (2) The birth parents (or parent), (3) The adoptive parents (or parent)

VIN vehicle identification number

vital statistics birth, marriage, divorce, and death records. This information is usually open to the public

How the Records Are Kept

To begin your search, you'll first try to locate the records of adoption. Below, we'll give you an overview of the different kinds of records that may be involved; in later chapters we describe how you can obtain copies of these records.

Typically, both agency and independent adoptions proceed along the six steps outlined below, and records may exist from each step. If you find that these guidelines were not followed in your particular case—and that is rare—simply call our consultant hotline (see Appendix 1) or contact a search and support group located in the area where the birth took place (see Chapter Three). Either source should be able to put you back on the right track.

The six stages of most adoptions are:

Pregnancy

In many cases, the record-keeping process begins at this stage. If, for instance, the birth mother was unwed and knew she would be unable to provide for the child, chances are a doctor, lawyer, or social agency became involved early on. If so, records of the birth and of the prospective adoptive families may have been kept through the entire process.

Birth

By and large, most adoptive births took place either in a hospital or in a home for unwed mothers. Both of these institutions typically keep admittance, medical, and delivery records, which contain information regarding family members, various medical issues, and possibly a birth certificate bearing the birth parents' names. Even if the child was transferred to an orphanage or social agency immediately after birth, some documents concerning the relinquishment should exist.

Relinquishment or surrender

During the relinquishment, the birth mother (and possibly birth father) signs papers to surrender the legal rights and responsibilities of her parenthood to someone else. In an agency adoption, custody was probably transferred to either a state or private agency, which became the legal guardian until a suitable adoptive family was selected. Private adoptions, on the other hand, usually involve an attorney, who transfers custody from the birth parents directly to the adoptive parents.

Placement

Private adoptions and agency adoptions have different placement procedures. In a private adoption, the birth parents may know the names of the adoptive parents and may even have met them face-to-face. In an agency adoption, the agency selects a suitable family from screened and approved clients. Although agencies are required to keep complete files on both sets of parents and on the adoptee, they take great pains to keep identifying information away from the families involved (see the "useful terminology" section on page 4 if you have forgotten what exactly constitutes "identifying information").

Petitioning

This is the last stage before the adoption becomes final. At this point, the adoptive parents formally request custody of the adoptee through the court of jurisdiction. Records of this action are filed either separately or with the remainder of the adoption papers. These records almost always provide some useful information.

Finalization

The court hands down a final decree granting the adoptive parents full and legal custody of the adoptee. An amended birth certificate is then issued bearing the names of the adoptive parents and the new name of the adoptee. The original birth certificate is sealed in the court records.

Now you know the stages of the adoption process, and you have a feel for the variety of records that may exist pertaining to your case. Don't worry about the official terminology for the different kinds of paperwork. For one thing, record-keeping will vary from state to state. And at this point you need only a basic overview; in later chapters we go over specific strategies for identifying and obtaining the proper records.

Your Basic Rights

If you have made any attempt to find an adoptee or birth parent, undoubtedly you've run into all sorts of barriers. Many times you've probably felt it was hopeless, and that you had no legal right to the information you are seeking. Not so! In many cases, had you been aware of your rights and the proper ways to exercise them, you could have received more help than you realized.

Each state originates and enforces laws regarding adoption and its related records. Their laws are wide and varied, with little uniformity.* In all the laws there are gray areas that may require the officials you contact to make personal judgment calls. Therefore, we (with the assistance of many search experts from across the country) have compiled a detailed state-by-state directory of specific laws, along with the names and addresses of organizations that can help you in your search. When used in combination with the checklists and guidelines provided in later sections, you will be armed with the knowledge and insight necessary to conduct an effective search.

As of August 1994, three states—Kansas, Hawaii, and Alaska—have passed laws requiring open adoption records. Most of the remaining forty-seven states follow a vague guideline of withholding any information that could be considered identifying.

So what are your rights? Both the federal government and various federal agencies probably have files on you. While you do not have the right to see all these files, you can see some of them if you request them. This policy came into being under the Freedom of Information Act (5 U.S.C. 552) and the Privacy Act of 1974 (5 U.S.C. 552A).

According to the Freedom of Information Act, the federal government must release to an individual, upon request, certain information (in accordance with published regulations) pertaining to that individual and filed in federal agency or department records. Once a request is received, the agency involved has ten working days to decide whether to release the information, and then must immediately notify the inquiring party of its decision (see Chapter Eight, "Requesting Information from the Federal Government," on page 98 for a further explanation of this process).

* We at the International Locator, Inc./BigHugs.com are personally committed to fighting for open records in the United States and have commissioned a full-time lobbyist to begin the long battle of educating our state and federal politicians on the necessity for open records.

The Privacy Act of 1974 also provides for individual access to information held in government files. It primarily regulates the federal government, dictating how it can collect and use information on its citizens. Normally, this act cannot be used to protect the privacy of deceased individuals; however, it is up to the person making the request to provide proof of death.

Your search will start by targeting the institutions relevant to your case and writing letters to them with requests for information. When writing these letters to federal agencies, it will probably be beneficial to mention your rights under both laws (more on this in Chapter Three).

As with all searches, the most important trait to exhibit will be persistence. Keep looking, stay optimistic, and never give up!

T W O

Your Personal Search Planner

In order to find anyone, the first thing you need to do is to get—*and stay*—organized. You must keep accurate records. Every search is a building process, not unlike putting together a puzzle. You will undoubtedly come into contact with people, documents, and bits of information that may seem useless and unimportant, but you should keep track of every detail, no matter how insignificant it seems. Nothing is too insignificant to save. Believe us. There may come a time when one of these unimportant details turns out to be the missing piece you need to put everything together.

Nothing is more frustrating than knowing you had something once, and being unable to remember where you put it. This chapter teaches you how to avoid that problem entirely. After reading this chapter and following its techniques, not only will you always have a handle on where things are, you will also have a map of your entire search, and a compass that will keep you pointed in the right direction every step of the way.

Always, *always* make working copies of any information and documentation you find. *Don't* keep original letters or documents lying around your desk; don't *refer* to originals; *don't file* originals; *don't use originals for anything*. (Look at all those italicized words—can't you tell how serious we are about this?) As soon as you get a letter or a document, *copy it*! Copy it, put the original in a safe place, where it cannot be damaged or lost—placing it in a safe deposit box is ideal. *Now,* with the original safely locked up, you can use the "working copy" you made and do whatever you want with it. You can put the working copy in the filing cabinet, you can keep the working copy in your desk, you can index it in your search workspace, you can add it to your notebooks—anything you want, because you'll never lose the original.

Being organized can be tedious, and it can be annoying. But it's the only way you'll be successful in your search. If you're serious about finding this person, get serious about organization.

Source and Document Checklist

There are two reasons to keep a source and document checklist (a copy of the actual checklist is printed below—we'll get to that in a minute). The first reason is to keep a running total of which documents and which pieces of information you have requested and received. The second is to give yourself a useful outline of which sources have already been explored, and where to turn when a particular avenue seems exhausted.

We suggest copying the source and document checklist from this book. Copy it rather than leave it in the book, because you'll want to keep the checklist with your other logs and not have it stuck between these covers. Also, as your search progresses and you discover new avenues to pursue, you will want to add documents and sources that we have not anticipated. Every search is different—this book, at best, can give you ideas for where to start. When you get into the thick of your search, you'll have to rely on your own creativity to guide you.

At this point, don't worry about understanding what all of these documents are for, or how to get them. That's not important yet. What's important is that you recognize the need to keep an accurate list of every document you've tried to access, every document you've seen a copy of, and the dates you obtained each piece of information.

A quick explanation of the columns.

Category/Item lists possible sources. Not all these documents will apply to your search, but the average person who exists in this country has generated most of these documents at one time or another. Finding any one of them may give you a clue as to where that person is now, or may give you the name of a person who will have more information about your search.

Source of information is the agency, department, church, school, or person you wrote to in order to obtain a copy of the document.

Date requested refers to the date you wrote the letter requesting information (you will, of course, keep copies of every letter you write!).

Date received—you'll fill in this column when you receive the record you were looking for. Sometimes you'll forget you've asked for something—this will help to remind you which document requests to follow up.

Source and Document Checklist

Category/Item	Source of information	Date requested	Date received
Personal and Family Memorabilia			
list of my personal memories of person			
interviews with family members			
photographs			
scrapbooks, family records			
medical and legal records			
Public Resources			
Library of Congress			
National Archives			
local libraries			
historical libraries			
genealogical societies			
state and federal census bureaus			
newspapers			

Category/Item	Source of information	Date requested	Date received
telephone directories			
city directories			
cross-street directories			
postal records			
voting records			
Real Estate Records			
situs file			
grantor/grantee index			
abstracts			
property tax records			
rental records			
Employment and Trade Records			
employment applications			
interviews with coworkers			
payroll records			
work histories			

Category/Item	Source of information	Date requested	Date received
professional licenses			
labor union records			
accomplishment announcements			
Educational Records			
enrollment records			
attendance records			
accomplishment records			
yearbooks			
graduation records			
census records			
alumni foundation records			
school newspapers			
fraternities/sororities			

Category/Item	Source of information	Date requested	Date received
Reunion Registries			
individual state reunion registries			
international soundex (ISRR)			
search and support group registries			
Motor Vehicle Records			
driver's licenses (past)			
driver's licenses (present)			
motor vehicle registrations			
license plate numbers and VINs			
marine license/boat registrations			
pilot license/plane registrations			
Marriage Records			
wedding announcements			
license applications			
ceremony records			
church records			

Category/Item	Source of information	Date requested	Date received
public indexes			
marriage license			
state and archive records			
religious records of engagement			
public announcement of engagement			
Divorce Records			
petition for divorce			
public announcements			
property records			
financial arrangements			
divorce decree			
religious records			
divorce indexes			
Death Records			
death certificate			
medical records			

Category/Item	Source of information	Date requested	Date received
insurance records			
funeral home records			
cemetery records			
obituaries			
probate records			
legal and public announcements			
wills			
neighbors and friends			
religious records of death			
Religious Records			
birth records			
baptismals/christenings			
attendance records			
marriage records			
divorce records			
death records			

Category/Item	Source of information	Date requested	Date received
weekly program records			
financial ledgers			
Sunday school records			
group and/or family portraits			
Hospital Records			
admittance records			
medical backgrounds			
delivery room records			
statement of birth			
nursery reports			
financial arrangements			
discharge records			
attending physician files			
Birth Records			
original birth certificate			
hospital statement of birth			

Category/Item	Source of information	Date requested	Date received
christenings/baptismals			
birth announcements (news)			
Adoption Agency Records			
original birth certificate			
amended birth certificate			
medical histories			
case studies and profiles			
relinquishment papers			
baptismal certificate			
legal agreements			
adoption petition			
adoption decree			
follow-up reports			
court records			
request for name change			

Search Maps

Your search will generate hundreds of pieces of information. Forgetting where to find a specific piece of information is one of the most common problems you'll face. Since many items (dates, names, etc.) will appear in several places, knowing where to turn can get fairly confusing unless you have a solid reference to follow.

That's where your search maps come in. During each stage of your search, you'll be looking for specific items. Your search maps allow you to identify quickly which documents and sources contain the desired information. It may seem silly now, but your search will probably produce more documents and records and copies and pieces of information than you could ever imagine—and eventually, finding an important fact will become a nightmare if you don't have a list of which facts appear on which documents. Trust us.

You'll make the search maps yourself. The "map" is really nothing more than a regular sheet of paper. Down the length of the paper on the left-hand side, you'll list each document you have obtained. Going across the width of the paper, you'll list the pieces of information contained on that document. As you get each new document, make a new entry describing what is on the document. Later, you'll be able to scan your search map quickly to find the information you're looking for. Believe us—it's going to be a lot easier than pawing through twenty or thirty documents and trying to decipher the fine print on each one.

Conversation Log

It has been estimated that most people remember less than half of what they see and only about thirty percent of what they hear. However, they remember more than seventy percent of what they see *and* hear. That is why we strongly recommend keeping a conversation log *and* tape recording of all your telephone calls (within the limits of the law).

A conversation log can be any notebook, tablet, or binder. Since you will be talking to many people and making valuable contacts during your search, it is of the utmost importance to maintain an accurate log of all the telephone calls you make and receive. Each page of your conversation log will serve as a record of a phone call. At the top of each page of the log, you will write down the date and time of the call, the organization or person you called (or who called you), the name of the person you talked to (it is always important to get the full name of the person you are talking with, especially when you are dealing with a large organization), and his or her phone number.

On the rest of the page, you should note important details of each call. Was a particular individual helpful or unhelpful? Might he or she be a source of information in the future? Did you learn any details about this person personally? In many instances, remembering someone's name and referring to a previous conversation will make the person feel more comfortable with you the next time you call. It can also save you the time and expense of trying to re-explain your situation to another person, who may not be as sympathetic.

Obviously anything you learn about the person you're looking for must be written down in this log too, so you'll remember who told you the information and when you obtained it. If there is a need for you to follow up on anything and get back to the person you spoke to, write that down as well. And if the person you're talking to is going to get back to you, write down what he's doing for you and when he says he'll get back to you. That way, you won't forget to follow up.

It will also be to your advantage to record your telephone conversations. This can be done quite easily by obtaining an ordinary tape recorder and a telephone pickup jack, which usually costs around five dollars and can be purchased at almost any electronics store. It's completely legal, although some states require you to inform the other party that they are being recorded.

Try to record every telephone conversation you make in connection with your search. During conversations, it's easy to get caught up in the moment and forget to listen to what is being said. When this happens, you will undoubtedly miss bits of information that would be lost if not recorded. Once the tape is played back, you will be astonished at the details you missed the first time around.

Even if you are tape recording your phone conversations, you *must still* take detailed notes in your conversation log. Why? Because if you forget a piece of information, it's not going to be any fun to go back and listen to thirty-seven taped phone conversations to try to find the information again. It will be much easier to flip through your conversation log and find the relevant fact, and then, after you know which conversation the fact came from, refer to the specific tape for more details.

Correspondence Log

The correspondence log is much like the conversation log, only it keeps track of the letters you write and receive rather than the phone calls.

Because many of the offices you will be writing to are either government bureaucracies or large private agencies, they can be slow to respond. We show you how to avoid these kinds of delays in chapter eight, but it's still necessary to know exactly where you are at all times during your search, to keep things moving in a timely manner.

As with the conversation log, any notebook or binder will do for your correspondence log, although we strongly recommend that you keep separate books (in separate colors) for each kind of log, so that you don't get them mixed up.

Divide each page of your correspondence log in half by drawing a line straight down the middle of the paper from top to bottom. At the top of the left side, write "Correspondence." At the top of the right side, write "Response." Now, at the top of each page on the correspondence side write the date you sent or received each letter, whom the letter was from or to (both organization name and individual name), the subject of the correspondence, the method of correspondence—first class, return receipt requested, certified mail, or any of the overnight services. On the "Response" side, write the date you received a response (if the letter on the correspondence side was *from* you) or the date you sent a response (if the letter on the correspondence side was *to* you).

On the rest of the page, make notes of any significant facts or details you learned as a result of this correspondence. Once again, this is not meant to replace the correspondence itself, nor should you ever, under any circumstances, throw out copies of your letters or the letters you receive. You aren't keeping this log to replace your copies of correspondence; you're keeping it so you can refer to it later on and speedily determine which letter contains what information.

Library Log

As you will see in later sections, libraries will be invaluable sources for your search. As a result, it is extremely important to keep accurate records of everything you come across in the library. Your library log will allow you to record important reference data, such as authors, publishers, page numbers, identification numbers, and brief descriptions of vital information.

The library log can be any notebook, which you'll take with you every time you go to a library during your search. Across the top of each page in the notebook, you'll keep a record of the name and location of the library you're visiting, the librarian's name, the date, the title of the reference book you have found helpful, any reference numbers associated with that book at that library, and the author or publisher of the reference. On the page itself, you should copy down the useful information and the page numbers where you found the information. Even if you are making copies of the reference pages on the library's copy machine, you should still keep accurate records in the library log. It will be much easier to locate a piece of information by referring to your library log than by plowing through all the copies you've made from various reference books.

Progress Journal

In addition to tracking specific details, it is also helpful to keep a record of your daily thoughts and activities, just as you would in a personal diary. Your progress journal will serve as the diary of your search. Reviewing it from time to time will almost always provide new ideas and food for thought, and will undoubtedly open new doors and avenues to success.

At the end of each day you spend searching, write down what you have achieved, what you have not achieved, any new sources you found, any costs you incurred, any important names or events you discovered, what your hopes are, what you plan to do next, how you feel, and so on. This is not a touchy-feely exercise that you can consider optional to your search; it is a necessary aid to processing your goals and your ideas. It may seem dumb at first, but you have to trust us: Eventually the progress journal will become an invaluable resource to you during your quest.

Initial Information Reports (for adoptees only)

If you are an adoptee, this is where your search will begin. Buy yet another notebook (searching for missing people is great for the notebook industry). This is your memory notebook. You need to find a quiet place, give yourself plenty of time, and do what you need to do to insure that you won't be interrupted. Take this book—your memory notebook—and a pen. Nothing else. What you're about to do will be done entirely from your own memories, without any outside help. There will be plenty of time to refer to documents and family members later.

Don't get discouraged if you know very little. It's unusual to know more than your own date and place of birth. The only source of knowledge for most adoptees is what their adoptive parents told them as they were growing up.

The two purposes of this memory log are to create a list of everyone who may know something about your adoption and to write down every shred of information you can remember. Be sure to include any casual remarks you may have heard over the years. The important thing is to write down everything you remember. At this point, you have no idea of what is important.

Okay, take out your memory log, which at this point is nothing more than an ordinary blank notebook. Copy each of the questions below in your notebook, then write out as much of an answer as you can manage, *completely* from your own memories.

1. Was I named? What was my original name?
2. What have I heard about my birth parents?

3. How old were they when they had me?

4. Where was I born?

5. What was the name of my adoption agency?

6. What is the name of the doctor who delivered me?

7. What are the names of every person I can remember who was involved in my adoption in any way?

Once you've done this, the next step is to make copies of the Adoptee Family Interview Sheet (see page 26) for every individual in your family and every individual you can remember who was involved in your adoption. Ask each of them to sit down *separately* and fill in as many of the blanks as they can. By doing this independently rather than in a group, no one person's judgment or memories will override another's. After they've finished, go over each of their answers with them to the extent you feel comfortable. Keep in mind that valuable information can often come from the most unlikely sources.

If you plan to tell your adoptive parents about your search, now is the time to do it, not only for information—but also to share each other's feelings.

Our experience has been that adoptive parents will generally have a positive reaction to your search. Adoptive parents often feel uncomfortable bringing up the issue of searching and decide early on to wait until the child asks before discussing it. Often your adoptive parents will provide valuable support, and you will become closer in the process.

The fact is, adoptive parents and family members can be very helpful in your search. Many times, either as a matter of procedure or by pure chance, they were exposed to documents that contained the names of your birth family. In some cases they may even have kept the documents without realizing their significance. It makes sense to involve your adoptive parents, if possible. Everyone's situation is different. Use your own judgment about whom you're going to tell. Keep in mind that your search will probably be much easier with the help and support of those around you.

Finally, you'll need to fill out your Birth Family Tree (see page 28). This will give you an ongoing picture of where you are and which directions to take as you learn more information. As you will learn as you read *The Locator,* this Tree can be extremely useful, since it is often easier to get detailed information about extended birth family members, such as aunts, grandparents, and siblings, than it is to get information about the birth parents themselves.

Adoptee
Family Interview Sheet

(Make copies of this form for every family member/friend who is going to be interviewed. Fill in every blank with either an answer or "unknown." Star (*) the answers that are known for certain. Use this list as a basic guide and attach any questions of your own on the last page.)

1. Exactly where was I born? ______________________________

2. What was the name of the hospital? ______________________________

3. Do you have a copy of my amended birth certificate? ________ Where? ______________

4. Do you have a copy of my original birth certificate? ________ Where? ______________

5. What were you told about my birth parents? ______________________________

	Birth Mother	**Birth Father**
Names:	______________	______________
Ages:	______________	______________
Exact DOB's:	______________	______________
Places of Birth:	______________	______________
Nationalities:	______________	______________
Education Levels:	______________	______________
Religions:	______________	______________
Military Service:	______________	______________
Physical Descriptions:	______________	______________
	______________	______________
Marital Status:	______________	______________
Other Children:	______________	______________
Their Parents:	______________	______________
	______________	______________
Their Bro's/Sis's:	______________	______________
	______________	______________
Deaths in Family:	______________	______________

6. Was there an agency or attorney involved?______ Who? ______________________________

____

____

7. How old was I when I was adopted?____

8. Was I baptized before being adopted?______ What religion? _________ Where?_______

____

9. What were the circumstances behind my adoption?_____________________________

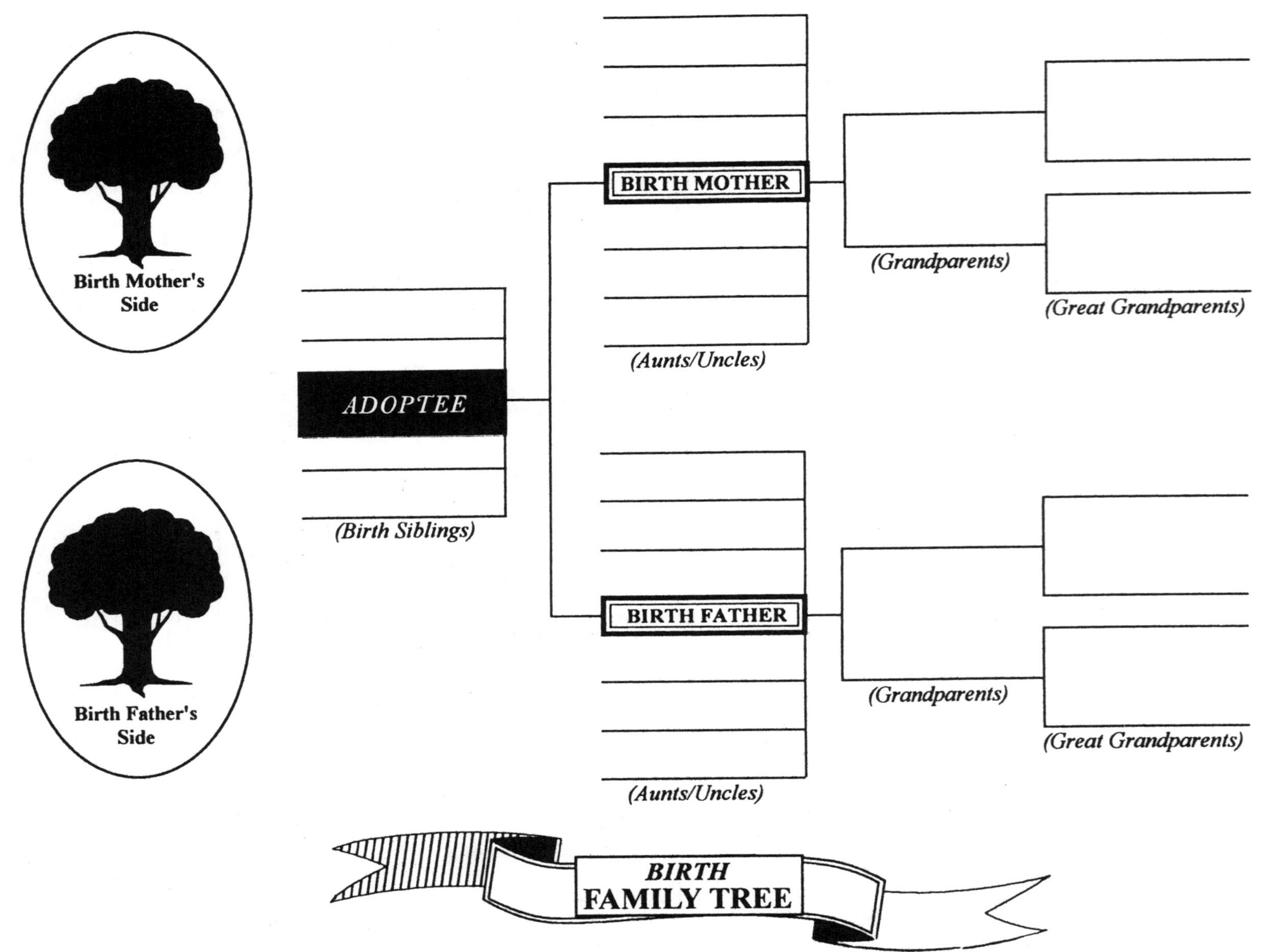
Birth Mother's Side
Birth Father's Side
ADOPTEE
(Birth Siblings)
BIRTH MOTHER
(Aunts/Uncles)
(Grandparents)
(Great Grandparents)
BIRTH FATHER
(Aunts/Uncles)
(Grandparents)
(Great Grandparents)
BIRTH
FAMILY TREE

Initial Information Reports (for birth parents only)

As a birth parent, this is where your search will begin. Read over the "Initial Information Reports (for adoptees only)" section on page 24, because the same arguments used there apply to your case. You do not want any help from family members or documents when filling out your memory log; you should do this completely on your own. For birth parents especially, it's unusual at this stage to remember more than your child's date and place of birth and his or her birth name, if given. Typically, the only source of this information is your own memory, since most birth parents received little or no documentation to show the event even occurred.

The two purposes of this log are to create a list of everyone who may know something about your relinquishment and to write down every shred of information you can remember—even if you're not sure about it. The important thing at this stage is to write everything down.

Okay, with your memory log in hand, following the directions here and those listed in the previous section, answer the following questions:

1. What was my name at the time of the birth?
2. Where and when did I give birth?
3. What did I name my child?
4. What was the name of the adoption agency?
5. What was the name of the attorney involved?
6. What was the name of the doctor involved?
7. What are the names of every person I can remember who was involved in my adoption in any way? Include the names of *all* doctors, hospitals, clergy members, lawyers, state or private agencies, and officials you can remember.

Once you have done this, the next step is to make copies of the Birth Parent Family Interview Sheet (see page 30) for every *family member* or *friend* named in your memory log. Do not contact any officials (i.e., doctors, agencies, lawyers, etc.) at this point; do not send the interview sheet to any officials you named. You will be able to contact them later, in different ways. Do ask your family and friends to sit down separately and fill in as many of the blanks as they can. After they've finished, go over each of their answers with them to the extent you feel comfortable. Keep in mind that valuable information can often come from the most unlikely sources.

Birth Parent
Family Interview Sheet

(Make copies of this form for every family member/friend who is going to be interviewed. Fill in every blank with either an answer or "unknown." Star (*) the answers that are known for certain. Use this list as a basic guide and attach any questions of your own on the last page.)

1. Exactly where did I give birth? ____________________
2. What was the name of the hospital? ____________________
3. Do we have a copy of my child's amended birth certificate? ________ Where? ________
4. Do we have a copy of my child's original birth certificate? ________ Where? ________
5. What were we told about the adoptive parents? ____________________

	Birth Mother	**Birth Father**
Names:	________	________
Ages:	________	________
Exact DOB's:	________	________
Places of Birth:	________	________
Nationalities:	________	________
Education Levels:	________	________
Religions:	________	________
Military Service:	________	________
Physical Descriptions:	________	________
	________	________
Other Children:	________	________
	________	________
Their Parents:	________	________
	________	________
Their Bro's/Sis's:	________	________
	________	________
Deaths in Family:	________	________

6. Was there an agency, social worker, doctor, or attorney involved?____ Who? ______________

7. How old was my child when he or she was relinquished?____________________

8. Was he or she baptized before being adopted? _____ What religion? _________ Where?___

9. What were the circumstances around my child's relinquishment?____________________

If you plan to tell your husband, wife, children, or anyone close to you about relinquishing your child, now is the time to do it. While they probably won't be able to provide any new information, they can be an invaluable source of emotional support. If there's one common denominator found in all the birth parents we've reunited, it is guilt. Keep in mind that until even a few years ago, an unwed pregnancy was looked upon by society as a terrible and shameful thing. Unfortunately, this misguided stigma has scarred many birth parents, and in the back of their minds they still carry around a lot of guilt. Because of this, many birth parents, mothers in particular, have gone through life being torn between their feelings for their child and their fear that their own family members will think less of them or even disown them.

It's common for a birth mother to be concerned about how to tell her husband and children what happened. When faced with this situation, our advice is always the same. Out of all the cases we've solved and all the birth parents we've reunited, never have we had a single birth mother regret telling her family. Never. Not only does the family accept it, most of the time they jump in wholeheartedly to help in any way they can. Children especially are delighted to find out they have another brother or sister out there and usually can't wait to meet him or her. By telling your family, not only will you suddenly be overwhelmed with helping hands, you will set yourself free from years of guilt and pain you never deserved in the first place.

The fact is, having your friends and family members on your side can be extremely helpful. However, we do recognize that everyone's situation is different, and what may work for someone else may not work for you. Use your personal judgment about who you're going to tell.

The last form you need is the Adoptive Family Tree. This gives you an ongoing picture of where you are and which directions to take as you learn more information. You will find that it is easier to get detailed information regarding extended family members, such as aunts, grandparents, and siblings, than it is to get information about the adoptees themselves.

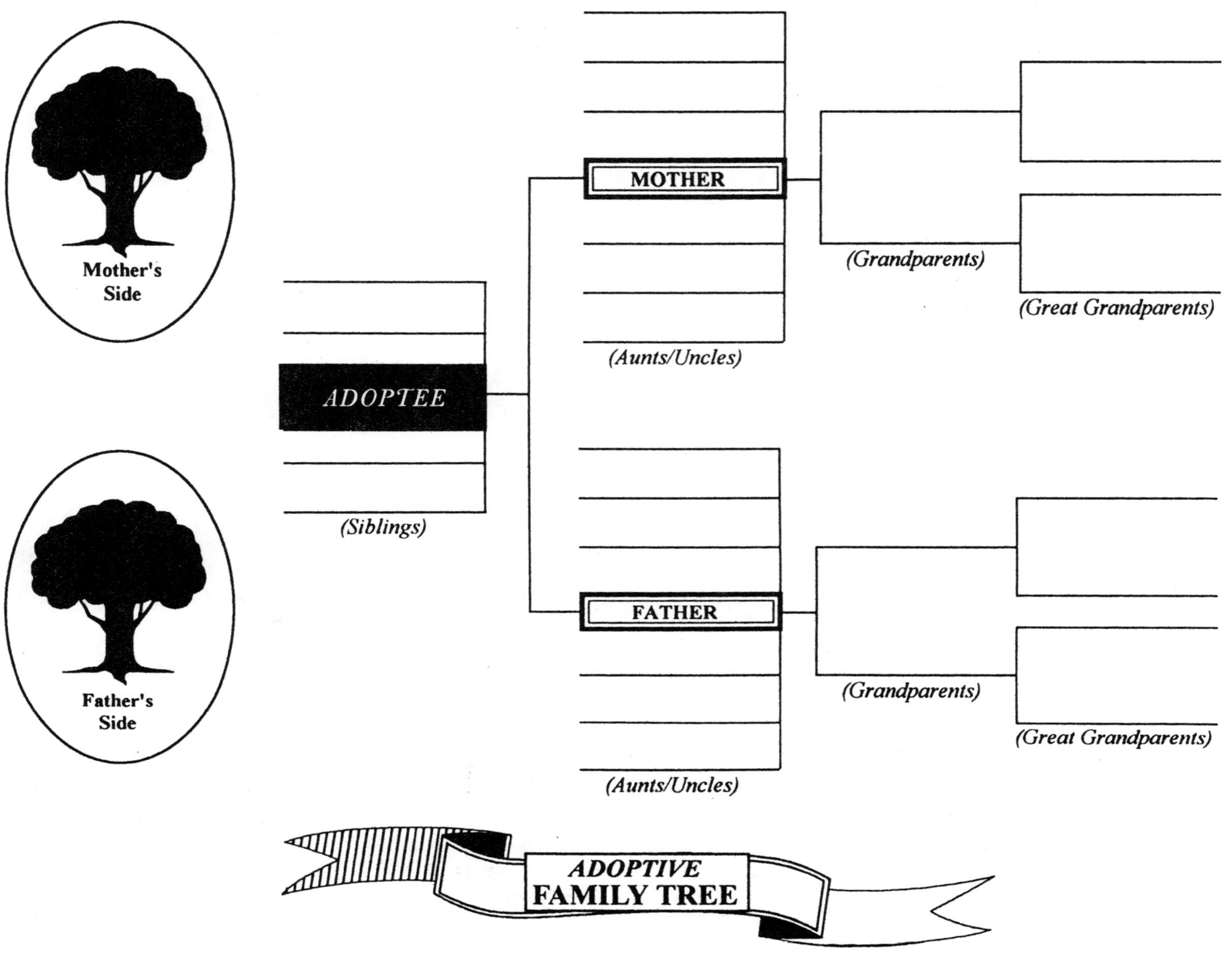
Mother's Side
Father's Side
ADOPTEE
(Siblings)
MOTHER
(Aunts/Uncles)
(Grandparents)
(Great Grandparents)
FATHER
(Aunts/Uncles)
(Grandparents)
(Great Grandparents)
ADOPTIVE
FAMILY TREE

THREE

Beginning an Adoptive Search

Adoption records are sealed. So how is it possible to get information from them?

The answer to that question is what this chapter is all about. It's true that forty-seven states currently have sealed adoption records. However, in most cases there are many other places where a person can find the same information (or pieces of it), and the majority of the time it's public information. You just have to know where to look.

We're going to start by examining the *sources* of information, then we'll describe how you can successfully *use* them to find the person you're looking for. We will not explain how to write letters and make phone calls to obtain these documents; those topics are covered in chapters eight and nine. To help you navigate the book, we frequently refer to the relevant sample letters in chapter eight, *but please don't dive in and write any of these letters without first reading this entire book, including all of chapter eight.* We understand your eagerness to get started right away, but it won't do you any good to start searching until you know how the entire process is supposed to work!

Since these are the same strategies we use in our offices every day, we'll be using actual examples and documentation from our files throughout part two of this chapter to give you a clear picture of what you'll be looking for and how you can get it.

Part One: What Are the Information Sources?

Personal and Family Memories

In chapter two we explained the importance of writing down your own memories as well as those of everyone around you who may have important information. If you haven't done this yet, we strongly suggest that you do so. Where your search will begin depends on how much information you have to start with. Therefore, it's important at this stage to gather everything you know into one place (this will be your search planner) so you can start formulating the next steps.

Legal Notices

Legal notices are a little-known but extremely valuable source of information in many searches. A legal notice is basically the announcement of an event or legal action. To meet the requirements of the law in some legal proceedings, legal notices often must be printed in a newspaper. Many types of legal actions, such as foreclosures, judgments, and liens, require this kind of published announcement, but the two that directly relate to what we'll be doing are the notice of adoption and the termination of parental rights.

The notice of adoption, sometimes referred to as a citation of adoption, normally includes the full names of the adoptive parents and the birth name of the adoptee. The second type of legal notice, termination of parental rights, is also called an abandonment citation. In most cases, this will reveal the full birth name of the adoptee and the names of the birth parents. In many areas, adoptive parents are required by law to place a legal notice in the newspaper notifying the alleged birth father of the impending adoption hearing. These notices are often placed even when the birth father had consented to the adoption. The purpose is to avoid the potential problem later on of a birth parent claiming he did not know about, or consent to, the adoption.

It's easy to see how finding this kind of information early in your search can make your job a lot easier. The only catch is that legal notices aren't required by every state. In some areas the placement of such notices even varies by county and year. Appendix 2 outlines which states currently require these notices. If the birth and adoption took place in two different counties or two different states, you'll want to check them both. The challenge of legal notices is that there is no rule of thumb regarding if or when they are required. Even if a given county does not currently require legal notices for adoptions, perhaps it did back when you were involved in the adoption. (In a few paragraphs, we'll tell you the best way to find out whether they were required in your area.)

Most often, these notices were placed by the attorney representing the adoptive parents. They were generally placed in obscure newspapers or legal journals. Sometimes they provide no identifying information about the adoptee, but if you are lucky, they may refer to the adoptee as "Baby Boy" or "Baby Girl" followed by their birth surname.

Legal notices are required to be published in a "newspaper of general circulation." Depending on individual state requirements, this usually means a county legal paper—although notices sometimes appear in public newspapers as well. The fastest way to find out if legal notices were required in a particular county and year, and where they were published, is to contact either a public librarian, a legal librarian, or a county clerk in the area where the event took place. In addition to pointing you in the right direction, sometimes, if you're nice, a clerk or librarian will even do a bit of the legwork for you.

If a particular librarian is unfamiliar with these types of notices or is unable to help you, another easy way to locate this type of information is to contact a local attorney who handles adoptions. In most cases, this can be done through the local yellow pages or chamber of commerce. When making this contact, you can often talk to a staff member in the office rather than directly to the attorney. Ask if legal notices of adoption were required in that county around the time of your birth or the birth of your child. If so, ask which paper they were normally published in, and where back issues are stored.

Going through the newspapers or legal journals, it can be difficult to determine which notice may be yours. Look at all notices within a year after the birth. Be inclusive in your search. Don't look for an exact fit; look for anything that seems to fit your case. In addition to writing down the names of possible birth parents, look for attorney names as well (in many instances legal notices will list the name of the attorney who represented the adoptive parents). Your goal is to get as much information about as many possible adoptions as you can. After you have a long list and have searched everything available, you can start narrowing the list down until you find the right notice (you will narrow the list using strategies we'll discuss later on).

Researching legal notices is a tedious process and may require looking through *thousands* of notices . . . but don't give up. Finding the correct legal notice can often be the turning point in your search.

State Department of Vital Statistics

Throughout *The Locator,* we will be referring to certain documents as "vital" records. Vital records are birth certificates, marriage licenses, divorce decrees, and death certificates. Every state and many counties and cities have agencies set up to keep vital records on the people residing within their borders. Depending on state requirements, many times these copies of documents are available to the public or to family members for a small fee (see Appendix 2). Forms, guidelines, and letters for requesting specific documents are detailed throughout the following sections.

State Adoption Department

Every state has an adoption department that, by law, must maintain records of all adoption proceedings. In most cases their files contain:

- original birth certificates
- amended birth certificates
- surrender papers
- adoption petitions/decrees
- parental case studies

Exactly which documents they have and how willingly they'll cooperate with you varies greatly from state to state. A lot will depend on *how* you make contact and request information—as discussed, that is covered in chapter eight.

Court of Jurisdiction

A court of jurisdiction is simply the court—usually on the county level—that handled the adoption proceedings. Some states have several courts that do this (see Appendix 2 for a detailed breakdown). These courts are required by law to keep copies of their records. Generally their files contain legal records ranging from original birth certificates to final adoption decrees.

Most states have a provision for opening these files to an individual, and in the majority of cases this can be done without hiring an attorney. The process of gaining access to these files is called petitioning. It typically involves (1) contacting the clerk of court in the appropriate court of jurisdiction, (2) completing an application (the petition), and (3) submitting it for approval. The person requesting these records will be required to provide a reason of "good cause" (see Chapter Eight).

Once a petition is submitted, it will go before a judge. If the judge determines there is good cause, a court order will be issued to release the files to either a confidential third-party intermediary or an officer of the court. That person will then attempt to contact the person being sought. Once this person has been located and signed a consent form, the judge will release the requested information to you.

As you can imagine, this process can be quite lengthy. Fortunately, in most cases it will not be necessary. We will show you faster methods that usually result in getting the same information.

Adoption Agencies

Exactly where your records are being held depends on whether or not the agency who handled your adoption is still in business.

If you were adopted—or if you relinquished a child—through an existing public or private adoption agency, your records will be in their files. If that agency no longer exists, all their records will have been transferred to the state adoption department. If you're not sure which agency was involved, the state adoption department can check its files and/or give you a list of all state and private adoption agencies operating within its borders.

Adoption agencies keep a gold mine of information in their files. This normally includes:

- original birth certificates
- amended birth certificates
- limited medical histories
- ethnicity of the birth parents
- dates, times, and places of birth
- psychological profiles of birth and adoptive families
- names and addresses of birth and adoptive families
- names and descriptions of relatives
- case studies of birth and adoptive families
- relinquishment papers
- adoption petitions/decrees

Attorneys

Almost all legal adoptions involve at least one attorney in some capacity. The attorney's files contain much of the same information that is held by the courts. The important distinction is that attorneys' records are not sealed by law. However, there is also nothing that requires an attorney to show you anything in his or her files.

In your quest for information about your birth parents, you may come across the name of the attorney who worked on the adoption. At this point, it may be a good idea to contact that attorney in an effort to obtain more information about the birth parents. (If you are a birth parent, you probably already know the attorney and can more easily get in contact.) If at all possible, it is best to visit an attorney in person. The amount of information he or she will disclose is usually at the attorney's discretion, so appearing in person will show your sincerity and will make it harder for the attorney to turn you down. If this is not possible, write the attorney an urgent letter stressing your "good cause"; this will usually accomplish the same goal.

If you're wondering whether or not a particular attorney is still practicing, contact the state bar association that licenses attorneys in that state (see Appendix 2); it can point you in the right direction.

Adoptees, adoptive parents, and birth parents who want to be located should send a notarized letter to the attorney who handled the proceedings, giving them full permission to release all information in their files. This will eliminate any gray areas of liability for the attorney in the likely event that someone is also looking for you.

Hospital Records

Records kept by the hospital of birth can provide both the medical background of the birth family and identifying information. They typically reveal a wide variety of items and facts, ranging from footprints to the full names of everyone involved.

When requesting hospital information pertaining to a birth, keep in mind that admittance records, delivery records, and nursery records are often filed separately. Enlist the help of your family physician if you can, since some hospitals will release records only to other physicians. Specific sample letters for requesting this information are included in chapter eight (Letters 26, 27, and 28). In many cases, hospital records can be accessed easily—especially by another physician.

It's important also to remember that doctors who deliver and/or care for infants often keep their own records apart from those of the hospital. This doctor's name normally appears near the bottom of the birth certificate, and a simple call to the state medical board, which licenses physicians, will tell you if the doctor on your birth certificate is still practicing.

The American Hospital Association has a directory of all hospitals in existence today, along with their names, addresses, and telephone numbers.

American Hospital Association
1 North Franklin, Suite 2700
Chicago, IL 60606
(312) 422-3000

If a hospital has closed, the American Hospital Association would unfortunately *not* be able to provide you with the name of the hospital that now has the records from that hospital. For that information, you would have to contact the hospital licensing agency (where this is and what it is called will vary from state to state). The hospital licensing agency can tell you how long hospitals are required to keep their records in that particular state.

If you need assistance in locating a doctor, the American Medical Association will give you background information on physicians.

American Medical Association
515 North State Street
Chicago, IL 60610
(312) 464-5000

They presently have information on any physician who was alive or who was licensed in 1969 and after. Much of this information could be obtained at your local library from the *American Medical Directory*.

Reunion Registries

At this stage of your search, we recommend that you enroll in a few *specific* reunion registries. A reunion registry is a computerized service that attempts to match your information with that of others who are also registered with them. In most cases, this is a simple process of filling out a form and sending it in. The reunion registry will then put your data into its computer. If someone with similar information has already registered (or registers in the future), the computer will make a match between the two.

Reunion registries are a great concept, and they're getting better every day. However, in order to get the most use out of them, there are a few important things you'll need to know. First, there are two kinds of registries: state reunion registries, which are owned and operated by a specific state, and privately owned operations.

Know up front that all registries are long shots. They work only if the person you are looking for has registered with that specific registry. However, thanks to a growing public awareness of searching, more and more people are getting registered every day.

Also, very few registries, state or private, *share* information with other registries, and most charge a small enrollment fee. Therefore you should avoid wasting money and carefully select the ones you will belong to.

The following guidelines are based on our experience and will help you make the best selection. There are four key things to look at when considering a registry: size, location, longevity, and price. Let's discuss each of these for a moment.

Size

Your odds of succeeding with any registry depend directly on how many other people are registered with that registry. Therefore, it's very important to consider the size of a registry before enrolling. Generally speaking, the more names in a registry, the better your chances of success.

Location

Another important consideration is the geographic area a registry covers. Most state-run registries are open only to people (or relatives of people) who were born or who relinquished a child within that state's borders. At the present time, twenty-eight states have reunion registries, and within the next five years we fully expect the rest will follow suit. Appendix 2 lists the states that currently have reunion registries.

Adoptees and birth parents should strongly consider registering their information in both the state where the birth took place and the state where the adoption was finalized. In some cases these are two different states. At this point you may not know which states were involved, but we will show you how to get that information.

We strongly encourage you to register with your appropriate state registries and with one international registry. Be aware that many privately owned reunion registries claim to be national or even international. In reality, most of these cover only a specific geographic region and have a few scattered registrations from outside that area.

Longevity

Since most state-sponsored registries are permanently established, this consideration is targeted primarily toward those that are privately owned. If you're considering joining a registry that charges a fee, do yourself a favor in advance and call the Better Business Bureau in the town where that registry is located. Ask how long they've been in business and if they have a satisfactory business rating. (If you don't know how to reach the Better Business Bureau in that town, call the Better Business Bureau in your own town and ask them for the telephone number of the B.B.B. office in the area where the registry is located.)

Price

The general rule of thumb is this: It never hurts to enroll in a reunion registry if it doesn't charge a fee. During the course of your search, you may come across some small private organizations and/or individuals who run their own little registries. If it's free, go ahead and put your name in. However, whenever a fee is involved, take a closer look at all the considerations we've just outlined before making your decision. At the time of this writing, about half the state-run registries charge a fee. It's been our experience that they're worth it—especially since more and more people are becoming aware of them.

While state-owned registries are generally a good bet, privately owned operations that charge a fee can be an entirely different story. It's an unfortunate fact, but over the last couple of years there have been a lot of fly-by-night registries popping up all over the country. Our experience has been that most of them go out of business within a year, so *check with the local Better Business Bureau office before doing anything.* If they haven't been around very long, we don't suggest using them.

One last important thing to look at when deciding to use a registry is *how* the fee is structured—especially when there is an *annual* fee. If a registry charges an annual fee, it means that you will have to pay more money every year if you want to keep your name in their computer. The bottom line is this: Once you're in a registry's computer system, it doesn't cost them anything to keep your name on file—so it doesn't make sense for you to pay a renewal fee every year.

Internet registry services are listed in chapter eleven.

The largest, most successful *international* registry is:

The International Soundex Reunion Registry
P.O. Box 2312
Carson City, NV 89702-2312
(702) 882-7755

Founded in the mid-1970s by Emma Mae Vilardi, the International Soundex Reunion Registry (ISRR) is a nonprofit reunion registry funded solely by donations. It has several hundred thousand registrations on file and currently accepts about 1,200 new registrations every month. They will keep your name on file forever—and it's completely free.

Write to the above address to receive a free current registration form. Due to processing requirements, you must enclose a self-addressed stamped envelope with your request—and photocopies of registration forms cannot be accepted. If you choose to make a small donation, it will be greatly appreciated.

Understand that the majority of reunion registries are legitimate operations. Therefore, we won't discourage you from using any particular registry. If you choose to enroll in a registry that charges a fee, follow the guidelines on pages 42–43 and you should avoid any problems.

Search and Support Groups

In addition to enrolling in reunion registries when you get stuck or when you just need some help, you may also turn to one or more qualified search and support groups in your area.

A current list of knowledgeable, qualified persons in your area is available through our Consultant Hotline (see Appendix 1). Because our trained staff is actively solving cases and developing new sources of information every day, this list is constantly being updated to reflect the latest search assistance.

Like reunion registries, many less-than-qualified search and support groups have appeared around the country claiming to have lots of experience helping adoptees and birth parents. Despite their claims, most of the time these people can't do anything you can't do yourself—and for a lot less money. The fact is, after reading this book you will know more about searching than ninety-nine percent of the so-called experts.

The search and support list provided through our hotline is a continually screened and updated source of expert advisers. In most cases, these individuals charge little or no fee whatsoever. If in doubt about the legitimacy of a particular person or group not on this list, contact the local Better Business Bureau or call our Consultant Hotline* and we'll use our resources to check them out.

Part Two: Understanding and Using Information Sources

The Issue of Nonidentifying Information

Laws differ from state to state, but most follow the same general policy of withholding from an adoptee or birth parent any piece of information considered to be identifying. Basically that means anything that could allow you to *directly* identify or locate someone. No agency will give you the full name or current address of your birth parent or birth child, because that would allow you to almost immediately figure out who the person is and where he or she lives. Agencies *may* supply you with nonidentifying information (but they are not required to).

The trick is that it's hard to determine what information will allow an enterprising person to identify someone. What if the agency gave you the state the person lived in? Would that be enough information for you to identify someone? Some people might think so; others might not. What about giving only the person's last name, not the first name? Would that be enough to identify someone? Some agencies might think so. The law isn't always clear, so it's often up to an individual's discretion. It's your job to try to wrest as many little pieces of nonidentifying information from these sources as possible, and to put all those pieces together until you have the puzzle assembled completely.

Some states now have regulations regarding what qualifies as nonidentifying information. Generally speaking, this includes items such as age, race, physical description, educational background, religious background, marital status, hobbies, talents, and medical history. Still, you can see

* The cost of the Consultant Hotline is $3.99 per minute; the average call lasts six to eight minutes.

that even under those regulations (and certainly under some states' vague laws), a lot of room has been left for individual interpretation. By carefully following the plans and strategies laid out in *The Locator,* you will successfully make the interpretive factor work in your favor.

Now we'll jump in and examine specific documents and records that contain the information you'll need. After explaining the documents, we'll discuss some successful methods for obtaining them. The examples used are actual documents from our files.

State Adoption Records

Searchers who don't even know if an agency was involved should start here. Almost every state has a state adoption department that keeps track of all state and private adoptions (see Appendix 2). If an agency was involved, the state adoption department can either tell you which agency it was or give you the telephone numbers of all licensed agencies currently operating. In those cases where a particular agency no longer exists, the state adoption department will have retained the defunct agency's files. And if the birth and adoption took place in different states, the state of birth will normally have the records you are seeking.

The following information will most likely be found in agency (or state) files:

- original and amended birth certificates
- relinquishment/surrender papers
- petition papers
- adoption decrees
- case studies of the birth and adoptive families
- additional court documents

For the most part, officials at these agencies are instructed to withhold any information they consider to be identifying. If you're going to be contacting these people by telephone, be sure to write out a list of carefully prepared questions (see Chapter Nine) in advance.

As an adoptee with very little information, your first step should be to write to the state adoption department where the birth occurred (see Chapter Eight, Letters 29, 30, and 31). They can provide a lot of basic information that will give you a solid place to start.

Birth parents usually remember where the birth and adoption took place. However, over the years it's possible that the records were moved to a different location. If this has happened, the state adoption department should be able to find the records for you—as long as you are persistent.

Adoptive parents almost always remember how and where the adoption was handled. When they write to request information, the agencies will probably worry that anything they release will constitute identifying information. For this reason, requests directly from adoptive parents are frequently denied. However, if this same information is requested by an attorney, he or she usually receives a better response.

Adoption Agency Records

Once you've established that your adoption was handled by an agency that is still in business, the next step is to contact that agency. (Remember, if the agency no longer exists, the state adoption department either will have your records or can tell you where to find them.)

Files kept by adoption agencies are often the most complete of any source; they can include extensive backgrounds on both the birth and adoptive families. However, adoption agencies also maintain the most rigid guidelines about identifying information. A few agencies honor only written requests for information; they feel that reading the requests rather than hearing them will reduce the emotional factor of the request. By dealing with letters only, they believe they will minimize their own errors in judgment.

The first thing you'll need to do is write a brief letter to the agency requesting nonidentifying information about the person you're looking for. We cover exactly how to go about that in chapter eight. The document on page 47 is a typical example of the kind of nonidentifying information adoptees can expect to receive from their first contact. Birth parents will usually get the same range of information about the adoptee and the adoptive family.

Although it may seem kind of sloppy and hard to read, this is often the way documents will come. Take a minute to read both columns of data closely, and you'll begin to get a clearer idea of what is normally considered nonidentifying information.

As you can see, the person who made out this report gives a general outline of the birth parents and their families but never reveals enough to identify any of them directly. This is the standard range of information most agencies will release, so let's see what we can do with it.

Looking closely at the document, we now know each of the birth parent's first names: Pamela and Richard. We also know how old they were at the time of birth. With a little calculating, we can determine that Pamela was born in either 1946 or in January 1947—probably in 1946. We also know she was in her sophomore year of college at the time of the adoption. This would mean she graduated from high school in 1963, when she was seventeen. We also know her father's employment.

On the birth father's side, we can calculate that Richard must have been born between 1943 and early 1944. We also know that he was studying science and engineering at a private college in Virginia but flunked out of school only two weeks before graduating. His father was a fireman and his mother a bank teller.

Adoptees Date of Birth

Birthmother's Age Calculation

1) Adoptee's Date of birth 1/18/65

2) Birthmother's Age at the time: 19

3) Birthmother was born between: 1/18/46 & 1/18/47

MONTGOMERY COUNTY DEPARTMENT OF SOCIAL SERVICES

Adoption Unit

NON-IDENTIFYING INFORMATION ABOUT MOTHER AND FATHER OF female (male or female) chi born on 1-18-65 (birth date).

	MOTHER	FATHER
Age at birth of child	19	~~22~~ 22
Race	W	W
Ethnic Heritage	IRISH	unknown
Religion	Prot.	Prot.
Education	was in sophomore year of college	was in senior year of college but "flunked out"
Occupation	student	
Physical Description (coloring, height, weight, etc.)	Brown eyes, Brown hair, fair skin, 5'6½", 125 lbs.	6'2", 180 lbs. Blue eyes, med. skin, lt. brown hair
Personality, Temperament, Skills, Interests	Horseback riding, knitting, cooking, music, above average student, Excellent in sciences, Verbal - outgoing	Good student with a heavy schedule - lost interest athletic - golf, tennis liked music - played + guitar - outgoing, singer
Medical History	usual Childhood diseases no other known physical or mental illnesses	pneumonia as a child
Significant social information about other family members (physical descriptions, medical problems, education, occupation, talents, etc.)	mother's father Naval Academy grad - high level navy position. mother's mother 2 yrs. college, No known health problems for either. (home ec.)	father's father - health fireman. father's mother - bank teller healthy.
Remarks	(Pamela (6/90) G. W. Medical Center	flunked out last couple wks. of school before grad. (Richard)
Please indicate the date this information was received and the source. (family member, worker, etc.)	DATE: 8-9-85 SOURCE: Record	DATE: 8-9-85 SOURCE: Record

(If more space is needed, please write on the back of this form.)

No contacts made by parents
Both private colleges
- VPI -
Father - science/engineering in VA (not liberal arts) - good school
Dean called in mother at 7/8 months

Birthfather's Age Calculation

1) Adoptee's Date of birth: 1/18/65

2) Birthfather's Age at the time: 22

3) Birthfather was born between: 1/18/43 & 1/18/44

Birthparent's Family Background

Birthparent's First Names

Important Additional Notes

Nonidentifying Information

Even though we may not have a complete picture at this point, we definitely have a good start. When we take this and combine it with data we'll be gathering from other sources, you'll see how valuable this kind of information can turn out to be.

Relinquishment Records

Like most legal proceedings, adoptions have several layers of paperwork. Much of this documentation is available when requested properly; the trick is that most state and private agencies black out what they consider to be identifying information. But don't let that discourage you. These documents can still provide a wealth of information: legal reference numbers, names of agencies, judges, attorneys, social workers, foster parents, and so on. The specific documents you are entitled to will depend on which role of the adoption you've played, birth parent or adoptive child, but generally court files contain documents such as:

- surrender/relinquishment papers
- interlocutory decrees
- formal requests for a name change
- adoption petitions
- adoption decrees
- investigative studies
- general correspondences between attorneys/social workers

The court of jurisdiction in the county where the event occurred normally retains these records in their files (see Appendix 2).

It may not be possible as an adoptee to access these files, but before trying to go through the courts you should ask your adoptive parents for any and all documents they might have. Courts can be notoriously slow to respond to requests of any kind. Many times adoptive parents or their attorneys have copies of legal records and letters that contain valuable information. Sometimes they even have an original baptismal certificate or birth certificate tucked into a file, and they just don't realize what it is.

If your adoptive parents are unable to help you (or, as the case may be, if they are unaware of your activities), your next step should be to write to the court for a copy of your adoption decree (see Chapter Eight). Depending on the state involved, and sometimes even who processes the paperwork, relinquishment papers may not be available without petitioning the court. It's best to write first and see what you get back.

In addition to requesting the adoption decree (see page 51), make sure to ask for the adoption petition (see page 50) by name. The adoption petition often contains additional information that may not be blacked out on the adoption decree.

Remember that any information in these records thought to be identifying will probably be blacked out when you get it. This decision is usually nothing more than the result of a clerk's individual judgment—and it doesn't always make sense. We've found that sticking to the following guidelines is the best way to decrease blackouts and get as much information as possible.

The courts are more likely to help if a reason of good cause is provided in your request. (The definition of good cause and the explanation of how to use it in your search are covered in Chapter Eight.) Many times, copies of the adoption decree and relinquishment papers are available to birth parents—although most laws are vague when it comes to this issue.

An adoptive parent can usually get copies of the adoption decree, interlocutory papers (temporary papers that are in effect between the court order and the issuance of the adoption decree), and petition papers from the attorney who handled the adoption or the court of jurisdiction in the county where the adoption was finalized (by writing letters; see Chapter Eight). There is also a small chance that adoptive parents can gain access to their child's birth and relinquishment records.

Courts and hospitals are usually more helpful toward adoptive parents than to adoptees. For example, courts generally black out less information on a document when it is requested by the adoptive parents. Who knows why—they just do. So if your adoptive parents know about your search, ask for their assistance when requesting documentation.

One final tip about requesting court documents: If you receive a document that has been blacked out, look closely to see if the markings were made directly on the copy that was sent. If they were, and sometimes even if they weren't, a local printer or photographer might have some equipment that can help you.

Let's now take a close look at the adoption petition on page 50. In addition to noting the adoptive parents' names in several places, this particular document reveals six other important pieces of information. Two numbers at the top right-hand corner are important: the date of finalization and the petition (or reference) number. These will come in handy later if you need to request more court documents. Having the names of the judge and the adoption agency also opens two new possible sources of information.

The most important clue on this document is the adoptee's partial birth name. It's very common for petitions to refer to the adoptee as "Baby Boy/Girl" surname or "Male/Female" surname (for example, "Baby Boy Smith"). Therefore, many times this information is left untouched on court doc-

At a Surrogate's Court held in and for the County of Queens, at Jamaica, in said County, on the 23rd day of April one thousand nine hundred and sixty-eight.

Date of Finalization →

Present:
HON. JOHN T. CLANCY, Surrogate

In the Matter of the Adoption by Steve B. Cain and Alice McCarthy-Cain of a minor under the age of fourteen years having the first name of female whose last name is contained in the verified schedule annexed to the petition hereto.

FILE No. 376/68 — Reference Number

Order

On the petition of Steve B. Cain and Alice McCarthy-Cain, his wife, adult*, duly verified before me the 23rd day of April, 1968, and the affidavit of ALICE HALL DOWLING duly sworn to the 25th day of January, 1968; affidavit of JEROME SHELBY

duly sworn to before me the 23rd day of April, 1968 except ALICE HALL DOWLING and the above named parties having severally appeared before me together with female a minor child whose full name is female Reddin as appears from the verified Schedule annexed to the petition herein, and said parties constituting all of the parties required to appear before me pursuant to the provisions of an act relating to the domestic relations, constituting Chapter Fourteen of the Consolidated Laws, as amended, and said parties having been examined by me, as required by said law, and said parties having presented to me an instrument containing substantially the consents required by said law, an agreement on the part of the foster parent* to adopt and treat the minor as their own lawful child, and a statement of the date and place of birth of the person to be adopted, as nearly as the same can be ascertained, the religious faith of the parents and of the child, the manner in which the foster parent* obtained the child, and said instrument having been duly signed, and acknowledged as required by law by Steve B. Cain and Alice McCarthy-Cain his wife, foster parents, and THE SPENCE-CHAPIN ADOPTION SERVICE by ALICE HALL DOWLING, President thereof, the officer authorized by the directors thereof to sign the corporate name to such instrument in accordance with Section 113 of the Domestic Relations Law,

each person whose consent is necessary to the adoption, and the said Steve B. Cain and Alice McCarthy-Cain his wife, foster parents, having acknowledged said instrument before me and the acknowledgment of the said institution having been duly presented to me and JANE D. EDWARDS of the SPENCE-CHAPIN ADOPTION SERVICE having been designated to make an investigation to verify the truth of the allegations set forth in the petition, the instrument or agreement of adoption and other papers in this

Name of the Adoption Agency

* If citation has issued, recite facts relative thereto. If no citation has issued, make no insertion.

proceeding and such other facts relating to the said infant FEMALE REDDIN and to the foster parent* as would give me full knowledge as to the desirability of approving said adoption, and the said investigator, Jane D. Edwards having made her report in writing dated November 16, 1967 and the same having been filed with the Clerk of this Court; and said investigator having reported that the facts and conditions as set forth in the petition, the instrument or agreement of adoption and other papers in this proceeding are true and are fairly stated, and further reporting that in her opinion the adoption of said infant FEMALE REDDIN as prayed for in the petition herein would be for the best interests of said infant.

And it appearing to my satisfaction that the moral and temporal interests of the infant FEMALE REDDIN will be promoted by granting the petition of said Steve B. Cain and Alice McCarthy-Cain his wife, and approving the proposed adoption; and it appearing to my satisfaction that there is no reasonable objection to the change of name proposed,

NOW, ON MOTION OF JEROME SHELBY attorney for the petitioner* herein, it is

ORDERED, that the petition of Steve B. Cain and Alice McCarthy-Cain, his wife, for the adoption of FEMALE REDDIN, a minor, born on or about the 18th day of January, 1965, at George Washington Univ. Hospital District of Columbia be and the same is hereby granted and that such adoption and the agreement therefor submitted upon this application be and the same hereby are in all respects allowed and approved, and it is

FURTHER ORDERED, that the minor, FEMALE REDDIN shall be henceforth regarded and treated in all respects as the child of said Steve B. Cain and Alice McCarthy-Cain his wife, and be known and called by the name of Virginia Marie Cain

JOHN T. CLANCY
Surrogate.

Adoptee's Partial Birth Name

Adoptee's Amended Name

Name of the Presiding Judge

Adoption Petition

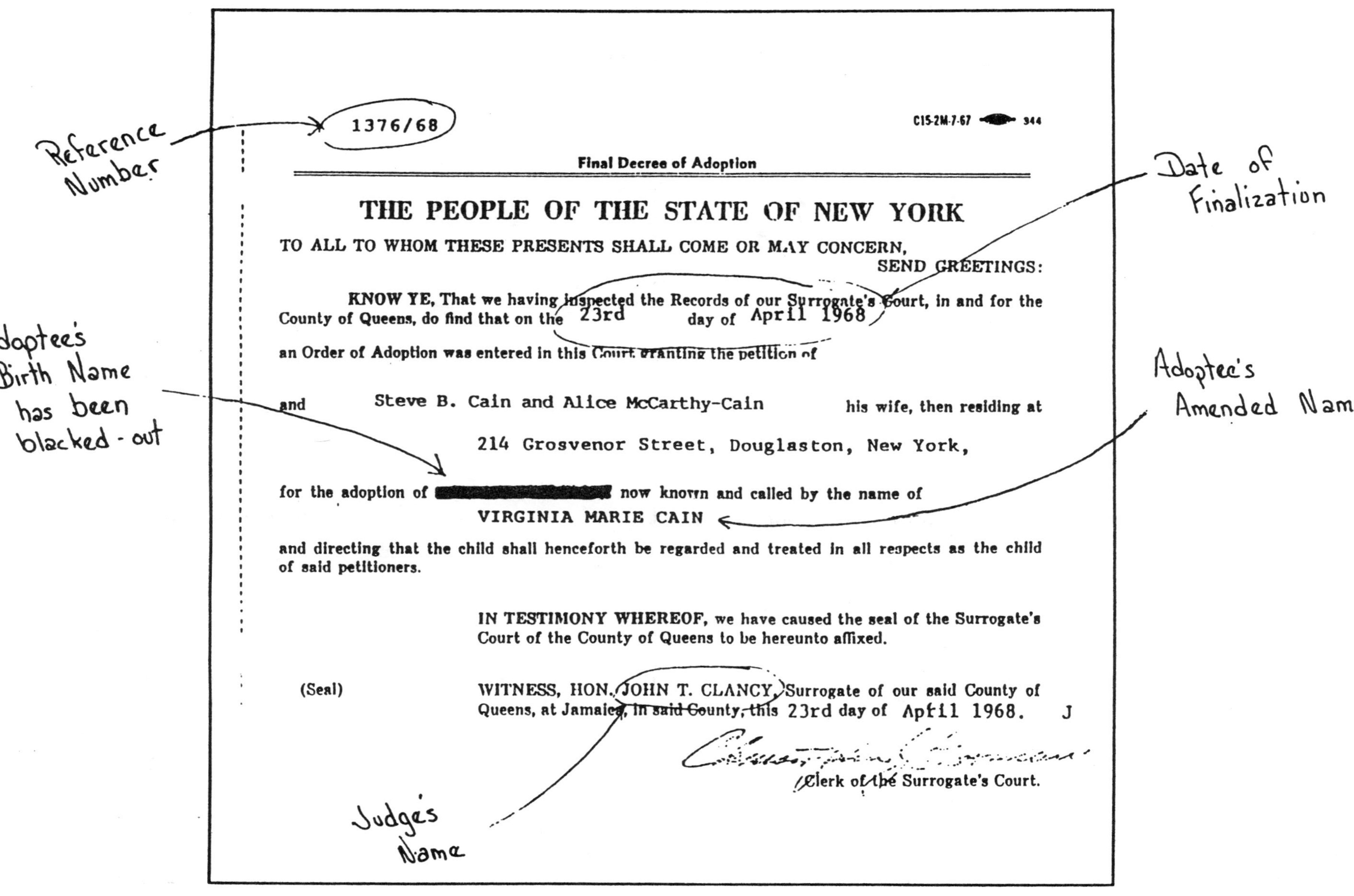

1376/68

C15-2M-7-67 344

Final Decree of Adoption

THE PEOPLE OF THE STATE OF NEW YORK

TO ALL TO WHOM THESE PRESENTS SHALL COME OR MAY CONCERN,

SEND GREETINGS:

KNOW YE, That we having inspected the Records of our Surrogate's Court, in and for the County of Queens, do find that on the 23rd day of April 1968

an Order of Adoption was entered in this Court granting the petition of

Steve B. Cain and Alice McCarthy-Cain and his wife, then residing at

214 Grosvenor Street, Douglaston, New York,

for the adoption of [blacked out] now known and called by the name of

VIRGINIA MARIE CAIN

and directing that the child shall henceforth be regarded and treated in all respects as the child of said petitioners.

IN TESTIMONY WHEREOF, we have caused the seal of the Surrogate's Court of the County of Queens to be hereunto affixed.

(Seal)

WITNESS, HON. JOHN T. CLANCY, Surrogate of our said County of Queens, at Jamaica, ~~in said County~~, this 23rd day of April 1968. J

Clerk of the Surrogate's Court.

Adoption Decree

uments, since a last name by itself isn't usually considered identifying (if the last name is extremely uncommon, it may be considered identifying).

Moving to the final adoption decree (page 51), you'll see that it contains much of the same information as the petition (reference numbers, names, dates, etc.). The important distinction is that in this case adoptee's birth name has been blacked out. This was probably because the adoptee's full original name rather than "Female Reddin" was used in the document.

Looked at separately, each piece of information seems insignificant. However, this will be a building process, like putting together a puzzle. Each document you come across can provide valuable new clues that will get you one step closer to solving the mystery of your life. Stay with this; we'll put it all together after a few more documents.

Hospital Records

If you don't know the name of the hospital that was involved in the adoption, you can usually get it from either the amended or the original birth certificate. Most hospitals keep several types of records throughout the birth process: delivery records, nursery records, and discharge records, for example. (The documents on pages 53 and 54 are made up of a general birth record, a medical information sheet, and an obstetrical record.)

Hospital records can be an important part of your search because they usually contain as much, if not more, identifying information than court documents. The important difference is that they are not sealed by law. Hospital files contain facts like:

- birth data (length, weight, sex, date, time)
- birth parents' names
- background information on birth parents (dates of birth, addresses, occupations)
- medical histories of birth parents
- footprints
- names of attending physicians
- discharge and financial arrangements (may include the names of adoptive family)

Although sometimes it will take a few attempts, you can usually get hospital records, as long as they still exist. Some states require hospitals to save their records for only seven years; but most hospitals keep them on microfilm indefinitely. Some have policies of releasing information only to a physician or to the people directly involved.

Adoptee's Full Birth Name

From records of ______________________
(Local Department)

Date 4-20-65

CHILD'S NAME Virginia Reddin

BIRTH INFORMATION:
Birthdate 1-18-65 Birthweight 6 lbs. 7 oz.
Birth measurements (inches): Length 19½"
Head circumference 13"
Chest circumference 12"
Condition at birth Good--cried at once
term Full - 40 weeks Delivery Normal

DEVELOPMENTAL RECORD:
First tooth ______ Sat alone ______
Pulled to feet ______ Walked ______
First words ______

LAST PHYSICAL EXAMINATION: Date 3-17-65
Height 22" Weight 12 lbs. Abdomen N
Temperature ______ Liver O
Skin Essentially Spleen R
Head - Circumference ______ Glands M
Fontanel Negative Genitals A
Other ______ Reflexes L
Eyes Child Well Extremities ______
Ears ______ Posture and spine ______
Nose ______ Nutrition Good
Mouth ______
Teeth ______ Recommendations ______
Throat - Pharynx ______
Tonsils ______
Adenoids ______
Chest - Circumference ______
Heart ______
Lungs ______

ILLNESSES:

Date	Nature	Treatment
None		

OPERATIONS:

Date	Nature
None	

SDPW-858

TOXIODS AND VACCINATIONS:

Date	Kind	Result
3-17-65	DPT #1	
3-17-65	OPV - Type #1	

LABORATORY TESTS AND X-RAYS:

Date	Kind	Result
None		

DAILY SCHEDULE AND HABITS (Feeding, etc.)

Virginia is an alert attractive and happy little girl who sleeps and eats on a regular schedule. She generally awakens at 6:00 in the morning, cries a bit, is changed and given a bottle. She sleeps for half an hour to an hour, rising at 10:00 for her breakfast of cereal (dry cereal, rice, oatmeal, etc.) At about 10:30 or 11:00 she has her bath after which she may sleep until noon or perhaps enjoy being cuddled. From noon til 2:00 she sleeps rather contentedly and soundly. At 2:00 she is again fed her milk after which she may play with her rattle or in bed and then goes to sleep until 6:00 p.m. Again at 6:00 p.m. she has a feeding and sleeps intermittently til 10:00 p.m. After her 10:00 feeding she sleeps straight through the night til morning, 6:00 a.m.

As of now she has developed no particular preferences for food, nor any allergies. She is on Tri-Vi-Sol vitamins, and her formula proportions are: 1½ cups Carnation milk, with 2 cups water and a bit of Karo Syrup.

Virginia is a warm, alert and receptive child who readily adapts to new people and situations. She is beginning to babble a bit and likes to be cuddled, rocked, and talked to.

General Birth and Medical Information

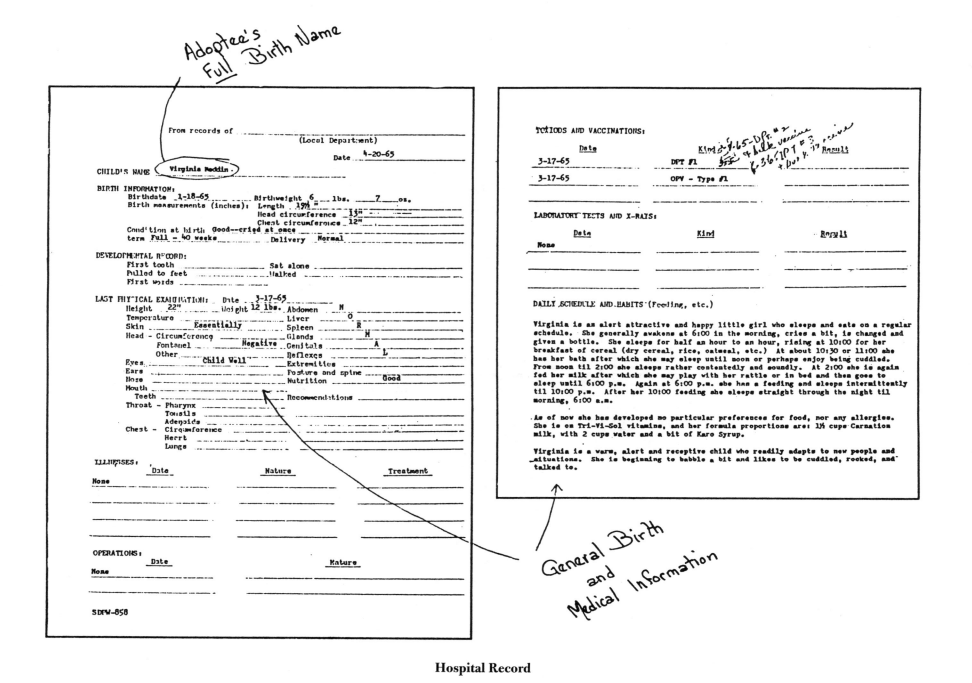

Hospital Record

B C

NAME

HUSBAND: Father: Richard S

Age 19 - 3/29/46 ADDRESS

Age OCCUPATION

OBSTETRICAL RECORD

CONTRIBUTORY PAST HISTORY: Family History Diabetes Epilepsy Sib. twins

Serious illness. Surgery

OBSTETRICAL HISTORY: Pregnancies: 1 2 3

Toxemia Swelling mild severe High blood pressure Convulsions Albuminuria

Hemorrhage yes no transfused Urinary symptoms yes no

Episiotomy last time yes no Largest baby's wt.

Hours in labor Longest Shortest

PRESENT PREGNANCY LMP 19 Quickening 19 Poss EDC 8-21-70

Menses regular (yes) no Serology 5-2 19 70 pos (neg

Rh and other special studies Blood type A2 B Rh Positive

Polio vaccine Booster

Troublesome symptoms

ABNORMAL PHYSICAL FINDINGS: (Pelvis adequate) doubtful inadequate

Coccyx free. Sacrum hollow. D.C. 12.5. T. O. 9.0. Pubic Arch V. Intercrest-1.

EDUCATION:

Circumcise yes no Breast yes no Hypno. Literature

[illegible handwriting]

DATE	TEMP	PULSE	BP S	BP D	WT	FUNDUS	FHT	POS	URINE S	URINE A	PVB	Hb	EDEMA	SYMPT.	MEDICINE
5-2-70			118	80	21[illegible]	5½ M			11	0	0	11	0		
5-29-70			108	80	[illegible]	6½ "	Ω	Vx	0	0	0		0		
7-3-70			108	60	218	33 W	Ω	Vx	0	0	0		0		
7-17-70			98	80	21[illegible]	35 W	Ω	Vx	0	tr	0		0		

Birthmothers' Name is Blacked-out

Birthfather's first Name and last Initial

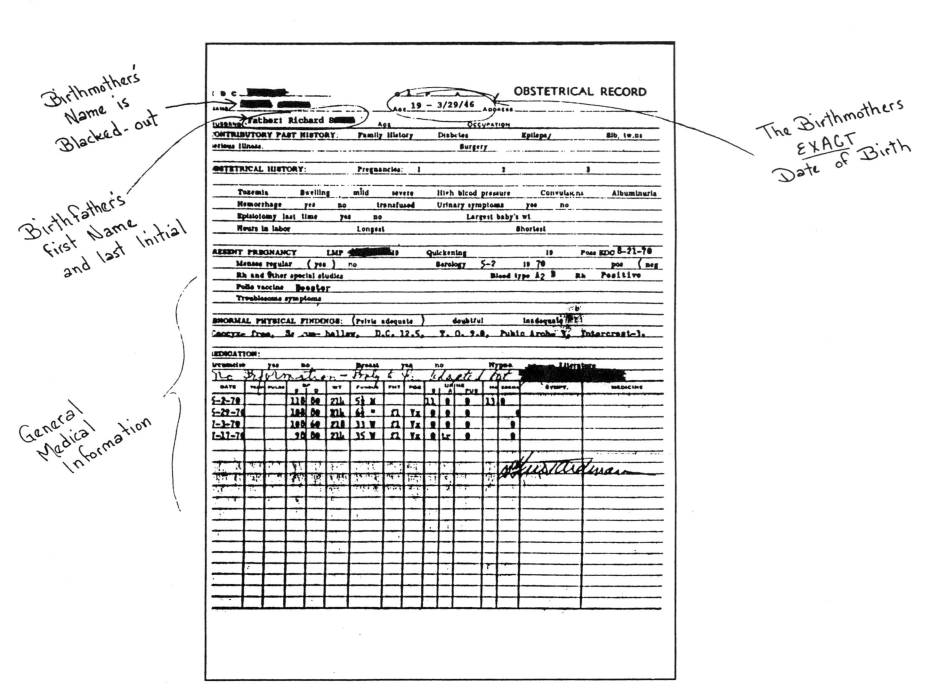

The Birthmothers EXACT Date of Birth

General Medical Information

Hospital Record

If you cannot obtain these records on your own, ask your family doctor to help. Armed with the proper information (dates, times, birth certificate numbers, etc.), he or she should have little trouble getting these records.

Records from hospitals and homes for unwed mothers are a valuable source of both identifying information and medical information for adoptees. These records are usually filed under the adoptee's birth name, so you will need to know it. They may also be filed under the name of the birth mother. When requesting these records, even if you don't yet have this information, you should still give it a try. If your request turns up nothing, you can try again when you have more to work with.

As a birth parent, you are usually entitled by law to copies of your hospital records and those of your child (see Chapter Eight, Letter 27). You may have to do a little pushing, but with persistence you should succeed—*as long as you don't mention the word "adoption."* If the hospital marked your birth file for adoption, they may try to stall you and deny access on the grounds that you are no longer the legal parent, or, more frequently, that "the records no longer exist." For this reason, we strongly suggest that you have a physician request this information for you—and have it sent directly to the physician's office. The clerks that process these types of requests usually give priority to other medical personnel and rarely question their motives.

Fortunately, many hospitals now recognize the importance of medical histories. As a result, adoptive parents, with the possible help of their family physician, can often get copies of their child's hospital records (see Chapter Eight, Letter 28).

If you receive a reply from a hospital saying "the records were destroyed in a fire or flood" or "we don't keep records going back that far"—chances are they just don't have the time or desire to go back into the microfilm and look for them. If this happens to you, wait a few weeks and have a physician try again. You'll be amazed at how often the records suddenly appear out of nowhere.

Now look at the hospital records on pages 53 and 54 again. Most of the time, you'll be looking for identifying names and dates in the hospital records. While the general medical information is interesting, it usually doesn't reveal anything that will directly help you with your search. In this case, a doctor requested these records on behalf of the adoptee (who was unable to get them on her own). Therefore, the clerk blacked out some information. As you can see, it doesn't make much sense why some things were blacked out in one area and left unchanged in others, but that's just the way it works sometimes. People are moving quickly over these records and they make mistakes.

In any event, we now know the adoptee's *full* birth name: Virginia Reddin. Had the birth mother been a minor, her parents' or guardians' names would probably have been listed as well. We know from the obstetrical record that the birth father's last name begins with an S. From the same record we get a bonus, because we also now know the birth mother's exact date of birth. Apparently, whoever "edited" this document decided it was okay to leave in the birth date since they had blacked out the birth mother's name. We'll see what we can do with this information later on.

Birth Certificates

Even though we've already mentioned this briefly, it is important to emphasize that every adoptee has *two* birth certificates—an original and an amended one. Since these two certificates contain different information, we'll review each of them separately to point out exactly what you should look for.

Also note that some states have two different types of birth certificate. The first is called a certificate of live birth and the second is called a birth certificate. The difference is subtle but substantial. A certificate of live birth is an abbreviated form, which the state normally issues when a request for the record is made. It is about a third of a page in length and does not contain much detail. A full-blown birth certificate, on the other hand, looks similar to the examples given on pages 57 and 59, and contains detailed information about the place of birth and the parents. All states have this general format on file, but because of time constraints, the state will issue it only if it is specifically requested. When making a request for a birth certificate, always be sure to ask for the long form of the certificate.

Original Birth Certificates

The original birth certificate on page 57 is issued at the time of birth and is valid until the adoption becomes finalized. It is a valuable source for any adoptive search (birth parent or adoptee). In addition to the birth parents' names, it typically provides the:

- adoptee's birth name
- date and time of birth
- name of the hospital and attending physician
- location of birth (county, city, state)
- birth parents' ages, origins, residences, and occupations

Once the adoption decree is approved and becomes final, the original birth certificate is sealed in the court records and a new, amended birth certificate is issued in its place.

As an adoptee, until you know your birth name it will be difficult to get a copy of this document. However, once you have that information, try writing to the department of vital statistics using your birth name in the state where you were born to request a certified copy.

Most states require a court order to release this document. However, we know from experience that mistakes happen quite often. In fact, you would be amazed at how many times a clerk just forgot to seal the original records, or accidentally sent a copy of the original birth certificate. The key

DEPARTMENT OF PUBLIC HEALTH
VITAL STATISTICS

STANDARD CERTIFICATE OF BIRTH

20569

1. PLACE OF BIRTH. Dist. No. 1901

County of Montgomery

City or Rural Registration District

No. G.W.U. Hospital

LOCAL REGISTERED No.

2. FULL NAME OF CHILD Virginia Reddin

3. Sex Female | 4. Twin, triplet, or other | 5. Number, in order of birth | 6. Premature / Full term X | 7. Date of birth (month, day, year) January 18, 1965

FATHER	MOTHER
8. Full name Richard Span	17. Full maiden name Pamela Reddin
9. Residence (usual place of abode; if nonresident, give place and State)	18. Residence (usual place of abode; if nonresident, give place and State)
10. Color or race Cauc · 11. Age at last birthday 22 years	19. Color or race Cauc · 20. Age at last birthday 19
12. Birthplace Virginia (State or country)	21. Birthplace Washington D.C. (State or country)
13. Trade, profession, or particular kind of work done, as spinner, sawyer, bookkeeper, etc. Student	22. Trade, profession, or particular kind of work done, as housekeeper, typist, nurse, clerk, etc. Student
14. Industry or business in which work was done, as silk mill, sawmill, bank, etc.	23. Industry or business in which work was done, as own home, lawyer's office, silk mill, etc.
15. Date (month and year) last engaged in this work ....19 · 16. Total time (years) spent in this work	24. Date (month and year) last engaged in this work ....19 · 25. Total time (years) spent in this work

26. If stillborn, period of gestation — months or weeks · 27. Cause of stillbirth — · Before labor / During labor

28. Was a prophylactic for Ophthalmia Neonatorum used? Yes · If so, what? AgNO3 · 29. Specify congenital crippling deformities None

30. Number of children of this mother (At time of this birth and including this child) 1 (a) Born alive and now living 1 (b) Born alive but now dead (c) Stillborn

31. CERTIFICATE OF ATTENDING PHYSICIAN OR MIDWIFE*

I hereby certify that I attended the birth of this child, who was born alive *at* 2:58 A. *on the date above stated.*

(Born alive or stillborn)

(SIGNED) C. A. Christman

Physician
(Physician, midwife, father, etc.)

*When there was no attending physician or midwife, then the father, householder, etc., should make this return. A stillborn child is one that neither breathes nor shows other evidence of life after birth.

Given name added from a supplemental report ______ Date of ______ Registrar

Address

32. Filed ______ Date ______ Registrar

Place of Birth
Adoptee's Birth Name
Birthfathers Full Name
Birthfather's General Background Information
Number of Other Children Born to this Mother
The Original Birth Certificate Number
Hospital of Birth
Exact Date of Birth
Birthmother's Full Name (Maiden)
Birthmother's General Background Information
Exact Time of Birth
Name & Address of the Attending Physician

Original Birth Certificate

to making this type of request is in how you ask for the information. It should be handwritten and include as much knowledge about your birth as possible (for more details see Chapter Eight).

As a birth parent, you may have been told that your name would be erased from all documentation and that you technically "never existed." Not true. You do exist, and your name appears not only on the original birth certificate, but also on many other documents. If you do not have a copy of your child's original birth certificate, you are entitled to a copy of it by law in most states. If it has been sealed, you will have to get a court order to release it, but the process is fairly straightforward. Write to the State Department of Vital Statistics in the state where the birth occurred. If that doesn't work, request a court order using Letters 23, 24, or 25 in Chapter Eight. It may take a little time, but eventually you should get it as long as you're persistent and follow up politely.

An adoptive parent will have a difficult time obtaining an original birth certificate if he or she doesn't know the child's birth name. When you get this information, ask your adoptive parent to request a copy from the State Department of Vital Statistics (see Chapter Eight, Letters 17, 18, 19, and 20).

If the request comes back with the response "record not found," ask your parent to write a follow-up letter thanking the clerk for his or her kind assistance, and ask him or her to "please check the delayed birth registrations." Many states file these separately from other birth certificates, and the clerks often forget to check them.

Amended Birth Certificates

The amended birth certificate on page 59 is issued to the adoptive parents when the adoption is finalized. It contains approximately the same range of data as the original, with the exception that all information pertaining to the birth family is replaced with that of the adoptive parents.

Depending on when and where the adoption occurred, a variety of additional data may have been erased or altered (such as dates, hospitals, names of physicians, etc.). However, this is very rare.

As an adoptee, you should already have a copy of your amended birth certificate. It's the one you grew up with. However, if you can't find it, your adoptive parents may have a copy, or you can write to the State Department of Vital Statistics (see Chapter Eight, Letter 21). Adoptive parents can also get a copy of the amended birth certificate in this manner (see Chapter Eight, Letter 22).

Now let's compare the original (page 57) and amended (page 59) birth certificates reprinted here. As you would expect, all names and personal information about the birth and adoptive families have been changed (for instance, note that Virginia Marie Cain was originally named Virginia Reddin). All other information, from the birth certificate number to the name of the attending physician, remains the same.

If you're an adoptee, you probably don't have a copy of your original birth certificate. There-

Place of Birth

Adoptee's Amended Name

Adoptive Father's Full Name

Adoptive Fathers General Background Information

Number of Other Children Born to this Mother

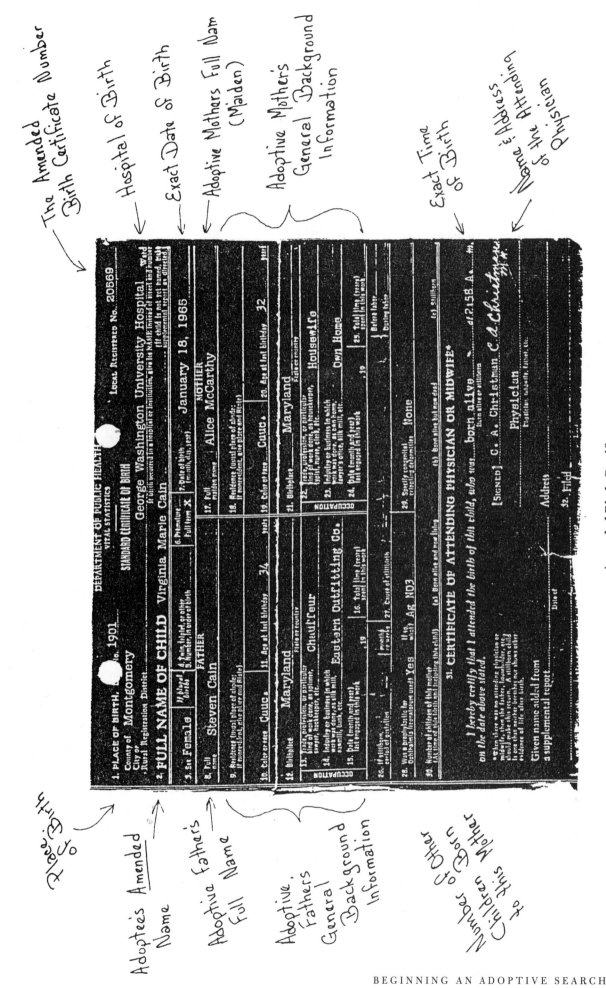

The Amended Birth Certificate Number

Hospital of Birth

Exact Date of Birth

Adoptive Mothers Full Nam (Maiden)

Adoptive Mother's General Background Information

Exact Time of Birth

Name & Address of the Attending Physician

DEPARTMENT OF PUBLIC HEALTH
VITAL STATISTICS
STANDARD CERTIFICATE OF BIRTH

1. PLACE OF BIRTH. No. 1901 LOCAL REGISTERED No. 20569

County of / City or / Rural Registration District Montgomery George Washington University Hospital Ward

If birth occurred in a hospital or institution, give its NAME instead of street and number

2. FULL NAME OF CHILD Virginia Marie Cain (If child is not yet named, make supplemental report as directed.)

3. Sex Female | If plural births | 4. Twin, triplet, or other 5. Number, in order of birth | 6. Premature — Full term X | 7. Date of birth (month, day, year) January 18, 1965

FATHER | MOTHER

8. Full name Steven Cain | 17. Full maiden name Alice McCarthy

9. Residence (usual place of abode: If nonresident, give place and State) | 18. Residence (usual place of abode: If nonresident, give place and State)

10. Color or race Cauc. | 11. Age at last birthday 34 years | 19. Color or race Cauc. | 20. Age at last birthday 32 years

12. Birthplace Maryland (State or country) | 21. Birthplace Maryland (State or country)

OCCUPATION 13. Trade, profession, or particular kind of work done, as spinner, sawyer, bookkeeper, etc. Chauffeur | OCCUPATION 22. Trade, profession, or particular kind of work done, as housekeeper, typist, nurse, clerk, etc. Housewife

14. Industry or business in which work was done, as silk mill, sawmill, bank, etc. Eastern Outfitting Co. | 23. Industry or business in which work was done, as own home, lawyer's office, silk mill, etc. Own Home

15. Date (month and year) last engaged in this work , 19 | 16. Total time (years) spent in this work | 24. Date (month and year) last engaged in this work , 19 | 25. Total time (years) spent in this work

26. If stillborn, period of gestation months or weeks | 27. Cause of stillbirth | Before labor / During labor

28. Was a prophylactic for Ophthalmia neonatorum used? Yes If so, what? Ag NO3 | 29. Specify congenital crippling deformities None

30. Number of children of this mother (At time of this birth and including this child) (a) Born alive and now living (b) Born alive but now dead (c) Stillborn

31. CERTIFICATE OF ATTENDING PHYSICIAN OR MIDWIFE*

I hereby certify that I attended the birth of this child, who was born alive (Born alive or stillborn) at 2:58 A. m. *on the date above stated.*

*When there was no attending physician or midwife, then the father, householder, etc., should make this return. A stillborn child is one that neither breathes nor shows other evidence of life after birth.

[SIGNED] C. A. Christman C A Christman M.D.

Physician (Physician, midwife, father, etc.)

Given name added from a supplemental report .... Date of

Address

32. Filed

Amended Birth Certificate

fore, one of your goals will be to get it. As you can see from this comparison, your amended birth certificate provides many clues that can help you to do this.

To begin with, your amended birth certificate will tell you exactly where (the name of the hospital) and when (the time of day) you were born. It will also give you the name of the doctor who delivered you. However, something you probably don't realize is that *your amended birth certificate also reveals your original birth certificate number.* At least, it does in almost all cases. The original and amended certificate numbers are almost always the same.

As a birth parent who's just getting started, one of your ultimate goals will be to get a copy of your child's *amended* birth certificate, so you can figure out what his or her new name is. In most cases, you will need to get a copy of the original first. This will help you verify a lot of information (time and hospital of birth, physician's name, etc.). You might remember most of this already, but there is one thing you probably don't recall—the original certificate number. As you now know, since this is almost always the same as the amended certificate number, you have a valuable piece of information there on the original certificate. Remember, only the original birth certificate is sealed—not the amended.

Throughout this section, we've used real documents from one of our average cases to give you a realistic idea of what to look for. Some documents are of particular importance to birth parents and others to adoptees. Rarely will you get all of them, but by now you can see there are many places where you can find bits and pieces of the information you'll need. The key to success is persistence. Once you've got enough pieces, it's just a matter of putting the puzzle together.

F O U R

How to Find Old Friends and Relatives

This chapter and the next three are meant to give your search a start. When it comes right down to it, there is often not much difference between locating, say, a third cousin you've lost contact with and a woman you used to date twenty years ago. Many of the techniques are the same, and the general strategies for finding them are discussed throughout this entire book.

No, these four chapters will not provide you with the quick answers; rather, they'll give you a rough overview of the kinds of searching you will do in each of these cases. Since every search is unique, we suggest that you read all these chapters, even if you're looking for someone who falls squarely under one specific chapter heading. The techniques for every kind of search apply to every other kind of search.

Friends and Relations

There are literally hundreds of ways to find old friends or relatives. We've found from experience that the easiest rule for starting this kind of search is simply to go back to the time and place where you left off. For example, if you and your friend went to school together, then the best place to begin is usually the institution you both attended. In general, this is the easiest kind of search. You have the person's name, you have a lot of information about the person, and you are not looking for someone who wants to avoid you or who doesn't know you exist.

To get started, you list everything you know about the person, no matter how insignificant. (See Chapter Two for more details on how to do this.) When you're looking for a friend or relative, the facts you'll most likely write down are these:

name — Be sure the spelling is correct, and if you're not sure, list all the possible spellings. If the person used a nickname such as Rick or Peggy, also be sure to list his or her legal or proper name, if known. A middle name or initial can be helpful too, especially if the first and last names are common.

age and date of birth — If you know the date of birth, list it. If you're not sure, try to determine the approximate birthday based on the person's age and anything else you might remember.

last known address — What's the last address you have for this person? (Often going to old neighbors will give you valuable clues.)

names of relatives/ friends — Do you know the name of your subject's father or mother? Siblings? These are people who, if located, might be able to tell you where the subject is currently. This may be the quickest way to locate someone.

school last attended — The school or alumni group may have current information, although they aren't required to release any data to you. More about this on page 64.

hobbies or interests — For example, if the relative was an avid fisherman, he would most likely have a license—as is required in all states.

occupation — There are hundreds of occupations that require professional licensing, and all licenses are available to the public. (See Chapter Ten.)

possibly deceased — If there's a chance the person is dead, you should check that first. Death records are fairly easy to get hold of, and doing so will save you time and energy (see Chapters Ten and Eleven). Obituaries always provide the names of surviving relatives and residences.

military service — If your subject was ever in the military, be sure to scour chapter seven. The military keeps excellent records on its active and reserve personnel (and veterans).

church attendance Did this person attend a particular church? Church records not only have helpful information, but often note if the person has requested their membership be transferred to another church. A church will usually provide you with the forwarding church's address.

In all searches, you need to be creative and use your imagination. Try to project yourself into thinking like the person you're looking for. What did this person like to do? Where did he want to live? What were her goals in life? What career did he or she hope to get into?

Lost Family Members

There are a few variables to consider in the search for a missing family member. If you're trying to fill in the holes on your family tree, then you are running a traditional genealogical search. You will utilize a number of genealogy resources (see Chapters Ten and Eleven). Without a doubt, you will find your closest Family History Center (Chapter Ten) to be a most valuable resource.

However, if you are looking for a relative who broke off contact with the family on purpose—a sibling who ran away, an aunt who cleared out after a family crisis, a cousin who just up and left with no forwarding address—in that case, you have a very different type of search.

People who don't want to be found try not to create a paper trail—at least not if they're smart, and are serious about not being found. Your search is going to be much like the other searches described in this book; the one advantage you have is that you probably know more about your missing family member than most people know about their old friends.

You or another one of your relatives probably has a date of birth and a social security number. As you will see elsewhere in this book (primarily in Chapters Ten and Twelve), having a social security number is a big step in the right direction.

It's crucial that you take care when making contact with a relative who disappeared on purpose. Whether you do it by phone or by letter, help this person feel safe. Give her the ability to choose to speak with you or not, as well as when and how. It is sometimes helpful to let the person know that it doesn't have to be a "package deal"—you'll respect her wishes if she still doesn't want to talk to a particular family member. You won't bring the entire clan knocking at her door. Bridges are built in sections to span large gulfs. Take it a step at a time and be sensitive and caring to the dynamics of the situation.

Because we believe deeply in the value and joy of family, we think that finding missing family members is the most satisfying search of all.

Using School Records to Find a Friend

In almost all cases, your missing friend is someone you knew in school but with whom you have lost touch since you both graduated. Remember the number-one rule of finding a missing person: Go back in time to the place you last knew that person. In this case, it's probably going to be your school.

Most schools are now on the Internet. If your lost friend is from your high school or college days, be sure to check "Searching for Former School Friends," on page 199. However, checking the school's Web site and posting a notice for your friend is a fairly passive way to search—you leave a message in hopes that he or she will visit the school Web site as well. So you will want to consider more active approaches to school records.

Normally, you will not be given access to another person's school records or transcripts, but if you explain that your motive is simply to reunite with an old friend, you will almost always be able to get valuable pieces of information about him or her (i.e., date of birth, address, family name, etc.). These pieces of data can be used later in combination with other techniques (which you will learn about as you read farther into *The Locator*), either to find your friend directly, or to find someone who knows where your friend is.

When calling a school, the first thing you need to discover is where the records are kept for the years you will be searching. Most schools keep only the last four to five years of records within reach. Older records are normally kept in a designated archive or records department. Either way, a quick call to the superintendent's office should point you in the right direction.

Once you have identified the location of the records, simply give the clerk a call and tell him or her that you want to reconnect with an old friend and would like some help. Give your friend's name and the years he or she attended the school, and see what the clerk comes up with. Once the file has been pulled, politely ask for your friend's date of birth, parents' names, any addresses at the time, and social security number, if listed (it rarely is). Also inquire if the employment of either parent is listed. Ask if the school has any record of where your friend may have gone. If your friend moved to another school, or if your friend's transcripts were at any time requested for employment purposes, chances are the school will have a note of where the records were sent (and therefore where your friend was).

If you know where your friend or relative graduated from college, another helpful source is that school's alumni association. Most colleges and universities spend a great deal of time and energy keeping track of their alumni, since a large part of their funding comes from donations. They're usually very willing to help if they can.

Other Ideas

Armed with some or all of this information, you have dozens of options to choose from to locate this person. For example, you could take your friend's name and date of birth and call the department of motor vehicles in several states where he or she might live. If your friend is driving in one of those states, the department will have an address that is usually not more than five years old. Keep in mind that these people do not have to help you—but as long as you're very polite and courteous, they will normally at least let you know if you're looking in the right state.

Men are usually easier to find than women, because their names don't change. Therefore, if your friend is female, the quickest way to find her may be to find her family first (her father, brothers, etc.).

There are several ways to do this. First of all, if you know where the father worked, or what he did for a living, start there. He may still be with the same company, even if he was transferred to another location. If not, he may still be in the same career. Many professions (lawyer, doctor) require some sort of state licensing that can be checked out with a quick phone call. Blue collar employees, on the other hand, often belong to a union or trade organization that keeps membership records. To give you an idea of just how far you can take this approach, we've even found people through their fishing, hunting, and pet licenses—all of which are faithfully maintained by our state and city governments.

If by chance you end up with your friend's social security number, you could call our staff and request a Social Security Trace* (see Appendix 1). This will probably solve your search instantly. Many documents and records today require people to list their social security numbers, so remember, if you somehow come across this during the course of your search, it is worth its weight in gold.

Another tried and true method for locating old friends and relatives is to contact neighbors or townspeople who may have known them. If you have the city or address where your friend lived years ago, try calling the local library in that town. Many libraries keep phone books and city directories from years past, which will list the neighbors who were living in the town at the same time your friend was. You can take a list of names from the old phone book or from the old city directory and compare that list to the current books, to determine which people have stayed in the town up to the present time.

The possibilities go on and on. It is important to remember that every search is unique and therefore requires different resources and methods. But in an effort to try to help you recognize some of the most helpful and often easy means to use for finding your missing person, we've provided a few

* Currently, the cost for a Social Security trace is $59.95.

case studies here and throughout the following chapters, to give you ideas that may be relevant to your search, and to show you how the techniques explained throughout *The Locator* can be put together.

Two Sample Searches

Every search is different, which is why this chapter (along with Chapters Five, Six, and Seven) is meant to prime you for the search, to suggest possibilities but not to dictate a methodology. We can't emphasize enough that you really need to read the entire book to get a complete picture of how to go about searching for an old friend or a missing relative.

That said, here are two sample searches, one for a missing relative, and another for a missing friend. These cases are from the International Locator, Inc./BigHugs.com files, which means we helped these people with their searches, but the cases have been rewritten to show you how, if these people had read this book and followed its techniques, they could have succeeded on their own.

Karen wanted to find her uncle John, who had disappeared nearly ten years earlier as a result of a family argument; after he moved, both sides of the family broke off contact, and neither one had ever given either a forwarding address. Now the two branches were hopelessly out of touch, and probably several moves away from each other.

Karen's grandmother was very ill, and her dying wish was to know that her son John was okay, and for John to know how much she loved him. The grandmother probably had only a few months to live, so time was of the essence.

The first thing Karen did was to get organized. She created a space in her home that would serve as her "search headquarters." She obtained binders for search maps, conversation logs, correspondence logs, library logs, and progress journals. She got a tape recorder and a jack to record phone calls. (See Chapter Two.)

The next step Karen took was to gather all the information she had, and all the information her relatives had, and to write it all down, along with all their memories of her uncle John's likes and dislikes, hobbies, friends' names, school names, and occupations.

Because John was a relative, and because so many of Karen's other relatives had known him for so long, she actually had a lot more information than the average searcher starts out with. She had his full name, his date of birth, and even had his social security number. Knowing that a social security number can be the key to any search, she had a professional searching company run a database check on the number (see Chapter Twelve). Given the time constraints she was under, and the importance of the search, it was a worthwhile expenditure for her. Unfortunately, database searches reported his address as the one where he had resided ten years before—there was nothing more current.

What was wrong? Could he be dead? Could he have changed his name for some reason? Could he be in prison? These all seemed like highly unlikely scenarios, but Karen knew she should consider all options, no matter how far-fetched.

Karen called the office of the Social Security Administration (see Chapter Ten). They were able to tell her that there had been no death claims filed on her uncle. Since John had been in the military, Karen called the veteran's association (see Chapter Seven), who reported no death claim or benefit claims. So it looked like Uncle John was still alive.

At this point, all of her surefire leads had turned up nothing. Going back to everything people had written down, Karen realized that she had some information listed under hobbies and occupations. She knew John had been a pilot and that he loved aviation.

Karen contacted the Federal Aviation Agency, where she discovered that John had a civilian pilot's license. The FAA gave her the address listed on his license, which was almost certain to be current. Rather than place a phone call, Karen sent John flowers with a card that said, "I promised Grandma I would find you and tell you how much she loves you. She is dying. *Please* call me."

He did.

Pamela wanted to reconnect with Lucy, who had been her best friend from grade school up through their sophmore year of high school. After sophomore year Lucy and her family had moved to Dallas, Texas, and the two girls had lost touch.

It had been fourteen years since they last saw each other. Pamela was now thirty years old. She assumed Lucy had married but had no idea what her married name was, or if she'd kept her name.

After making the required first steps—creating search maps, conversation logs, correspondence logs, library logs, a progress journal, and a tape recorder—she sat down and tried to remember as much as she could. Unfortunately, it was hardly anything. She did not remember Lucy's birthday, nor did she remember her parents' first names.

It made sense for Pamela to check *www.reunionregistry.com*; she and Lucy had been such good friends, there was definitely a chance that Lucy was looking for her too (see Chapter Eleven). Lucy was not registered under her maiden name, but Pamela went ahead and registered her own name—under both her current name and her maiden name—in case Lucy came looking for her later on. She also tried to look up Lucy Rozelle under *members.aol.com/maydyn/index.htm*, the maiden name index (see Chapter Eleven) that can often reveal what a woman's new name is, or what her old name used to be. No luck there either, but Pamela once again registered her maiden name and her current name at that site in case Lucy came looking for her.

It looked like the Internet was not going to turn up any solid leads, so Pamela moved on to other ideas. (She knew that the two best allies in every search are patience and persistence!) Next she checked voter registration records (see Chapter Ten). She contacted the Board of Elections for Dallas and was able to quickly discover a voter's registration for a Lucy Rozelle, with a social security number and a date of birth that seemed about right.

However, a call to Dallas information did not turn up a Lucy Rozelle, so Pamela was once again stymied. Could she be listed in the voting records under her maiden name and in the phone book under her married name only? It was entirely possible, especially if she'd kept her maiden name for professional purposes but used her married name socially.

However, armed with Lucy's date of birth, maiden name, and social security number, Pamela had enough information to write a letter that sounded urgent to the Social Security Administration, asking them to forward her letter to Lucy Rozelle's current address. The SSA will do this for you if the reason is urgent and seems legitimate (see Chapter Ten for more details). The SSA always informs the people being contacted that they are under no obligation to respond, but Pamela assumed Lucy would call her (or at least write back) when she got the letter.

As it turned out, Lucy was thrilled to hear from her old childhood friend and called her immediately. They agreed to meet the next time Pamela was in Dallas, and the reunion was a happy one; they've been in touch ever since.

In these two examples we've briefly introduced techniques and strategies that you will be able to use easily after reading this book. The idea here was just to get you familiar with the kind of creative thinking that goes on in these searches. We'll give you the tools, we'll give you some ideas, we'll provide the starting points—but the persistence, patience, drive, and creativity are all your own. And if you run up against a brick wall, or just need someone to talk to, see Appendix 1, and remember that the International Locator's experts are always available to you.

FIVE

How to Find Lost Loves

It is not unusual for a person to reflect and wonder, "What ever happened to . . ." or "What would my life be like now if . . ." Sometimes old loves still seem to have a permanent place in our hearts.

These reflections sometimes motivate a search for both the old love and those old feelings. Often this kind of search is really an attempt to find closure, so life can go on with less fantasizing about what might have been. Finding a lost love rarely results in the rekindling of an old flame, but it does often provide peace of mind.

What's Different About This Search?

Searching for an old boyfriend or girlfriend is much like searching for a missing friend or lost family member, but with one major difference: the manner in which inquiries are made, and the method of making first contact.

It is important to remember that you are not aware of the dynamics in your ex's life now. For example, he or she may be married, and an insensitive phone call or letter could create problems for this person and his or her spouse. We certainly hope you value the sanctity of home and family, as we do, and will maintain healthy and appropriate boundaries in your search for this old love.

That said, let's get into the strategies that we use for this kind of search every day. Locating a former boyfriend or girlfriend is not as difficult as it may seem. First, you should go back and read

Chapter Four, "How to Find Old Friends and Relatives," if you haven't already done so. In most cases these two searches are basically the same. Still, it is important for you to be aware of the slight differences between the two.

As you look for your old flame, you will be gathering various bits of information from people like former employers, school secretaries, and even members of his or her family (the methods for this kind of information-gathering are explained in subsequent chapters of this book, primarily in Chapter Ten).

In most cases, it's best to keep the story of your past romance to yourself when you're trying to get information. The "lost love" angle only confuses things, and may make people nervous, so keep it simple and proceed as though you are looking for an old friend. If you tell the whole story, we've found, people who are close to the individual you're seeking tend to pass judgment on your motives. And if they judge you and your motives negatively, they may deny you the information you are requesting.

For example, a sister of your former love may choose not to tell you where her "happily married" brother is now living, for fear that you might interfere with his marriage. If, however, she considers you just an old friend, the threat isn't quite as apparent. With this in mind, we recommend that you play it safe.

In some cases, it may even make sense to have someone of the same sex as the person you are seeking make phone calls for you. In other words, if you're seeking a former boyfriend, it helps to have a man make the phone calls. In the mind of whomever you are calling for information, this will almost entirely eliminate the possibility that an old flame is behind the search. If you are seeking a former girlfriend, remember that she has probably changed names at least once. For this reason, it is usually easier to focus on finding her family *first* and then having a female friend make the call.

How to Make Contact

Be sensitive to all the possible dynamics when making contact. This person might not only be happily married, he or she could be married to a very jealous person. Proceed with caution and with care. You can usually determine from a person's tone of voice if he or she is pleased to hear from you—be especially alert to tone of voices and other cues if you make first contact over the phone.

It's usually best to test the waters a bit and say something along the lines of "I've thought about you often, wondered how your life was, and hoped you were happy." Gauge the response to that—friendly? lukewarm? curt? antagonistic? Based on the answer and the *style* of the answer, you ought to be able to determine what is appropriate.

If you're really nervous about making contact, or have reason to believe it might not go well, a letter might work best, or even asking a third party to make the call.

Good luck with your search, and may you find a happy ending—or at least closure, so that you can move on with your life without looking backward!

A Sample Search

Every search is different, which is why this chapter (along with Chapters Four, Six, and Seven) is meant to prime you for the search, to suggest possibilities, but not to dictate a methodology. You really need to read the entire book to get a complete picture of how to go about searching for a lost love.

That said, here is a sample case. This case is from the International Locator, Inc./BigHugs.com files, which means we helped this person with his search, but it has been rewritten to show you how, if he had read this book and followed its techniques, he could have succeeded on his own.

Robert, aged forty-two, wanted to find his high school sweetheart, Tracie Marie Black, also forty-two. They had graduated from St. George High School together in 1974, in St. George, Utah.

The first thing Robert did was to follow the instructions laid out in this book. He bought some folders and marked them for the future search maps, conversation logs, correspondence logs, and library logs he knew he'd be creating (see Chapter Two). He also bought a tape recorder and a phone jack, to record conversations.

Next, he tried to get all his memories about Tracie down on paper. He remembered her parents' names, Don and Nancy Black. He remembered that she had three sisters, Tonya, Terrie, and Tiffany, and that she had a little brother, but he couldn't think of the brother's name.

Robert located Tracie's dad, who still lived in St. George. Don Black had never liked Robert. He refused to give him any information about Tracie, refused even to deliver a message to Tracie, and he told Robert not to bother him about this matter again. Not wanting to make trouble, or to prejudice Tracie against him by antagonizing her father in any way, Robert did not press the issue with Mr. Black, and he completely dropped that avenue of the search, realizing it would only be detrimental to him to continue.

Next he contacted their old high school (see Chapter Ten) and asked if the school had Tracie's address on any alumni reunion mailing lists. Unfortunately, they did not. The next step was to check her old school records. He learned from the secretary that records of the school's transcripts from the 1970s were kept at the downtown district office.

Robert called the downtown office and got a clerk on the phone. He explained that he was trying to find an old friend from high school, and while he didn't want to see any confidential information, he wondered if the clerk could answer some general questions. The clerk agreed to do some checking for him.

Had Tracie ever asked St. George High School to send her transcript anywhere? The clerk discovered she had not. So much for finding out which colleges she might have applied to, or which jobs she might have worked at after graduation.

Did the clerk have any papers that indicated Tracie's birthday? Yes, he was able to confirm that her birthday was April 19, 1956.

So now Robert gathered the information that was readily available to him: He had Tracie's maiden name, date of birth, parents' and siblings' names (except one), and her last residence as of twenty-four years ago.

Then he turned to the Internet, filing his name at *www.reunionregistry.com* as well as several online high school registries (see Chapter Eleven). He found no registration for any Tracies on any of those sites—he had no idea if she had been married, or whether she had kept her name if she did, so he had to assume that any Tracie could be the old Tracie Black. However, one other person, a woman in their graduating class, had registered at the school's online page. He e-mailed her, but she replied that she had heard nothing about Tracie since graduation.

He considered going to the library and searching through the microfiche records of the wedding announcements from 1975 through 1985, to see if he could find her name and, therefore, discover what her new name was. But first he wrote a letter (Chapter Eight) to the county recorder's office and the state department of vital statistics. Marriage licenses are available to the public, and he knew that the county might even let him search the records himself (Chapter Ten).

Following up on his letter to the county, he phoned the office to see if there had been any progress, and asked if he could come in to search the marriage licenses himself. The clerk said that would be fine, and even showed him how to use the files when he came in. After several hours, he came up with his answer: Tracee Black (it was not until this point that Robert realized he had been spelling "Tracee" wrong throughout his search) had married Jason Johnston on June 15, 1979. Mr. Johnston's address—in Mobile, Alabama—was given on the license, as was his occupation, engineer. There were also the names of two witnesses, although they were both women, so their names might have changed since 1979 as well.

At this point, Robert had a lot of options. He could call information in St. George and perhaps Salt Lake City, and then call information in Mobile and the surrounding suburbs asking for a Jason and/or Tracee Johnston. He could check around St. George for the names of the two witnesses, to see if they knew what had happened to Tracee. He could check with national societies of engineers to see if Jason Johnston was listed anywhere. He could check all the Johnstons in Mobile, in hopes of finding Jason Johnston's parents (this path seemed particularly time-consuming and unlikely to yield results, but Robert was brainstorming all the possibilities).

Robert followed up on the witnesses first but could not find their names in St. George or in any of the nearby towns. He checked some Utah towns and cities for Johnstons and turned up nothing; then he called Mobile information and found no listing for Jason or Tracee Johnston there either.

He did turn up a J. Johnston in Mobile. Not wanting to make anyone nervous, he had a female friend call the Mobile listing to see if J. Johnston was actually Jason, and if he was married to Tracee. Unfortunately, J. Johnston's name turned out to be Jasper, and he had never heard of a Jason Johnston marrying a Tracee from Utah.

Hmm . . . time for some more creative thinking. As he reflected upon Tracee and her family, Robert wondered if he could find her little brother. Maybe the brother would be more cooperative than the father had been; maybe if he were slightly vague about why he was trying to find her, he wouldn't make the brother suspicious.

But how could he figure out the brother's name? He knew only that the brother was younger than his sisters, that his last name was Black, and that he had lived in St. George, Utah, in 1979, and probably in the early 1980s as well. This was a safe assumption, since the parents still lived there, and the younger brother was a few years behind Tracee in high school.

Robert went back to the library and searched a current phone disc for all of Utah. He looked for Blacks with a first name starting with T, because it seemed likely that after naming four daughters Tracee, Tonya, Terrie, and Tiffany, the parents would stay with tradition in naming their son.

Bingo! Todd Black was listed as living in Cedar City, a town only a short distance from St. George. It was worth a shot. Robert called Todd and explained that he was going to be visiting Utah in a couple of weeks (a slight stretch of the truth) and was hoping to look up a few old friends he had lost track of over the years. Was Todd by any chance related to Tracee Black? (It wouldn't make sense for Robert to ask for Tracee Johnston—if Robert knew the details of her marriage, he would also know that she didn't live in Utah any longer.) Todd immediately said, "Yeah, she's my sister, only she's Johnston now." To which Robert quickly replied, "I'd heard a rumor she was married and living in the South somewhere, but I wasn't certain." Todd confirmed that, and said that she was in Atlanta. If Robert didn't mind waiting a minute, he would get her phone number.

So, there Robert was, ready to make the initial contact call to Tracee. He did so in a sensitive and discreet way, not knowing who would answer the phone, and certainly not wanting to cause any problems. He approached the phone conversation as one between old friends, and did not bring up their dating past, instead inquiring as to her health and telling her that he'd gotten her number from her brother. Tracee was quite flattered that Robert would care enough to go to such lengths to find her; however, she was quick to point out that she was also quite happily married. Robert said he was glad to hear she was happy. She mused that it had been nearly a quarter of a century, three kids, and one grandson since they'd last seen each other.

Perhaps Robert had hoped that Tracee would be available, or would warm up to him immediately; instead, it seemed that she was quite settled in her current life. Robert was happy that he had found the person he was looking for and soon realized it was time to say good-bye to her and get on with his life. Case closed.

S I X

How to Find Deadbeat Parents

It is an unfortunate fact of our society that each year literally millions of parents fail to live up to their family obligations, choosing not to provide for the well-being of their children and former loved ones. Locating the parent is not usually that difficult. Getting the parent to pay—that's another story. Collecting has to be left to the proper authorities.

Not All Deadbeats Are Dads—or Even Deadbeats!

Although the familiar term is "deadbeat dad," it has been our experience that the issue of an ex-spouse abandoning parental responsibilities is not limited to dads. So in fairness, we will address this issue as one of searching for a "deadbeat parent."

Over the years, we've located many deadbeat parents, and throughout our experiences, we have found that very few of them were actually what you'd consider real losers or deadbeats. For the most part, they've felt that if they could live life in reverse they would do a number of things differently. Most of them would love to go back and change the decisions that resulted in the loss of contact with their child. Often they intended the separation to last only a few weeks—but one thing led to another, and they let weeks turn into months. After a while, their guilt over the missed months overrode their common sense, and so they painted themselves into a corner. At that point, they knew the kids might have been told negative things about them, and they were scared to make a reentry.

There are other understandable scenarios we have come across as well: times when the relationship with the other parent was so hostile that the missing parent thought it might be better not to stir up a hostile environment for their children. In many instances, the custodial parent had remarried, and the estranged parent felt that he had no right to upset a happy and stable home. If the divorce or abandonment happened early enough in the child's life, many of these estranged parents nuture a real fear that the child might not even know they exist; the child might think a stepparent was actually a biological parent.

In other words, don't jump to conclusions about the deadbeat parent. People do change, and usually for the better! You can't turn the clock back, so why get stuck in the past? Many wonderful reunions have taken place when adult children are willing to keep their minds and hearts open; meaningful relationships have been reestablished without letting blame or guilt rob anyone of a future. Focus your efforts on locating the person, and reserve judgment until you have an opportunity to discover for yourself who that person is and has become. Then you can decide if you simply want answers and closure, or if you would like to make a new beginning with this person in your life.

What's Different About This Search?

If you've been reading *The Locator* straight through (which you should be, no matter what kind of search you are pursuing), you know by now that chapters four through seven are merely "starter" chapters, meant to give you a basic idea of the elements of your specific kind of search. You should read all four of these chapters, because every search shares elements with every other search, even though each one is individually unique. You will find no quick answers to finding a deadbeat parent in this chapter—but it will put you in the right mind-set for reading the other chapters of *The Locator.*

If the purpose of your particular search is primarily to locate an individual who is not paying child support, you should contact this government agency:

The Federal Office of Child Support
370 LaFont Promenade, SW
Washington, DC 20047
(202) 401-9271

Unfortunately, at the present time there is no national headquarters you can contact about the person you are seeking. The federal office noted above can provide phone numbers for each state's child support office. You will then call the office in your own state (call your own state, not the deadbeat dad's state). The child support office will instruct you about how to open a case, and will refer you to a local office.

When contacting these offices, you will have to provide the name, date of birth, and social security number of the person you are seeking. His or her last known address will also be helpful to these agencies.

Although the above-mentioned agencies want to assist, they are often backlogged. It will be in your best interest, after initiating your case, to pursue your own search using the various resources provided in *The Locator.* However, before you start your own search, go through the official motions and open your case with the proper child support office. You want the proper channels to be already open and ready to go; that way, when you do find the deadbeat parent, there won't be any delay in getting the state on your side.

Deadbeat dads are much easier to find than deadbeat moms, because men do not change their names. Deadbeat moms often remarry and change names, sometimes more than once. If you don't know the name of the person you're looking for, you will have to rely on the other techniques listed in *The Locator,* which explain many, many ways to track down a person's name when you don't know it. If you do know the person's name, your search will be much easier.

Searching for a deadbeat ex-spouse is typically not that difficult, simply because the people who are looking for the deadbeats know a great deal of information about them. Since you were married to this person, you will presumably know his full name, exact date of birth, social security number, and the names of most of his family and friends. As we have continuously stated throughout *The Locator:* Once you know the person's name, you've won a huge part of the search battle.

If you do not have the parent's social security number or exact date of birth, the best place to start will be with his family. If you and they are not on speaking terms, or if you feel they are hiding something, have someone else call for you. Give the calling friend a "creative" reason for calling the deadbeat's family: Have your friend say he is an old high school friend, a military buddy, a schoolmate planning a reunion, and so on. It is a fact that almost all families know where the "missing" person is.

If you are a former spouse of this man or woman and do not have your ex's social security number, there are several places you can get it, many of which you probably have at home and just don't realize it. For example, old tax returns, bank account records (which are kept on file at the bank), mortgage papers, credit reports, medical bills, and divorce documents all contain this valuable piece of information.

If you have a lot of statistical information about the deadbeat parent, there are literally hundreds of ways to track him or her down. For example, if you have his full name and exact date of birth, you can try calling the department of motor vehicles in several states where you think he may be living. If you have his social security number, you could call our staff and have them do a social security trace for $59.95. Most people are not sophisticated enough to change their social security number, so if you have this piece of information, it is usually only a matter of time before he or she pops up on some computer.

Other Ideas

We've found that there are certain things most deadbeat parents do when they are trying to hide. For instance, they normally put their apartment, phone, and utility bills in a roommate's or friend's name—rather than going to the trouble of legally changing their own name. However, most deadbeats make certain mistakes over and over again.

Let's say that Dad took off two years ago with the pickup. In most cases, all you have to do is call your insurance agent and have him give you a copy of the old policy. On that policy will be the pickup's vehicle identification number, or VIN. Once you have this number, you can go to law enforcement or the department of motor vehicles and get the current address associated with that vehicle. It's public information.

Here's another approach. Even though Dad may have disappeared, his likes and dislikes probably haven't changed. These hobbies and habits can be a powerful locating tool. If he was an outdoorsman, hunting and fishing licenses can provide a wealth of information—just contact the licensing agencies in the relevant states, or in the states where you think he may be living.

One of our clients recently wrote us that he'd located his son's mother (who had disappeared six years earlier) simply by calling the publisher of a magazine his wife had subscribed to when they were married. He figured she was probably still a subscriber. On the phone to the magazine, he said that his wife hadn't received last month's issue, and asked which address they had on file. Sure enough, she was still subscribing to her favorite magazine, and the subscription clerk gave him his ex-wife's current address.

If the deadbeat ex-spouse belonged to any club that has chapters around the country, many club headquarters will have national directories. Was the deadbeat in any professional organizations? Many national associations keep national files of their members. Was the deadbeat a boater or a pilot? These licenses are traceable too. As you can see, the possibilities are endless.

Collecting Money from Deadbeat Spouses

Finally, a note about collection. If you have not received satisfaction from the proper government authorities in the past, there are several private companies out there who will, for a fee (usually thirty percent of all collected moneys), handle the collection end of this problem for you. One company that reports substantial success rates in this type of work is Child Support Enforcement based in Austin, Texas. They can be reached by phone nationwide at (800) 801-KIDS, or write to:

Child Support Enforcement
P.O. Box 49459
Austin, TX 78765

A word of caution: No matter what company you choose to do this for you, be sure that they get paid only when *you* get paid. Anyone who asks for money up front should not be trusted.

A Sample Search

Every search is different, which is why this chapter (along with Chapters Four, Five, and Seven) is meant to prime you for the search, to suggest possibilities, but not to dictate a methodology. You really need to read the entire book to get a complete picture of how to go about searching for a deadbeat parent.

That said, here is a sample search. This case is from the International Locator, Inc./BigHugs.com files, which means we helped this person with her search, but it has been rewritten to show you how, if she had read this book and followed its techniques, she could have succeeded on her own.

Susan, a thirty-year-old woman, contacted us for help in locating her birth father. His name was Eugene Raskin. Susan knew very little about him. Her mom had told her they'd never been married but had lived together for a year. They'd met on the beach in Fort Lauderdale, Florida; he'd worked a job in construction. Gene, as he liked to be called, was about two or three years older than Susan's mom, Ellen, who was born in 1950.

Ellen either remembered little or else refused to provide any additional information when her daughter questioned her. She always replied, "I really don't remember much. I think his family lived in the Midwest. Maybe Kansas or Nebraska. He left when he found out I was pregnant, and I never heard from him again."

If you've read the other sample searches in the previous chapters, you know what Susan did now. She put together some notebooks for search maps, conversation logs, correspondence logs, and library logs; she also borrowed a friend's tape recorder and bought a jack with which to make recordings (see Chapter Two).

Next, Susan pushed her mother to come up with any memories she had about her father's past—anything at all—knowing that every little detail could potentially be useful in her search. Ellen did say that she thought he might have been "Eugene Raskin, Jr.," and that she thought she remembered him saying his father had been killed in a train accident, maybe when Gene was in his late teens.

That was all Susan had to work with. There were several ways she could have solved this case, but here is what she chose to do. First, she checked *www.reunionregistry.com,* and a few other free reunion registries to see if her father was registered in an effort to find her. He wasn't at the moment, but she registered herself in case he came looking for her there.

After reviewing the facts that she had (and the possible facts that she had), Susan guessed that her father had probably been born between 1946 and 1948. Therefore, if indeed his father were Eugene Raskin, Sr., then she guessed he would have died between 1961 and 1967, the years when Eugene Raskin, Jr., might have been in his late teens. Taking these dates and these names, she decided to check the Social Security Death Index, which was available at her local Family History Center (see Chapter Ten).

There were a number of Eugene Raskins listed in the index; however, there was only one who would have been the right age to be Gene's father. He was also listed as a "Sr.," which gave Susan some hope that she was on the right track.

The Social Security Death Index listed the date of death, along with the city where the final benefits were paid: Olathe, Kansas.

Susan called the public library in Olathe and spoke to a helpful and friendly librarian, who was more than happy to look up the obituary in the library's microfiche files of the local paper. The librarian found a copy of the obit, printed the day after Eugene Raskin, Sr., died. She read it to Susan over the phone, and then faxed her a copy. It stated that Eugene Raskin, Sr., of Olathe, Kansas, had been killed in a train accident! That matched Susan's mother's memory perfectly. The obituary provided the names of his surviving widow and his children, and also listed the city in which they currently resided—Lawrence, Kansas.

Well, it was a piece of cake from that point. A simple call to directory assistance located Gene's brother (Lloyd Raskin of Lawrence, Kansas). Susan called Lloyd Raskin (Chapter Nine) and explained that she was trying to find an old friend, Gene. She didn't want to make anyone nervous at this point by mentioning that Gene was her father—probably his family members had no idea of his past and would be protective of him, and potentially uncooperative if she explained the whole story.

Lloyd was more than cooperative and gave Susan Gene's current address and phone number.

Rather than call him out of the blue, she wrote him a very nice letter (Chapter Eight), gently explaining who she was and how much she wanted to see him, and reassuring him that she wanted nothing more than to talk to him. Within days, she received a phone call from him. He tried to talk, but started sobbing and said, "Is this Susie, Ellen's daughter?" When Susan confirmed that it was, he went on to say that he had vicariously watched her grow up by secretly keeping tabs on where Ellen was. He had even managed to get a copy of her senior picture out of a yearbook! He knew that Ellen had married in 1970, and always assumed that Susan didn't know her stepfather wasn't her real dad. He would have tried to contact her, but he was afraid of hurting her or destroying her life. And he had never married or had any other children. Needless to say, a very happy reunion took place within days!

S E V E N

Finding Someone Who Was or Is in the Military

Locating someone who is or has been in the military is one of those rare cases where we can be grateful for government red tape. Active military personnel cannot make a *move* without a mountain of paperwork following them, and our government's system of veteran benefit programs makes locating former military personnel relatively simple.

If the person you are seeking cannot be located through traditional military record sources, or if you don't have his or her full name, you will have to rely on the strategies used elsewhere in this book to track the person down. But as soon as you have his or her name, social security number, and geographical information, you will be able to turn to the military records and find the person successfully.

The Most Common Search

The most common military search is initiated by a person looking for a missing father. It is also not unusual for people to look for old military buddies with whom they have lost touch over the years. In either case, regardless of the motivation, implementing some resources unique to the military can often offer a jump start. Information hard to come by in other searches is much easier to get a hold of in a military search.

Here is a typical scenario: You are looking for your dad but have very little information on him. Your mom met him while he was stationed at a particular military facility, but she either does not know or will not tell you where he was from originally. She doesn't remember or very possibly never knew his date of birth, and she knows nothing about his family. In other words, you have only a name and an approximate age; you know which branch of the military he served in; and you know which base he was stationed at, and the year he was there. Doesn't sound like much, does it? It is probably enough to get you started . . . read on!

Military Records

Special thanks to Lieutenant Colonel Richard S. Johnson for allowing us to base portions of this section on his book *How to Locate Anyone Who Is or Has Been in the Military.*

If you are looking for a long-lost love, an old friend, a birth parent, or anyone else, find out, if possible, if that person was ever in the military. If he or she was, then use the techniques in this chapter before going anywhere else. It truly is much easier to track down someone who has been in the service.

A note about adoption searches: Most adoption agencies and related organizations do not consider military backgrounds to be identifying information. Therefore, it's often easy to find out if the person you're looking for is or ever was in a branch of the service—just ask. Even if you don't have a name yet, knowing that your birth father or birth mother was in the military will give you a huge advantage in your search.

You have several options available to you when trying to search military records. First of all, limited information from military personnel files is available to everyone under the Freedom of Information Act (see page 98, "Requesting Information from the Federal Government"). This information typically includes:

- rank/grade
- name
- duty status
- date of rank/grade
- service number
- dependents (including name, sex, and age)
- gross salary

- geographic locations of duty assignments
- military/civilian education level
- awards and decorations
- official photograph
- city and state of last known residence
- date and place of induction and discharge

If the veteran is deceased, the place of birth, date and location of death, and the place of burial can also be released. Complete personnel and health records are also available to next of kin. Because of the Privacy Act, the general public will not be provided with medical information, social security numbers, or present addresses.

If you suspect that the person you are searching for may have died while enlisted, contact your nearest Family History Center for assistance (see Chapter Ten). The Family History Center keeps a set of records called the Military Index, which can be extremely helpful and can provide many of the details you'll need to continue your search. The Military Index is a list of deceased persons who served in Korea, Vietnam, and World War II. Every Family History Center has the index available, on site, at no charge to the public. It provides a date of birth and a date of death, and most often a place of death. If you find the place of death, you'll be able to go to that town's local newspaper files and find a copy of the obituary.

To obtain official records or specific information, send a copy of Standard Form 180: Request Pertaining to Military Records (pages 86 and 87) to the National Personnel Records Center (NPRC). Their address is provided below. On this form, you must state if you are requesting information under the Freedom of Information Act. There is no charge to former service members or their next of kin; however, others may have to pay a small fee for research and photocopying. If you plan to take this route, be patient. Since the NPRC receives 200,000 letters and requests every month, a reply can take as long as six months. Send requests regarding military personnel to the first address, and requests regarding civilians employed by the military to the second address.

National Personnel Records Center
Military Personnel Records
9700 Page Boulevard
St. Louis, MO 63132-5100

REQUEST PERTAINING TO MILITARY RECORDS

Please read instructions on the reverse. If more space is needed, use plain paper.

PRIVACY ACT OF 1974 COMPLIANCE INFORMATION. The following information is provided in accordance with 5 U.S.C. 552a(e)(3) and applies to this form. Authority for collection of the information is 44 U.S.C. 2907, 3101, and 3103, and E.O. 9397 of November 22, 1943. Disclosure of the information is voluntary. The principal purpose of the information is to assist the facility servicing the records in locating and verifying the correctness of the requested records or information to answer your inquiry. Routine uses of the information as established and published in accordance with 5 U.S.C.a(e)(4)(D) include the transfer of relevant information to appropriate Federal, State, local, or foreign agencies for use in civil, criminal, or regulatory investigations or prosecution. In addition, this form will be filed with the appropriate military records and may be transferred along with the record to another agency in accordance with the routine uses established by the agency which maintains the record. If the requested information is not provided, it may not be possible to service your inquiry.

SECTION I—INFORMATION NEEDED TO LOCATE RECORDS (Furnish as much as possible)

1. NAME USED DURING SERVICE *(Last, first, and middle)*	2. SOCIAL SECURITY NO.	3. DATE OF BIRTH	4. PLACE OF BIRTH

5. ACTIVE SERVICE, PAST AND PRESENT (For an effective records search, it is important that ALL service be shown below)

BRANCH OF SERVICE *(Also, show last organization, if known)*	DATES OF ACTIVE SERVICE		Check one		SERVICE NUMBER DURING THIS PERIOD
	DATE ENTERED	DATE RELEASED	OFFI-CER	EN-LISTED	

6. RESERVE SERVICE, PAST OR PRESENT *If "none," check here* ▶ ☐

a. BRANCH OF SERVICE	b. DATES OF MEMBERSHIP		c. Check one		d. SERVICE NUMBER DURING THIS PERIOD
	FROM	TO	OFFI-CER ☐	EN-LISTED ☐	

7. NATIONAL GUARD MEMBERSHIP *(Check one):* ☐ a. ARMY ☐ b. AIR FORCE ☐ c. NONE

d. STATE	e. ORGANIZATION	f. DATES OF MEMBERSHIP		g. Check one		h. SERVICE NUMBER DURING THIS PERIOD
		FROM	TO	OFFI-CER ☐	EN-LISTED ☐	

8. IS SERVICE PERSON DECEASED ☐ YES ☐ NO *If "yes," enter date of death.*

9. IS (WAS) INDIVIDUAL A MILITARY RETIREE OR FLEET RESERVIST ☐ YES ☐ NO

SECTION II—REQUEST

1. EXPLAIN WHAT INFORMATION OR DOCUMENTS YOU NEED; OR, CHECK ITEM 2; OR, COMPLETE ITEM 3

2. IF YOU ONLY NEED A STATEMENT OF SERVICE *check here* ☐

3. *LOST SEPARATION DOCUMENT REPLACEMENT REQUEST (Complete a or b, and c.)*

☐	a. REPORT OF SEPARATION *(DD Form 214 or equivalent)*	YEAR ISSUED	*This contains information normally needed to determine eligibility for benefits. It may be furnished only to the veteran, the surviving next of kin, or to a representative with veteran's signed release (item 5 of this form).*
☐	b. DISCHARGE CERTIFICATE	YEAR ISSUED	*This shows only the date and character at discharge. It is of little value in determining eligibility for benefits. It may be issued only to veterans discharged honorably or under honorable conditions; or, if deceased, to the surviving spouse.*

c. EXPLAIN HOW SEPARATION DOCUMENT WAS LOST

4. EXPLAIN PURPOSE FOR WHICH INFORMATION OR DOCUMENTS ARE NEEDED

6. REQUESTER

a. IDENTIFICATION *(check appropriate box)*

☐ Same person identified in Section I ☐ Surviving spouse

☐ Next of kin (relationship) ____________

☐ Other (specify)

b. SIGNATURE *(see instruction 3 on reverse side)* | DATE OF REQUEST

5. RELEASE AUTHORIZATION, IF REQUIRED *(Read instruction 3 on reverse side)*

I hereby authorize release of the requested information/documents to the person indicated at right (item 7).

VETERAN SIGN HERE ▶ ____________

(If signed by other than veteran show relationship to veteran.)

7. *Please type or print clearly —* COMPLETE RETURN ADDRESS

Name, number and street, city, State and ZIP code

TELEPHONE NO. *(include area code)* ▶

180-108 NSN 7540-00-142-9360 STANDARD FORM 180 (Rev. 7-86) Prescribed by NARA (36 CFR 1228.162(a))

Standard Form 180—Request for Military Records

INSTRUCTIONS

1. Information needed to locate records. Certain identifying information is necessary to determine the location of an individual's record of military service. Please give careful consideration to and answer each item on this form. If you do not have and cannot obtain the information for an item, show "NA," meaning the information is "not available." Include as much of the requested information as you can. This will help us to give you the best possible service.

2. Charges for service. A nominal fee is charged for certain types of service. In most instances service fees cannot be determined in advance. If your request involves a service fee you will be notified as soon as that determination is made.

3. Restrictions on release of information. Information from records of military personnel is released subject to restrictions imposed by the military departments consistent with the provisions of the Freedom of Information Act of 1967 (as amended in 1974) and the Privacy Act of 1974. A service person has access to almost any information contained in his own record. The next of kin, if the veteran is deceased, and Federal officers for official purposes, are authorized to receive information from a military service or medical record only as specified in the above cited Acts. Other requesters must have the release authorization, in item 5 of the form, signed by the veteran or, if deceased, by the next of kin. Employers and others needing proof of military service are expected to accept the information shown on documents issued by the Armed Forces at the time a service person is separated.

4. Location of military personnel records. The various categories of military personnel records are described in the chart below. For each category there is a code number which indicates the address at the bottom of the page to which this request should be sent. For each military service there is a note explaining approximately how long the records are held by the military service before they are transferred to the National Personnel Records Center, St. Louis. Please read these notes carefully and make sure you send your inquiry to the right address. Please note especially that the record is not sent to the National Personnel Records Center as long as the person retains any sort of reserve obligation, whether drilling or non-drilling.

(If the person has two or more periods of service within the same branch, send your request to the office having the record for the last period of service.)

5. Definitions for abbreviations used below:
NPRC—National Personnel Records Center PERS—Personnel Records
TDRL—Temporary Disability Retirement List MED—Medical Records

SERVICE	NOTE: (See paragraph 4 above.)	CATEGORY OF RECORDS — WHERE TO WRITE ADDRESS CODE		▼
AIR FORCE (USAF)	*Except for TDRL and general officers retired with pay, Air Force records are transferred to NPRC from Code 1, 90 days after separation and from Code 2, 150 days after separation.*	Active members (includes National Guard on active duty in the Air Force), TDRL, and general officers retired with pay		1
		Reserve, retired reservist in nonpay status, current National Guard officers not on active duty in Air Force, and National Guard released from active duty in Air Force.		2
		Current National Guard enlisted not on active duty in Air Force.		13
		Discharged, deceased, and retired with pay.		14
COAST GUARD (USCG)	*Coast Guard officer and enlisted records are transferred to NPRC 7 months after separation.*	Active, reserve, and TDRL members.		3
		Discharged, deceased, and retired members *(see next item).*		14
		Officers separated before 1/1/29 and enlisted personnel separated before 1/1/15.		6
MARINE CORPS (USMC)	*Marine Corps records are transferred to NPRC between 6 and 9 months after separation.*	Active, TDRL, and Selected Marine Corps Reserve members.		4
		Individual Ready Reserve and Fleet Marine Corps Reserve members.		5
		Discharged, deceased, and retired members *(see next item).*		14
		Members separated before 1/1/1905.		6
ARMY (USA)	*Army records are transferred to NPRC as follows: Active Army and Individual Ready Reserve Control Groups: About 60 days after separation. U.S. Army Reserve Troop Unit personnel: About 120 to 180 days after separation.*	Reserve, living retired members, retired general officers, and active duty records of current National Guard members who performed service in the U.S. Army before 7/1/72.*		7
		Active officers (including National Guard on active duty in the U.S. Army)		8
		Active enlisted (including National Guard on active duty in the U.S. Army) and enlisted TDRL.		9
		Current National Guard officers not on active duty in the U.S. Army.		12
		Current National Guard enlisted not on active duty in the U.S. Army		13
		Discharged and deceased members *(see next item).*		14
		Officers separated before 7/1/17 and enlisted separated before 11/1/12.		6
		Officers and warrant officers TDRL.		8
NAVY (USN)	*Navy records are transferred to NPRC 6 months after retirement or complete separation.*	Active members (including reservists on duty)—PERS and MED		10
		Discharged, deceased, retired (with and without pay) less than six months, TDRL, drilling and nondrilling reservists	PERS ONLY	10
			MED ONLY	11
		Discharged, deceased, retired (with and without pay) more than six months *(see next item)*—PERS & MED		14
		Officers separated before 1/1/03 and enlisted separated before 1/1/1886—PERS and MED		6

**Code 12 applies to active duty records of current National Guard officers who performed service in the U.S. Army after 6/30/72.*
Code 13 applies to active duty records of current National Guard enlisted members who performed service in the U.S. Army after 6/30/72

ADDRESS LIST OF CUSTODIANS (BY CODE NUMBERS SHOWN ABOVE)—Where to write / send this form for each category of records

Code	Address	Code	Address	Code	Address	Code	Address
1	Air Force Manpower and Personnel Center Military Personnel Records Division Randolph AFB, TX 78150-6001	5	Marine Corps Reserve Support Center 10950 El Monte Overland Park, KS 66211-1408	8	USA MILPERCEN ATTN: DAPC-MSR 200 Stoval Street Alexandria, VA 22332-0400	12	Army National Guard Personnel Center Columbia Pike Office Building 5600 Columbia Pike Falls Church, VA 22041
2	Air Reserve Personnel Center Denver, CO 80280-5000	6	Military Archives Division National Archives and Records Administration Washington, DC 20408	9	Commander U.S. Army Enlisted Records and Evaluation Center Ft. Benjamin Harrison, IN 46249-5301	13	The Adjutant General *(of the appropriate State, DC, or Puerto Rico)*
3	Commandant U.S. Coast Guard Washington, DC 20593-0001	7	Commander U.S. Army Reserve Personnel Center ATTN: DARP-PAS 9700 Page Boulevard St. Louis, MO 63132-5200	10	Commander Naval Military Personnel Command ATTN: NMPC-036 Washington, DC 20370-5036	14	National Personnel Records Center (Military Personnel Records) 9700 Page Boulevard St. Louis, MO 63132
4	Commandant of the Marine Corps (Code MMRB-10) Headquarters, U.S. Marine Corps Washington, DC 20380-0001			11	Naval Reserve Personnel Center New Orleans, LA 70146-5000		

490-498 (m) STANDARD FORM 180 BACK (Rev. 7-86)

Standard Form 180—Request for Military Records

National Personnel Records Center—Civilian Records
111 Winnebago Street
St. Louis, MO 63118-4199
(314) 425-5722

Army: (314) 538-4122
Army (prior 1960): (314) 538-4144
Air Force: (314) 538-4218
Navy, Marines, Coast Guard: (314) 538-4200

In addition to providing general information, the NPRC will also forward correspondence to veterans at their last known address. Normally this service is reserved for situations considered "in the veteran's best interest." The NPRC will open your letter and read it. If the letter meets their requirements, they will forward it. You will not be informed of the outcome.

Unfortunately, in July 1973 a fire at the NPRC destroyed about eighty percent of the records for army personnel discharged between November 1, 1912, and January 1, 1960. About seventy-five percent of the records for air force personnel discharged between September 25, 1947, and January 1, 1964, were also lost. If your request is denied on these grounds, don't give up. Ask them to check alternate information sources at the state adjutants general and veteran's service offices.

War Babes

If you have reason to believe that you are the child of an American serviceman, the NPRC is required to forward your letter. In November 1990, a group named War Babes brought suit against the NPRC in federal court. The terms of this settlement now permit, under the provisions of the Freedom of Information Act, the children of American servicemen to try to locate their fathers by utilizing records kept at the NPRC.

The Department of Veterans Affairs

The Department of Veterans Affairs (formerly the Veterans Administration) will also forward letters to veterans of the armed services. Before sending a letter, contact your local library and ask for the address and telephone number of the nearest VA office, or call (800) 827-1000 for your closest VA regional office. Call that office and tell a counselor you wish to verify if a veteran is listed in their files before mailing any correspondence. Give the individual's full name, service number, social security number, and VA file number or claim number. If you do not have this information, your counselor can sometimes still identify the right person from a date of birth, branch of service, or possibly even the name alone if it is uncommon. If they find the individual, ask for his or her VA claim number and anything else they'll tell you. You will need the claim number later on (see page 90); and any other tidbits are always welcome. As you read this book, you'll see how every piece of information, no matter how small, can add up.

If your regional office can't find the individual in their files, contact the VA insurance office in Philadelphia at:

Department of Veterans Affairs
P.O. Box 13399
Philadelphia, PA 19101
(215) 842-2000

This office has insurance information in its files that is not readily available in the regional offices.

The VA does not have all veterans listed in their files, only those who have at some time applied for VA benefits. The benefits are wide ranging, and the odds are good that your person may have applied for educational assistance, disability compensation, pensions, home loans, or insurance. The address in the VA's files will be the last one where the veteran received benefits.

To have a letter forwarded, place your correspondence in an unsealed stamped envelope *without* your return address. Put the veteran's name and VA claim number on the front of this envelope. Next, prepare a short fact sheet, and request that the VA forward this letter to the individual. Tell them you were given the VA claim number by their regional office. Include all the information you know about the veteran to help make sure they identify the right person. Place all of this in a large envelope and mail it to the regional VA office you spoke with. If they cannot find the individual, they will return your letter to you. They will also inform you if the letter was undeliverable by the post office. In general, the VA is very cooperative in providing assistance in locating veterans.

If you know a veteran's full name, date of birth, and service number, it may be possible to obtain his or her social security number, if he applied for benefits after April 1973, by writing:

Department of Veterans Affairs
VA Records Processing Center
P.O. Box 5020
St. Louis, MO 63115

Enclose a check or money order for $2.00 payable to the Department of Veterans Affairs. Request the veteran's claim number. If the veteran has applied for some type of VA benefit, Veterans Affairs will be able to provide you with a nine-digit claim number preceded by "C," or "XC" if the person is deceased. After April 1973 this number is the same as the veteran's social security number.

The Military's Worldwide Locator Offices

If you have reason to believe that the person you are looking for is *still in* the military, each branch of the service maintains a worldwide locator office that will either forward a letter or provide you with the current military unit of assignment within the United States.

If you want a letter forwarded, place it in a sealed stamped envelope. Put your name and return address in the upper-left corner. In the center of the envelope put the full name of the individual, rank, and social security number (if known—not absolutely necessary). On a separate sheet, list everything you know that may help the agency identify this person.

In a legal-size envelope, enclose: the fact sheet with all the identifying information you have, the letter you want forwarded, and a check for $3.50 made out to the United States Treasury. If you state that you are a family member on the fact sheet, then sending a fee will not be necessary. Be sure to include your return address on the outside of this envelope. Address it to the appropriate locator office listed below. Even though they will try to find the person, they cannot require a reply. If they cannot find the person, they will notify you and tell you why.

Marine Corps Worldwide Locator
HQMC-MMSB-10
2008 Elliot Rd. #20
Quantico, VA 22134-5030
(703) 784-3942

Navy Worldwide Locator
Bureau of Navy Personnel
2 Navy Annex P-02116
Washington, DC 20370-0216
(703) 614-3155

Air Force Worldwide Locator
AFPC-MSIMDL
550 C Street W., Suite 50
Randolph AFB, TX 78150-4752
(210) 652-5774 or 652-5775

Army Worldwide Locator
USAEREC
Indianapolis, IN 46249-5301
(317) 542-4211

Coast Guard Worldwide Locator
Personnel Commander CGPC-ADM-3
2100 2nd St. SW #1616
Washington, DC 20593-0001
(202) 267-1340

Other Ideas

On September 16, 1940, President Franklin D. Roosevelt signed into law the first peacetime Selective Service Act. It required all men between the ages of twenty-one and thirty-five to register for the draft. These records are available to the public for men who registered for the draft from 1940 to 1975 under the Selective Service Act. The records typically list the person's name, date of birth, draft classification, induction address, and sometimes date of separation. For information about searching these records, write:

National Headquarters—Selective Service System
1550 Wilson Blvd., #400
Arlington, VA 22209-2426

If you have or obtain a service number for the person you are seeking, you may well have his or her social security number. The armed forces began using social security numbers for service numbers in the following years:

Army: April 1969

Air Force: April 1969

Coast Guard: October 1974

Navy: April 1972

Marine Corps: April 1972

Your local library (or the local library in your search area) may be a valuable source of information. Libraries often have copies of draft registration records for their county. These records contain legal names, addresses, and dates of birth. The libraries also often have voter registration lists, which may provide the same information and may also provide a social security number.

In addition to these traditional methods of tracking someone with a military background, a new service called V.E.T.S. has recently become available from a private firm in Missouri. This firm claims a tremendous success rate in locating veterans; they can be reached at (800) 449-VETS. In most cases, the fee does not exceed fifteen dollars, and results can be expected within three to six weeks. Because of the minimal cost and short response time, you might wish to try this organization before pursuing other avenues.

There are literally *hundreds* of additional ways to locate someone who has been in the military. The above guidelines should be sufficient to help you get the information you need. However, if it looks like a large portion of your search is going to be focused on getting military information, we strongly suggest that you obtain the following book: *How to Locate Anyone Who Is or Has Been in the Military* by Lieutenant Colonel Richard S. Johnson. Send a check or money order for $24.00 (South Carolina residents must add $1.00 sales tax), to:

Military Information Enterprises
P.O. Box 17118
Spartanburg, SC 29301
(800) 937-2133

A Sample Search

Every search is different, which is why this chapter (along with Chapters Four, Five, and Six) is meant to prime you for the search, to suggest possibilities, but not to dictate a methodology. You really need to read the entire book to get a complete picture of how to go about searching for someone who was or is in the military.

That said, here is a sample search for a military buddy. This case is from the International Locator, Inc./BigHugs.com files, which means we helped this person with his search, but it has been rewritten to show you how, if he had read this book and followed its techniques, he could have succeeded on his own.

Rob wanted to find his old army buddy, "Gunny" Martin Ferrell. Rob guessed that Gunny was about a year or two younger than he. He knew where Gunny had served and when, and thought he remembered Gunny saying he was from Kansas City . . . whether that was Kansas City, Kansas, or Kansas City, Missouri, he wasn't sure! Furthermore, he wasn't sure of the correct spelling of the last name (Ferrell? Ferrel? Farrell? Farrel? etc.).

Of course, before diving into his search, Rob knew he had to get organized. He cleared off a desk in a back room and declared it his search area. In it he created files for search maps, conversation logs, correspondence logs, and a progress journal. He had a tape recorder handy, but went out and bought a jack so he could record conversations. (See Chapter Two.)

Now Rob was ready to start looking. There were several things that occurred to him. He knew he should first try to confirm the spelling of Gunny's last name. However, there didn't seem to be any direct way to do that outside the normal methods for a military search, so he proceeded and hoped the name issue would sort itself out.

He called the VA and asked if any death or benefit claims had been filed for a "Gunny" Martin Ferrell, explaining that he wasn't sure how to spell the last name. They asked him for a date of birth, which he didn't know, so he bluffed and just made one up, trying to get the year as close as possible. He was close enough—the helpful clerk corrected him on the date of birth (he was ten months off), and confirmed that a Martin Farrell had filed a benefit claim for continued education. In addition to giving him the correct birthday, they gave him a claim number.

Rob looked at the claim number and realized that given the date it was issued, it must also be Gunny's social security number. Examining the number and comparing it to the SSN geographical chart (see Chapter Ten)—which allows you to determine where a number was issued based on the first three digits—Rob realized that this social security number had been issued from Missouri. That piece of information jibed with his memory that Gunny was from Kansas City. Martin Farrell was looking more and more like Gunny!

The next step was to send a letter to the VA, asking them to forward it to his buddy (since he had the social security number, he also could have run a database check, which would have been substantially faster—see Chapter Twelve). After a few months of patient waiting, he got a call from Gunny, who was now living in Little Rock, Arkansas.

Within minutes these two army buddies were reminiscing about their past, and the years and miles that had separated them instantly disappeared.

EIGHT

The Key to Success: Letter-Writing that Gets Results!

There are two basic ways you'll be gathering information: writing letters and making telephone calls. Sometimes you'll be requesting public information; other times (especially in the case of an adoption search) you'll be requesting information that falls into the hard-to-categorize gray area between identifying and nonidentifying.

This chapter prescribes specific guidelines for increasing the efficacy of your requests. The thirty-five sample documents are actual letters that the International Locator, Inc./BigHugs.com uses successfully every day to get information. Developed over time, by trial and error, these specific letters have played a key role in reuniting thousands of families.

Throughout this chapter, you'll find instructions on when to use a certain type of letter, how to use it, and what you'll need to do to tailor one of our examples to your individual situation. Additionally, you'll find specialized tips and guidelines at the beginning of each letter. With a little creativity, you'll have no problem converting our examples into effective personal letters.

Ten Rules of Writing Letters

Both inheritance and medical urgency are normally considered reasons of good cause. However, since no firm definitions exist, the final decision still rests in the hands of whoever receives your request. Therefore, showing good cause is only *one part* of writing letters that get results.

We follow ten general rules in all our letters. They were originally developed by Mary Louise Foess, an author and Michigan schoolteacher. Over the past few years, we've fine-tuned them to fit our specific needs, and now we share them with you.

1. Whenever possible, always make your first contact to an agency or organization in writing. This allows you to plan each question and statement carefully. It also doesn't give the one from whom you're requesting information the chance to quiz you with uncomfortable, probing questions.

2. Put yourself in the position of the person opening your letter. Anticipate that person's response. We recommend that your first requests be handwritten and informal, to set the recipient at ease. Cursive penmanship in black ink on a yellow, legal-size paper works best.

   When writing a state department of vital statistics for birth, marriage, divorce, or death records, always make your first attempt in this format.

3. If you're claiming urgent reasons such as a medical emergency or a legal proceeding, send your request overnight or second-day delivery. Mailing an urgent request by regular post gives the recipient a mixed message (how urgent could your request be?). Along these lines, it also makes sense to include extra postage in your request to cover express *return* shipping.

4. Never ramble. Don't give the recipient too much information. Use integrity and sincerity, but don't give your life history.

5. Send a wallet-size color photo of yourself and your family (if any). The recipient will automatically attach a face to your request, which will make it more personal.

6. Be as accommodating as possible. Offer to pay any search and duplication fees. Use a money order; do not use cash or a personal check to pay fees. (Cash can be lost or stolen; personal checks are typically held until they clear, often delaying a response.) When using a money order, attach the receipt to your copy of the letter, and place them in your correspondence file.

   Send all letters with a self-addressed stamped envelope. This will demonstrate your sincerity and encourage a timely response.

7. Try to include two character references—one from a clergy member if possible.

8. Notarizing a letter or sending a request by certified mail will make it seem more important and will catch the recipient's attention. Generally, a letter should be notarized when you:

(A) want to prove that the contents of the letter are factual

(B) need to verify that you are the person making the request

(C) haven't received satisfactory cooperation in your previous attempts.

Your bank will typically have a notary public on staff to do this. Notary publics can also be found in the yellow pages of your telephone directory. If you are a member of AAA, you may have free notary services available at the nearest office. Do not forget to make copies of these letters for your search planner *after* they have been notarized.

Mailing a letter certified mail/return receipt requested is a good idea when sending important items such as certified documents and legal papers. It costs a little more (usually under five dollars), but you will have written proof that your request was received and the signature of the person who accepted it. The postmaster will give you a receipt, which should be put in your search planner.

9. Do not mention adoption search as a reason for your request unless it is absolutely necessary. Clerks may feel uncomfortable helping with an adoption search, which will lead them to prejudge your intentions and refuse to give you information they might otherwise routinely release.

   We use the term "genealogy search" in place of adoption search when making a request. The goals are the same in terms of the information you'd be looking for, and following this rule can greatly increase your chances of success. You may want to say something along these lines: "I am an active genealogist doing a family research project. Since I was not raised by my natural family, I depend on people like you to help me find my roots."

10. Include effective phrases in your letter, such as:

   "I'm an ordinary person who cannot afford costly private detectives or attorneys. I depend on your good faith and effort to help me. Please don't let me down."

   "A few moments of your time may unlock the door to my true bloodline. This will affect my happiness, and my family's, for a long time."

   "Don't ignore my letter, please. I have no one else to turn to."

   "No clue is insignificant. Any help, however small, will be deeply appreciated."

   "Please go the extra mile for me. I'm depending on you."

   Even though the officials receiving your letters may be somewhat conservative, they are nonetheless human and have emotions and a conscience. If your first correspondence is unsuccessful, keep trying different variations and the chances are good that you'll eventually get the information you need.

Requesting Information from the Federal Government

The following are some helpful guidelines from *12 of the Most Often Made Mistakes* by W. E. Siegmond. For more details, consult *How to Use the Freedom of Information Act: FOIA* by L. G. Sherick (New York: Arco Publishing Co., 1978) in your local library.

(1) The first step when requesting information from the federal government (and sometimes the most difficult) is locating the correct agency to address. To simplify this process, the name, address, and telephone number of each state's central information agency is listed in Appendix 2. These agencies should be able to refer you to a public information or Freedom of Information Act officer who can help with your requests—although you may have to be persistent.

(2) Always state in writing that you are making this request "pursuant to the Freedom of Information Act."

(3) Offer to pay any reasonable standard charges for actual search time and duplication fees. You will be charged anyway, but this clarifies your intentions.

(4) Set a limit on charges you are willing to pay. Ask the agency to contact you for approval if the costs exceed that amount. (The Department of Agriculture once billed a hapless questioner $90,000 in search fees!)

(5) Ask for a response within ten working days. This is the length of time a federal agency has by law, but it lets them know that you understand your rights.

(6) There are nine classifications of information to which you *do not* have access under the Freedom of Information Act. These include information that would jeopardize national security; commercial trade secrets; and financial information. If your request falls into one of these classifications, there is nothing you can do. However, there may be some common excuses for not providing information, which there are ways to overcome.

"Your request is not specific enough."
The law requires only that you be reasonable. Do the best you can and *insist* that the information be produced.

"The records are not in our files."
Write back and ask where they are.

"We cannot find them."

Write back and ask the agency to clarify the extent to which they have searched.

"We need more time."

In certain instances, the agency is allowed more than ten working days, but generally you can insist the information be produced on time, because it is your right under the law.

"Why do you want these?"

You do not have to (and should not) answer this question. It only gives the agency reason to turn down your request. Pleasantly respond that you're afraid you'd rather not say, and that it is your understanding of the law that they don't have the right to ask you that question.

There are times when the only way to get information about yourself from certain organizations, schools, or hospitals is to employ the Freedom of Information Act. The FOIA is not a threat, it is the law. Use it! The Federal Information Center, (800) 688-9889, can help you locate any federal agency.

Writing Letters to Adoption Agencies

Once you've established that your adoption was handled by an agency that is still in business, your next step will be to contact them. (If you're not sure if your agency is still operating, a quick call to the state adoption department in the state where the birth occurred will answer this question and point you in the right direction. See Chapter Three, "State Adoption Records," for more information about this.)

Before diving straight into the instructions and samples, however, we need to familiarize you with some of the issues involved in the decision to grant information.

The Issue of Good Cause

You can greatly increase your chances of getting a positive answer from a government organization or an adoption agency when your request is considered to show good cause. While most states do not have specific guidelines as to exactly what good cause means, it is generally considered to be anything that constitutes a legal necessity or a legitimate health hazard.

You may not have a law-related motivation or a pending medical emergency behind your search, but if you do, you need to know how to utilize it in your letter writing.

Your Medical Need to Know

One of the most important and widely accepted reasons to start an adoption search is your medical need to know.

Scientists have made many great advances in the area of genetic research over the last twenty years. Only recently did medical experts realize that thousands of illnesses, from epilepsy to heart disease to some forms of cancer, have a hereditary component. Situations as severe as retardation and untimely death can, in some cases, be treated if medical experts know the birth family's medical history.

To the millions of adoptees who possess little or no family medical histories, these facts are alarming. Many of these hereditary diseases lie dormant between generations and can be passed down to loved ones unknowingly.

Fortunately, there is an increasing awareness among lawmakers about the importance of this issue. Some adoption agencies and states have even made the medical histories of adoptees and birth parents (to the extent it is known) available upon request. Unfortunately, these records are often incomplete, since illnesses in the birth family may not surface until long after the adoption is finalized.

In October 1990, the American Society of Human Genetics addressed the seriousness of this issue by adopting a public policy designed to "encourage state and private agencies to collect helpful genetic histories." A segment of that statement reads as follows:

1. Every person should have the right to gain access to his or her medical records, including genetic data that may reside therein.

2. A child entering foster care or the adoption process is at risk for losing access to relevant genetic facts about himself or herself.

3. The compilation of an appropriate genetic history and the inclusion of genetic data in the adoptee's medical files should be a routine part of the adoption process.

4. Genetic information should be obtained, organized, and stored in a manner that permits review, including periodic updating, by appropriate individuals.

5. The sharing of information should be bi-directional between the adoptive and biological parents until the child reaches an appropriate age to receive such information himself or herself.

The truth is, every adoptee, birth parent, and family member has a legitimate medical need to know, whether there is any hint of an upcoming medical condition or not; any unknown situation can be considered urgent by the adoptee. When writing letters, using the phrase "urgent medical reasons" will help to give you good cause consideration. Your request will carry more weight if it details a specific medical emergency and includes a letter from a physician on his or her stationery.

Inheritance and Estate Settlement

In some states, adoptees still have inheritance rights relating to their birth parents—even though all other forms of interaction are cut off. Individual state laws pertaining to inheritance are listed in Appendix 2. If the laws in your situation are favorable, birth parents and adoptees alike can use phrasing such as "probating a will" and "urgent matters of estate settlement" as good cause reasons for requesting information.

No agency has successfully created a set of rules to govern *exactly* what information can be given out, or *exactly* what information must be kept in closed files, simply because there are too many different situations and experiences to regulate. Nine times out of ten, the people whom you will contact—bureaucrats, clerks, volunteers, assistants, whoever is reading letters and answering phones—will have to use their personal judgment when deciding whether or not to tell you what you want to know. Therefore, a great deal depends on *how* you make your request. A good letter can tip the balance in your favor; the people reading it will decide that in this case, they *will* fulfill the request. Conversely, a bad letter can fail to be persuasive, and your request for information could be denied because of it.

Files kept by adoption agencies are often the most complete of any source; they generally include extensive backgrounds on both the birth family and the adoptive family. Unfortunately, they also have the strictest definitions of what qualifies as identifying information.

Therefore, *how* you make your first contact to an adoption agency is very important. Your first letter should have two parts: (1) a brief introduction of your circumstances, which must follow the "Ten Rules of Writing Letters" presented on pages 95 to 97, and (2) a list of specific questions asked in several different ways.

Along with the letter to the adoption agency, it is absolutely essential that you include a waiver of confidentiality (see Letters 32, 33, and 34). Have it notarized and ask the agency to put it in your file. This document allows someone who is looking for *you* to access your information—even if you can't get theirs. Birth parents should also enclose updated copies of their medical records and a summary of their family medical history with this waiver.

You will probably need to follow up your first or second letter with a phone call—whether you received a semihelpful reply, a flat-out rejection, or no reply at all (more about this in chapter nine). The purpose of making the first contact in writing is to get a feel for how cooperative the agency is going to be—without giving it a chance to ask you questions. Don't volunteer any information you may already know about the person you're looking for. Generally speaking, the less they think you know, the more cooperative they'll be. Keep your hopes up even if they don't release as much information initially as you'd like. This letter is just the first step.

Once the ice is broken, you'll start clearing the way for some meaningful progress. The purpose of the first letter is to get your foot in the door, so to speak. Once it's written and mailed, you have initiated a dialogue. You plan to continue that dialogue as long as necessary, so the best way to do this is to make the first contact as positive and pleasant as possible. Then, any future contacts will have a better chance of falling on receptive ears. When you establish a more personal and personable rapport with someone, it is more difficult for that person to refuse to help you. So first, make him like you; then, make him want to help you, and then find a way he *can* help you without fear of reprisal from his superiors (remember, if he gives out any identifying information, he could lose his job).

Every detail of your letter should be considered part of the "package"—from the postage on the envelope right down to how each sentence is phrased. Pay close attention to the small details most people overlook. Once you've completed a letter, step back and put yourself in the shoes of the person who will be opening it. Ask yourself, "If I got this letter, how would I respond to it?" As long as you're persistent, chances are you'll eventually get the information you need.

The Sample Letters and How to Use Them

In all these samples, where it says "give approximate date if known," you should certainly give the exact date if you know that. It's just that in most cases you will be lucky to know the approximate date.

Letter 1	Contacting a Possible Neighbor or Relative
Letter 2	Request for Marriage Records
Letter 3	Request for Divorce Records
Letter 4	Request for Death Records
Letter 5	Request for Probate Records
Letter 6	Request for Cemetery Records
Letter 7	Request for Funeral Home Records
Letter 8	Request to a Newspaper for Obituary Records
Letter 9	Request for School Records
Letter 10	Request for Alumni Organization Records

LETTER 1

Contacting Possible Neighbor or Relative

(Note: This letter should appear friendly and casual. It could be handwritten.)

Date

Dear ______,

I know this is an unusual letter to receive. I am hoping you can help me. I am looking for a friend, ____________________. (Or you can say, "I am looking for a friend of my parents.")

(Go on to provide some details based upon your information, i.e., date of birth, age, where subject lived or worked in a certain year.)

I really appreciate your time and help. It has been too long and I am eager to reconnect with this special friend (or, "I am eager to surprise my parents by reuniting them with ________________"). Any help you can offer will be greatly appreciated. Please drop me a note in the enclosed self-addressed stamped envelope, or you are welcome to call me collect at ____________________ (give phone number).

Hope this finds you and yours doing well. Thanks again.

Sincerely,

Your signature
Address
City, State, Zip

LETTER 2

Request for Marriage Records

(Note: This letter should be handwritten on regular notebook paper. It should appear urgent yet informal. You may also want to enclose a family photo.)

Date

County Clerk (see state directory)
County
Address
City, State, Zip

Dear County Clerk,
Would you please search your records for the marriage license and application for the following person:

–give full or partial names, both maiden and married, if known
–give dates of birth, if known
–give the date of marriage, within five years each way, if not known

My (husband/wife) and I are trying to locate this individual for urgent matters of inheritance. Please find a money order for (see state directory for amount) to cover any search and duplication fees. I have enclosed a self-addressed stamped envelope for your convenience. A great deal depends on your helping me as quickly as possible. All your efforts will be greatly appreciated. Thank you.

Sincerely,

Your signature, along with your husband's or wife's signature
Address
City, State, Zip

LETTER 3

Request for Divorce Records

(Note: This letter should be handwritten on regular notebook paper. It should appear urgent yet informal. You may also want to enclose a family photo.)

Date

County Clerk (see state directory)
County
Address
City, State, Zip

Dear County Clerk,
Please search your records and send me the full divorce records for my (put relationship here). The information I know is as follows:

-give parties' maiden and/or married names, if known
-give their address, if known
-give ages, if known
-give date and place of marriage, if known
-give approximate date of divorce with five years either way

My (husband/wife) and I are trying to locate this person to pass on urgent inheritance information. Please enclose any additional documents you may have. A great deal depends on your helping us as quickly as possible. We have enclosed a self-addressed stamped envelope and a money order for (for appropriate fee, check state directory). All your efforts will be greatly appreciated. Thank you.

Sincerely,

Your signature, along with your husband's or wife's signature
Address
City, State, Zip

LETTER 4

Request for Death Records

(Note: This letter should be handwritten on regular notebook paper. It should appear urgent yet informal. You may also want to enclose a family photo.)

Date

County Clerk (see state directory)
County
Address
City, State, Zip

Dear County Clerk,
Please search your records and send us copies of the death records for our (put relationship here). The necessary information is as follows:

–give full or partial name of the deceased and spouse, if known
–give their last address, if known
–give approximate date of birth, if known
–give date and place of marriage, if known
–give approximate date of death within five years either way

My (husband/wife) and I are trying to locate this information for urgent medical reasons. Please enclose any additional documents you may have. A great deal depends on your helping us as quickly as possible. We have enclosed a self-addressed stamped envelope and a money order for (for appropriate fee, check state directory). All your efforts will be greatly appreciated. Thank you.

Sincerely,

Your signature, along with your husband's or wife's signature
Address
City, State, Zip

LETTER 5

Request for Probate Records

(Note: This letter should be handwritten on regular notebook paper. It should appear urgent yet informal. You may also want to enclose a family photo.)

Date

County Clerk (see state directory)
Probate Records
County
Address
City, State, Zip

Dear County Clerk,
Please search your records and send us copies of the probate transcripts for our (put relationship here). The necessary information is as follows:

-give full or partial name of the deceased and spouse, if known
-give their last address, if known
-give approximate date of birth, if known
-give date and place of marriage, if known
-give approximate date of death, if known

My (husband/wife) and I are trying to locate this information for urgent medical reasons. Please enclose any additional documents you may have. A great deal depends on your helping us as quickly as possible. We have enclosed a self-addressed stamped envelope. All your efforts will be greatly appreciated. Thank you.

Sincerely,

Your signature, along with your husband's or wife's signature
Address
City, State, Zip

LETTER 6

Request for Cemetery Records

(Note: This letter should be handwritten on regular notebook paper. It should appear urgent yet informal. You may also want to enclose a family photo.)

Date

County Clerk (see state directory)
County
Address
City, State, Zip

Dear County Clerk,
Please search your files and send us copies of all the cemetery records for our (put relationship here). The necessary information is as follows:

–give full or partial name of the deceased
–give their last address, if known
–give approximate date of birth, if known
–give approximate date of death within five years either way, if known

My (husband/wife) and I are trying to locate this information as a part of our genealogical research. Please enclose any additional documents you may have, including payments. Please help us as quickly as possible. We have enclosed a self-addressed stamped envelope, and five dollars to cover any costs. All your efforts will be greatly appreciated. Thank you.

Sincerely,

Your signature, along with your husband's or wife's signature
Address
City, State, Zip

LETTER 7

Request for Funeral Home Records

(Note: This letter should be handwritten on regular notebook paper. It should appear urgent yet informal. You may also want to enclose a family photo.)

Funeral Home
Address
City, State, Zip

Dear Sirs and Madams,
Please search your records and send us copies of the funeral transcripts for our (put relationship here). This information is as follows:

-give full or partial name of the deceased and spouse, if known
-give their last address, if known
-give approximate date of birth, if known
-give approximate date of death within five years either way

My (husband/wife) and I are trying to locate this information for our genealogical research. Please enclose any additional documents you may have, including payments. A great deal depends on your helping us as quickly as possible. We have enclosed a self-addressed stamped envelope and five dollars to cover any costs. All your efforts will be greatly appreciated. Thank you.

Sincerely,

Your signature, along with your husband's or wife's signature
Address
City, State, Zip

LETTER 8

Request to Newspaper for Obituary Records

(Note: This letter should be handwritten on regular notebook paper. It should appear urgent yet informal. You may also want to enclose a family photo.)

Date

Name of Newspaper
Address
City, State, Zip

Dear Sirs and Madams,
Please search your past records and microfilm, and send us a copy of the obituary for our (put relationship here). The necessary information is as follows:

–give full or partial name of the deceased and spouse, if known
–give their last address, if known
–give approximate date of birth, if known
–give date and place of marriage, if known
–give approximate date of death within five years either way

My (husband/wife) and I are trying to locate this information for urgent judicial purposes. Please enclose any additional documents you may have. A great deal depends on your helping us as quickly as possible. We have enclosed a self-addressed stamped envelope and five dollars to cover any costs involved. All your efforts will be greatly appreciated. Thank you.

Sincerely,

Your signature, along with your husband's or wife's signature
Address
City, State, Zip

LETTER 9

Request for School Records

(Note: This letter should be handwritten on regular notebook paper. It should appear urgent yet informal. You may also want to enclose a family photo.)

Date

Name of school (elementary, junior high, high school, or university)
Address
City, State, Zip

Attention: Registrar

Dear Registrar,
My wife and I are trying to locate our (give relationship) for urgent inheritance matters. We understand that (give full name if known) was a student between the years of (give approximate dates within five years either way). We know that some information is not available, but are aware that the following can be released:

- -Student's full name
- -Ages during attendance and dates of attendance
- -Birth date
- -Primary field of study (if university)
- -Grades (or degrees) completed
- -Social security number
- -Past and current addresses
- -Names of next of kin
- -Names of any organizational affiliations

A great deal depends on your helping us as quickly as possible. Also please include the names of any friends, teachers, or alumni groups that might be helpful. All your efforts will be appreciated more than you could ever know. Thank you.

Sincerely,

Your signature, along with your husband's or wife's signature
Address
City, State, Zip

LETTER 10

Request for Alumni Organization Records

(Note: This letter should be handwritten on regular notebook paper. It should appear urgent yet informal.)

Date

Name of School (high school and/or university)
Address
City, State, Zip

Attention: Registrar

Dear Registrar,
My wife and I are trying to locate our (give relationship) for urgent inheritance matters. We understand that (give full name, if known) was a student between the years of (give approximate dates within five years either way). We are aware that the following can be released:

–Student's full name
–Ages during attendance and dates of attendance
–Birth date
–Primary field of study (if university)
–Grades (or degrees) completed
–Social security number
–Past and current addresses
–Names of next of kin
–Names of any organizational affiliations

A great deal depends on your helping us as quickly as possible. Also please include the names of any friends, teachers, or additional organizations that might be helpful. We have included a self-addressed stamped envelope for your convenience, and five dollars to cover any costs. All your efforts will be appreciated more than you could ever know. Thank you.

Sincerely,

Your signature, along with your husband's or wife's signature
Address
City, State, Zip

LETTER 11

Request for Yearbook Information from Library

(Note: This letter should be handwritten on regular notebook paper. It should appear urgent yet informal. You may want to enclose a family photo.)

Date

Name of School Library (high school, local public, or university)
Address
City, State, Zip

Attention: Registrar

Dear Registrar,
My wife and I are trying to locate our (give relationship) for urgent inheritance matters. We understand that (give full or partial name, if known; otherwise request all pages for the possible grades and corresponding years) was a student between the years of (give approximate dates within five years either way).

A great deal depends on your helping us as quickly as possible. Also please include the names of any family, friends, teachers, or alumni groups that might be helpful. We have included a self-addressed stamped envelope for your convenience, and five dollars to cover any duplication costs. All your efforts will be appreciated more than you could ever know. Thank you.

Sincerely,

Your signature, along with your husband's or wife's signature
Address
City, State, Zip

LETTER 12

Request for Real Estate Records

(Note: This letter should be handwritten on regular notebook paper. It should appear urgent yet informal. You may want to enclose a family photo.)

Date

County Clerk
County
Address
City, State, Zip

Attention: Real Estate Records

Dear County Clerk,
My wife and I are trying to locate any land or tax records for our (give relationship). We understand that (give full or partial name, as known) was a resident of your county between the years (give approximate dates within 10 years either way). Please search the following records and send us copies of any information that even remotely relates to this person.

–All property and tax records
–Deed records
–Mortgage records
–Grantor/grantee indices
–Situs files
–City directories

A great deal depends on your helping us as quickly as possible. Also please include any other records that might be helpful. We have included a self-addressed stamped envelope for your convenience, and five dollars to cover any costs. All your efforts will be appreciated more than you could ever know. Thank you.

Sincerely,

Your signature, along with your husband's or wife's signature
Address
City, State, Zip

LETTER 13

Request for Religious Records

(Note: This letter should be handwritten on regular notebook paper. It should appear urgent yet informal. You should definitely include a family photo.)

Date

Name of Religious Organization
Address
City, State, Zip

Attention: (Pastor, Priest, etc. . . .)

Dear (Pastor, Priest, etc.),
My wife and I are trying to locate our (give relationship) for urgent medical reasons. We understand that (give full name, if known) was a member of your congregation between the years of (give approximate dates within ten years either way). Please provide us with any or all of the following:

–Birth records
–Baptismal records
–Marriage records
–Divorce records
–Death records
–Full name and addresses of friends or family.

A great deal depends on your helping us as quickly as possible. Also please include any other records that might be helpful. If you are unable to find these records, please ask among your congregation and other churches in the area. We have included a self-addressed stamped envelope for your convenience, and five dollars to cover any duplication costs. All your efforts will be appreciated more than you could ever know. Thank you.

Sincerely,

Your signature, along with your husband's or wife's signature
Address
City, State, Zip

LETTER 14

Forwarding Request to Social Security Administration

(Note: This letter should be handwritten on regular notebook paper. It should appear urgent yet informal. You may want to enclose a family photo with the unsealed letter. The address listed here is different from the one in Chapter Ten [under Social Security Administration] because that listing was for their main office, whereas this listing is for their letter-forwarding office.)

Date

Social Security Administration
300 N. Greene St.
Baltimore, MD 21201

Attention: Location Services Department

Dear Sirs and Madams,
Please forward the enclosed unsealed correspondence to the following individual. Their information is as follows:

–give full or partial name of person and spouse, if known
–give last address, if known
–give full or partial social security number, if known
–give date and place of marriage, if known

My (husband/wife) and I are trying to locate this person for urgent matters of inheritance. A great deal depends on your helping us as quickly as possible. All your efforts will be greatly appreciated. Please let us know of your results. Thank you.

Sincerely,

Your signature, along with your husband's or wife's signature
Address
City, State, Zip

LETTER 15

Enclosed Correspondence to Social Security Administration

(Note: This letter should be handwritten on regular notebook paper. It should appear urgent yet informal. *Definitely* enclose a family photo with this letter; it will set the recipient at ease.)

Dear (give name of individual in question),
Although you may not know who we are, my wife and I recently became aware that you are entitled to urgent information regarding matters of inheritance. As strange as this probably sounds, we assure you that this is in no way a joke or game of any kind. Since we are not one hundred percent sure that you are indeed the person in question, it would not be appropriate to mention this in any more detail at this time. Please contact us at (give telephone number or address) between (give specific dates and/or times). A great deal depends on your urgent reply. Thank you.

Sincerely,

Your signature, along with your husband's or wife's signature
Address
City, State, Zip

LETTER 16

Freedom of Information Act Request Letter

Date

Agency Head or FOIA Officer
Name of Agency or Agency Component
Address
City, State, Zip

Dear (put person's name here; obtain name from phone call to agency):
Under the **Freedom of Information Act,** 5 USC. Subsection 552, I am requesting access to or copies of (identify the records you are requesting as clearly and specifically as possible).

If there are any fees for copying or searching for the records, please let me know before you fill my request. (Or, you could write "Please supply the records without informing me of the cost if the fees do not exceed $____, which I agree to pay.")

(Optionally, you could say: "I am requesting this information because ____." State this reason only if you think it will help you obtain the information.)

I understand that you have ten working days to respond to this request. If you deny all or any part of this request, please cite each specific exemption that you think justifies your refusal to release the information, and please notify me in writing of appeal procedures available under the law.

(Optionally, you could say: "If you have any questions about handling this request, you may telephone me at [home phone] or at [office phone].")

Sincerely,

Your signature, along with your husband's or wife's signature
Address
City, State, Zip

LETTER 17

Adoptee's Request for an Original Birth Certificate

(Note: This letter should be handwritten on regular notebook paper. It should appear direct yet informal. Also include a picture of yourself and/or your family.)

Date

Vital Statistics Agency
Address
City, State, Zip

Dear Registrar,
I find myself in need of another copy of my birth certificate for medical purposes. My name is (give birth name), and I was born on (give date and time, if known) in (give hospital, if known).

I have enclosed a self-addressed stamped envelope and a money order for (for appropriate fee, check state directory). My need is rather urgent, and a few moments of your time would help me greatly. Thank you very much.

Sincerely,

Signature of birth name
Address
City, State, Zip

LETTER 18

Birth Parent's Request for Original Birth Certificate

(Note: This is just one approach. You should state whatever need you feel comfortable with. This letter should be handwritten on lined notebook paper. The letter's main purpose is to project your true need and your sincerity. You should enclose a picture of yourself.)

Date

Vital Statistics Agency
Address
City, State, Zip

Dear Registrar,
In setting up my last will and testament, I discovered that I no longer have an original birth certificate for my child whose name is (give name as it appeared on original certificate).

(He/she) was relinquished on (give date), and I am her natural (mother/father). The following is the information you'll need. Please note that I am not requesting any identifying information, or an amended birth certificate.

-give child's birth name
-give place, date, and time of birth
-give other birth parent's name, if included in certificate

I have enclosed a self-addressed stamped envelope and a money order for (for appropriate amount—see state directory). I have recently found that it is urgent for me to put together my will, and am depending on you to help me in this situation. Any efforts you could lend would be appreciated more than you could ever imagine. Thank you very much.

Sincerely,

Your signature
Address
City, State, Zip

LETTER 19

Birth Parent's Follow-up Request to Court for Original Birth Certificate

(Note: This letter should be typed formally. It should be notarized and sent certified mail, return receipt requested. Attach the receipt to the copy of this letter you keep in your correspondence file, to serve as proof that it was received. It would also be very helpful to enclose a copy of a confirmation letter from your doctor on his or her letterhead.)

Date

Presiding Judge
Court of Jurisdiction
Address
City, State, Zip

Your Honor,
I recently became aware that it is necessary for me to create a last will and testament, and find myself in great need of the original birth certificate for my child, who was given up for adoption.

I am the child's natural (mother/father) and did not receive a copy of this document at the time of birth. It is now urgently needed for the purpose of creating a trust. Please provide a copy of this transcript. I am aware of the laws relating to adoption information, and am in no way requesting any data regarding identifying information or the amended birth certificate. The necessary information is as follows:

-give child's birth name, along with date, place, and time of birth
-give birth mother's/father's full names, if known
-give time of relinquishment

I am depending on you to help me in a timely manner. All efforts are greatly appreciated. Thank you.

Sincerely,

Your signature
I (give present full name), a.k.a. (give name at time of surrender if different), hereby swear that I am the natural (mother/father) of the child named (give child's birth name). Said child was born (give date) and relinquished (give date).
(Your signature)

Type Your Name, Address, City, State, and Zip

Notary Public:

LETTER 20

Adoptive Parent's Request for Original Birth Certificate

(Note: This should be handwritten on notebook paper. You should convey a sense of urgency by sending it certified mail, return receipt requested. Enclose a picture of yourself and the child. It would also be helpful to enclose a copy of a confirmation letter from your doctor on his or her letterhead.)

Date

Vital Statistics Agency
Address
City, State, Zip

Dear Registrar,
I have recently become aware that it is critical for me to obtain another copy of my child's original birth certificate for urgent medical purposes. The necessary information is as follows:

-give child's full birth name, if known
-give time, date, and place of birth

I have enclosed a self-addressed stamped envelope, along with a money order in the amount of (for appropriate fee, check state directory). A great deal depends on receiving this information as quickly as possible. All your efforts will be appreciated more than you could ever know. Thank you.

Sincerely,

Your signature
Address
City, State, Zip

LETTER 21

Adoptee's Request for Amended Birth Certificate

(Note: It should not be necessary to provide many details about the cause for your request, because you are entitled to this document by law. This letter should be typed and notarized. If you are planning to request a copy of your original birth certificate, do so *before* sending this letter. The reason is that clerks occasionally send the wrong [i.e., original, non-amended] birth certificate, which can be a huge help.)

Date

Vital Statistics Agency
Address
City, State, Zip

Dear Registrar,
I find myself in urgent need of my amended birth certificate. I am an adopted child and fully aware of the laws regarding identifying information. The necessary information is as follows:

- -give full adopted name
- -give date, place, and time of birth and relinquishment, if known
- -give full names of adoptive parents

I have enclosed a self-addressed stamped envelope, along with a money order in the amount of (for appropriate fee, check state directory). Your urgent attention to this matter is greatly appreciated. Thank you.

Sincerely,

Name (your adopted signature)
Address
City, State, Zip

LETTER 22

Adoptive Parent's Request for Amended Birth Certificate

(Note: It should not be necessary to provide details about the cause for your request, since you are fully entitled to this document by law. This letter should be typed and notarized. If you are planning to request a copy of the child's original birth certificate, do so *before* sending this letter. The reason is that clerks occasionally send the wrong [i.e., original, non-amended] birth certificate, which can be a huge help.)

Date

Vital Statistics Agency
Address
City, State, Zip

Dear Registrar,
I find myself in urgent need of my child's birth certificate. The necessary data is as follows:

–give child's full adopted name
–give date, place, and time of birth and relinquishment, if known
–give full names of adoptive parents

We have enclosed a self-addressed stamped envelope, along with a money order in the amount of (for appropriate fee, check state directory). Your urgent attention to this matter is greatly appreciated. Thank you.

Sincerely,

Your signature, along with your husband's or wife's signature
Address
City, State, Zip

LETTER 23

Adoptee's Request for Court Records

(Note: This should be handwritten on regular notebook paper. It should appear direct yet convey a sense of urgency. To best convey its urgent nature, send it by overnight mail. Also include a picture of yourself and/or your family. It would be helpful to include a confirmation letter from your doctor on his or her stationery.)

Date

Vital Statistics
Address
City, State, Zip

Dear Registrar,
I find myself in need of a copy of my adoption records for urgent medical reasons. My name is (give full adopted name), and I was born on (give date and time, if known) in (give hospital, if known). My adoptive parents are (give full names), and I was adopted on (give exact date, if known; otherwise give the year). I am requesting my adoption decree, interlocutory order, adoption petition, and any other records you may have.

For your convenience, I have enclosed a self-addressed stamped envelope. My need is rather urgent, and I am depending on you to help me. If any fees are involved, simply contact me at (telephone number) between the hours of (give times), let me know the amount, and I will send it immediately. Thank you very much.

Sincerely,

Your signature, along with your husband's or wife's signature
Address
City, State, Zip

LETTER 24

Birth Parent's Request for Court Records

(Note: This should be handwritten on regular notebook paper. It should appear direct and urgent, so you may want to send it by overnight mail. Also include a picture of yourself. It would be helpful to include a confirmation letter from your doctor on his or her stationery.)

Date

Court of Jurisdiction
Address
City, State, Zip

Dear Registrar,
I find myself in urgent need of a copy of my (son/daughter's) adoption records for the purpose of putting together my last will and testament. I am requesting the adoption decree, interlocutory order, adoption petition, all surrender and relinquishment papers, consent to adopt, and any other records you may have. The necessary information is as follows:

–give child's full birth name, or adoptive name, if known
–give date, time, and place of birth
–give date, time, and place of relinquishment, if known
–give your full name

For your convenience, I have enclosed a self-addressed stamped envelope. I find myself in the unfortunate situation of my need being rather urgent, and a great deal depends on your helping me as quickly as possible. If any fees are involved, simply contact me at (telephone number) between the hours of (give times), let me know the amount, and I will send it immediately. Thank you very much.

Sincerely,

Signature
Address
City, State, Zip

LETTER 25

Adoptive Parent's Request for Court Records

(Note: This should be handwritten on regular notebook paper. It should appear direct and urgent, so you may want to send it by overnight mail. Also include a picture of yourself and/or your family, circling the child in question. It would be very helpful to include a confirmation letter from your doctor on his or her stationery.)

Date

Court of Jurisdiction
Address
City, State, Zip

Dear Registrar,
I find myself in need of a copy of my (son/daughter's) adoption records for urgent medical reasons. My wife (husband) and I are requesting the adoption decree, interlocutory order, adoption petition, all surrender and relinquishment papers, consent to adopt, and any other records you may have. The necessary information is as follows:

-give child's full adoptive name
-give date, time, and place of birth
-give date, time, and place of relinquishment, if known
-give your full names

For your convenience, we have enclosed a self-addressed stamped envelope. I find myself in the unfortunate situation of my need being rather urgent, and a great deal depends on your helping us as quickly as possible. If any fees are involved, simply contact us at (telephone number) between the hours of (give times), let us know the amount, and we will send it immediately. Thank you very much.

Sincerely,

Your signature, along with your husband's or wife's signature
Address
City, State, Zip

LETTER 26

Adoptee's Request for Hospital Records

(Note: This letter should be typed in formal fashion and notarized. It should convey extreme sincerity and urgency, so you should probably send it by overnight mail. Also include a picture of yourself. It would be extremely helpful to enclose a confirmation letter from your doctor on his or her stationery.)

Date

Hospital
Maternity Records
Address
City, State, Zip

Dear Administrator,
I find myself in urgent need of all my medical records as quickly as possible. Please forward all of the following: admittance, nursery, delivery room, discharge, and any other records you may have. The necessary information is as follows:

-give your full name at the time of birth, if known
-give date, time, and place of birth
-give birth mother's full or partial name, if known
-give name of attending physician, if known

I have enclosed a self-addressed stamped envelope for your convenience. As I mentioned before, this information is extremely critical and a great deal depends on your helping me as quickly as possible. Please check all microfilm records as well. If a fee is involved, please bill me with the records and I will send payment immediately. Thank you very much.

Sincerely,

Signature of the name you used above
Address
City, State, Zip

LETTER 27

Birth Parent's Request for Hospital Records

(Note: This letter should be formal, typed, and notarized. It should convey extreme sincerity and urgency, so you should send it by overnight mail. Also include a picture of yourself. It would be extremely helpful to enclose a confirmation letter from your doctor on his or her stationery.)

Date

Hospital
Maternity Records
Address
City, State, Zip

Dear Administrator,
I find myself in urgent need of all my medical records as quickly as possible. Please forward all of the following: admittance, nursery, delivery room, discharge, and any other records you may have. The necessary information is as follows:

–give your full name at the time of birth
–give child's full birth name
–give date, time, and place of birth
–give name of attending physician, if known

I have enclosed a self-addressed stamped envelope for your convenience. As I mentioned before, this information is extremely critical and a great deal depends on your helping me as quickly as possible. Please check all microfilm records as well. If a fee is involved, contact me at (give number) between the hours of (give times) and I will send payment immediately. Thank you very much.

Sincerely,

Signature of your name at the time of birth
Address
City, State, Zip

LETTER 28

Adoptive Parent's Request for Hospital Records

(Note: This letter should be formal, typed, and notarized. It should convey extreme sincerity and urgency, so you should send it by overnight mail. Also include a picture of yourself. It would be extremely helpful to enclose a confirmation letter from your doctor on his or her stationery.)

Date

Hospital
Maternity Records
Address
City, State, Zip

Dear Administrator,
My (husband/wife) and I find ourselves in urgent need of all our (son/daughter's) medical records as quickly as possible. Please forward all of the following: admittance, nursery, delivery room, discharge, and other records you may have. The necessary information is as follows:

-give your child's full adoptive name and birth name, if known
-give date, time, and place of birth to the best of your knowledge
-give name of attending physician, if known
-give birth mother's full/partial name, if known

We have enclosed a self-addressed stamped envelope for your convenience. As we mentioned before, this information is extremely critical and a great deal depends on your helping us as quickly as you can. Please check all microfilm records as well. If a fee is involved, contact us at (give number) between the hours of (give times) and we will send payment immediately. Thank you very much.

Sincerely,

Your signature, along with your husband's or wife's signature
Address
City, State, Zip

LETTER 29

Adoptee's Request for Basic Information from State

(Note: This letter should be typed formally and notarized. It should convey extreme sincerity and urgency, and you should provide a copy of your amended birth certificate, if possible. Also include a picture of yourself.)

Date

State Adoption Department
Address
City, State, Zip

Dear Registrar,
I urgently need your assistance in locating the agency that processed my adoption. Please forward any information to me as quickly as possible, as an urgent medical need exists. If you do not have my records, it is important that you provide the name, address, and telephone number of the organization that is in possession of them. The necessary information is as follows:

–give your full adoptive name and birth name, if known
–give date, time, and place of birth to the best of your knowledge
–give full names of adoptive parents

I have enclosed a self-addressed stamped envelope for your convenience. Please check all microfilm records as well. If a fee is involved, contact me (give number) between the hours of (give times) and I will send payment immediately. A great deal depends on your helping me as quickly as possible. All efforts will be appreciated more than you could ever know. Thank you.

Sincerely,

Your adoptive signature
Address
City, State, Zip

LETTER 30

Birth Parent's Request for Basic Information from State

(Note: This letter should be typed formally and notarized. It should convey extreme sincerity and urgency, and you should enclose a confirmation letter from your doctor on his or her stationery, if possible. Also include a picture of yourself. If you have a copy of your child's original birth certificate, enclose this as well.)

Date

State Adoption Department
Address
City, State, Zip

Dear Registrar,
I urgently need your assistance in locating the agency that processed the adoption of my child. It has recently come to my attention that it is critical for me to draw up my last will and testament, and I need this information very badly. If you do not have my records, please provide the name, address, and telephone number of the agency that is in possession of them. The necessary information is as follows:

–give the child's full birth name
–give date, time, and place of relinquishment as known to you
–give your full name
–give date, time, and place of birth as known to you

I have enclosed a self-addressed stamped envelope for your convenience. Please check all microfilm records. If a fee is involved, contact me at (give number) between the hours of (give times) and I will send payment immediately. A great deal depends on your helping me as quickly as possible. All efforts will be appreciated more than you could ever know. Thank you.

Sincerely,

Your signature
Address
City, State, Zip

LETTER 31

Adoptive Parent's Request for Basic Information from State

(Note: This letter should be typed formally and notarized. It should convey extreme sincerity and urgency, and you should enclose a confirmation letter from your doctor on his or her stationery, if possible. Also include a picture of your family, circling the child in question. If you have a copy of your child's amended birth certificate, enclose this as well.)

Date

State Adoption Department
Address
City, State, Zip

Dear Registrar,
For urgent medical reasons, my (husband/wife) and I are requesting your assistance in locating the agency that handled the adoption of our child. We need this information very badly. If you do not have these records, please provide the name, address, and telephone number of the agency that is in possession of them. The necessary information is as follows:

-give the child's full adoptive name
-give date, time, and place of relinquishment as known to you
-give your full names
-give date, time, and place of birth as known to you

We have enclosed a self-addressed stamped envelope for your convenience. Please check all microfilm records. If a fee is involved contact us at (give number) between the hours of (give times) and we will send payment immediately. A great deal depends on your helping us as quickly as possible. All efforts will be appreciated more than you could ever know. Thank you.

Sincerely,

Your signature, along with your husband's or wife's signature
Address
City, State, Zip

LETTER 32

Adoptee's Waiver of Confidentiality

(Note: This letter *must* be notarized. It should be typed formally and sent certified mail, return receipt requested. Keep the receipt in your correspondence file attached to a copy of this letter. You may wish to have an attorney review this letter before you send it, as it is a legal document.)

Date

Adoption Agency, State Adoption Department, Hospital of Birth
Address
City, State, Zip

To All Concerned Parties:
I hereby formally request that this letter and/or copies hereof be immediately placed in all records and files pertaining to my adoption as follows:

–give full adopted name
–give date, time, and place of adoption and relinquishment, if known

This is to be considered my legal authorization to waive the confidentiality guaranteed to me by any laws and/or organizations of the state of (give name); and includes all court records, agency records, hospital records, and anything considered to be identifying information.

The effects of this waiver are to extend only to my birth parents, birth siblings, and any other blood relatives, and/or their legal representatives. The following information may hereby be released in full to the above mentioned parties:

–my full name (present and maiden)
–my current address (give address) and telephone number (if desired)

This waiver gives my full and legal permission to release my present identity, with the exclusion of any reference to my adoptive parents, and/or adoptive relatives. Please respond to this request, and should you refuse it, denote the state law that supports such an action. This letter is to remain in full effect until otherwise revoked by myself in writing.

Sincerely,

Your signature
Address
City, State, Zip

LETTER 33

Birth Parent's Waiver of Confidentiality

(Note: This letter *must* be notarized. It should be typed formally and sent certified mail, return receipt requested. Keep the receipt in your correspondence file attached to a copy of this letter. You may wish to have an attorney review this letter before you send it, as it is a legal document.)

Date

Adoption Agency, State Adoption Department, Hospital of Birth
Address
City, State, Zip

To All Concerned Parties:
I hereby formally request that this letter and/or copies hereof be immediately placed in all records and files pertaining to my child who was surrendered for adoption as follows:

-give full birth name of child
-give date, time, and place of birth and relinquishment
-give your full name at the time of birth and relinquishment

This is to be considered my legal authorization to waive the confidentiality guaranteed to me by any laws and/or organizations of the state of (give name); and includes all court records, agency records, hospital records, and anything considered to be identifying information.

The effects of this waiver are to extend only to my relinquished child, and any of (his/her) adoptive relatives or legal representatives. The following information may hereby be released in full to the above mentioned parties:

-my full name (present and maiden)
-my current address (give address) and my current telephone number (give number)
-all medical records in your files, including those enclosed with this waiver

This waiver gives my full and legal permission to release my present identity as described above. Please respond to this request, and should you refuse it, denote the state law that supports such an action. This letter is to remain in full effect until otherwise revoked by myself in writing.

Sincerely,

Your signature
Address
City, State, Zip

LETTER 34

Adoptive Parent's Waiver of Confidentiality

(Note: This letter *must* be notarized. It should be typed formally and sent via certified mail, return receipt requested. Attach the receipt to a copy of this letter, and place them in your correspondence file.)

Date

Adoption Agency and/or State Adoption Department
Address
City, State, Zip

To All Concerned Parties:
We hereby formally request that this letter and/or copies hereof be immediately placed in all records and files pertaining to the child we legally adopted as shown below:

–give child's full adopted name
–give date, place, and time of birth and relinquishment

This is to be considered our full legal authorization to waive the confidentiality guaranteed to ourselves and our adopted child by any laws and/or organizations of the state of (give name); and includes all court records, agency records, hospital records, and anything considered to be identifying information.

The effects of this waiver are to extend only to our adopted child's birth relatives and/or their legal representatives. The following information may hereby be released in full to the above mentioned parties:

–our full names (present and maiden)
–our current address (give address)
–our current telephone number (if desired)

This waiver gives our full and legal permission to release our present identity as described above. Please respond to this request, and should you refuse it, denote the state law that supports such an action. This letter is to remain in full effect until otherwise revoked by us both in writing.

Sincerely,

Both husband's and wife's signature
Address
City, State, Zip

LETTER 35

Writing a Letter to Make First Contact with Birth Parent or Adoptee

This is probably the only letter we can't write for you. What you choose to say will largely depend on why you began searching in the first place. However, there are a few general guidelines that should always be followed. They are listed below:

1) Open your letter by verifying all the facts you know in a nonthreatening manner. Assure the person that you have no hidden agenda for writing to him or her.

2) Follow immediately by saying that you wrote this letter, rather than calling, because you were concerned about protecting his or her privacy. This will set the recipient of your letter at ease, letting the person know that you are not going to come crashing through the front door without consent.

3) Always be positive in your letter. Nobody has lived a perfect life, but your first letter is not the time or place to unburden any problems.

4) Include lots of pictures. If you're an adoptee, enclose a photo from every five-year interval of your life. No matter how cold someone may be, it's impossible not to look at a picture of your own flesh and blood.

5) Don't come on too strong. Reasons like "passing along medical information" or "needing medical information for my family" are good icebreakers. Ease into the relationship slowly.

6) Mention that you'd like to say hello if they'd like to. Saying hello is a nonthreatening wording that doesn't imply starting a full-blown relationship.

7) Include your address and a day and nighttime phone number where you can be reached. Also give specific times of the day that you will be available. This will avoid many stressful hours of sitting and waiting for the phone to ring.

If you would like an expert opinion when it comes time to write this letter, give one of our consultants a ring on the Consultant Hotline.* Most of us have been in this situation personally, and we know that sometimes it helps to have an understanding ear before taking the final step. Also, remember that if you would like us to make the call for you, we'd be happy to do it at no charge! Good luck!

* The cost of the Consultant Hotline is $3.99 per minute; the average call lasts six to eight minutes.

NINE

The Power of Persuasion: The Best Telephone Techniques

Good phone skills are key to any successful search. Part of these skills depends on the kind of preparation you do before dialing; part depends on knowing what to say and how to say it. However, before any of these issues arise, you need to understand the most valuable phone lesson there is: learning when to use the telephone to get what you need, and knowing when to write first.

Writing a Letter vs. Making a Phone Call

At the start of your search, most of your tracking efforts will involve writing. The majority of documents and records can be obtained only by writing letters to the appropriate organizations and agencies. In general, the only times you'll need to ask for information by telephone are when you're following up on letters.

There's a good reason you shouldn't hit the phones at the start of your search. Using the telephone is an easy and immediate way to reach someone. It's also something all of us in today's world are intimately familiar with. Most of us make phone calls every day, while we write letters only once every few months, if that. If there's a problem with a bill, a complaint to be lodged, a question about a company, or a friend who hasn't been heard from in a while, we'll just pick up the phone and place a call. Odds are, the phone call will do the trick no matter what the circumstances.

When you're looking for someone, however, the phone will not yield such simple and quick results. Oftentimes, you'll be calling someone you don't know, someone who has no interest in helping you, no reason to trust you, and no inclination to spend much time on the phone with you at all. You won't get very far unless you've laid careful advance groundwork with letters.

In a letter, you can better control the terms of the dialogue because there really is no dialogue. A letter seems more official, and appears more trustworthy. It is an excellent introduction, as opposed to a first-time phone call, which can seem intrusive. A letter is harder to ignore than a phone call: If you call and leave a message, it may be ignored, whereas a letter will most likely be placed in a to-do pile, to be attended to later on. Further, when you call to follow up on the letter, the person you wrote to may feel beholden to you, because he or she has thus far failed to respond to your pleasant and reasonably worded request.

As you go about your search, you will find, as we have, that the most successful phone calls are the ones that follow up on letters. However, even after you've paved the way with some preliminary written correspondence, you will still need to put a lot of study and work into each phone call before you make it.

Here are some basic guidelines you should follow whenever you are requesting information by telephone.

The Five Rules of Telephone Conversations

Since a telephone call is a free-form, two-way exchange of information, it's basically anyone's guess what will happen once the conversation begins. Therefore, since a great deal depends on *how* you ask for the information you need, it is extremely important to prepare yourself in advance (both mentally and physically) for these contacts. By following the guidelines presented below, you will maintain control of each call and get the maximum amount of information.

1. Before making any contact, prepare a detailed list of questions. Address every issue you want to cover, and think about the best order in which to ask these questions. Write out your questions in your own words, so that you won't have to work to make them sound natural in the middle of your conversation. Keep this list in front of you during the entire call. Obviously, there will be some give and take during the phone call—no matter how much preparation you've done, you won't be able to predict everything the person on the other end of the line is going to say—but keeping the list where you can see it will help

you stay on track, and will help you incorporate unexpected detours into your overarching plan.

2. Phrase all your questions in an open-ended manner, so that you leave the other person plenty of room to respond. We can't stress enough the importance of asking open-ended questions. A question that can be answered by saying yes or no is a closed question—that's not the kind you should be preparing. For example, if you asked your mother, "Was my father in the military when you met him?" she might answer no. Don't lead the witness—don't insert information you know, or think you know, into the question. Instead, ask her, "How did you meet my father?" That way, you'll get far more information, and you won't restrict the answer with your own assumptions.

3. Always record your conversations within the limits of the law. During conversations, it's easy to get caught up in the moment and forget to listen to what is being said. When this happens—and it *will* happen—you will undoubtedly miss important slips, and bits of information would be lost forever if they hadn't been recorded. Once the tape is played back, chances are you will be astonished at the details you previously overlooked.

   Getting the equipment to record conversations is inexpensive and well worth the cost. In most cases all you'll need is a basic tape recorder and a telephone pickup jack. A pickup jack is essentially a small suction cup that attaches to the receiver of your phone. You can find one at almost any electronics store; they cost about five dollars.

4. Don't ramble. Work hard to keep your talking to a minimum without seeming rude. You need to be friendly, you need to build a rapport with the individual you're talking to, but you don't want to volunteer too much information (which is what will happen if you talk too much or if you feel the need to talk in order to fill a silence). Remember, the less a person *thinks* you know, the more cooperative that person will be.

5. For adoption searches: Unless you're in a situation where it's obvious (such as talking with an adoption agency), never mention the word "adoption" in your conversation unless it's absolutely necessary. We've found that using reasons like "doing a family genealogy" or "matters of estate settlement" are very effective, whereas "trying to locate my birth parents" merely serves to make people nervous. Use sentences like:

   "My family is in the process of doing our family genealogy, and we're trying to trace a few distant branches of our family."

   "Our family is trying to find this person in order to settle an estate. All we have is some sketchy information, but we know . . ."

In addition to all these rules, don't forget what you learned in Chapter Two. Throughout all phone conversations you will want to have your conversation log handy, so that you can take notes on the calls you make and the things you learn from the person you talk to.

Contacting Adoption Agencies

Your first contact with a state and/or private adoption agency should be in writing. The reasoning behind this is that a carefully written letter gives you the opportunity to get a feel for how cooperative the agency is going to be—without giving it a chance to quiz or probe you with questions you might not be ready for.

After writing your first letter, you will receive some kind of reply—positive, negative, or neutral. Regardless of the type of reply and its tone, use it as an opportunity to follow up and keep the dialogue open. Send a note thanking the writer for his or her time and effort on your behalf. Explain that it really means a lot to you to have people trying to assist you in such an urgent matter. And then, go for it again! Use this second letter, under the guise of a thank-you note, to ask another question, or to rephrase your previous request.

We have found that many times people become so uncomfortable repeatedly saying no and being so obviously uncooperative that they actually *want* to find something positive they can tell you. Help them help you!

After your second letter, or perhaps after your third, you may feel comfortable enough to do your follow-up on the phone. You may even have a person's name at the agency by then. Give that person a call. This call has two purposes: (1) to begin building a rapport with the person who has your file, and (2) to start asking creatively for specific pieces of information.

Introduce yourself, and say something like, "I really appreciate the time and effort you've put into our correspondence. I wondered if I could take a minute of your time . . ."

Be sure to make notes of any personal comments the person has made. For example, if she (or he) comments that she hadn't returned your call for a few days because she was out sick, the *next* time you talk to her, be sure to ask if she is feeling better. If she mentions a vacation, or having once lived in a town near you, bring it up again the next time you talk. Build a relationship. It is much easier for this adoption-agency employee to say no to a piece of paper than to a voice or a face; and it is much easier to say no to a stranger than to someone you have a more personal relationship with.

These three techniques have been especially successful when dealing with adoption agencies:

1. Whenever you are denied *specific* information, request pieces of it. For example, if they won't tell you someone's name, ask for their initials. After all, initials alone can't be con-

sidered identifying information. If they refuse to give you a specific date of birth, ask for the month, or the time of year.

2. Play on the person's desire to help you out. Sometimes people want to help you even though they know the law doesn't allow them to. You could try to phrase your questions so that they have "true/false" answers, and suggest to the person that he (or she) could simply remain quiet if the answer is "true." To do this, you need to have a little bit of outside information, or else you'll get a lot of "false" replies. What you want, of course, is to find out what the truth is—but on the other hand, knowing that something isn't true can be helpful too. For instance, you could ask, "Is it true that my mother lived in Philadelphia?" If the clerk remains silent, you know what city and county to start searching, which is a great confirmation. If the clerk says, "Well, I guess it's not identifying information for me to answer that—she did not live in Philadelphia," then at least you know that your assumption was incorrect, and it's time to go back to another avenue.

3. Ask "yes or no" questions to pinpoint general information, such as, "It would be really helpful to me if you could just give me the smallest of starts in the right direction. Nothing that's identifying, just a little piece of information. Okay? Please, does the first initial of my mother's first name come before the letter M?" ("Well . . . um . . . no, it doesn't come before M.") "Does it come after T?" ("Well, yes, it's after T . . .") "After W?" At this point the person may say, "Look, we can't go over this name letter by letter all day long!" But at least you've narrowed down the first initial to a fairly small group. (The first initial of the first name won't be all that helpful, of course, unless you have your mother's last name already.)

These same general techniques can work equally well when talking with a doctor or attorney who was involved in the adoption. Be informal and unthreatening in your first contacts. It may take *several* calls to successfully build a relationship and get the information you need.

If one clerk or official seems rigid and unsympathetic, try a different one. Be persistent throughout the entire conversation, but always remain calm and polite. If you are refused information, rephrase the question. The important thing is that you can never give up. If the official tells you that the information you're requesting would be identifying, ask him exactly *why* or *how* the information is identifying. Ask him what *wouldn't* be identifying; is there some broader question you could ask that would give you a general sense of the answer and be nonidentifying?

Use open-ended questions that leave a lot of room for response. Don't get discouraged. If you have the desire and determination to succeed, you eventually will!

One final note regarding state and private adoption agencies. Whenever you request borderline identifying information from an official, understand that you are really asking that person to jeopardize his or her job. In the course of solving thousands of searches using these same techniques, we've gotten to know many people who work in adoption agencies. In most cases, their story is the same. They are human and often genuinely feel for the person who is calling or writing. The problem is that they could get fired if they were caught releasing identifying information. Since their office guidelines regarding what they can (and can't) say are often unclear, they are stuck in a very awkward position.

Put yourself in their shoes before you start asking questions. Would you risk losing *your* job to help someone you don't know? Be creative and positive. You'll get a lot further if you take time to establish a relationship with this person. Then use the techniques we've just outlined and phrase your questions in a way that won't be threatening. The key to getting what you want is mixing compassion with creativity.

Agency Questionnaires

In the five rules of telephone conversations we listed above, rule number one is that before you make any contact, you need to prepare a detailed list of questions. In this section we've given you some topics you might want to cover when you are calling agencies and looking for information.

Not all these questions will apply to you; nor will you want to bring up every one of them in any single phone call. But this will give you a place to start. We talked above about creating a list of questions, written in your own words, to help guide your phone conversations. *Don't* use these questions for that list. Instead, look these over, and use our questions as a guide to write your *own* questions onto your *own* list in your *own* words. Again: This is just a basic guide for devising your own questions based on your specific situation.

Adoptee

Did my birth mother name me? What was the name?

Was I a twin? Did I have other siblings?

In what hospital was I born? What is the name of the doctor who delivered me?

What were my birth parents' ages? What were their names?

What did my birth parents look like (height, weight, eye and hair color, etc.)?

What religion(s) were my birth parents?

What nationality were my birth parents? What were their occupations?

What were my birth parents' education levels (high school, college, graduate school)?

Did they graduate? Where? When?

Were my birth parents married to each other? To someone else? Where? When?

Were there any divorces? Where? When?

Where were my birth parents born (city, county, state)? When were they born (date of birth)?

Were any members of my birth family in the military? What branch? Where? When?

Was my birth father living at the time of my birth?

Were my grandparents alive at the time of my birth? What were their names?

How old were my grandparents when I was born? When did they die?

Did my grandparents participate in the relinquishment?

Who gave the consent for my adoption?

What were the circumstances behind my relinquishment?

Was I baptized before the relinquishment? When? Where?

Which court finalized my adoption (state, county, city)? When?

Was I ever in foster care? Where? When? For how long?

Were there any other deaths in my birth family? When? Where? How?

What medical information is in my file? When was it last updated?

Does your agency have a specific waiver of confidentiality that I can file?

Birth Parent

What name was the child given?

Does the child have any brothers or sisters? What are their names? Ages?

What nationality are the parents?

How long had they been married at the time of the adoption?

What were their occupations?

What are the parents' names?

How old were they at the time of the adoption?

Why did they want to adopt?

Where were they born (city, county, state)? When (date of birth)?

What did they look like (height, weight, eye and hair color, etc.)?

What was their religion (if Protestant, be sure to get specific denomination)?

Were there any divorces? Where? When?

What were their educational levels (high school, college, graduate school)?

Did they graduate? Where? When?

Were any members of the family in the military? What branch? Where? When?

Was the child baptized after relinquishment? When? Where?

Was the child ever in foster care? When? Where? How long?

Were there ever any court actions affecting the child? When? Where?

Has this agency ever made contact with the child or parents since finalization? When? Where?

What is the best way for me to update the medical information in my file?

Does your agency have a specific waiver of confidentiality that I can file?

How can you help me contact the parents or child?

T E N

Strategies for Tracing and Locating

Fortunately for us, the United States has always placed a high value on keeping accurate and extensive records of its citizens. Beginning with birth and continuing throughout our lives, almost all our experiences and activities are recorded in some manner, whether we realize it or not. Records of family, education, driving histories, telephones, utilities, medical records, professional records, voting registrations, tax filings, legal proceedings . . . the list is endless.

The mountains of documentation in public records will now open up countless avenues for tracing. This chapter examines most of the sources that are available to ordinary citizens. Whenever applicable, we will include sample documents from our files to give you a clear idea of what you'll be looking for.

Libraries and Family History Centers

As you begin piecing together your search puzzle, an important resource will be your local library and the services of its reference librarian. Most reference librarians truly enjoy taking on a challenge. They can be invaluable, helping you sift through the maze of available reference materials and directories.

Here's a list of helpful sources normally available through your city or county library:

- maps and city cross-street directories
- old telephone books
- books on local history
- professional directories listing the names and addresses of doctors, lawyers, organizations, colleges, universities, etc.
- specific family records and histories available through the Library of Congress
- microfilm of newspaper articles, obituaries, etc.
- the *American Library Directory* of national, state, city, and county libraries
- the *Directory of Special Libraries and Information Centers*
- old voter registration records
- genealogy departments
- the *Guide to American Directories,* which lists directories published by all business and professional organizations.
- the *Encyclopedia of Associations,* which lists labor unions, sororities, fraternities, and trade, alumni, and religious organizations

Don't be discouraged if some or all of your search must be conducted outside the county or state where you live. Your librarians can get almost any documentation or microfilm you need through the interlibrary loan program. The loan program gives each library access to materials from other libraries across the country, including the Library of Congress. It typically takes two to four weeks to get information in this manner.

Whenever possible, it's best to enlist the help of a genealogist local to the area of your search. If this is not possible, you can locate a board-certified genealogist who may be able to assist you through:

The Board for Certified Genealogists
P.O. Box 5816
Washington, DC 24403

Another source of genealogists is the Church of Jesus Christ of Latter-Day Saints (the Mormons). Ask where their nearest genealogy library (also called a Family History Center) is located. For decades the Mormons have diligently gathered genealogical records from around the world and transferred them to microfilm. In fact, some of these records now exist nowhere else. The depth of the Family History Centers' records is unparalleled. These records include, but are not limited to, newspapers and periodicals, vital record announcements, all sorts of published directories, obituary indexes, census records, military records, church and parish records, birth indexes, and the Social Security Death Index. Furthermore, staff members at Family History Centers are extremely knowledgeable, very helpful, and free! Their librarians are usually highly skilled researchers who often have access to amazing amounts of information. If you do not have a Mormon church in your area, you can call the Family History Services Center in Salt Lake City, Utah, at (800) 346-6044. They will be able to give you the address and telephone number of the nearest Mormon genealogical library. You may also want to try the Mormons' new Web site, an incredible trove of genealogical information, at *www.familysearch.com.*

County Offices

County public records are available at county courthouses and other county offices. These records can be invaluable to your search. The following is a list of records that are typically kept on the county level.

- voter registration records
- birth, marriage, divorce, and death records
- tax records
- business and professional licensing records
- civil and criminal court records
- draft registrations

Because the availability and range of information contained in these records varies widely, each of these valuable sources is discussed separately, in great detail, later in this chapter.

State and National Archives

The National Archives is a federal repository whose public records date back to the 1700s. It holds a wealth of information, including military, census, and other family background records. There are twelve branches of this agency in addition to their national headquarters in Washington D.C.

Each state also maintains its own state archives, where all state, county, and local records are sent, as opposed to all federal records, which are housed in the National Archives.

Some regional branches of the National Archives have certain types of records unique to their region. One can either call and inquire if a particular type of information or record is available at a regional branch, or go to *www.nara.gov* to find information about each regional archive.

To give some examples: all criminal, civil, and bankruptcy court records are kept in the National Archives. All city directories are housed in the State Archives. Many of the records we've talked about here, while held at particular agencies, can also be found at the National and State Archives.

Headquarters
National Archives
7th & Pennsylvania Ave. NW
Washington, DC 20408
(202) 501-5400; (202) 501-5410

Northeast Region:
National Archives
380 Trapelo Road
Waltham, MA 02154-6399
(617) 647-8104

Mountain States
National Archives
P.O. Box 25307
Denver, CO 80225
(303) 236-0801

Southwest Region
National Archives
P.O. Box 6216
Ft. Worth, TX 76115-0216
(817) 334-5515

Pacific Alaska Region
National Archives
6125 Sand Point Way NE
Seattle, WA 98115-7999
(206) 526-6501

Great Lakes Region
National Archives
7358 S. Pulaski Road
Chicago, IL 60629-5898
(312) 581-7816

Alaska Region
National Archives
654 W. 3rd Avenue
Anchorage, AK 99501-2145
(907) 271-24431

Mid-Atlantic Region
National Archives
14700 Townsend Road
Philadelphia, PA 19154-1025
(215) 671-9027

Pacific Region—Laguna
National Archives
P.O. Box 6719
Laguna Niguel, CA 92656-6719
(714) 360-2618

Central Plains Region
National Archives
2312 E. Bannister Rd.
Kansas City, MO 64131-3071
(816) 926-6920

Pacific Region—San Francisco
National Archives
1000 Commodore Drive
San Bruno, CA 94066
(415) 876-9249

Southeast Region
National Archives
1557 St. Joseph Ave.
East Point, GA 30344-2593
(404) 763-7477

Northeast Region—NYC
National Archives
201 Varick St.
New York, NY 10014-4811
(212) 337-1300

If you're wondering what kinds of records your State Archive houses, consult your local reference librarian, or contact the State Archives directly (see Appendix 2).

When contacting National and State Archives, always say you are doing "genealogical research on your family tree." They hear this request all the time, and it will avoid any problems that might come up if you mentioned adoption.

If you wind up looking for information dating back to the 1920s or earlier, state and national census records are another source of good historical data. Most State Archives and Family History Centers have updated census information. Keep in mind that in addition to the national census, many states maintain their own censuses, whose records may contain more detailed information than those conducted by the federal government.

The Government Printing Office (GPO) is another federal agency that can be of assistance to searchers, although pursuing this avenue will take some work on your part. Each year this agency publishes thousands of pamphlets on almost every subject imaginable—the majority of which cost less than $3.00. Your local librarian can probably tell you if any information in these pamphlets can be of help in your situation.

The Government Printing Office is the printer for the federal government and makes public all congressional information products: the Congressional Record (the daily record of congressional proceedings), the Federal Register (a listing of all government agencies), the decisions of the Supreme Court . . . they print tens of thousands of federal publications, with an annual operations budget of $800 million. Probably your best approach would not be to scour their Web site for clues to your particular situation. Instead, just remember that they exist. If at any point in your search you come across a clue leading to a government publication, know that you can buy a copy from the GPO to peruse it further.

Information about GPO publications is available on the Internet at *www.access.gpo.gov,* by e-mail at *gpoaccess@gpo.gov.* by telephone at (202) 512-1530 or toll free at (888) 293-6498; by fax at (202) 512-1262.

Telephone Directories

The first place many people look to try to find someone is the telephone book. After all, there is a slim chance the person you're looking for may still be living in the same area. However, most of the time this doesn't work. Usually the person has moved, and, if not, may have married, or may have an unlisted number.

If you think you know the town where your person lives, and you believe he or she has an unlisted number, simply call directory assistance and ask for the name. If directory assistance tells you there is no listing under that name, then the object of your search doesn't live in the town. However, you may be told that the number is unlisted and cannot be released. Either way, you'll know if the person you're looking for lives in the area or not.

If you don't get lucky enough to find the person you're looking for listed in the current phone book, don't despair. Most libraries, telephone companies, and State Archives keep old telephone directories. You may find what you're looking for in these volumes. If you're on an adoption search, keep in mind that birth parents often come from a town near where the birth or adoption took place. By looking through directories from around the time of the adoption, you should be able to get one, or possibly several, matching names. Water, gas, trash removal, and utility companies also keep similar records.

The idea behind looking through old telephone directories is to find an address—any address, no matter how old—where someone once lived. As soon as you have an old address, you can use it to track down those people still in the neighborhood who used to know the person you're looking for.

Thanks to recent computer technology, there are also faster ways for professional searchers to get this kind of information on a national basis (see Chapter Twelve, "National Name Sweeps," page 204).

City and Cross-Street Directories

City Directories

City directories are similar to telephone books, except their records are normally much more detailed (see page 154). Typical information found in these volumes includes:

- complete names of all family members in residence over age eighteen
- addresses and telephone numbers of residence
- occupations and places of employment of those in residence
- length of occupancy
- whether residence is owned or rented
- names, addresses, and telephone numbers of neighbors

The Cross-Street Directories section (page 155) gives a good example of how to apply this kind of research. Past and present issues of city directories are usually kept in State Archives and local libraries. These volumes, also called Polk directories, are typically divided into six sections. They use a lot of symbols and shorthand, so it's best to have a reference librarian help you decode the information.

If you are having trouble finding the directories you need on a state or local level, your librarian can usually get the necessary information from the Library of Congress. Their National Reference Service telephone number is (202) 707-5522. If this doesn't get satisfactory results, you can also contact the largest publisher of these directories:

R. L. Polk & Company
Customer Service
(800) 275-7655

53 **RESIDER**

BEIGH

Beigh Gerry L Jr util sup spec County r9821 Westberry Ct N Ft Myers

Beights Howard E & Loraine; retd h5575 Beacon Blvd Apt 117

Beijnen Froukje M winter res h7430 Lake Breeze Dr SW Apt 210

Beilodeau Jean & Nicole; retd hA44 Page Mobile Vil

Beilsten Jas W & Gladys; retd h347 Doubloon Dr

Beiner Dolores A winter res h4790 S Cleveland Av Apt T2002

Beirch Raymond emp Gulfcoast Beveling r930 S W 47th Cape Coral

Beireis Clarence W Rev & Emma L; retd h28 Homestead Dr

Beisel Chas A & Linda; body shop mech Dixie Buick r10953 Goodwin St Bonita Springs

Beisner Neoma h19701 N Tamiami Trl Lot 63

Beiter Danl F & Jean M h13264 White Marsh La SE Apt 18

" Danl H & Christine h5975 Briarcliff Rd

Beitz Lawr N & Rosella; retd h621 Elephant Way

Bejger Cheryl L support State Attorney r2449 Kent Av

" Gerald J r2449 Kent Av

Beking Gerrit H & Dina W; winter res h18961 N Tamiami Trl Lot 335

Bekins Van Lines Bob Bergner Mgr 2633 Anderson Av

City Directory

Cross-Street Directories

Cross-street directories are sometimes referred to as "Criss-Cross," "Haines," or "Bressers" directories. These invaluable sources allow you to locate a name and address from a telephone number, and vice versa. They can also be an excellent way to identify ***neighbors*** of the person you're looking for. If your library doesn't have one, you can usually find them at the local police or fire department. Copies of old directories can also be found in local libraries and at the State Archives in your search area.

Let's take a minute and go through an example of how to apply this kind of information:

Assume that you're an adoptee. After diligently writing letters and making calls, the only information you've been able to get is: (1) your exact date and place of birth (which you obtained from your amended birth certificate), (2) your birth mother's last name, "Hennessey" (which you found on a copy of the hospital records), and (3) your grandfather's first initial, "P" (which you cajoled a clerk at the adoption agency into giving you). This doesn't seem like much, does it? Well, let's see how to utilize the knowledge you have so far.

The first thing to do is to look through city and cross-street directories from the year you were born, plus the five years before you were born and the five years after. You are looking for the name Hennessey in these city and cross-street directories. As we said earlier, birth parents often live in the general area where they give birth, so this is a good place to start. If no Hennesseys are listed, call or write the county library to check the directories of nearby towns.

Let's assume that you find four Hennesseys listed in a nearby town and one of them is named Peter. Since you know your grandfather's name was P. Hennessey, this may be he. But now you run into a new problem: The directory doesn't mention that Peter Hennessey has any children in the household. This could mean any number of things. He may not be the right P. Hennessey, but it may be that your birth mother was old enough to be living on her own when she gave birth.

In any event, the chances are still good that some or all of the Hennesseys listed are *relatives* of your birth mother. Therefore, you should continue to look through directories for the following years—making note of any changes as well as the names and addresses of neighbors who might know something.

At this point, there are dozens of ways you could proceed. For example, it would be easy to check high school yearbooks in the area for Hennesseys (see "Educational Records," page 168). You could also check local church records to see if any Hennesseys were members. If they were, it's a fairly easy process to identify children and/or close relatives (see "Religious Records," page 171). Since city directories also typically list occupations or places of employment, you could even look at Peter Hennessey's occupation, and then check with local townspeople or employers in that field. The important thing is to be creative—and never mention the word "adoption."

One last note regarding city and cross-street directories. If a name suddenly disappears from a directory, it usually means the individual has either died or moved. In either event, the directory will give you a list of neighbors, whom you can then call. At least one of them should know what happened. (You would call the neighbor, identify yourself as a relative of the missing person, tell the neighbor you are doing genealogical research, and ask if he or she remembers what happened to the person in such-and-such a year). If the person died, it is a fairly routine process to identify the family members (see "Death Records," page 160). If the person moved, a quick trip or letter to the county courthouse should tell you how to proceed (see "Real Estate Records," page 169).

Even though this example is from an adoptee's perspective, it should be clear that directory information is also a powerful tool for anybody who is searching for anybody else.

One final note: When using directories of any kind, *be sure to make copies of relevant pages and keep them in your search planner.* This information could become important at a later stage in your search, and taking this precaution on the spot can save you a great deal of time in the long run.

Vital Statistics Records

Vital statistics are birth, marriage, divorce, and death records. This information is usually open to the public, or at least somewhat open, and a small fee may be charged for making copies.

Whenever you request vital statistics records, be as specific as possible (unless you are running an adoption search; in that case, as always, do not mention the word "adoption"). Identify the individual as clearly as you can. You will get the best results if you state a "legal" or a "medical" need rather than genealogical search as the reason for your request. Keep in mind, these records are always more accessible to family members—so make your requests accordingly.

When requesting vital records, or any of the records mentioned in this chapter, be sure to do so only after thoroughly reviewing all of Chapter Eight. Also be sure to use the appropriate sample letter from Chapter Eight as a model for your own letter. As mentioned in Chapter Eight, your first requests should always be informal and handwritten.

Much of the information found in vital statistics records can also be obtained through local newspapers. In most cases, you will have to provide at least a partial name and an approximate date for the event. If you don't live in the area where you'll need to search, contact a local librarian and offer to pay him or her a few dollars on the side to scan the records for you.

Birth Records

Because of the criminal misuse of birth certificates to create new identities, it is becoming increasingly difficult to obtain these documents. Availability varies from state to state.

Birth certificates provide you with verification of exact spellings of names and exact dates of birth—which, for example, can then be used to trace driving and motor vehicle records in many states. Since birth certificates also routinely reveal the place of birth and parents' names, you will then be able to conduct a search in that geographic area for possible relatives through various local directories, and city and county records.

The occupation(s) of the parents are also listed on birth certificates in many states. This can be valuable, since many occupations require some form of licensing, which is normally available through the state. Many occupations also require membership in trade or union organizations, which in turn can be contacted for information (see page 176, "Professional Organizations and Unions," under "Alternate Sources").

When searching for these records, it is always important to assume that the information is available. Personnel and human resource departments will often provide helpful information, but you must ask for it, and ask with confidence (but politely). *If you don't sound like you expect to get what you're looking for, you may not get it.*

Another often overlooked source of birth information is the birth announcements page in local newspapers. Published birth announcements for children born out of wedlock or for children who were to be placed for adoption are relatively rare. However, mistakes have been known to occur, so always make copies of all the birth announcements that match the correct date and place of birth for the person in question, even if no exact match is found. This list can often be useful during a later stage of your search.

Marriage Records

Marriage records contain two documents of interest to searchers: the marriage license and the marriage license *application.* To get either of these, you'll need at least a partial name and a rough idea of where and when the wedding occurred. Some of the information you will find in these records includes:

- maiden name of the bride
- groom's name
- address, ages, and occupations of bride and groom
- wedding site and name of the minister or official who performed the wedding
- names of the couple's parents
- dates and places of birth
- names of witnesses

- previous marital status
- location of divorce

In most states, marriage records are open to the public. They are kept by the State Department of Vital Statistics and/or the county recorder. If you get turned down on the state level, try the county level—and vice versa. For a sample letter detailing how to write for this information, see page 105.

If you live in the same county as the one you are requesting information from, many times you will be allowed to search these records yourself on a county or city level. In most counties, marriage records are organized by decade (usually on microfilm with microfilm readers available). Often, you will have no idea who, when, or where the person in question got married. Nonetheless, the search is relatively easy and, if you mention genealogy as your primary reason for searching, you can easily get a nearby clerk to show you how to get started.

The records are usually organized alphabetically rather than chronologically and grouped by both bride's name and groom's name so that you can search either way. Searching marriage records can facilitate your quest in a variety of ways. You can obtain from a marriage license the full legal names of the bride and groom, their dates of birth, their state of birth, their permanent address, and often their social security numbers. Some jurisdictions ask if either of the couple have been previously married, and list all the names both spouses have used previously. Also on the license are the names of the witnesses, who are usually best friends or relatives of the couple. If you can't find your missing person, you may want to track down one of the witnesses to the marriage, to see if he or she is still in contact with the married couple.

Obviously, a marriage license is immensely helpful in the adoptive search as well. For instance, if you know only your birth father's last name and his approximate age, you can use marriage records to find candidates of the right age who share his last name. If you turn up one or two people with that last name, you now have discovered one or two possible first names for him, which will help your search elsewhere. Also, in the case of a birth mother, this information can help you determine a married name to trace, if she got married after giving birth to you and changed her name. Since marriage records contain so much additional information about the person you are looking for, and carry information about their relatives, they can help provide the missing link that will carry you to the final steps of your search.

Each marriage entry will also have a file number next to it. Copy down all the entries that are relevant and their file numbers. Then show the entries to the clerk and ask for both hard copies of the marriage licenses and *applications* for the marriage licenses belonging to the entries. There is a good chance your missing person got married in the county of his or her birth, so you should use this as your starting point. If you cannot locate anything, expand your search to surrounding areas.

Marriage License

KENT COUNTY, MICHIGAN — 7109 (Local File No.)

To any person legally authorized to solemnize marriage in the State of Michigan,

GREETINGS

Marriage May Be Solemnized In the State of Michigan Between

BOYD THOMKINS (Full Name of Male) and ETHEL KILMER FOREMAN (Full Name of Female)

Male	Female
40 (Age at last birthday) — White (Color)	26 (Age at last birthday) — White (Color)
------ (Residence No. Street)	------ (Residence No. Street)
Grand Rapids, Michigan (City Zone No. State)	Cascade, Michigan (City Zone No. State)
Bowne Twp. Kent County, Mich. (Birthplace - City and State)	Grand Rapids, Michigan (Birthplace - City and State)
Die Maker (Occupation)	None (Occupation)
Bishop Thomkins (Father's Full Name)	Elton Kilmer (Father's Full Name)
Katherine McVea (Mother's Maiden Name)	Jesica Shulman (Mother's Maiden Name)
None (Number of times previously married)	Once (Number of times previously married)
	Kilmer (Maiden name (if a widow))

and whose Parent's or Guardian's consent, in case she has not attained the age of eighteen years, has been filed in my office. An affidavit has been filed in this office, as provided by Public Act No. 128, Laws of 1887, as amended, by which it appears that said statements are true.

IN WITNESS WHEREOF, I have signed and sealed these presents,

this 17th **day of** August **A.D., 19** 18

ROBERT G. HILL
County Clerk

Jacob J. Kosten
Deputy County Clerk

L.S.

Between Mr. Boyd Thomkins **and M** Ethel Kilmer Foreman

I HEREBY CERTIFY that, in accordance with the above license, the persons herein mentioned were joined in marriage by me, at Grand Rapids**, county of** Kent**, MICHIGAN,**

on the 17th **day of** August **A.D. 19** 18**, in the presence of**

Blanche B. Miller (**Full Name**) **of** Grand Rapids, Michigan (**Residence City State**)**, and**

Ruth Miller (**Full Name**) **of** Grand Rapids, Michigan (**Residence City State**)**, and**

as witnesses.

H.C. Miller (**Signature of Magistrate or clergyman**) — Minister (**Official Title**)

Marriage License

Both local churches and local newspapers are additional sources of marriage information. Many times they provide even *more* identifying information than the records held by the state and county. Newspaper announcements and church registries can fill in a lot of missing pieces when combined with a partial name and/or religious affiliation found in other records.

Divorce Records

Since so many marriages today unfortunately end in divorce, these records have become another useful source for searchers. Most states and counties keep divorce records, and there is usually a small fee for accessing them. A sample request letter is provided on page 106 (Letter 3).

Divorce records usually contain the following information:

- names and addresses of persons involved (including children)
- date and place of marriage
- names of attorneys
- social security numbers
- references to any property held by the couple (homes, cars, land, businesses, bank accounts, etc.)

Newspapers are another good source of divorce information. Local libraries should have microfilm copies of local newspapers, which you can easily search.

Some religious denominations also keep records of persons in their congregations who have divorced. You'll have to ask at each relevant church individually—there's no rule of thumb to tell you which churches keep divorce records.

Death Records

One of the most effective ways to locate the individual you are seeking is through the death records and obituaries of his or her relatives. These documents contain a great deal of information and it is usually easier to get identifying data on related persons than on the individual directly in question.

Types of death records include death certificates; obituaries; and cemetery, funeral home, and probate records. Each type of death record summarizes the life of an individual to some extent and provides valuable clues about the person (see sample death certificate, page 162).

Here is a list of useful information you can expect to find in death records:

- name and last address of the deceased
- place and time of birth, death, and burial
- spouse's and parents' names
- social security numbers
- occupation and place of employment
- church and other organizational memberships
- name of funeral home and cemetery that handled the death
- military background (if any)
- names and addresses of surviving family members
- payment records of death benefits to widows or widowers, and any other dependents
- inheritance information

Death records are generally public information, and death certificates can usually be obtained by writing either the county or State Department of Vital Statistics where the death occurred (see Appendix 2). To make a request, you will need at least a partial name, an approximate date of death (plus or minus five years) and any additional identifying information. A sample letter of request is provided on page 107).

In many cases, most of this same information is available at your county or local library, and also at the Family History Centers run by the Mormon church (see "Libraries and Family History Centers," page 147). These institutions often have copies of the State Death Index on microfilm, and they may even have records for the entire county on computer, if they are linked to the Social Security Death Index.

Probate records are those records that address matters of inheritance and estate settlement. They are typically kept at the county level, and are open to the public in most counties. Probate records are indexed by the name of the decedent. New information they might contain would include names and addresses of other relatives involved in the estate; creditors at the time of death; locations of property and other assets; names of lien holders; and much more. And once you track down those items, they will all provide even more data.

Remember, quite often when we are looking for a living person, it is easier to find traces of a deceased relative, who can posthumously lead you to the living!

STATE OF IOWA
IOWA DEPARTMENT OF PUBLIC HEALTH
CERTIFICATE OF DEATH 114-

TYPE IN PERMANENT BLACK INK. FOR INSTRUCTIONS SEE HANDBOOK

BIRTH NUMBER

DECEDENT

1. DECEDENT'S NAME — FIRST — MIDDLE — LAST
2. DATE OF DEATH (Mo. Day, Yr.)
3. SEX: Male
4a. AGE LAST BIRTHDAY (Years): 63
4b. UNDER 1 YEAR — MOS — DAYS
4c. UNDER 1 DAY — HRS — MIN
5. DATE OF BIRTH (Mo. Day, Yr.): December 28, 1926
6a. COUNTY OF DEATH: Black Hawk
6b. FACILITY NAME (If not institution, give street and number)
6c. CITY, TOWN, OR LOCATION OF DEATH
6d. INSIDE CITY LIMITS (Specify yes or no): Yes
6e. PLACE OF DEATH (Check only one)
HOSPITAL: ☐ Inpatient ☒ ER/Outpatient ☐ DOA
OTHER: ☐ Nursing Home ☐ Residence ☐ Other (Specify)
7. WAS DECEDENT OF HISPANIC ORIGIN? (Specify No or Yes below) If yes, specify Cuban, Mexican, Puerto Rican, etc.: ☒ NO ☐ YES Specify
8. RACE - White, Black, American Indian, etc. (Specify): White
9. DECEDENT'S EDUCATION (Specify only highest grade completed) Elementary/Secondary (0-12) — College (1-4 or 5+): 8 grade
10. BIRTHPLACE (City & State or Foreign Country): Grundy Co., Iowa
11. CITIZEN OF WHAT COUNTRY: U.S.A.
12a. MARRIED, NEVER MARRIED, WIDOWED, DIVORCED (Specify): Married
12b. SURVIVING SPOUSE (If wife, give maiden name)
13. SOCIAL SECURITY NUMBER
14a. USUAL OCCUPATION (Give kind of work done during most of working life. Do not use retired.): Maintenance Supervisor
14b. KIND OF BUSINESS OR INDUSTRY: Americana Health Care
15. WAS DECEDENT EVER IN U.S. ARMED FORCES? (Specify yes or no): Yes

USUAL RESIDENCE WHERE DECEDENT LIVED. IF DEATH OCCURRED IN A LONG TERM CARE INSTITUTION GIVE INSTITUTION ADDRESS AS RESIDENCE

16a. RESIDENCE - STATE: Iowa
16b. COUNTY: Black Hawk
16c. CITY, TOWN, OR LOCATION: Cedar Falls
16d. STREET AND NUMBER OF RESIDENCE
16e. INSIDE CITY LIMITS (Specify yes or no): Yes

PARENTS

17. FATHER'S NAME — FIRST — MIDDLE — LAST
18. MOTHER'S NAME — FIRST — MIDDLE — MAIDEN

INFORMANT

19a. INFORMANT'S NAME: T
19b. MAILING ADDRESS (Street and Number or Rural Route Number, City or Town, State, Zip Code)

BURIAL

20a. METHOD OF DISPOSITION: ☒ Burial ☐ Cremation ☐ Removal from State ☐ Donation ☐ Other (Specify)
20b. PLACE OF DISPOSITION (Name of Cemetery, Crematory, or other place): Pleasant Valley Reformed Cemetery
20c. LOCATION (City or Town, State): Holland, Iowa
21a. FUNERAL DIRECTOR - SIGNATURE ▶ [signature]
21b. F.D. LICENSE #: 1855
21c. FUNERAL HOME - NAME AND ADDRESS (Street and Number or Rural Route Number, City or Town, State, Zip Code): THE DAHL-Van Hove-Schoof Funeral Home,

REGISTRAR

22a. REGISTRAR - SIGNATURE ▶
22b. DATE RECEIVED BY REGISTRAR (Mo. Day, Yr.)

23. MANNER OF DEATH: ☐ Natural ☐ Accident ☐ Suicide ☐ Homicide ☐ Pending Investigation ☐ Could not be determined
24a. DATE OF INJURY (Mo. Day, Yr.)
24b. HOUR OF INJURY — M
24c. INJURY AT WORK? (Specify yes or no)
24d. DESCRIBE HOW INJURY OCCURRED
24e. PLACE OF INJURY (Specify at home, farm, street, factory, office building, etc.)
24f. LOCATION (Street and Number or Rural Route Number, City or Town, State, Zip Code)

CERTIFIER

To the best of my knowledge, death occurred at the time, date and place due to the cause(s) and manner as stated
25a. (Signature and title) ▶
25b. DATE SIGNED (Mo. Day, Yr.)
25c. HOUR OF DEATH
26. NAME AND TITLE OF ATTENDING PHYSICIAN IF OTHER THAN CERTIFIER (Type/Print)
27. NAME AND ADDRESS OF CERTIFIER (Physician or Medical Examiner) (Type/Print)

CAUSE OF DEATH

28. PART I. Enter the diseases, injuries, or complications that caused the death. Do not enter the mode of dying, such as cardiac or respiratory arrest, shock, or heart failure. List only one cause on each line.

Approximate Interval Between Onset and Death

Final disease or condition resulting in death → IMMEDIATE CAUSE
(a)
DUE TO (OR AS A CONSEQUENCE OF)
(b)
DUE TO (OR AS A CONSEQUENCE OF)
(c)
DUE TO (OR AS A CONSEQUENCE OF)
(d)

Sequentially list conditions, if any, leading to immediate cause. Enter UNDERLYING CAUSE (Disease or injury that initiated events resulting in death) LAST

PART II. Other significant conditions contributing to death but not resulting in the underlying causes given in Part I

b. IF FEMALE WAS THERE A PREGNANCY IN THE PAST 12 MONTHS? (Specify yes or no)

29a. AUTOPSY (Specify yes or no)

29b. WERE AUTOPSY FINDINGS AVAILABLE PRIOR TO COMPLETION OF CAUSE OF DEATH? (Specify yes or no)

IDH 588-0021 Revised - 1/88

Death Certificate

Some cemetery and funeral home records are not open to the public. However, their keepers are usually quite helpful to family members wishing to trace their genealogical history.

If the funeral home clerk gives you access to the records, you will find a wealth of information. You will obtain the deceased's dates of birth and death, his or her social security number, last known address before passing away, the names of living family members, and any contact information the next of kin provided for living family members (or, occasionally, for other people the deceased was close to).

Also enclosed in the typical funeral home file is the location of the burial site and a copy of the deceased's obituary. In some cases an insurance company is listed, which will provide you with another source of personal information to be pursued if necessary.

Lastly, in the funeral home records you should be able to find a copy of the death certificate. A death certificate provides the following: date of birth, date and time of death, place of death, last address, cause of death, name of the person who informed authorities of the death, name of the doctor who signed the death certificate.

In contrast, a cemetery record is more difficult to get your hands on and doesn't have as much information. The typical cemetery record will list the dates of birth and death and usually the name of the funeral home involved. That may be all you'll get. Really, cemetery records are most useful in directing you to the funeral home (where you'll find far more informative files).

All death records can be valuable when combined with other scattered pieces of nonidentifying information. Here's a step-by-step example of how you could put information together if you were an adoptee:

You have managed to assemble the following clues.

1. From the state adoption department, you
   - A) learned that you were adopted through an agency
   - B) got the agency's name, address, and telephone number
2. According to the information on your amended birth certificate, you were
   - (A) born at Grundy County Hospital in Grundy Center, Iowa
   - (B) on August 14, 1965, at 12:43 A.M.
3. By writing a letter to your adoption agency, and then following it up with several conversations over the phone, you also learned that
   - (A) your mother was sixteen and unmarried at the time of your birth
   - (B) your maternal grandparents were German immigrants, and their first initials were P and A
   - (C) your maternal grandmother had been a widow for ten years prior to your birth

4. You were able to obtain a copy of your adoption petition (on your second request) which:
   (A) stated that your birth mother's last name was Hennessey

Let's start putting the pieces together. First, the adoption agency refused to provide your birth mother's last name and first initial on the grounds that this would be identifying information. This was a long shot anyway—but it was worth a try. However, because you were persistent and asked the right questions, the agency did eventually agree to release your *grandparents'* first initials.

Now, when you combine your grandfather's initial with the last name found in the adoption petition, you've got a partial name! That's *half* of what you'll need to get a death certificate.

The next piece of the puzzle is calculating an approximate date of death. To do this, we'll need to get a rough idea of how long your grandfather was dead before you were born. You prepare your question in advance, writing it out on a piece of paper. Next you call your contact at the adoption agency and learn that your grandfather died ten years before you were born. This means he passed away sometime between 1952 and 1958 (that's ten years before your birth, plus or minus three years on either side to allow for errors).

Now that you've got the partial name of your grandfather and an approximate date of death, the next step would be to

(1) Send a letter to the Iowa Department of Vital Statistics requesting a death certificate for a "P. Hennessey," who died between 1952 and 1958. You state "matters of estate settlement" as the reason for requesting your grandfather's death certificate, you enclose a self-addressed, stamped envelope, along with a photo of your current family (see page 107).

(2) Next, you write letters to all the newspapers in Grundy County and ask them to look for an obituary that fits your grandfather's description (following the model of the sample letter on page 111).

This example we've been using was a real case. In fact, we *did* write letters to all the newspapers requesting obituaries, and to the state requesting a copy of the death certificate. One of the newspapers came through, providing the obituary notice on page 165.

Within forty-eight hours of receiving the notice, our client was talking with her birth mother! Using the address from the obituary, our client visited the houses on either side of the grandfather's old home. A short conversation with one of the neighbors revealed where the family had moved after the grandfather's death—and the daughter, our client's birth mother, was still living there. They had a wonderful reunion.

HENNESSEY - Mr. Peter Edmund Hennessey, aged 41, of Dike, passed away Sunday, April 28, 1955 at his home after suffering a stroke. Surviving are his wife, Alice Hennessey; one son and one daughter, Lester P. Hennessey, 11 and Marlene Hennessey, 6; no grandchildren; many nieces and nephews. Mr. Hennessey was a long-time member of the First Christian Reformed Church in Stout. He had been a farmer all his life. A Christian Burial will be celebrated Tuesday at 12 noon at the First Christian Reformed Church in Stout, Reverend William Neiderman, Celebrant. Interment to follow. The family will receive visitors Monday evening from 6–10 p.m. at the Oberman-Rice Funeral Home.

Birthmother

About a month later we received the grandfather's death certificate in the mail. It would eventually have led us to the same place.

So you see how even the *smallest* shred of data can become revealing when combined with the right knowledge. The key is to be persistent, pursue many different avenues at once, use what little you have to the maximum advantage, and never give up.

Social Security Records

Since almost everyone has a social security number, it is likely that the Social Security Administration will have the employment records or the home address of the person you are looking for—especially if that person is old enough to be receiving benefits.

While the SSA will not allow you to contact a person *directly,* they will forward mail to that person for "humanitarian purposes." This normally includes matters of medical urgency, legal proceedings, inheritance, and estate settlement. Genealogical reasons are usually not considered to be sufficient cause, and "adoption search" is always a sure candidate for the trash can.

Assuming you are creative enough to come up with a reason that is acceptable, the SSA will then contact the individual, informing him that he is under no obligation to respond. So, even if you reach the person you're seeking through this route, he or she may not respond. But if he does, then you will have made contact with the person you were looking for. It is definitely worth pursuing.

To contact the SSA, address your request to:

Social Security Administration—Letter Forwarding Service
Office of Central Records Operations
300 N. Greene St.
Baltimore, MD 21201
General Inquiry Number: (800) 772-1213

Provide as much personal information as possible (name, approximate date and place of birth, employer(s), military history, etc.). Enclose an unsealed letter with your request, addressed to the person you are looking for. The SSA will read this letter to determine if its purpose meets their "humanitarian" guidelines (for sample letters, see pages 117 and 118).

The SSA is not a mailing service. *You can use this route only once for each person being sought.* The SSA will usually advise you, in writing, of the outcome of their search. If it's especially difficult, the agency might even charge you a small fee. This entire process can take anywhere from three to thirty-six weeks.

You may not know this, but the first three digits of any social security number reveal the state where it was issued. Typically this is the first state where the individual was employed and does not necessarily represent the person's place of birth. However, the information can give you a starting place. The following is a current list of numbers and the states they correspond to:

001–003 New Hampshire
004–007 Maine
008–009 Vermont
010–034 Massachusetts
035–039 Rhode Island
040–049 Connecticut

440–448 Oklahoma
449–467, 627–645 Texas
468–477 Minnesota
478–485 Iowa
486–500 Missouri
501–504 North Dakota

050–134 New York

135–158 New Jersey

159–211 Pennsylvania

212–220 Maryland

221–222 Delaware

223–231 Virginia

232–236 West Virginia

232, 237–246 North Carolina

247–251 South Carolina

252–260 Georgia

261–267, 589–595 Florida

268–302 Ohio

303–317 Indiana

318–361 Illinois

362–386 Michigan

387–399 Wisconsin

400–407 Kentucky

408–415 Tennessee

416–424 Alabama

425–428, 587–588 Mississippi

429–432 Arkansas

433–439 Louisiana

505–508 Nebraska

509–515 Kansas

516–517 Montana

518–519 Idaho

520–524 Colorado

525, 585, 648–649 New Mexico

526–527, 600–601 Arizona

528–529, 646–647 Utah

530 Nevada

531–539 Washington

540–544 Oregon

545–573, 602–626 California

574 Alaska

575–576 Hawaii

577–579 District of Columbia

580 Virgin Islands

580–584, 596–599 Puerto Rico

586 American Samoa

586 Northern Mariana Islands

586 Guam

586 Philippines

The only two exceptions are railroad workers (700–729) and some military personnel inducted in the 1970s; in these cases, the social security numbers are ten digits and begin with the number 0.

Passport Records

In most cases, these records will not be available, but some searchers have received them by citing their rights under the Freedom of Information Act and Privacy Act of 1974 (see page 98, "Requesting Information from the Federal Government"). When you compose a letter to the Department of State, be sure to cite these rights.

Information found in these files includes birth certificates, social security numbers, addresses, and birth dates. To file a request, write to:

The Department of State
National Passport Information Center
1425 K Street NW
Washington, DC 20524

Education Records

Most Americans have some level of formal education. School records from elementary school through college often provide valuable clues to a person's identity and location. Sources include:

- old yearbooks
- school records
- alumni association records
- fraternal organizations
- reunion committees
- classmates and teachers

To pursue this avenue, contact a local reference librarian, or write a letter to the State Archives asking for a list of all schools operating in your search area around the time your individual went to school.

Alumni records and reunion committees are another good source of information. High school and college reunion committees spend a great deal of time tracking down classmates, and they may be able to save you a lot of time. If you have reason to believe that the person you're looking for went to college, that institution's alumni association may be of assistance. For a listing of all universities, colleges, and junior colleges, ask your library for a copy of *Patterson's American Education Directory.*

School records can provide a great deal of information, but some schools are less cooperative than others. If a particular school is unable or unwilling to help, contact the district school office and repeat your request. If that office refuses to release any information to you, explain that in accordance with the Family and Educational Rights and Privacy Act, Public Law 380, Title 5, enacted August 1974, they are "allowed to release directory information." This information should give you correct spellings of full names, old addresses, old phone numbers, and possibly dates of birth and parents' names. If you've read *The Locator* from the beginning, by now you should know what to do if you get any of these pieces of data. (With an old phone number, try the local cross-street directory or city directory to find an old address; with an old address, contact the neighbors to see if they remember the residents; with parents' names, expand your search to include the parents, since they may be easier to track down than their children; and so on.)

One final note about requesting school records; *Never* mention the words "adoption search." This will always make people suspicious. "Genealogical research" or "inheritance matters" usually meet the most success. The people working at educational organizations may have their own biases and prejudices, so it's best to use genealogical, reunion, or inheritance matters as the reason for your inquiries. For samples of letters to schools, see pages 112, 113, and 114.

Real Estate Records

The buying and selling of real estate has created one of the most thorough forms of record-keeping worldwide. Property and tax records are open to everyone and are usually kept by the county recorder, the tax assessor, or somewhere at the county courthouse. To request real estate records, you'll need to know the county where the sale took place, an approximate year, and at least a partial name of the people involved. To write a letter based on this information, follow the sample outlined on page 115.

The following is a list of what you might expect to find in real estate records:

- full names
- addresses
- birth dates and places

- occupations
- names and addresses of mortgage holders
- marital status

The situs file and grantor/grantee index are two records of special importance to searchers. The situs file is an alphabetical list of who owns what in a county. It's usually kept on microfilm and is available for the asking. The records will be kept by the county recorder, the tax assessor, or somewhere at the county courthouse, it varies from county to county.

The grantor/grantee index is organized alphabetically in chronological order by year. It lists the file (or document) number where more information can be found about any given transaction. The grantee is the buyer of the property, the grantor is the seller.

Both these sources normally contain a great deal of legal terminology. If you get confused, simply ask a clerk for help. The clerks are usually very good at finding this kind of information and can cut through the red tape if you tell them exactly what you're looking for.

Here's a closer look at how to apply this kind of information:

Assume that you have the full name of the person you're looking for. While researching old city directories, you notice that after a certain year an individual with the name you are looking for disappeared from a city in the area you think he lived. This means he probably died or moved.

Taking note of the address, you use the city and cross-street directories to find the addresses and names of the neighbors (see "City and Cross-Street Directories," page 153). After making a few calls to neighbors, you discover that your candidate did not die, but did move away from the town in that year.

Since the person moved, you have four possibilities:

He still owns the house and is renting it out.

He sold the house and may still be holding a mortgage.

He sold the house outright.

He was merely renting the property originally, and never owned the house.

In any of these cases, a little research at the county courthouse should narrow things down.

If he still owns the house and is renting it, then the county recorder will show no record of a transaction for that address in that year, or in any following years. If this is the case, contact the current tenants and ask them where, and to whom, they mail their checks.

If the person in question is holding a second mortgage, or has sold the property outright, then the county recorder will almost always have a record of this transaction. In the former case, the county recorder and the present owner should both have the seller's new address. In the latter case, the seller's new address will be harder to find. Go back to the new owner and the neighbors and ask them for the names of friends or relatives who might know where the seller went. Citing "reasons of inheritance" as your need to contact the seller works especially well when talking to people in this situation.

Up until now, we have covered how to proceed if the person you are looking for *owned* the property. What if he or she was just renting it in the first place?

In most cases, you will still be able to gather more information. Use the records kept by the county recorder to identify the owner of the property at the time your person was renting it. Contact that owner in the same way you would reach a friend or neighbor. The owner will often have the tenant's new address on file, because the owner probably mailed a deposit refund to the renter. You can also check with the post office for a change of address card (see "Post Office Records" under "Alternate Sources," page 177).

Religious Records

Records of religious and church affiliations are another good source of information for searchers. If you know the denomination of the person you are looking for, a local clergyman should be able to provide a list of corresponding institutions in your search area. (If you're in an adoption search and are unsure of the denomination, try asking the agency or attorney who handled the adoption. This isn't usually considered identifying information.) If you can't get the denomination narrowed down, you may want to mail a letter to every religious organization in the area and ask for their help (for a sample letter, see page 116). A local library should be able to provide you with names and addresses of all the religious institutions in the area.

Typical information found in religious files includes:

- birth records
- baptismal records (see page 172)
- marriage records
- divorce notations
- death records
- full names and addresses of family

Certificate of Baptism

ST. AMBROSE PARISH
18213 HAMPTON ROAD

GROSSE POINT PARK, ARKANSAS 49320

THIS IS TO CERTIFY

THAT Michele Lyn Bradey

CHILD OF John Bradey

AND Florence Oshman

BORN IN (not recorded)

ON THE 27th DAY OF December 1958

WAS BAPTIZED

ON THE 25th DAY OF January 1959

ACCORDING TO THE RITE OF THE ROMAN CATHOLIC CHURCH

BY THE REV. John Morande

SPONSORS Celeste Morande

Francis F. VanDenberg

AS APPEARS FROM THE BAPITSMAL REGISTER OFTHIS CHURCH

DATED February 11, 1986

Rev. Paul E. Rosenberg

LEGALLY ADOPTED - 1961 - by Harry and Dorothy Kay. Name changed to Joanne Margaret Kay. Catholic Social Services of Macomb County.

Baptismal Certificate

Religious organizations are often willing to help searchers. It would be wise, however, to avoid mentioning an adoption search, and instead give "family research" as the reason for your request.

Here is a list of national headquarters for some of the larger religious denominations:

Adventual Library
Aurora College
Aurora, IL 60507

Archives of Episcopal Church
606 Ratherdue Place
Austin, TX 78701

American Congregational Library
14 Beacon Street
Boston, MA 02108

LDS Church Archives
50 East N. Temple Street
Salt Lake City, UT 84150

Lutheran Archives Center
7301 German Ave.
Philadelphia, PA 19119

Southern Baptist Library and Archives
901 Commerce St. #400
Nashville, TN 37203

United Methodist Library
Beeghley Library
Ohio Wesleyan University
Delaware, OH 43015

American Baptist Historical Society
Samuel Colgate Baptist Library
11 S. Goodman St.
Rochester, NY 14620

American Jewish Archives
Hebrew Union College
3101 Clifton Ave.
Cincinnati, OH 45220

American Catholic Historic Association
Department of Archives
Catholic University of America
Washington, DC 20017

Mennonite Archives Library
Bethel College
N. Newton, KS 67117

Presbyterian Historical Association
425 Lombard St.
Philadelphia, PA 19147

Friends Historical Library
Swarthmore College
Swarthmore, PA 19081

Historical Society of the Reformed Church
21 Seminary Place
New Brunswick, NJ 08901

iminal Records

/hile it's not something most of us care to consider, there is a chance that you are searching for someone with a criminal record. Criminal records are open to the public, but you will need the full name, along with some idea of what the infraction was and when it occurred.

Local police departments have been known to help searchers, especially in situations of medical urgency. If you want to inquire whether an individual has ever been in the federal penal system, contact (202) 307-3126. This is the number for the Inmate Locator Service, which will find anyone who is or has been in the prison system. The service is run by the Federal Bureau of Prisons. Be prepared to wait a while, because their voice-mail system works slowly. Be patient—they can be very helpful.

If a military or former military person received a court-martial and was imprisoned in a United States disciplinary barracks (a military prison), call Fort Leavenworth, Kansas, at (913) 634-4629 for assistance.

Driving Records

Every state has a Department of Motor Vehicles (DMV), which maintains current and historical records of all drivers and their automobiles. A quick look at your own driver's license shows how much helpful information is recorded there.

Although these files may not be considered public information, most DMVs will eventually release this data if you can prove you have a good cause in asking for it. Some DMVs require as little information as the person's name and date of birth; others will need the driver's license number and written permission from the person you are looking for. Some states will provide you with "address verification" (i.e., they'll tell you where the person lives) if you can give them the date of birth and the presumed address of the person you're looking for. Most states keep transcripts detailing the drivers' records in that state, which are available by written request; there is normally a small fee for duplication.

In 1994 Congress passed the Driver's Privacy Protection Act, which provides individuals with a "limited veto" over public access to their personal information in DMV files. As a result, DMV records have become increasingly more difficult to obtain. States have put the Privacy Protection Act into varying degrees of effect, so you may or may not have trouble getting the address information you are looking for.

On the other hand, a different congressional law has created *greater* availability—we refer to the recently passed "motor voter" legislation. The motor voter law allows people to register to vote when they apply for a driver's license. This has resulted in an interesting situation: Many people have unknowingly made personal information accessible to the public just by registering to vote through the motor voter program. The voter registration data from this program is routinely entered into commercial databases across the country by public record providers, thus offsetting the privacy restrictions on DMV records. This information won't help the individual who writes to a state DMV, but it does help any public record provider with access to public information databases. (When selecting a provider, be sure to choose one who is licensed and bonded.)

As we've said before, obtaining a social security number for the person in your search can open doors to all sorts of other information. Some states give drivers the option of using their social security numbers as their driver's license number. They are:

Hawaii	Georgia	Virginia
Massachusetts	Missouri	Iowa
Nevada	Arkansas	North Dakota
Idaho	Mississippi	Washington, D.C.
Kentucky	Oklahoma	
South Dakota	Indiana	
Kansas	Montana	

In order to request an abstract of a person's driver's license, you will usually need a social security number, but sometimes you can be successful with only a name and date of birth. The information you can expect to learn: the address at the time the license was issued or renewed; a physical description; and, in some states, a social security number. When making such a request, be sure to ask specifically for "the abstract of [the person's] driving history."

If the person you're searching for has moved and obtained a new driver's license in a different state, that information will appear on the driving record from the state he left. At present, Texas is the only state that does not notify other states when a driver is issued a new license.

If you have trouble getting driver's license information, you could contact our Consultant Hotline (see page 233 for number; charge is $3.99 per minute). Some state driver's license reports are available to us via our computer databases (giving us the person's name, address, license violations, accidents, traffic tickets, etc.) and can be obtained within a few days. In many cases, these databases also allow us to trace license plates and/or vehicle identification numbers. It is important to note that vehicle registration records are often more current than driver's license information, since the registration must be renewed every year.

Alternate Sources

Your individual situation will always dictate which search techniques work best. Listed below are several additional sources that many people have found to be useful.

Townspeople

Local townspeople can often provide valuable clues to the identity and whereabouts of the person you are seeking. While you shouldn't take this type of information as gospel, keep in mind that almost every community has someone with a good memory for people and events—and that person is usually not hard to find. Remember that giving "inheritance reasons" as the purpose for your search usually gets the best response.

Professional Organizations and Unions

If you suspect that the person you're searching for could have belonged to a trade or labor union, write to that union and request the person's records, which might offer some valuable clues. A local library should be able to provide addresses and telephone numbers for the unions in the area you are searching.

Professional organizations and state licensing offices are also good places to look. A large reference guide to over 6,000 of these organizations is published by Columbia Books, titled *National Trade and Professional Associations of the U.S. and Canada and Labor Unions.* Most libraries, especially those affiliated with universities and technical schools, will have it. Once you have identified an occupation (through city directories, friends, neighbors, etc.), look in this book to find out how to contact the appropriate organizations. They are usually happy to check membership records for you.

Classified Ads

If you feel certain you're searching in the correct geographical area, you may want to run a classified ad in the personals. When placing an ad in a public newspaper that is read by the local townsfolk, don't identify the person you are seeking by name; that could be embarrassing for the person, and will discourage him or her from getting in touch with you. Here are some examples that have worked in the past:

Looking for lost relative in the ________________ family for urgent medical reasons. If you have any information, please contact ____________ immediately.

(Male/female) born on ____________ urgently seeks any information regarding parents! Call ________.

REWARD: Genealogist searching for members of the ___________ family who lived in _____________ (area) between ________-________ (dates). Anyone with information, please contact _________________.

Post Office Records

Each local branch of the United States Postal Service retains change of address cards for one year after they are filed. These are usually available on request for a $1.00 fee and may prove useful if you believe the person has recently moved. Another technique for obtaining a current address is to mail an empty sealed envelope to the old address marked "Address Correction Requested—Do Not Forward." Be sure to put your return address on the envelope! You will normally receive the new address within three to four weeks.

Voter Registration Records

If you believe that the person you're looking for is a regular voter, then voter registration cards can be a simple way to pinpoint information. Usually kept at the county courthouse, these records normally include full name, date of birth, address, and social security number.

For Adoptees and Birth Parents: Agency Searches

In the last couple of years, some states have passed laws requiring adoption agencies to begin doing searches on behalf of adoptees and birth parents. Also, some adoption agencies themselves have voluntarily begun doing searches. In theory, this is a great thing. However, there are certain issues you should be aware of.

First of all, most agencies charge a fee for this service. It can range anywhere from $25.00 to $500.00. Depending on the price and on your circumstances, it might be worth it. If you're considering letting an agency conduct a search, make sure you understand what the agency will do—and ask them what their restrictions and limitations are—before making a decision. For instance: Even though an agency may do searches, they are still bound by their state law. This means that *regardless of whether or not you paid a fee,* the agency will not release any information to you without the other person's written consent.

Second, understand that while agencies normally have the name, age, and some general background information about the person you're looking for, most of them know very little about how to find anybody. Many times an agency search consists of nothing more than writing a letter to the address where that person was living when the adoption was finalized. That address is usually twenty to thirty years old. If the letter is returned or comes back with no new information, in many cases the agency considers the search to be over.

Third, many of the agencies that have begun doing searches are backlogged several months with requests, so they can't afford to spend much time on any one search. They may sincerely *want* to do more, but in most cases the social workers are severely overworked and underpaid, and your case becomes just another number.

Adoptees and/or adoptive parents who are considering having an agency do a search on their behalf should be aware of one more thing. If a birth parent is located, and is unsure about what to do, or is not absolutely thrilled and excited about being found, many social workers will *mistake* that as a negative response. If that happens, you will probably be told that the birth parent "does not want any contact"—and you're out of luck. Even though they may locate a birth parent, most agencies do very little to counsel or encourage contact.

Birth parents who are considering having an agency do a search on their behalf face a similar dilemma. Most states require agencies that conduct searches to make contact *directly* with the adoptee—as long as the adoptee is an adult. This looks great on paper, but in reality it rarely happens. Since most of the information in the agency's files pertains to the adoptive *parents,* they will usually find the adopted parents first. If even *one* of the adoptive parents shows any sign of concern or hesitancy, many social workers will stop the search. They'll simply go back to the birth parent and say the adoptee "does not want any contact."

In general most agencies are honest and as diligent as they can be when it comes to doing searches. Therefore, if you're presented with the opportunity and it doesn't cost too much, give it a try. Just make sure you clearly understand the limitations up front. Whatever you do, don't stop your own search efforts. You could wait several months for an agency search to be completed, only to hear that the search was unsuccessful, or that the person was found but wasn't interested in making contact. In either case, you'll have no way of knowing what really happened—regardless of whether or not you paid a fee. The fact is, nobody will care about your case as much, or give it as much attention as you.

Special Provisions for Adopted American Indians

The Indian Child Welfare Act of 1978 (Public Law 95-608) entitles adoptees of American Indian heritage, including Eskimos and Aleuts, to special rights.

Under this legislation, persons of American Indian descent are exempt from sealed-records laws, and can therefore obtain their sealed adoption files by following the correct procedures. Section 107 reads:

> Upon application by an Indian individual who has reached the age of eighteen and who was the subject of an adoptive placement, the court which entered the final decree shall inform such an individual of the tribal affiliation, if any, of the individual's biological parents and provide such other information as may be necessary to protect any rights flowing from the individual's tribal relationship.

American Indian adoptees also retain their rights of inheritance. Section 301(b) reads:

> Upon the request of the adopted Indian child over the age of eighteen, the adoptive or foster parents of an Indian child, or an Indian tribe, the Secretary of the Interior shall disclose such information as may be necessary for the enrollment of an Indian child in the tribe in which the child may be eligible for enrollment for determining any right or benefits associated with that membership.

Adoptees must be at least twenty-five percent Native American to qualify under this act. For further information about your rights, contact your local library and ask for the address and telephone number of the nearest Bureau of Indian Affairs office or call the Federal Bureau of Indian Affairs Office at (202) 219-4150 for a wealth of information.

Searching Internationally

Whatever the reason for an international search, conditions surrounding it will vary depending on the amount of information available, the nature of your search, and the legal and social situation in the country you are searching.

Appendix 2 provides general information and specific document request forms for over fifty countries and their provinces. However, because international searching can become extremely complex (and the fact that it is often complicated further by changing political/social issues), we strongly suggest that searchers enlist qualified assistance in addition to their own efforts. In most cases, the organizations listed below will charge little, if any, for their services.

The availability of international search assistance in a specific country depends greatly on how many, if any, organized groups or individuals operate within its borders. The following is a review of the type of search assistance and the amount of assistance available as of 1999. All these sources are knowledgeable about locating individuals and obtaining records within their country.

It is quite common for new international sources of assistance to become available and to disappear without notice. If during the course of your search you come into contact with any groups, organizations, or individuals not mentioned here, please write to us at:

The International Locator, Inc.

Attn: Foreign Services Dept

2503 Del Prado Blvd., Suite 435

Cape Coral, FL 33904

If during the course of your search you find it necessary to obtain translation assistance via telephone, AT&T has an invaluable service called AT&T Language Help, which is available around the clock, seven days a week. The number is (800) 628-8486. Call this and AT&T will provide you with a translator.* It does cost money, but in many cases it will be worth it.

Immigration Resources

If you believe the person you are looking for emigrated to this country, two types of records will be helpful.

The first is documentation associated with becoming a United States citizen. Also known as naturalization records, these usually include the following:

- declaration of intention
- petition
- certificate of naturalization

Three separate sets of these records are issued for every new citizen who entered the United States after 1906. One copy is given to the citizen himself. The second is filed with the court of jurisdiction, usually in the county where the individual first established residency. The third copy is retained by the United States Immigration and Naturalization Service (INS). These records typically include:

- name and address of the applicant
- nationality and country of immigration
- age and/or birth date
- marital status
- names of spouse and children, if any
- occupation

* This service costs $2.50 plus $3.75 per minute.

Public access to INS records filed after 1906 is restricted. However, if you are an adoptee, you should know that all adoptees brought into—or taken out of—the United States are entitled to obtain copies of their INS records under the Freedom of Information Act. These records will usually contain a great deal of information about the birth family and the adoptive family. You will need to request an original Form G-639 from:

Immigration and Naturalization Service (INS)
U.S. Department of Justice
425 "I" Street NW
Washington, DC 20536

To obtain a copy of the birth certificate of a United States citizen in a foreign country, request an original Form FS-240 from:

Passport Services
Correspondence Branch
U.S. Department of State
Washington, DC 20524

You can also get information from the INS regarding where and when a particular individual was granted citizenship by requesting Form G-641. Since naturalization documents are filed in the county that granted citizenship, this can provide clues about where to start looking for county court records.

Even though INS records are restricted on a *federal* level, the copies kept by county courts usually aren't. To get these records, you will need a name, an approximate date of entry into the United States, and the court of jurisdiction. Once you've located the correct county, a local clerk should be able to help you find the necessary files.

If you are looking for the death record of a United States citizen who died in a foreign country, write to the above address for Passport Services and request a Form OF-180, which is a Report of the Death of an American Citizen Abroad.

Another type of immigration documentation searchers often find useful is the passenger and immigration arrival list. Records kept since the early 1900s typically include the following data:

- passenger's name
- age, race, and sex

- occupation and marital status
- name and address of nearest foreign relative
- last residence
- port of arrival
- final destination

This information is kept on microfilm at the National Archives. To obtain microfilm data about a particular immigrant, request several copies of NATF Form 81 (Order for Copies of Ship and Passenger Arrival Records). A small fee will be charged when the information is located.

The National Archives also publish a catalogue titled *Immigrant and Passenger Arrivals.* Check with your local library first, but if the library doesn't have a copy, you can request one by writing a letter and sending a $2.00 money order to:

Catalog
Department G05
National Archives
Washington, DC 20408

This catalogue indexes reels of microfilm in an easily understood format. The reels themselves can be purchased for $23.00 apiece. Check with your local library and/or Family History Center to see which reels might already be available locally.

Experience has shown that foreign embassies and consulates located in the United States are uniquely *un*qualified to help searchers. It is not recommended that you contact such offices, except to request updated names of groups or individuals in that country who are qualified to do genealogical research.

Whenever possible, correspondence with foreign sources should be made in *their* language. This helps to shorten response time in case they don't speak or read English. The following international organizations usually have English-speaking persons within each country. Their experiences and previously established relationships could very well save you a great deal of time and money. As always, remember never to mention "adoption search" as the reason for your inquiries unless absolutely necessary.

International Organizations

The following international organizations have a history of helping searchers. They have offices and resources in many different countries. Even if these organizations don't know of a specific search group in the country you are seeking, they still may be able to provide either direct assistance or a referral.

The Church of Jesus Christ of Latter-Day Saints

As we mentioned on page 147 (in "Libraries and Family History Centers"), this organization can be very helpful when you are conducting any type of genealogical research. Because they place so much importance on family history, the Mormons have for decades diligently gathered genealogical records from all around the world and transferred them to microfilm. The librarians in these institutions are exceptionally skilled researchers who often have access to amazing amounts of information.

On an international level, branches of the Mormon church have expanded around the world. Persons living in a specific country can often be very helpful to searchers, due to their specialized knowledge of the region and its sources of information. In most cases, people at these branches speak English and have access to translator services if necessary. To find out if there is a branch in a specific country, call the Family History Center in Salt Lake City, Utah, at (800) 453-3860 and ask for Boundary Services. They will be able to give you the name and addresses of specific churches or individuals living in a particular region.

Always contact your nearest Family History Center *before* trying to enlist international assistance. Whenever possible, extensive microfilmed copies of international records have been sent to the main Family History Center in Salt Lake City. Your local branch can tell you what's available, and even get the records shipped directly to them, which may save you some international letter-writing and phone-calling.

The Red Cross

Founded by Clara Barton after the American Civil War, the Red Cross is a worldwide organization with a long and respected history of assisting people who have become displaced or otherwise separated from loved ones through war or other events. The Red Cross is also experienced at locating missing persons on an international level. United States residents who wish to make use of the Red Cross's locator services should contact their local chapter and request an appointment to fill out an application to the organization's Central Tracing Agency.

International Social Services (ISS)

The ISS is another international organization that has been known to help searchers. United States residents should write to the American branch to request assistance:

International Social Services (American Branch)
95 Madison Avenue
New York, NY 10016
(212) 964-7550

The Salvation Army

The Salvation Army has four regional missing persons bureaus. They do not generally forward letters or handle requests relating to genealogy or adoption. However, if you are looking for someone for humanitarian reasons (such as trying to reunite with an estranged family member or a runaway), they can be helpful.

You can contact the Salvation Army at the following addresses:

Eastern: The Salvation Army
Social Services Department
Missing Persons Bureau
120 W. 14 St.
New York, NY 10011

Central: The Salvation Army
Social Services Department
Missing Persons Bureau
860 N. Dearborn St.
Chicago, IL 60610

Southern: The Salvation Army
Social Services Department
Missing Persons Bureau
1424 NE Expressway
Atlanta, GA 30329

Western: The Salvation Army
Social Services Department
Missing Persons Bureau
30840 Hawthorne Blvd.
Rancho Palos Verdes, CA 90274

Australia

The following information regarding recent legislation changes in Australia is taken from a letter from Mary Iwanek to William Gage. Mary Iwanek works at Victoria University of Wellington in the Department of Social Work, and William Gage is the publisher and editor of the twin adoption- and search-related newsletters *Geborener Deutscher*® (an English-language newsletter) and *Das Adoptionsdreieck* (a German-language newsletter).

> In 1990, the states of Queensland and New South Wales, Australia, passed legislation accepting all the recommendations made in the report by the New South Wales, Australia, Standing Committee on Social Issues (see "New Zealand" page 310). These Australian states now have the most open legislation giving access to identifying information to adopted peo-

ple age eighteen and over and their birth parents. There is no compulsory counseling, and support services are optional at a nominal fee which can be waived if the applicant is unable to pay for some reason.

The Australian states have the same parliamentary system as the U.S. It is interesting to note that in 1987, Queensland passed legislation setting up a passive contact registry whereby all three parties to an adoption had to register before contact was able to be made. When passing the latest legislation, the Government admitted that passive contact registries do not work. In New South Wales, out of 154 politicians in both houses, only one voted against the legislation.

Mary Iwanek
Dept. of Sociology and Social Work
Victoria University of Wellington
P.O. Box 600
Wellington, New Zealand

Sources of search assistance currently available in Australia include:

Adoption Jigsaw (S.A.), Inc.
20 McKenzie Road
Elizabeth Downs, South Australia 5113

Adoption Jigsaw (W.A.), Inc.
Glennis Dees
P.O. Box 252
Hillarys
Perth, Western Australia 6025

Adoption Jigsaw (Victoria) Ltd.
G.P.O. Box 5260BB
Melbourne, Victoria 3001
Australia

Canada

Adoption laws in Canada vary so much from province to province that it would take an entire book to explain them. Thankfully, there is an *abundance* of qualified search assistance available. Since many of Canada's laws are currently undergoing change, we suggest you contact one or more of the following groups for individualized special assistance. In most cases the fee, if any, is minimal.

Edmonton: **Parent Finders**
Ruby E. Miller
P.O. Box 12031
Edmonton, Alberta T5J 3L2
Canada

National Capital Region: **Parent Finders**
P.O. Box 5211, Station F
Ottawa, Ontario K2C 3H5
Canada

Hamilton: **Parent Finders**
Lou Kuttschrutter
36 Woodbridge Rd.
Hamilton, Ontario L8K 3C9
Canada

St. Catherine's: **Parent Finders**
Margaret Hertzberger
146 Richmond St.
Thorold, Ontario L2V 3H4
Canada

Parent Finders
2279 Yonge Street, Ste. 11
Toronto, Ontario M4P 2C7
Canada

***Mervin:* Parent Finders**

Muriel Linette Concacher

P.O. Box 123

Mervin, Saskatchewan SOM 1Y0

Canada

International Message Bank

27 Willesden Rd.

Willowdale

Toronto, Ontario M2H 1V5

Canada

Missing Pieces Through Adoption

12551-77B Avenue

Surrey, British Columbia V3W 8L9

Canada

Missing Pieces Through Adoption

P.O. Box 3674

2307 E. Hastings Street

Vancouver, British Columbia V5L 1V6

Canada

Missing Pieces Through Adoption

2278 Irvine Avenue

Port Coquitlan, British Columbia V3G 3H2

Canada

Society for Truth in Adoption

Wayne Schultz

P.O. Box 5114, Station A

Calgary, Alberta T2H 1X1

Canada

Germany

The following are German branches of the Red Cross and International Social Services (ISS). East and West Germany were officially reunified in November 1990. However, use of the terms "East" and "West" are still recommended as of this writing to ensure proper processing.

A note about adoption searches in Germany: Germany opened adoption records to adoptees age sixteen or older in 1977. The social structure of Germany makes searching easy, since the population tends to be less mobile than that of the United States.

Frau Ingrid Baer, Direktorin
Internationaler Sozialdienst Deutscher Zweig e.V.
Am Stockborn 5-7
D-6000 Frankfurt/Main 50
(West) Germany

Deutsches Rotes Kreuz
Generalsekretariat
Suchdienst Muenchen
Zentrale Auskunfts-und Dokumentationsstelle
Infanteriestrasse 7A
D-8000 Muenchen 40
(West) Germany

United Kingdom (including England, Scotland, Wales, and Northern Ireland)

Adoption records in the U.K. were opened to adult adoptees in the 1970s. The National Organization for the Counseling of Adoptees and Birthparents (NORCAP) is a registered charitable group in Great Britain. As such, it offers search advice and assistance to persons seeking to be reunited in the U.K.

Among the services NORCAP offers is: 1) "Recordscan"—a service available to members who cannot conduct records research themselves, 2) a quarterly newsletter, and 3) a professional, not-for-profit intermediary service.

Membership in NORCAP is required to obtain assistance. Annual membership costs vary depending on each individual's needs. Persons wishing assistance should contact:

(In the U.S.)

England and Ireland Search Help
M. Catherine O'Dea
P.O. Box 360074
Cleveland, OH 44136

(In the U.K.)

Pamela Hodgkins
3 New High St.
Headington, Oxford OX35AJ
England

War Babes is another group that helps searchers in the U.K. In November 1990, a lawsuit was brought in the U.S. by this group against the National Personnel Records Center in St. Louis, Missouri (see page 88). The terms of this settlement now permit the son or daughter of an American serviceman (whether the offspring was British or American) to try to locate his or her father using records kept at the NPRC under the provisions of the Freedom of Information Act. Anyone wishing assistance should contact:

War Babes
15 Plough Avenue
South Woodgate
Birmingham, B323TQ
England

E L E V E N

Using the Internet in Your Search

You may not know anything about the Internet; perhaps you have never touched a computer in your life. Don't let that deter you from giving the Internet a try in the course of your search. However, if you are one of the many people with no Internet experience, you should ask someone familiar with computers to give you a few quick lessons about the World Wide Web before you read this chapter and follow its instructions. You'll probably be surprised at how easy it is to use the Web; and, while the Internet is not a surefire solution to your missing person problems, it's definitely worth exploring.

If you don't have a computer at home, you might be able to find one at your public library, local community college, or university. If none of those institutions has a public hookup, inquire at the nearest computer store. Many copy centers and computer service stores will provide access to the Internet for a small hourly fee.

We're not going to take the time and space to teach Internet basics here, but we will make a few general observations.

First of all, no single authority controls or regulates the Internet, and any person with a little computer knowledge can post a site on it. While this democratic approach gives Internet users instantaneous access to incredible amounts of information, the free-for-all nature of the medium has also provided new arenas for scams and con artists. Most sites are completely aboveboard, just as most businesses on the city streets are trustworthy. However, you should maintain a degree of skepticism about claims made online. If it sounds too good to be true, be cautious. When giving out personal information online, be sure you have checked a site's credentials. This chapter provides you with recommendations, but you may find sites we don't mention, and you may want to use them. We encourage you to explore—just use common sense.

Second, be aware that the Internet is continually evolving. Since the publication of this book, some of the sites we've listed below may have moved to new locations. (Often when a site has moved, the old site will list a forwarding address; but sometimes it won't, and you'll need to use a search engine to track the site down at its new locale.) Some sites in this chapter may not exist anymore; perhaps the people maintaining them could no longer afford to do so, or they may have moved on to other projects. And, of course, new and better sites may have cropped up *after* this chapter was written. If you find any of the above to be true, *please* take the time to e-mail us at *Locator@BigHugs.com;* we will add your tips and discoveries to the next edition of *The Locator.*

Our company, the International Locator, Inc./BigHugs.com, has a Web site of its own. You'll find us at *www.BigHugs.com. We update Internet information at that site constantly, so you'll find the latest news and the most recent sites there.* If you have an e-mail address, you can go to *www.BigHugs.com* and sign up for our free newsletter, which will e-mail you on a regular basis, lists of new and helpful sites found by other readers.

Just to reiterate this point: The Internet is rapidly changing. Use this chapter as a guide to the best sites, but refer to our site, *www.BigHugs.com,* to get the most recent, constantly updated list of recommended sites.

As you go through the chapter and surf the Internet, you should get in the habit of bookmarking sites. This is most helpful when you find sites you don't have time to explore at the moment but that might be useful later on. If you don't bookmark them (or write down their address), you might not be able to find them again! It is also helpful to organize your bookmarks and favorite Web sites into folders, by topic. Also, the Web site names may be clear now, but when you go back to scan your list of bookmarks, you may forget which site does what. Naming the folders something that makes sense to you will save you the frustration of having a number of bookmarks and being unable to remember why you marked them!

What Makes a Good Site?

When choosing sites to include in this chapter, we used a specific set of guidelines. Each Web site we mention in *The Locator* has been reviewed and approved by our team of licensed investigators and certified researchers. Here are our guidelines; they will be useful to you as well if you need to evaluate a new site you found on your own that isn't listed in this book:

1. The sites must have a good mix of content and commerce—not just commerce. We're looking for people who are more interested in providing information for a good cause than in selling a product or service.

2. Information must be current and accurate. If, reading through the text of the site, you don't find any dates or referents from the current year, you may not be dealing with a frequently updated site.

3. The site must *not* have any data, tips, or suggestions that are illegal or unethical.

4. The site must be easy to navigate and understand.

5. The site must be outstanding and unique in its specific category.

Throughout this chapter we've provided you with our investigators' favorite sites, based on the above criteria. You can easily find these sites on your own, but we have also placed all of them on a current links page, which you can access at the International Locator's Web site, *www.BigHugs.com/locatorlinks.htm.*

The White Pages

There are numerous white-page services on the Net. It can be a bit confusing to navigate them all, because there is no definitive white-page service. Our recommendation is the Ultimates' site, at *www.theultimates.com/white/.* It checks for a name in six different and popular white pages (Yahoo, WhoWhere, Switchboard, Four11, Anywho, and Worldpages). This makes it user friendly, and saves you the time and frustration of trying to compare results from multiple white-page sources. Under the white pages section of the site, you will find search engines that facilitate reverse lookups—that's when you have an address but not a name; or when you have a telephone number but don't know who the number belongs to. For instance, you type in the address in question, and the reverse lookup will tell you who lives there currently. Several other features that may be helpful in your search are also available at this site. To name a few of them: The Ultimate Yellow Pages can give you information about almost any business in the United States. The Ultimate Trip Planner gives detailed maps of any area in the country. The Ultimate E-mail Directory should be able to give you the e-mail address of an individual, if you have that person's full name.

Why doesn't this Web site solve everybody's search problems immediately? Because the search engines, while large, are not exhaustive. The information available on this site, and sites like it, represent only a small portion of the population. Still, they are a good and free place to start your search.

Don't be discouraged if you can't find your missing person listed on any of the white pages. You may at least be able to find people with the same surname as the person you are looking for; then, you can use those people as a starting point in your search, on the chance that they are related.

For searches in Canada, we recommend the excellent Canadian 411, which you can reach by going to *canada411.sympatico.ca/*. Once again, not everyone in Canada will be included in these white pages, but they do have over ten million listings, and it's a good, free place to start.

Without a doubt, the best site for international one-stop shopping is the International Pages, found at *www.eu-info.com/inter/world.asp?country=* (yes, that's really the site address). This site offers resources for over 180 countries. It's an impressive collection of white pages, but remember: Most of the world has not embraced database technology to the degree the United States has. You won't necessarily find other countries' versions of the white pages to be as comprehensive as ours. Some countries have only yellow pages on line (i.e., business listings but no personal residence listings). Don't get frustrated—there are many other avenues available to you, explained elsewhere in this book.

Registries and Databases

A registry is a database of people who are looking for someone. The idea behind the registry is simple: If you are looking for someone, it's possible that person is also looking for you. When both people sign up with the same registry, the registry links up their names and a match occurs. (For non-Internet registries, see Chapter Three.)

Www.ReunionRegistry.com is the largest online mutual-consent registry for anyone: friends, family members, lost loves, birth families, the gamut. It is absolutely free, and at the present time it is averaging two matches a day, and growing. It's easy to sign up, as you'll see from a quick visit to the site. Regardless of what direction you take in your search process, you should register at *www.ReunionRegistry.com.*

Keep in mind that using a registry is a passive way to search. You register, and then you sit back and hope to get lucky. We strongly suggest that you register and then continue conducting an organized search through other avenues.

In addition to the registry databases, there are some powerful databases that can be used to access public records. *Www.knowx.com* and *www.BigHugs.com* are both excellent resources. BigHugs is run and owned by the International Locator; KnowX is owned by Information America.

The public records these services access will most likely provide helpful information for your search. These databases are more than just white pages. Through sophisticated computer techniques, they plug into all the different kinds of public records we have discussed in earlier chapters: real estate records, death records, courthouse records, marriage licenses, and so on.

Both these recommended sites charge a fee for their search service. Prices range from $5.00 to $150.00, depending on the source being searched and how extensive the search will be. You might have only a small amount of information—for instance, a name and an approximate age—and still have a chance to find that person with a database search. We strongly suggest you look at the options offered on each of these sites. It could save a lot of time and money—which is why we often refer to them as shortcuts (for more information about these shortcuts, see Chapter Twelve).

Beware of sites that make exaggerated claims or promises for their database results. Many sites whose services we tested simply passed off basic white pages data as "powerful information." Another frequent abuse we found when testing the services offered on other sites was that the data was blatantly outdated. Don't get ripped off . . . stick with the services we've listed here.

Searching for Background Information

Background checks are becoming routine in this day and age, whether your subject is a potential employee, a nanny, fiancé, renter, or birth parent. We have found this site, *www.FullReport.com,* to be run by professional investigators who take great pride in their work and their vast resources. At the International Locator, Inc./BigHugs.com we have worked with them for years, and consistently found them to be extremely thorough. They are able to check assets, liens, employment, education, professional licensing, aliases, and many other sensitive areas. While there are other sites that offer background checks, this site delivers!

Perhaps this goes without saying, but the more information you can provide about the person you are seeking or checking on, the more information your results will contain. Be sure that all the facts you supply to the background checker are accurate, especially with regard to spelling and dates.

How would a background check be useful in your search? Many people, as they get close to finding someone, will want to know more about the person they're about to contact. Let's say you were looking for a lost love from high school. After you have found the person's city and address, you may suddenly find yourself nervous about making contact. How much has he or she changed? What if he just got out of prison? Let's say you are an adoptee finding your birth father. What if he is deeply in debt and unemployed—would he use this reunion to hit you up for money? These are all unpleasant scenarios, but if it's been a long time since you last saw the person you've been searching for, a background check could be in order.

This is all above board—it may seem like an invasion of privacy, but, in fact, it is all public information, which the public has a right to, according to our government's laws. Sometimes patients use background checks to see if their doctor has ever been sued for malpractice; rental car companies in many states run quick background checks on their renter's driving record; landlords run them on tenants; newspaper reporters run them on people in the news. Technically, you don't need a background-check company to get any of this information. You could track it down yourself in public records, but most of us don't have the time to check everything ourselves.

Running a background check is not free; it can cost anywhere from fifty to two hundred dollars, depending on a number of things: the information the client provides initially, the type of information needed, the number of records that need to be accessed. Most states charge the background checker fees, so, depending on how much searching is going on, the cost can vary.

Searching for Abducted Children and Missing Persons

When a child has been abducted or is missing, every parent's first step (after calling their local law enforcement agency) should be to contact the National Center for Missing and Exploited Children. See Appendix 4 for a detailed discussion about what to do.

When it comes time to enlist the aid of the Internet in your search, the most helpful sites are *www.missingkids.org/* and *www.childquest.org/*. Missing Kids is run by the National Center for Missing and Exploited Children. Child Quest International, a nonprofit organization, has run its site since 1995. Both sites allow for photos and information to be distributed to law enforcement and the media almost instantly. They also provide many support services and procedures that will prove helpful in such a critical time.

Other excellent sites are:

hollywoodnetwork.com/hn/mpc/index.html

This is a missing persons network named the Missing Persons CyberCenter. It makes a wealth of knowledge available, and maintains a bulletin board where you can post information about the person for whom you are searching.

www.pollyklaas.org/Missing Children's Resources

Run by the Polly Klaas Foundation, this site provides public education on the prevention of child abduction, and also allows you to report a missing child, whereupon a representative will contact you. Among other things, the foundation will post a photo of your child on its Web site.

www.securityadvisors.com/center.htm

Security Advisors, Inc., has teams of specially trained and experienced persons (usually former military and intelligence agents) who will actually go to rescue the abducted child. While this is a very controversial approach, any parent whose child has been abducted will undoubtedly want to identify and consider every option.

nch.ari.net/

This site is run by the National Coalition for the Homeless. The organization addresses the growing problem of locating people who may be living on the streets or in shelters. In addition to contacting them for assistance, if you feel your child (or anyone else) is homeless, you can contact the Salvation Army at *www.salvationarmy.org.*

One final note about this topic (which is echoed in Appendix 4). The majority of all abducted children are taken by their noncustodial parent. You may find that all you need to do is contact the powerful databases listed above (on page 194, under "Registries and Databases"), and do a search for the name of the noncustodial parent. When you find that parent, often you will have found your child.

Genealogical Sites

We cannot discuss genealogy without emphasizing how vital are the resources that can be found at your closest Family History Center. You can use the Internet to find your closest FHC: Go to *www.cyndislist.com/lds.htm* and follow the instructions. This is a quick way to locate any Family History Center worldwide . . . and it's free! This site will also explain what you can expect to find at the FHC and how to use this great resource. For related information, a broader knowledge is offered at *www.lds.org/.* And, of course you should read "Libraries" on page 147 to discover more about FHCs.

There is an overwhelming number of genealogy sites online, but in an effort to save you some surfing time and get you to a few really comprehensive and extremely helpful sites, we are listing our favorites. Our preference for these sites is based upon several factors. First, they are well maintained and their data is kept current. This is extremely important, as nothing can be more frustrating than thinking you now have a current source that will help you in your search, only to find it is outdated. Second, these sites offer numerous resources that you, therefore, won't have to worry about finding again on your next "surfing adventure." You can find your closest Family History Center, a census, a library, an obituary source, military indexes, the Social Security Death Index, and a zillion other helpful sources all within the same site simply by clicking via their index. Which brings us to the last factor that we consider vital . . . these particular sites are user-friendly and easy to navigate.

www.ancestry.com/

A commercial but excellent genealogy site. Also provides a direct link to the Social Security Death Index for locating a person who is possibly deceased.

www.gengateway.com/

This is a gateway to thousands of genealogy resources. It also includes the largest online obituary search.

www.cyndislist.com/

Cyndislist gives a comprehensive listing of almost 40,000 search sites. This is a great help for locating the sites that contain city directories, phone directories, e-mail listings, postal zip codes and addresses, and many more worldwide resources.

www.usgenweb.org/

An excellent site for locating specific state and county resources and data.

searches.rootsweb.com/cgi-bin/Genea/rslsearch.pl

This free site allows you to find people who do genealogical research on the particular surname you are interested in. For example, if you want to know about the Peterson family of Wisconsin in the 1950s, you could plug those names and dates into this site, and the site would put you in touch with the Wisconsin-area Peterson family experts.

http://members.aol.com/maydyn/index.htm

A directory to people's maiden names.

http://www.nara.gov/

The site of the National Archives and Records Administration. This site (and organization) makes governmental records available to the public. There are a wealth of historical information and research tools at this site.

http://vitalrec.com/index.html

If you are looking for information contained in any of the vital records that are publicly kept, this site will tell you where to find those records. There is a list of states and territories at the site;

you just click the area you are searching, and the site will tell you where to go to find the vital records.

http://www.piperinfo.com/state/states.html

All states and many local governments maintain Web sites. Here is a comprehensive listing of all those sites—a good place to start if your search requires you to investigate in a state you know nothing about.

http://www.ecola.com/news/press/

A massive listing of all the newspapers in the world that are online, and how to find the sites for those papers.

http://www.acpl.lib.in.us/genealogy/genealogy.html

The Allen County Public Library of Allen County, Indiana, keeps a genealogy archive online (run by the Fred J. Reynolds Historical Genealogy Department of the Allen County Library). The library's collection of genealogical resources is nationally renowned.

http://dbase1.lapl.org/pages/barrett.htm

The Los Angeles Public Library (whose main site is at *http://www.lapl.org/*) maintains a genealogical search program on their Web site.

Please review other links listed in this chapter, because it is impossible to limit the application of any particular link to a particular type of search. All the sites we list in this chapter tend to have multipurpose applications. For example, your genealogical search might require you do a military search. Check a wide range of sites, but remember: The challenge to Internet searching is to stay focused and not become fragmented as you bounce around the Web.

Searching for Former School Friends

Just about everyone has lost track of an old friend from childhood or school days. The Internet is making this type of search easier and easier. Visit the following sites and see if any of your old friends or lost loves are listed . . . and don't forget to register yourself! We suggest three sites:

www.classmates.com/ (charges a small fee)

www.nowandthen.com/reunion/Highschool/College registry

www.alumni.net/

These three sites basically work in the same way. Go to the site and key in your state and city. You will most likely find a listing for your school. You can then submit your name, post messages on a bulletin board, and search the listings for classmates who have posted their names as well.

Searching for a Military Buddy

This type of search is quite similar to the search for an old friend. The following links address specific military resources:

www.militarycity.com/newsroom/databases.html

The main site is *www.militarycity.com,* a large online service for military personnel. At the section of the site we list here *(www.militarycity.com/newsroom/databases.html),* you'll find the personnel locator. To use this locator, you *must* know the last name of the person for whom you are searching. They *request* two other pieces of information: the first name of the person, and the person's current duty status (active, reserve, or veteran).

www.thewall-usa.com/cgi-bin/mboard.cgi

The main site, *thewall-usa.com,* lists all the names on the Vietnam Memorial in Washington, D.C. This section of the site features a message board that you can use to post "looking for information regarding . . ." queries.

www.gengateway.com/milifile.htm

This site has an especially good listing of deceased military personnel.

Adoption Searches

Without a doubt, there is no search more difficult and more sensitive than an adoption search. As you fill in the clues to your search, you may be able to use some of the other sites recommended in this chapter. However, at the beginning of your quest, you may not even know the name of the person you are looking for. If that is the case, you will need to go to Web sites that are specifically oriented toward the adoption search. There are several good ones:

www.angelfire.com/va/tenniris/bparnt.html

This is a large list of adoptees' searching resources available on the Internet, along with tips and Internet strategies. This site connects to . . .

www.angelfire.com/va/tenniris/ST.html

An excellent site providing all states' adoption laws, listings of search and support groups, state registries, and locations of vital records.

www.BigHugs.com

The International Locator's site contains, in addition to everything else we do, an immense amount of expertise in the area of adoption searches.

www.ligraphixs.net/adoption/index.html

This site allows you to contact people who have yearbooks for certain states and certain high schools. Searching through yearbooks can be useful in your adoption search if you know only a first name, or only a last name, and you know the town where your birth parent lived and the approximate dates your birth parent went to school. Searching the town's yearbooks can give you possible candidates' full names. The site also contains many other adoption links.

And again, at the risk of sounding like a broken record: Go to *www.ReunionRegistry.com* and register. This is a totally free registry and is the largest and most successful (as measured by number of matches) online mutual consent registry. For more information about this site, see the "Registries and Databases" section on page 194.

If you are searching the Net for other sites, do not be timid about using key words—i.e., "adoption," "adoptees," "birth mother," "birth family." The Internet offers you a community of others who are passionate about adoption searches. But beware of those who might exploit your needs or have hidden agendas. They are usually easy to spot because they make promises and guarantees that sound amazing and are impossible to keep.

You will find many bulletin boards on which to post information and queries. The average post guidelines will ask you for a date and place of birth, your position in the triad (adoptee, birth mother, birth father), and who you are looking for. *Don't give too much information and do not post your address or phone number (e-mail responses are best.)* Why withhold some information? Because you need to keep secret some pieces of information that only your birth parent or birth child would know. That way when someone contacts you by e-mail, you can ask specific questions. If he or she can answer your questions correctly, you will know it is, in fact, the person you are looking for, and not a con artist.

Seldom is searching on the Internet the definitive method. Still, it offers many valuable resources and networking opportunities that were not available even a few years ago. Cyberspace may not hold all the answers, but it certainly has become a vital tool in helping people like you find your missing piece (and peace).

T W E L V E

Shortcuts of the Pros

This is a bonus chapter. You could tear it out of the book and *still* have everything you need to successfully locate your missing person. The national computerized record searches that are outlined over the next few pages are simply shortcuts we often use; they drastically reduce the amount of time it takes to find people.

Making the Most of Computerized Databases

Over the last few years, the International Locator, Inc./BigHugs.com has invested tens of thousands of dollars in a state-of-the-art computer system. Our computerized network allows us direct access to special databases of information on *millions* of people across the country. We use these databases to eliminate expensive and time-consuming tasks like reading through thousands of old phone books, city directories, newspapers, and so on.

After a great deal of consideration, we decided to make these databases available to the public at drastically reduced rates, if people wish to use them. You won't need a computer, nor do you need *anything* for that matter. To get access to our databases, all you have to do is call the consultant hotline (listed in Appendix 1). Once you describe the information you have, the consultant will be able to tell you which database search could help solve your problem. He or she will then process your request through our computer system and either mail or fax you the results. In most cases, it takes less than forty-eight hours to process a request. You will be charged a fee for each report, but it is nominal. We don't do this as a profit-making tool; we do it because we believe it will help people.

There are literally hundreds of databases available from our computer system; at the present time, we have the ability to generate over 850 different types of computerized record searches (the cost for each varies), but many are so obscure that they are only effective in specific circumstances. If you come across a situation where you think a particular database may exist that can help you, call the Consultant Hotline and one of our searchers will advise you about its availability.

Using the databases that are explained in this section does cost money, but they offer incredible shortcuts that can often end up saving you money in the long-run. We use them *hundreds* of times every week to solve our own searches in record time. Here are some examples of our most commonly used reports, and explanations of how they can help save you time. You'll quickly understand why we call them shortcuts.

National Name Sweeps

This database is an incredible time-saver in many searches. It contains the names, addresses, and telephone numbers of 85–90% of all the people in the United States! Once you have a name, *and it can be a last name only,* you can use this as a shortcut to locate the addresses of either your missing person, or the person's relatives.

Let's take a look at how to *apply* this kind of information. In the case illustrated here, we were looking for a man with the first initial "C" and the last name Canterbury. We entered this information into our computers and within minutes had the following list of twenty-two people across the country who fit that description. As you can see, they all contain an address, and eighteen of them even list a telephone number (we've blotted out portions of this report to protect the identities of those listed).

At that point we started calling these individuals, saying that we were doing a "Canterbury family tree." Within a half-hour, we had our man!

Our computers are capable of giving you a print-out similar to this one for any name you have. Of course, the less common the name, the better the database works (a National Name Sweep requested for someone named "Smith" would generate thousands of responses. The same type of sweep for a name like "Klunder" would probably generate fewer than ten.)

A National Name Sweep can be run even if you only have a last name. Chances are that if this list doesn't identify the *specific* person you're looking for, it will almost always find a relative who knows where that person is.

Last, First Name	Phone Num	St	ZIP	Street Address, City
CANTERBURY C	703	VA	22018	9 SANDERS LN ATHARPIN
CANTERBURY C	3043 571	WV	25271	1 #-32, RIPL
CANTERBURY CARL	3044 638	WV	25186	#-72, SMITH
CANTERBURY CARTER	3096 353	IL	61614	1 N HUMBOLDT E, PEORIA
CANTERBURY CHARLES	508	MA	02760	MAY ST, NOR ATTLEBORO
CANTERBURY CHARLES	7162 215	NY	14092	THE CIR, LE TON
CANTERBURY CHARLES	2169 129	OH	44092	5 294TH ST, KLIFFE
CANTERBURY CHARLES	2167 531	OH	44305	5 ADELAIDE B , AKRON
CANTERBURY CHARLES	2148 888	TX	75201	0 ROUTH ST, LAS
CANTERBURY CHARLES C	3045 650	WV	25045	GABE RD, CL ENIN
CANTERBURY CHARLEY	2032 620	CT	06492	YLVAN WAY, W INGFORD
CANTERBURY CHARLIE	3138 947	MI	48216	7 25TH ST, D OIT
CANTERBURY CHUCK	6194 737	CA	92040	29 TOPO LN, ESIDE
CANTERBURY CHUCK	7133 827	TX	77469	6 FAIRDALE C RICHMOND
CANTERBURY CLARENCE	3045 637	WV	25286	#-117, WALT
CANTERBURY CLARENCE	3044 528	WV	25676	#-448, LENO
CANTERBURY CLAYTON	8136 018	FL	33980	25 HARBOR VI RD #-26C, PORT CHARLOT
TE				
CANTERBURY CLAYTON	2153 287	PA	19454	HICKORY LN, RTH WALES
CANTERBURY CLIFFORD	5033 113	OR	97402	5 S BERTELSE D #-22, EUGENE
CANTERBURY CLIFFORD	304	WV	25661	1 #-168, WIL MSON
CANTERBURY CURTIS	304	WV	25676	#-83, LENOR
CANTERBURY CURTIS	3045 224	WV	25840	1 #-246, FAY EVILLE

National Name Sweep

National Death Sweeps

If you suspect that the person you are looking for is deceased, this database will give you a great deal of useful information. To use it, you need a partial or full name.

In the example on page 207, using the same name as in the previous cases, we did a National Death Sweep on the name "C. Canterbury." You will see that there were twelve deceased persons with that name.

To the far left is the social security number of each deceased individual and the name of the state where that number was issued (portions have been blotted out to protect privacy). The next two columns contain the person's name. The following columns give each person's exact date of birth *and* death. The last three columns reveal the state and zip code where that person died (if two zip codes are listed, the second is the address where the deceased's last social security check was sent). Each zip code is listed again at the bottom of the report next to the name of the corresponding town.

Once you have the date and place of death, it's a fairly simple process to obtain a person's obituary (from the local papers, kept at the local library, in the town where the death occurred, within three or four days of the time of death); which will usually contain the names of family members.

Social Security Number Traces

During your search, you may come across the Social Security number of the person you're looking for. When this happens, our experience shows that this report will give you that person's current address over 95% of the time! We must make it clear that this report does NOT get you a person's social security number. It simply traces an existing number to the person who is using it and to *where* that person is now.

In the example on page 208, you will notice that we did a Social Security Number Trace on the fictitious SSN: 123-45-6789. The report from that trace shows us the fictitious name: Charles Canterbury. In this case, it also gave us his spouse's name: Martha. Their current address is in Livingston, TX. Charles's date of birth is 1/9/29. He is currently employed at "Dimark Industries." All of this information is accurate as of March 1992 (you can tell from the "first reported" row under the most recent address).

Beneath the first section of this report, you will see a list of three *former* addresses where Mr. and Mrs. Canterbury have lived. Once again, all this information is available from his social security number alone.

```
CANTERBURY   ,C          Born: 7-01-1911 ( ± 5 yrs)  Died:1930 to 1992
Last name must match Exactly;      First name matching   C*        ;
States: All
Out of 58 records satisfying initial criteria, 12 are retained.
Listing sorted by First-Name
```

St	Soc Sec Num	Last Name	First Name	Birth Date	Death Date	Resi	Zip1	Zip2
WV	236-10-6	CANTERBURY	C	02/02/1906	08/00/1974	(TX)	77568	
WV	235-68-9	CANTERBURY	CESSEL	04/27/1911	08/00/1986	(IL)	62864	
WV	235-09-7	CANTERBURY	CHAFFIN	09/23/1907	11/00/1976	(WV)	25118	
AL	423-12-9	CANTERBURY	CHARLES	06/24/1910	05/00/1978	( )		35630
WV	235-16-4	CANTERBURY	CHARLIE	04/05/1910	07/25/1991	( )	48216	
CA	568-28-2	CANTERBURY	CHESTER	05/10/1913	07/00/1974	( )	00000	
MO	494-07-3	CANTERBURY	CHESTER	09/11/1915	07/00/1971	(MO)	63110	
WV	236-16-4	CANTERBURY	CLARENCE	06/03/1914	12/30/1990	( )	25951	
WV	233-07-9	CANTERBURY	CLAUDE	01/29/1909	02/00/1978	(LA)	70358	70394
PA	178-28-1	CANTERBURY	CLAUDE	03/24/1912	01/00/1973	(PA)	18504	
PA	196-03-7	CANTERBURY	CLAYTON	03/24/1912	11/01/1988	( )	19454	
OH	289-09-6	CANTERBURY	CLYDE	06/14/1908	11/00/1979	(OH)	45619	45680

```
00000 Not Available . .    18504 PA Scranton  .....   19454 PA North Wales....
25118 WV Kimberly  .....   25951 WV Hinton    .....   35630 AL Florence  .....
45619 OH Chesapeake.....   45680 OH South Point....   48216 MI Detroit   .....
62864 IL Mount Vernon...   63110 MO Saint Louis....   70358 LA Grand Isle.....
70394 LA Raceland  .....   77568 TX La Marque .....
```

National Death Sweep

```
PAGE 1   DATE  7-29-92  TIME 12:23:42  PCX01  V602

SSN: 123-45-6789

SOCIAL SECURITY TRACE SUMMARY:
FROM 04/01/92

FULL NAME/ADDRESS:

CHARLES CANTERBURY SPOUSE: MARTHA
  109 RAINBOW DR                    SUB: 8940615
  LIVINGSTON TX 77351               DOB: 1/9/29
  FIRST RPTD:  3-92U
  EMPLOYMENT:  DIMARK INDUSTRIES

  ROUTE 1 BOX 510                   SUB: 3278165
  LIVINGSTON TX 77351               DOB: 1/9/29
  FIRST RPTD: 12-89U

  PO BOX 98                         SUB: 2201031
  SEA GIRT NJ 08750
  FIRST RPTD: 10-86


  29 CEDARHURST AVE                 SUB: 1114876
  WEST PATERSON NJ 07424
  FIRST RPTD:  5-89

END OF REPORT -- SOCIAL SECURITY TRACE
```

Social Security Number Trace

National Cross-Street Directory Traces

During your search, it's very likely that you'll find old addresses of the person you're looking for, or addresses of the person's relatives. When that happens, the National-Cross-Street Directory Trace will tell you who is living at that address now and how long they've been there.

The Cross-Street Directory will also give you the names, addresses, telephone numbers, and lengths of residence *for their ten closest neighbors!*

In this example on page 210 we've run a National Cross-Street Directory Trace on the following address: "794 Hickory Lane, North Wales, PA 19454". This report shows that there is a "Clayton Canterbury" living at that address. Below that information appears a list of his ten nearest neighbors.

As you can see in the last column (LOR means "Length of Residence"), four of these neighbors have been around for six years or longer. They might be excellent sources to contact if you were looking for someone who previously lived at Mr. Canterbury's address.

Whenever you have an address and your trail suddenly grows cold, we recommend this database primarily because it can be very helpful when trying to identify neighbors.

State-by-State Driver's License Traces

Appendix 2 gives you the address to write to in each state when requesting a driver's license search. If you do not get any cooperation from a particular agency, or if you just don't want to wait for the agency to process your request, then the State-by-State Driver's License Trace can probably help you.

The minimum pieces of information you need are the full name and exact date of birth of your missing person. This database report is designed to let you know if someone has a current driver's license in a particular state. If the person you're looking for shows up in the database, it will give you the address listed on that person's driver's license—and possibly even a social security number.

Not all states' records are available through this database, although the list is constantly growing. When you call the Consultant Hotline, the consultant will tell you which states are currently included.

```
REQUESTED     ... 9210011154
PROCESSED     ... 920011155   (yymmddhhmm)
REQUEST CODE ... Session # A1B5409 / Request # 01


**   NATIONAL CROSS-STREET DIRECTORY SEARCH   **
    REQUESTED ON Thursday,  October 01, 1992  ... 11:55:04
    REQUEST CODE ... Session # A1B5409 / Request # 01


                                              : CLAYTON CANTERBURY
SEARCH        ADDRESS:            794 HICKORY LANE
INFORMATION   CITY/STATE/ZIP:     NORTH WALES PA 19454
******************************************************************************
REQUESTED     CLAYTON    CANTERBURY       PHONE#........... (215) 362-5287
DATA          794 HICKORY LN              UNITS/LOR........
              NORTH WALES    PA 19454     AGE CODE/GENDER..

NEIGHBOR                                                      UNITS  LOR
WILLIAM     REED         795 HICKORY LN          215-368-8       1    05
FRANK     G HOEFLE       796 HICKORY LN          215-368-9       1    06
JOHN      I WEIERMAN     797 HICKORY LN          215-855-4       1    05
G           DECK         798 HICKORY LN          215-368-1       1    03
ROLAN     A SWEIGERT     799 HICKORY LN          215-368-0       1    06
E           DEFREHN      801 HICKORY LN          215-362-2       1    05
JAMES     W SCHOLES      802 HICKORY LN          215-368-6       1    03
S           UNZEITIG     803 HICKORY LN          215-361-1       1    01
GEORGE      MAAG         804 HICKORY LN          215-362-2       1    06
JOHN      N MILLER       805 HICKORY LN          215-855-2       1    06



******   E N D   O F   N E T W O R K   T R A N S M I S S I O N   ******
```

Cross-Street Directory Trace

Address Update Report

If you can supply the person's full name, along with any address he or she has had within the past seven years, this database will give you the person's current address. Once the old address is put into our computers, it will generate not only the most recent address, but also (usually) a social security number!

T H I R T E E N

A Closer Look at Adoptive Searches: Helpful Case Studies

With twelve chapters under your belt, you now know that there are hundreds of ways to locate someone. The twists and turns you take in your search will depend partly on how much information you have to begin with, and will depend even more on how creative you are along the way.

Up until now, we have been examining the search process one step at a time, breaking down each stage with examples to give you a clear idea of how to proceed and what to look for. In this chapter, we put the entire package together and walk you through two actual searches. In the first example, we look at how an adoptee found her birth mother. In the second, we see how a determined birth mother was finally able to locate the daughter she had given up for adoption fifty-five years earlier.

Both of these case studies represents an average search (if there is such a thing). They're intended to give you a sense of how the techniques and strategies detailed in the previous chapters are put together. With the knowledge you have up to this point, you will undoubtedly notice many *additional* avenues the people in these stories could have taken to complete their searches. Get into the habit of thinking creatively—it will help you put the pieces of your own search together.

Case One: An Adoptee's Search

As is the case with most adoptees, our client Virginia Cain didn't know anything about her birth mother when she started. About all she knew was that she had been born in Washington, D.C., and her adoptive parents lived in New York State when they adopted her. The only documentation she had was the amended birth certificate (page 215).

There really wasn't very much information on the amended birth certificate that Virginia didn't already have. However, she made a list of the important details, to help her brainstorm:

(1) Her exact place of birth was George Washington University Hospital. Although Virginia grew up knowing she was born in Washington, she had never seen the name of the hospital until she took a closer look at her birth certificate.

(2) Her exact time of birth (2:58 A.M.). This specific information, coupled with the name of the hospital, made up half the information she would eventually assemble to write for medical records.

(3) Her amended birth certificate number, 20569. As we learned in Chapter Three, this number is almost always the same as the number of the original birth certificate. Once she had a partial name to add to this number, she would be ready to write to the State Department of Vital Statistics to try to obtain a copy of her *original* birth certificate.

At this stage, Virginia sat down with her adoptive parents and told them about her desire to search for her birth parents. As is the case with most adoptive parents, once she explained her position, they agreed to help in any way possible. She asked each of them to sit down separately and write out everything they could remember about her adoption. Unfortunately, neither of them had any documentation or knew the birth mother's name. In fact, the only things they did remember were the name of the adoption agency, Montgomery County Department of Social Services in Maryland; that they had had to go through the courts in New York to make the adoption permanent, since they'd lived in New York State at the time; and that she had already been named Virginia before they adopted her. Each of these clues turned out to be very important.

Let's stop for a second and take an inventory of everything Virginia knew up to this point:

(1) Her exact time and place of birth:	January 18, 1965, at 2:58 A.M., George Washington University Hospital
(2) Her amended birth certificate number:	20569
(3) The name of her adoption agency:	Montgomery County Social Services, in Maryland
(4) Her partial birth name	Virginia
(5) The place where the adoption was finalized	New York State

DEPARTMENT OF PUBLIC HEALTH
VITAL STATISTICS

STANDARD CERTIFICATE OF BIRTH

1. PLACE OF BIRTH. No. 1901 — Local Registered No. 20569

County of Montgomery

City or Rural Registration District — George Washington University Hospital — Ward

If birth occurred in a hospital or institution, give its NAME instead of street and number

2. FULL NAME OF CHILD Virginia Marie Cain — (If child is not yet named, make supplemental report as directed)

3. Sex Female — If plural births: 4. Twin, triplet, or other — 5. Number, in order of birth — 6. Premature — Full term X — 7. Date of birth (month, day, year) January 18, 1965

FATHER

8. Full name Steven Cain

9. Residence (usual place of abode; if nonresident, give place and State)

10. Color or race Cauc. — 11. Age at last birthday 34 years

12. Birthplace Maryland (State or country)

OCCUPATION

13. Trade, profession, or particular kind of work done, as spinner, sawyer, bookkeeper, etc. Chauffeur

14. Industry or business in which work was done, as silk mill, sawmill, bank, etc. Eastern Outfitting Co.

15. Date (month and year) last engaged in this work , 19 — 16. Total time (years) spent in this work

MOTHER

17. Full maiden name Alice McCarthy

18. Residence (usual place of abode; if nonresident, give place and State)

19. Color or race Cauc. — 20. Age at last birthday 32 years

21. Birthplace Maryland (State or country)

OCCUPATION

22. Trade, profession, or particular kind of work done, as housekeeper, typist, nurse, clerk, etc. Housewife

23. Industry or business in which work was done, as own home, lawyer's office, silk mill, etc. Own Home

24. Date (month and year) last engaged in this work , 19 — 25. Total time (years) spent in this work

26. If stillborn, period of gestation — months or weeks — 27. Cause of stillbirth — Before labor — During labor

28. Was a prophylactic for Ophthalmia Neonatorum used? Yes — If so, what? Ag NO3

29. Specify congenital crippling deformities None

30. Number of children of this mother (At time of this birth and including this child) (a) Born alive and now living — (b) Born alive but now dead — (c) Stillborn

31. CERTIFICATE OF ATTENDING PHYSICIAN OR MIDWIFE*

I hereby certify that I attended the birth of this child, who was born alive (Born alive or stillborn) *at* 2:58 A. m. *on the date above stated.*

*When there was no attending physician or midwife, then the father, householder, etc., should make this return. A stillborn child is one that neither breathes nor shows other evidence of life after birth.

[Signed] C. A. Christman C A Christman M.D.

Physician (Physician, midwife, father, etc.)

Given name added from a supplemental report — Date of

Address

32. Filed

Amended Birth Certificate

At this point, Virginia did two things:

(1) She called the Maryland State Adoption Department and got the address and telephone number of her adoption agency. She wrote the agency a letter requesting nonidentifying information about her birth parents. She also included a waiver of confidentiality (Chapter Eight, Letter 32).

(2) Since she knew that her parents lived in Queens County, New York, when her adoption was finalized, she called the county courthouse to verify the correct court of jurisdiction (see Chapter Ten). She then asked her parents to send a letter to the Surrogate Court of Queens County, requesting copies of all their daughter's court documents (Chapter Eight, Letter 25).

Although it took several weeks, she eventually received responses to both requests. The first to come back was the nonidentifying information from Montgomery County Social Services (see page 217). As you can see, this document contains a wealth of information about each of the birth parents and their families. Take a moment to study it; we'll be referring to it frequently for important pieces of information.

About two weeks after Virginia received this list of nonidentifying information, the Surrogate Court of Queens County responded to the request made by her parents. Of the several documents they received from the court, only one provided any new information—the adoption petition shown on page 218.

One particularly interesting item appears on the first page of this document. It is the name of *another* adoption agency (Spence-Chapin Adoption Service). The most likely reason for this is simply that Virginia was born in one state, put up for adoption in a *second* state, and placed for adoption in a *third* state—three different states! This is a very unusual situation; most of the time only one agency is involved. Even so, this did give Virginia another possible source, in case she needed it.

As you can see, the second page of the adoption petition provides a crucial missing piece to the puzzle—the birth mother's last name, Reddin. Remember from Chapter Three that many courts will not black out partial names because they consider them to be nonidentifying. With this crucial piece of data, Virginia now had the answer to the first half of her search—she had her birth mother's full name, Pamela, from the agency's nonidentifying information, and Reddin from the adoption petition.

You may be asking yourself, "How do we know that Reddin is the birth *mother's* name? Couldn't it be the father's last name?"

The answer is yes, it could be, but it's highly unlikely. Over the last few years, we've learned

MONTGOMERY COUNTY DEPARTMENT OF SOCIAL SERVICES

Adoption Unit

NON-IDENTIFYING INFORMATION ABOUT MOTHER AND FATHER OF female chi
born on 1-18-65 (birth date). (male or female)

	MOTHER	FATHER
Age at birth of child	19	~~23~~ 22
Race	W	W
Ethnic Heritage	IRISH	unknown
Religion	Prot.	Prot.
Education	was in sophomore year of college	was in senior year of
Occupation	Student	College but "flunked out"
Physical Description (coloring, height, weight, etc.)	Brown eyes, Brown hair, fair skin, 5'6½", 125 lbs.	6'2", 180 lbs. Blue eyes, med. skin, lt. brown hair
Personality, Temperament, Skills, Interests	Horseback riding, knitting, cooking, music, above average student, Excellent in sciences, verbal—outgoing well-traveled	Good student with a heavy schedule—lost interest, athletic—golf, tennis, liked music & played the guitar—outgoing, singer
Medical History	usual childhood diseases no other known physical or mental illnesses	pneumonia as a child
Significant social information about other family members (physical descriptions, medical problems, education, occupation, talents, etc.)	mother's father Naval Academy grad—high level navy position. mother's mother 2 yrs. college. No known health problems for either. (home ec.)	father's father—healthy fireman. father's mother—bank teller healthy.
Remarks	Pamela (6/90) G. W. Medical Center	flunked out last couple wks. of school before grad (Richard)
Please indicate the date this information was received and the source. (family member, worker, etc.)	DATE: 8-9-85 SOURCE: Record	DATE: 8-9-85 SOURCE: Record

(If more space is needed, please write on the back of this form.)

No contacts made by parents
Both private colleges — VPI —
Father — science/engineering in VA (not liberal arts) — good school
Dean called in mother at 7/8 months

Non-Identifying Information

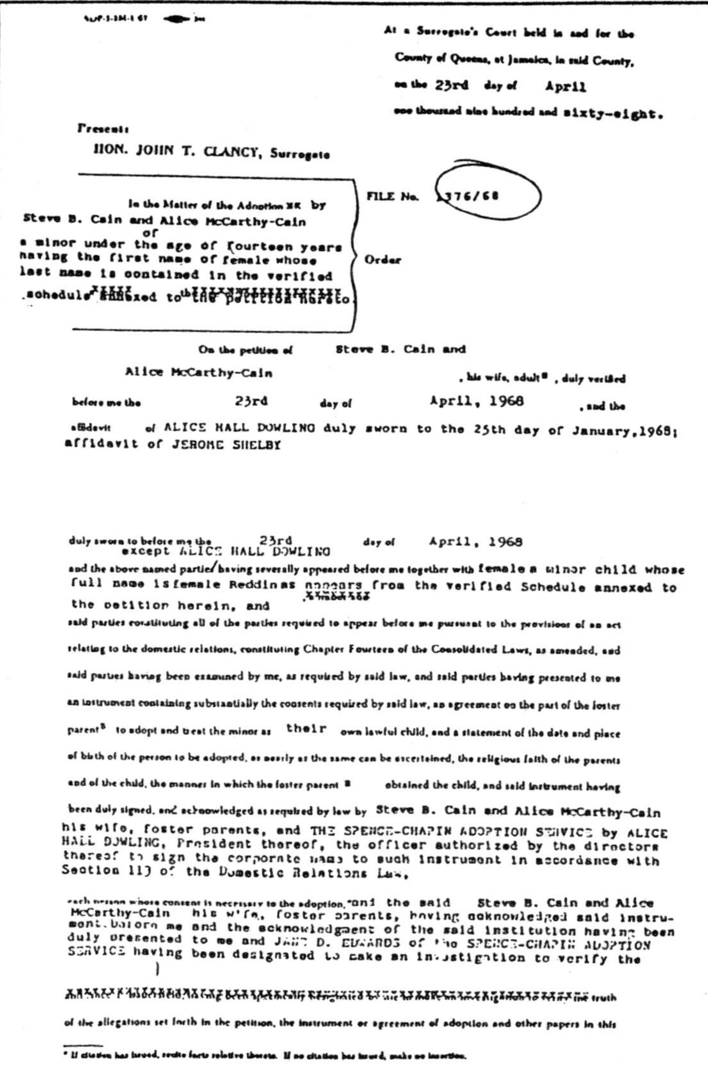

At a Surrogate's Court held in and for the County of Queens, at Jamaica, in said County, on the 23rd day of April one thousand nine hundred and sixty-eight.

Present:
HON. JOHN T. CLANCY, Surrogate

In the Matter of the Adoption by Steve B. Cain and Alice McCarthy-Cain of a minor under the age of fourteen years having the first name of female whose last name is contained in the verified schedule annexed to the petition hereto.

FILE No. 376/68

Order

On the petition of Steve B. Cain and Alice McCarthy-Cain, his wife, adult*, duly verified before me the 23rd day of April, 1968, and the affidavit of ALICE HALL DOWLING duly sworn to the 25th day of January, 1968; affidavit of JEROME SHELBY

duly sworn to before me the 23rd day of April, 1968 except ALICE HALL DOWLING and the above named parties having severally appeared before me together with female a minor child whose full name is female Reddin as appears from the verified Schedule annexed to the petition herein, and said parties constituting all of the parties required to appear before me pursuant to the provisions of an act relating to the domestic relations, constituting Chapter Fourteen of the Consolidated Laws, as amended, and said parties having been examined by me, as required by said law, and said parties having presented to me an instrument containing substantially the consents required by said law, an agreement on the part of the foster parent* to adopt and treat the minor as their own lawful child, and a statement of the date and place of birth of the person to be adopted, as nearly as the same can be ascertained, the religious faith of the parents and of the child, the manner in which the foster parent* obtained the child, and said instrument having been duly signed, and acknowledged as required by law by Steve B. Cain and Alice McCarthy-Cain his wife, foster parents, and THE SPENCE-CHAPIN ADOPTION SERVICE by ALICE HALL DOWLING, President thereof, the officer authorized by the directors thereof to sign the corporate name to such instrument in accordance with Section 113 of the Domestic Relations Law,

each person whose consent is necessary to the adoption, and the said Steve B. Cain and Alice McCarthy-Cain his wife, foster parents, having acknowledged said instrument before me and the acknowledgment of the said institution having been duly presented to me and JANE D. EDWARDS of the SPENCE-CHAPIN ADOPTION SERVICE having been designated to make an investigation to verify the truth of the allegations set forth in the petition, the instrument or agreement of adoption and other papers in this

* If citation has issued, recite facts relative thereto. If no citation has issued, make no insertion.

proceeding and such other facts relating to the said infant FEMALE REDDIN and to the foster parent* as would give me full knowledge as to the desirability of approving said adoption, and the said investigator, Jane D. Edwards having made her report in writing dated November 16, 1967 and the same having been filed with the Clerk of this Court; and said investigator having reported that the facts and conditions as set forth in the petition, the instrument or agreement of adoption and other papers in this proceeding are true and are fairly stated, and further reporting that in her opinion the adoption of said infant FEMALE REDDIN as prayed for in the petition hereto would be for the best interests of said infant.

And it appearing to my satisfaction that the moral and temporal interests of the infant FEMALE REDDIN will be promoted by granting the petition of said Steve B. Cain and Alice McCarthy-Cain his wife, and approving the proposed adoption; and it appearing to my satisfaction that there is no reasonable objection to the change of name proposed,

NOW, ON MOTION OF JEROME SHELBY attorney for the petitioner* herein, it is

ORDERED, that the petition of Steve B. Cain and Alice McCarthy-Cain, his wife, for the adoption of FEMALE REDDIN, a minor, born on or about the 18th day of January, 1965, at George Washington Univ. Hospital District of Columbia be and the same is hereby granted and that such adoption and the agreement therefor submitted upon this application be and the same hereby are in all respects allowed and approved, and it is

FURTHER ORDERED, that the minor, FEMALE REDDIN shall be henceforth regarded and treated in all respects as the child of said Steve B. Cain and Alice McCarthy-Cain his wife, and be known and called by the name of Virginia Marie Cain

JOHN T. CLANCY,
Surrogate.

Adoption Petition

some hard and fast rules about searching, and one of them is that the adoptee is almost always named after the birth mother, unless she was married at the time—and if she was married, the adoptee's last name was still the same as the birth mother's present name, it's just shared with the birth father as well. (The decision to use the mother's last name is usually made by the agency involved in the adoption; the purpose is to save confusion in their paperwork.)

Before jumping ahead to Virginia's next move, let's make a second list of everything she knows about her birth mother up to this point:

(1) full maiden name	Pamela Reddin
(2) approximate date of birth	1946–1947
(3) educational level	sophomore in a private college, possibly George Washington University
(4) her father's occupation	high-level navy; graduated from Annapolis

By now, the wheels in your head should have started spinning with ideas about how to start locating Pamela Reddin. At this point, there are a number of things Virginia could have done—looked in old phone books and city directories, searched for school records, etc. However, instead of jumping the gun, she wisely decided to gather more information before proceeding.

After carefully studying the known facts, she:

(1) wrote a follow-up letter to the adoption agency, thanking them for their kindness and asking for specific pieces of nonidentifying information (which would help her narrow down the search). Specifically, she requested the name of the school her mother had attended, her mother's place of birth, the ages of her birth grandparents, and the first names and ages of her birth mother's siblings.

(2) wrote a letter to the District of Columbia Department of Vital Statistics using her birth name to request a copy of her original birth certificate (see page 121).

(3) asked her family doctor to write a letter on his stationery requesting her birth records from George Washington University Hospital (using the name Virginia Reddin).

Even though it was difficult to wait patiently for responses to these letters, Virginia hung in there. Her first reply was rather disappointing. As you can see in the certificate on page 220, the District of Columbia was unable to find (or release) Virginia's original birth certificate. This probably

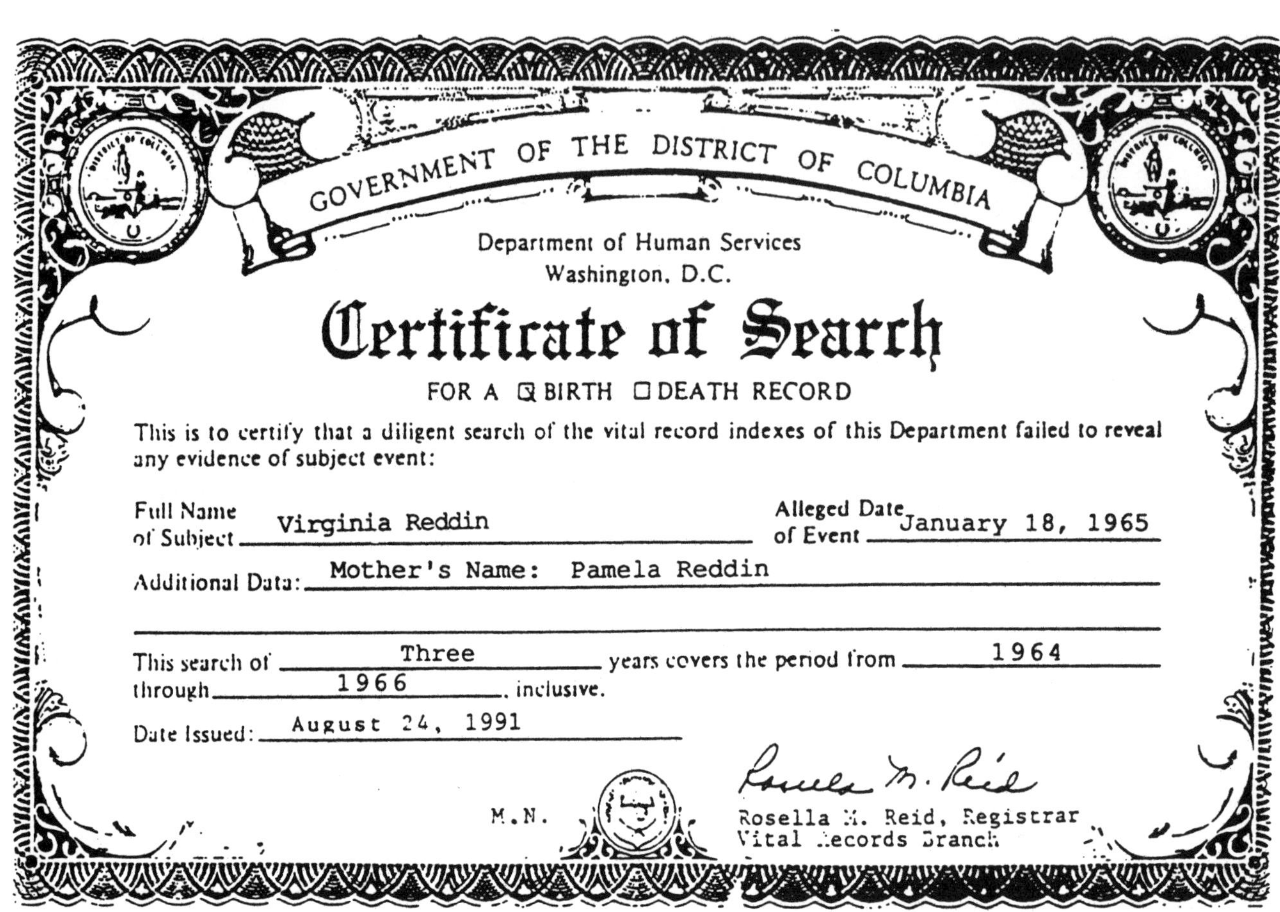
GOVERNMENT OF THE DISTRICT OF COLUMBIA

Department of Human Services
Washington, D.C.

Certificate of Search

FOR A ☒ BIRTH ☐ DEATH RECORD

This is to certify that a diligent search of the vital record indexes of this Department failed to reveal any evidence of subject event:

Full Name of Subject: Virginia Reddin
Alleged Date of Event: January 18, 1965

Additional Data: Mother's Name: Pamela Reddin

This search of Three years covers the period from 1964 through 1966, inclusive.

Date Issued: August 24, 1991

M.N.

Rosella M. Reid, Registrar
Vital Records Branch

Unfavorable Response

meant that it had, indeed, been sealed. As we said earlier, it *does* occasionally happen that clerks forget to seal these, so it was worth a try. But no big surprise that it didn't come through.

This brings us to an important point. Understand that your requests for information *will* get turned down. Count on it. By using the letters we've composed for you on pages 104 through 108, you'll receive some positive responses; but you should realize that only about one out of every three letters we write ends up leading to new information. That's why you should pursue more than one avenue at a time. And it's also why, if turned down for a specific piece of information the first time, you should just ask for it in another way. The hardest part of searching is waiting. As long as you don't give up, chances are you'll eventually get what you want.

In any event, over the next couple of weeks Virginia received replies from both the hospital and the adoption agency. As you'll see, they both turned out to be worth the wait.

Virginia now had just about every piece she needed to solve the puzzle. Her hospital records, shown on page 222, basically revealed two new pieces of information: her birth mother's exact date of birth, 3/29/46, and her birth father's last initial, S. As it turned out, her hospital file must have been marked "for adoption," because some information had been blacked out. At any rate, the fact that the birth father's last initial was S confirmed her earlier assumption that Reddin was her birth *mother's* name.

The letter from Virginia's adoption agency (page 223) was very informative. In fact, when combined with the information she already knew, it gave her more than enough answers to begin locating her birth mother.

Let's summarize the ever-expanding list of facts:

Birth mother's full maiden name	Pamela Reddin
Her exact date and state of birth	March 29, 1946; Washington, D.C.
Her educational level	Sophomore year at a private college in Washington, D.C.
Her father's occupation	Worked at a high level in the navy
Her family's state of residence	Maryland (possibly Bethesda)
Her siblings	brother, 17 at the time; sister, 12 at the time
Ages of her parents	mother, 45 at this time; father, 47 when he died a year earlier

You can probably think of several things for Virginia to do. One of the first things *she* thought of was to call directory assistance in the Maryland and D.C. area codes and ask for anyone with the last name Reddin.

: D C [redacted]

OBSTETRICAL RECORD

NAME [redacted] [redacted] AGE 19 – 3/29/46 ADDRESS

HUSBAND: Father: Richard S[redacted] AGE OCCUPATION

CONTRIBUTORY PAST HISTORY. Family History Diabetes Epilepsy Tb. twins

Serious Illness. Surgery

OBSTETRICAL HISTORY: Pregnancies: 1 2 3

Toxemia Swelling mild severe High blood pressure Convulsions Albuminuria

Hemorrhage yes no transfused Urinary symptoms yes no

Episiotomy last time yes no Largest baby's wt.

Hours in labor Longest Shortest

PRESENT PREGNANCY LMP [redacted] 19 Quickening 19 Poss EDC 8-21-70

Menses regular (yes) no Serology 5-2 19 70 pos (neg

Rh and other special studies Blood type A2 B Rh Positive

Polio vaccine Booster

Troublesome symptoms

ABNORMAL PHYSICAL FINDINGS: (Pelvis adequate) doubtful inadequate

Coccyx- free. Sacrum- hollow. D.C. 12.5. T. O. 9.0. Pubic Arch- V. Intercrest-1.

MEDICATION:

Circumcise yes no Breast yes no Hypno. [redacted] Literature

No Information – [illegible] [redacted]

DATE	TEMP	PULSE	BP S	BP D	WT.	FUNDUS	FHT	POS	URINE S	URINE A	URINE PUS	HG	EDEMA	SYMPT.	MEDICINE
5-2-70			118	80	214	5½ M			11	0	0	13	0		
5-29-70			108	80	214	6½ "	Ω	Vx	0	0	0		0		
7-3-70			108	60	218	33 W	Ω	Vx	0	0	0		0		
7-17-70			98	80	214	35 W	Ω	Vx	0	tr	0		0		

[illegible signature]

Hospital Record

February 19, 1991

Ms. Virginia M. Cain
P.O. Box 8388
Mew York, NY 10021

Dear Ms. Cain:

We have very limited information about your biological family that expands more on what you already have.

* In answer to your questions, your mother was going to college in the District of Columbia, I cannot give you the name.

* Your father's first name was Richard. Your mother was born in Washington, D.C.; however our guidelines do not allow us to release the name of the hospital. She and her parents were living in Maryland but had travelled widely. I beleive they were living in Bethesda.

* Your maternal grandfather was 47 when he died a year before your birth and your maternal grandmother was 45 at the time of your birth.

Your mother had a 17 year old brother and a 12 year old sister.

We hope this will be helpful.

Sincerely,

Suzanne P. Dunmire
Adoption Homefinder

Additional Non-Identifying Information

There were two people with that name, both in Maryland. Her first call was to a "Michael." Being careful to say she was doing "some distant family genealogy," she tactfully worked her way around to asking if he knew of a "Pamela, who would be in her forties." Michael told her that his mother was named Pamela, and that she was in her forties. Virginia's heart dropped down to her feet. Fighting to contain her excitement—*she was talking to her brother!*—she managed to get him to volunteer Pamela Reddin's current address and telephone number. And to make a long story short—the reunion went great!

Even though Virginia's first attempt worked, there were many additional routes she could have taken to find her birth mother, not to mention her birth father. Let's take a look at a few of the obvious ones.

To begin with, researching the school records and yearbooks of George Washington University from 1963 to 1965 probably would have been a smart move. Since Virginia was born in a university hospital, and since George Washington University happens to be a private university located in Washington, D.C., (which conforms to the facts known about her mother), searching the yearbook probably would have met with success.

Another good route would have been to research naval records for anyone named Reddin. Since it's a fairly uncommon name, a quick call to the archives at Annapolis probably would have given Virginia her grandfather's first name and his exact date and place of death (remember it was Pamela's father, not Virginia's father, who was in the navy). With this she could easily have requested his obituary from the newspaper in that area.

Before we move on to the next example, we'd like to stop and make a few key observations about Virginia's search. First of all, you may be wondering why she didn't just call directory assistance in Maryland and D.C. the minute she got the last name Reddin. Well, she could have done that, and with hindsight, things probably would have worked out the same way. But generally speaking, it wouldn't have been a good move.

Virginia was smart. She waited until she had enough information to ask intelligent questions on the telephone. Many times you'll only have *one* chance at getting information from somebody over the phone, so it pays to make sure you've got everything covered before you make that call.

The second thing Virginia did correctly in her telephone call was not to tell her brother who she was. As it turned out, Michael knew *nothing* about his mother's having had a child out of wedlock—and although Pamela immediately told her son the good news, it was still *her place* to tell him. As we have discussed throughout this book, you should always respect the privacy of the person for whom you are searching.

As is so often the case, Virginia's birth mother had also tried on several occasions to search for *her*. Although she did have a copy of Virginia's original birth certificate, unfortunately she just didn't know where to turn or what to do next.

Let's move on and take a closer look at how a birth mother, armed with determination and the right knowledge, eventually found the daughter she had given up for adoption *fifty-five* years earlier.

Case Two: A Birth Parent's Search

As is the case with almost all birth parents, Mrs. Kathy Wells-Peterson knew nothing about what had happened to the daughter she gave up for adoption. She, like most, never received any documentation proving that she had even *given birth* to a child. In fact, based on what she had been told, she believed her name had been erased from all the records.

The only details Kathy could remember after all these years were her daughter's exact date of birth, March 14, 1937, and the name of the agency that took her, Hillcrest Family Services in Oklahoma.

Armed with only these facts, Kathy called the state adoption department in Oklahoma and obtained the address and telephone number of Hillcrest Family Services. Using a prepared list of questions similar to those provided in Chapters Eight and Nine, she wrote the agency a letter requesting nonidentifying information about her daughter and the adoptive parents. With this letter she also enclosed a Waiver of Confidentiality (see page 136).

Next, she wrote a letter to the Oklahoma department of vital statistics requesting a copy of her daughter's *original* birth certificate. In this letter she listed her maiden name, the child's date of birth, and the birth name "Baby Girl Wells." She couldn't remember if she had named her daughter, which is not unusual.

Even though it took several weeks, she eventually got responses to both requests. The first to come back was the nonidentifying information from Hillcrest Family Services (see page 226).

As you can see, even though this document doesn't say much about the adoptee, it does contain quite a bit of information about each of the adoptive parents.

About two weeks after she received this document, she heard from the Oklahoma department of vital statistics. Unfortunately, this reply stated that they were not able to find a birth record with the information she provided. Kathy immediately sent another letter (including a copy of the nonidentifying information from the adoption agency) making note of her daughter's birth name, which she now knew from the Hillcrest letter, Lisa Marie Wells. Although it would come too late in her search to be of any assistance, Kathy *did* eventually receive a copy of the birth certificate from Oklahoma several months later.

In the last paragraph of the letter from Hillcrest Family Services, it's mentioned that the adoptive parents "live in a large town within the state." To a determined birth mother like Kathy, this was the only clue she needed to get started.

A ministry of the Presbyterian Church, USA Accredited by the Council of Accreditation, Families and Children, Inc.

January 20, 1991

Prepared for: Kathy (Wells) Peterson

DOB of Adoptee: March 14, 1937

POB: Stillwater General Hospital

Born as: Lisa Marie Wells

Non-Identifying Information on the Adoptive Parents gathered in 1937

Married: 7 years
1 male child, age six years

Adoptive Mother	Adoptive Father
Age 30	Age 36
Protestant	Protestant
Caucasian	Caucasian
Born in Arizona	Born in Texas
Raised in a small town	Raised on a farm
High School Graduate: attended teaching school	High School Graduate: attended 3 years of college
Homemaker/Teacher	Teacher
Interests are: sewing, cooking decorating, bridge, music	music, swimming, fishing hunting, camping

Misc: The adoptive father served in the military. Is a hard worker, good common sense. They live in a large town within the state. Are active in church and community activities.

Non-Identifying Information

Here and Now

Wednesday, March 23,

In Brief

Births

Mr. and Mrs. Frederick Raffetto gave birth to a healthy 9lb, 2oz boy, Mark Allen, at 2:45 am on March 20th.

Mr. and Mrs. Harold Anderson delivered a healthy 6lb, 9oz girl, Margaret Jean, at 8:57 pm on March 21st.

?! → Mr. and Mrs. Richard Owens welcome a new addition to their home, Victoria Luanne born March 14.

Mr. and Mrs. Milo Smith delivered

Birth Announcement

Immediately, she pulled out a map of Oklahoma and narrowed her search down to the five largest cities in the state: Oklahoma City, Tulsa, Enid, Lawton, and Muskogee. Knowing that each county is required to publish legal notices of adoption (see Chapter Three), she began a long, tedious search through these records.

At the same time, she also wrote a letter to the Oklahoma board of education, requesting the names of all teachers in the state licensed during the years 1935 to 1940. Unfortunately, this request was denied a week later, stating that "the records you requested are not indexed by date. If you have the name of a specific educator, we would be happy to assist you."

Along with searching legal notices, Kathy also began scanning birth announcements in the major newspapers of each city she had targeted. In every case, she started at her daughter's date of birth, March 14, 1937, and continued through June 15.

About three weeks into this process, she came across a particular birth announcement in Tulsa. Something in the *way* this announcement was worded caught her eye. All the other announcements used words like "delivered" or "gave birth to." But in the case of Mr. and Mrs. Richard Owens, not only did the *date* match, but the phrase "welcome a new addition to their home" was used instead (see above). Our experience has shown that while this kind of wording doesn't *always* mean an adoption occurred, it *is* usually a signal that justifies further investigation. And that's exactly what Kathy proceeded to do.

Counting on the fact that the Hillcrest Family Services is a Presbyterian adoption agency, and that the adoptive parents were Protestant (as listed in the letter from Hillcrest), Mrs. Peterson immediately got a list of all Presbyterian churches in Tulsa from the local library and wrote a letter to each church. In this letter she stated she was doing "her family genealogy" and was looking for the baptismal certificate of a "Victoria Luanne Owens who was born on March 14, 1937." Approximately two weeks later, her diligence paid off.

Kathy had hit the jackpot! As is the case in many baptismal records, when there is an adoption involved, both the adoptive *and* the birth names are listed. In this case, Kathy could now definitively see that Victoria Luanne Owens and Lisa Marie Wells were the same person (see page 229).

The wonderful thing about baptismal records is that they also provide a great deal of information about the *parents* of the person being baptized. With the information Kathy now had, she immediately tried the current directories, looking for the parents' names with no luck (assuming her daughter had been married and no longer had the last name Owens). Kathy next began rifling through old phone books and city directories, seeking an exact address for the Owens home. She also called the Oklahoma board of education and had them start a search for any record of *either* parent, since both were listed as teachers.

It didn't take long for Kathy to find something in the city directory. In fact, Richard and Martha Owens consistently appeared in every city and telephone directory up until 1950—when they both suddenly vanished. Now what?

Well, as you can see, the city directory listed the Tulsa Christian Elementary School as the Owens' single place of employment (see page 230). Would you like to take a wild guess at what Mrs. Peterson's next move was?

She immediately got on the phone to Tulsa Christian Elementary School and asked to talk to someone in records "who had been there for a while." She then proceeded to tell this person that she was trying to find one of their "retired teachers, a Mr. Richard Owens and/or his family, for urgent matters of estate settlement."

As it turned out, the person she talked to had been with the school for only twenty years and wasn't able to help. However, she *was* able to give Kathy the telephone number of a recently retired minister who had taught in the school system since the 1950s.

Later that evening, Kathy was finally able to reach the reverend. He remembered a man by the name of Owens who had taught at the school, but that person had moved away years ago. He thought Owens had moved to Muskogee, and was also pretty sure that he'd died sometime around 1970.

By now Mrs. Peterson had become very good at getting records out of libraries. She called the Muskogee Public Library, stating "urgent inheritance matters" as the reason for speed, and they faxed her an obituary notice (see page 231).

It looked like Owens's daughter, Victoria, was married to a Dr. Charles Lehew and living in Miami. Unfortunately, the rest didn't turn out to be as easy as it looked. Kathy's hopes were put on

He that believeth
and is baptized
shall be saved.
Mark 16:16

For ye are all the children of God
by faith in Christ Jesus.
For as many of you as have been
baptized into Christ
have put on Christ.
Gal.3:26,27

Certificate of Baptism

This certifies that:
Victoria Luanne Owens
(A.K.A Lisa Marie Wells)
Child of Richard Owens
~~and his wife~~ Marsha Tiste
Born at Stillwater, OK.
Date of birth March 14 1937
Was baptized in Presbyterian Parsonage
On the 1st. day of June
In the year of our Lord 1937

in the Name of the Father,
and of the Son,
and of the Holy Ghost

Rev. Eugene Brown
Pastor

Witnesses.. Mary E. Fuller
Laura Mae Brown

Baptismal Certificate

Earthmoving and Site Work • Clearing and Drainage
Excavation • Asphalt Materials
Land Development • Limerock and Crushed Stone Aggregates

PORATED REALTORS

h HOUSEHOLDER 376

Owen contd..
" Terry & Earline, res mgr Sun-N-Fun Mobile Home Park 1122 Lennox Ct.
" Thelma res. secret Greer Tractor & Implement 871 Marboro Avenue, #26
" Thomas pres Comm Title Servs r225 NE 18th Tr.
Owenberg
" Felix & Michelle retd. h383 Norwood Ct. SW
Owens
" Ann tradeswrkr Siton & Andresson I11680 Woodard Ave
" Arleta asst. mgr convention bur. 13191 Fairway cir.
" Beatrice retd. 15085 Pine Meadow Dr. SW apt 2
" Benjamin R contracting 4224 Pioneer Rd.
" Carley Jr emp. Bell engin. 322 French St.
" Celia & Joseph emp. mgr Joe's Buick 1503 Lafayette St. apt. 64
" Charles & Arliene emp Smythe Pharmacy 230 12th Ave SW

Owens, contd..
" Peggy R paralegal Marshon, Snow & Ass Blackwell Manors #12
" Peter & Janey slsmn Eagle Toyota, mgr N 229 Winker Ave.
" Peter & Kathleen retd 462 Brandywine D
" Randall & Melissa mgr Newburgs Gasolin 39th St.
" Randy W slsmn Tulsa Grain Supply Max
" Richard & Ann emp John Deere Imp. 693 Trail
" Richard & Barbara welder. Olson's Steel hawk Dr.
* Richard & Martha tchr Tulsa Christian El 14211 Grand Ave.
" Robert emp Roger's Tire & Auto 749 Old
" Robert & Betty lnwrkr John Deere 581 Da
" Robert & Darlene emp Bell Concrete 267

City Directory

DEATHS, FUNERALS

Information in the Deaths and Funerals Column is paid advertising.

GERTRUDE A. MOORE

Gertrude A. Moore, 84, of rural Muskogee died Saturday.

A retired housekeeper, she had resided here for the past 24 years. Formerly of Tempe, Arizona, Mrs. Moore was a member of the First Baptist Church.

Among her many survivors are three sisters-in-law, Ora Detmler of Spokane, Washington, Beryl Marsh and Winona Bingham both of Tulsa, and a son Willard Moore of Muskogee.

A funeral service will be held Tuesday at 2pm for the chapel of Eternal Memories Funeral home. Friends may call one hour prior to the service at the funeral home.

RICHARD ALVA OWENS

Richard Alva Owens, 67, of Muskogee passed away Friday evening.

A resident for the past 17 years and retired elementary school teacher, he was formerly of Tulsa.

He is survived by his wife, Martha; one son, Richard Jr., living with his wife and 3 children in Dallas, Texas; and one daughter, Victoria Lehew, living with her husband Dr. Charles Lehew in Miami, Florida.

Funeral services will be held at 1pm Monday at the Garden of Memories Funeral Home with Rev. Michael Ross officiating. Interment will follow in the Garden of Memories Cemetery. Visitation will be allowed from 10am until the services begin.

OLIVIA MILLER

Olivia Miller, 96, of Muskogee, died Saturday morning at her home.

A lifetime resident of Muskogee, she was preceeded in death by her husband, Otto. She is survived by two daughters, Nina Gerben and Edna Donahue; three grandchildren, Robert, Karen, and Allison; and one great-granchild, Olivia.

In lieu of flowers, donations may be made to the Senior Friendship Center in Muskogee. Arrangements are by the Windsor Chapel of Hope.

Obituary

hold once again when she called Miami directory assistance asking for Dr. Charles and/or Victoria Lehew, and turned up nothing. But at Kathy's insistence, the operator checked the entire area code and found Dr. Lehew just outside Miami. Kathy made the last call herself, and fifty-five years of separation and wondering came to an end!

As you have seen in each of these examples, locating the person you are looking for can take some pretty wild turns along the way. However, with each turn also come countless new opportunities for success. The search process is often compared to a roller-coaster ride, because there will be times when everything is charging ahead full-steam, and others when all you can do is sit and wait.

You now have the knowledge and skills you'll need to start solving your own search. Remember that the trick to winning is simply to *be persistent.* Never, never give up! We wish you all the best of luck.

A P P E N D I X 1

You're Not Alone: Ongoing Support and Search Services

We have structured *The Locator* to stand on its own. It's the only tool you'll need to complete your search. However, if you would like in-person advice, or a set of ideas specific to your situation, or if you'd like to save some time and take some shortcuts—you are welcome to call us here at the International Locator, Inc./BigHugs.com. Just dial our **consultant hotline** at **(900) 289-FIND.** That's (900) 289-3463.

At this number you'll be able to speak one-on-one with our search professionals. These are the very same people who solve cases every day, and they are available to you Monday through Friday, 9:00 A.M. to 5:00 P.M. eastern standard time.

These searchers are very busy and their time is valuable. As such, they must be compensated for their time. To do this, we have chosen to use a 900 number. We have set up this number not as a profit center, but as the *fairest* way possible for someone in your position to obtain on-the-spot, expert search assistance. The cost of this call is only $3.99 per minute (unlike most consultation lines, which range from $6.99 to $8.99 per minute), and the cost of the call will appear on your phone bill.

We provide the consultant hotline only as a service to you. Use it whenever you feel the need for advice, assistance, new ideas, shortcuts, or professional guidance.

When you call our consultant hotline, be sure to have your questions organized and ready (see Chapter Nine). That way the time you spend on the call will be minimal. At present, most calls to us are fewer than three minutes long.

Each member of our search staff has a copy of *The Locator* in front of him at all times. If you have a question regarding something written in *The Locator,* have the chapter and page number ready when you call. The staff knows all the ins and outs of searching and can answer virtually any question you may have.

If you decide to take a shortcut on your search (see Chapter Twelve) and want to get information out of our computer system, tell the consultant on the phone which databases you want to access, and have the minimal information requested for that type of search in front of you. The consultant will immediately give you the current cost of the report you are requesting and then expedite your request for information from the computer.*

Our searchers also keep updated lists of available support personnel in your area. These people come and go frequently, and some are more legitimate than others. Therefore, printed lists soon become outdated. If you're interested in a list of people in your area, call us and we'll be happy to provide it to you.

The International Locator, Inc./BigHugs.com also has a quarterly newsletter that updates readers on the newest changes in state laws and search techniques. The newsletter contains stories and photos of people just like yourself who've recently been reunited. When you call us, ask for a free copy and the consultant will gladly send it to you.

Our staff of search consultants have gone through months, and in many cases *years,* of extensive training; they've been personally involved in hundreds of reunions. Almost everyone on our staff is an adoptee or a birth parent who has been reunited. As such, they know firsthand what it means to be searching for someone important to you. If you ever need someone to listen to your feelings, or just want the opinion of somebody who's been there, feel free to call. We've established the consultant hotline to give you a constant companion in your search. We want you to know that you are never alone on this journey, and there is *always* hope and help.

* The average database search costs $99.00

APPENDIX 2

State-by-State Directories

This appendix summarizes everything you need to know about contacting the records departments, libraries, and archives of all fifty states, plus Washington, D.C. and Puerto Rico. For those of you who are adoptees or birth parents, you will find information on state laws pertaining to identifying information as well as details of state-run reunion registries.

Alabama

1. CENTRAL INFORMATION AGENCY:

State Capitol
64 N. Union
Folsom Admin. Agency Rm #111
Montgomery, AL 36130
(334) 242-8000

2. STATE ADOPTION DEPARTMENT:

Office of Adoption
Department of Human Resources
50 Ripley Street
Montgomery, AL 36130
(334) 242-9500

3. ADOPTION RECORDS: Closed; see #7

4. YEAR CLOSED: N/A

5. DEGREE OF AVAILABILITY: Alabama adoption records, including the adoption decree, are open when an adoptee reaches the age of majority (excluding the full names of birth parents). A court order is required to release further information. The state will try to contact the birth parents if requested by the adoptee, after they receive nonidentifying information.

6. AGE OF MAJORITY: 19 years old

7. ADOPTION LAWS: Sect. 26-10A-31: Adopting parents, as well as children who have attained the age of majority, may not inspect original birth certificates without a court order. Sect. 26-10A-31: Under subsection (J), an adult adoptee may petition the court for the disclosure of identifying information. The court then directs an intermediary to contact the birth parents to determine if they will consent to the release of their identity. If the natural parents are deceased, not located, or do not consent, then the court will weigh the interest of all concerned parties and may release the information without the consent of the birth parents.

8. COURT OF JURISDICTION: Probate Court

9. STATE REUNION REGISTRY: None. However, adoptees and birth parents can file a waiver of confidentiality with their agency and/or state adoption department. Adult adoptees can request a search for birth parents. If they are located, it is then determined if a contact is mutually desired, or if a release of all nonidentifying information will be possible.

10. STATE ARCHIVES:

Dept. of Archives and History
Archives and History Building
P.O. Box 300100 (36130-0100)
624 Washington Ave.
Montgomery, AL 36130
(334) 242-4435

11. HOSPITAL RECORDS AVAILABLE: Yes

12. LEGAL NOTICES REQUIRED: Varies by county

13. LAND RECORDS: Available through county probate records

14. DEPARTMENT OF MOTOR VEHICLES: Must be 16 years old to get a driver's license. At the present time, historical transcripts for the last 5 years cost $5.75. You must have the driver's full name and driver's license number. Payment must be in the form of a money order or cashier's check made out to the Alabama Department of Public Safety. Mail request to:

Dept. of Public Safety
Driver's License Division
Certification Section
P.O. Box 1471
Montgomery, AL 36102-1471
(334) 242-4400

15. LAWS REGARDING INHERITANCE: Sect. 26-10-5 (c): Unless specifically laid out in the adoption proceedings, adoptee has no legal rights of inheritance from birth family.

16. LAWS REGARDING TELEPHONE RECORDINGS: Sect. 13A-11-30: At the present time, private parties may legally record their own conversations without obtaining the other party's consent.

17. PHYSICIAN LICENSING BOARD:

Medical Licensure Commission
P.O. Box 887 (36101)
848 Washington Ave.
Montgomery, AL 36101
(334) 242-4116

18. ATTORNEY LICENSING BOARD:

Alabama State Bar Headquarters
415 Dexter Avenue
Montgomery, AL 36104
(205) 269-1515

19. VITAL STATISTICS AGENCY:

Bureau of Vital Statistics
State Dept. of Public Health
P.O. Box 5625
Montgomery, AL 36103-1701
(334) 206-5418

RECORD	COST	AVAILABILITY	SOURCE
A. Birth	$12.00**	Kept since 1908 Public information	STATE: Above COUNTY: Court of equity clerk
B. Marriage	$12.00*	Kept since 1936 Public information	STATE: Above COUNTY: Probate judge
C. Divorce	$12.00**	Kept since 1936 Public information	STATE: Above COUNTY: Court of equity clerk
D. Death	$12.00*	Kept since 1908 Public information	STATE: Above COUNTY: Court of equity clerk

* Plus search fee. Only money orders made out to Alabama State Board of Health will be accepted.

** Birth records are filed under the father's name by date and place the event occurred. Death records are filed under deceased named by date and place.

Alaska

1. CENTRAL INFORMATION AGENCY:
State Capitol
211 4th Street
Juneau, AK 99811-0650
(907) 465-2111

2. STATE ADOPTION DEPARTMENT:
Department of Health and Social Services
Office of Adoption; Attn.: Suzanne Maxson
P.O. Box 110630
Juneau, AK 99811-0630
(907) 465-3191

3. ADOPTION RECORDS: Open

4. YEAR CLOSED: N/A

5. DEGREE OF AVAILABILITY: Most adoption records are open to the adoptee upon reaching the age of majority. However, many agencies will release nonidentifying information to an adult involved party.

6. AGE OF MAJORITY: 18 years old

7. ADOPTION LAWS: Sect. 18-50-500: (identifying information) Adopted child may receive a copy of original birth certificate when he or she reaches age 18; child may also receive attached information about names and addresses of birth parents.
Sect. 18-50-510: (nonidentifying information) Adopted child may receive information about biological parents and relatives, physical characteristics, education, medical and social history, etc. when he or she reaches 18 years of age.
Sect. 25-23-150: (confidentiality) Disclosure of names and identities of adoptive parents or children may not be permitted without the consent of said adoptive parents, children over age 14, or without court orders.
Sect. 18-50-510: Medical information must be made available to the adoptive parents, and to the adoptee when adoptee reaches age 18.

8. COURT OF JURISDICTION: Superior Court

9. STATE REUNION REGISTRY: None. However, adoptees and birth parents can file a waiver of confidentiality with their agency and/or state adoption department.

10. STATE ARCHIVES/RECORDS DEPT.:
State Library of History and Archives
State Office Building
P.O. Box 110571
MS 0571
Juneau, AK 99811-0571
(907) 465-2928

11. HOSPITAL RECORDS AVAILABLE: Yes

12. LEGAL NOTICES REQUIRED: Varies by county

13. LAND RECORDS: Available from judicial recorder

14. DEPARTMENT OF MOTOR VEHICLES: Must be 16 years old to get a driver's license. At the current time, transcripts are $2.00. Payment must be in the form of a money order or cashier's check made out to the Alaska Department of Public Safety. Mail requests to:
Division of Motor Vehicles
2150 Dowling Road
P.O. Box 960
Anchorage, AK 99507-1225
(907) 269-5551

15. LAWS REGARDING INHERITANCE: Sect. 20-15-130: Adoption decree severs all rights and responsibilities—including inheritance.

16. LAWS REGARDING TELEPHONE RECORDINGS: Sect. 42.20.310: At the present time, private parties may legally record their own conversations without obtaining the other party's consent.

17. PHYSICIAN LICENSING BOARD:
Occupational Licensing
Alaska Medical Board
P.O. Box 110806
Juneau, AK 99811-0806
(907) 465-2534

18. ATTORNEY LICENSING BOARD:
Alaska Bar Association
510 L. St. Suite #602
P.O. Box 100279 (99510-0279)
Anchorage, AK 99501-1958
(907) 272-7469

19. VITAL STATISTICS AGENCY:
Bureau of Vital Statistics
Department of Health & Social Services
P.O. Box 110675
Juneau, AK 99811-0675
(907) 465-3391 (automated system)
(907) 465-3392
(907) 465-3038 (credit card orders)

RECORD	COST	AVAILABILITY	SOURCE
A. Birth	$10.00*	Kept since 1913 Immediate family	STATE: Above COUNTY: County clerk
B. Marriage	$10.00*	Kept since 1913 Immediate family	STATE: Above COUNTY: County clerk
C. Divorce	$10.00*	Kept since 1950 Immediate family	STATE: Above COUNTY: Clerk of Superior Court**
D. Death	$10.00*	Kept since 1913 Immediate family	STATE: Above COUNTY: County clerk

* Add an additional $10 for same day service; add $10 fee for credit card orders.
** In the judicial district where the divorce was granted. (1st District: Juneau and Ketchikan; 2nd District: Nome; 3rd District: Anchorage; 4th District: Fairbanks.)

Arizona

1. CENTRAL INFORMATION AGENCY:
   State Capitol
   1700 W. Washington St.
   Phoenix, AZ 85007
   (602) 542-4900

2. STATE ADOPTION DEPARTMENT:
   Administration for Children, Youth, and Families
   Attn.: Adoption Dept.
   P.O. Box 6123
   Phoenix, AZ 85005
   (602) 277-3564

3. ADOPTION RECORDS: Closed

4. YEAR CLOSED: Unknown

5. DEGREE OF AVAILABILITY: All adoption records held by the court are closed upon finalization, and a court order is required to release any information from them. Almost all agencies will release nonidentifying information to an involved adult party.
A "motion to open adoption file" is provided by the superior court in the county where the adoption took place. All superior courts will release nonidentifying information, but some might charge a fee. This may include birth parents' (and grandparents') first names, ages, birth dates, and educational backgrounds. Some courts will release the first names of adoptive parents and the adoptee. Very little medical information is available. Allow three weeks to three months to process.

6. AGE OF MAJORITY: 18 years old

7. ADOPTION LAWS: Sect. 8-129: (nonidentifying information) Health and genetic histories are available to prospective adoptive parents, and to the adoptee upon reaching the age of majority. The histories are also available to the adoptee's spouse and/or children upon death of adoptee. Background information regarding the adoption placement is available to the birth parents.
Sect. 8-110: (confidentiality) Any interested party may request that the child to be adopted be referred to by a fictitious name.
Sect. 8-120: "All files, records, reports, and other papers compiled in accord with this article, whether filed in or in possession of the court, an agency, or any person or association, shall be withheld from public inspection. . . . All files, records, reports, and other papers not filed in or in possession of the court shall be destroyed after a 99-year period."

8. COURT OF JURISDICTION: Superior Court in the county where the adoption occurred

9. STATE REUNION REGISTRY: None. However, adoptees and birth parents can file a waiver of confidentiality with their agency and/or state adoption department. Confidential Intermediary Program (Adoptee must be 21 years or older). $25.00 application fee: (800) 732-8193 or (602) 542-9580

10. STATE ARCHIVES/RECORDS DEPT:
   State Library, Archives and Records
   State Capitol
   1700 W. Washington St.
   Phoenix, AZ 85007
   (602) 542-3701

11. HOSPITAL RECORDS AVAILABLE: Varies by hospital. Some are destroyed after 21 years (contact a local support group).

12. LEGAL NOTICES REQUIRED: Typically

13. LAND RECORDS: Available from county recorder

14. DEPARTMENT OF MOTOR VEHICLES: Must be 16 years old to get a driver's license. At the current time, transcripts are $3.00. Payment must be in the form of a money order or cashier's check made out to the Arizona Department of Public Safety. Mail requests to:
   Motor Vehicle Division
   1801 West Jefferson
   Phoenix, AZ 85007
   (602) 255-0072
Unless you know a full name, birth date, driver's license number, or social security number, driving records are available only to the driver, to private investigators, and to government officials.

15. LAWS REGARDING INHERITANCE: Sect. 8-117: The finalization of adoption proceedings severs all legal rights and responsibilities—including inheritance.

16. LAWS REGARDING TELEPHONE RECORDINGS: Sect. 13-3005: At the present time, a person can record their own conversations without obtaining the consent of the opposite party.

17. PHYSICIAN LICENSING BOARD:
   Arizona Board of Medical Examiners
   1651 E. Morton Ave. Suite #210
   Phoenix, AZ 85020
   (602) 255-3751

18. ATTORNEY LICENSING BOARD:
   Arizona State Bar Association
   111 West Monroe, Suite 1800
   Phoenix, AZ 85003-1742
   (602) 252-4804

19. VITAL STATISTICS AGENCY:
   Division of Vital Records
   State Department of Health
   2727 West Glendale Ave.
   P.O. Box 3887
   Phoenix, AZ 85030
   (602) 255-3260

RECORD	COST	AVAILABILITY	SOURCE
A. Birth	$9.00**	Kept since 1909 Immediate family	STATE: Above COUNTY: Abstract records*
B. Marriage		Kept since 1909 Genealogical family	STATE: None COUNTY: Clerk of Superior Court
C. Divorce		Kept since 1909 Genealogical family	STATE: None COUNTY: Clerk of Superior Court
D. Death	$6.00	Kept since 1909 Immediate family	STATE: Above COUNTY: Abstract records*

* Birth and death records kept on a county level date prior to 1909.
** $9.00 for birth record (certified); computer certification: $6.00.

Send a certified check or money order as payment; also send copy of requestor's driver's license, or have request notarized.

Arkansas

1. CENTRAL INFORMATION AGENCY:
State Capitol
5th & Woodland
P.O. Box 3155
Little Rock, AR 72203-3155
(501) 682-3000

2. STATE ADOPTION DEPARTMENT:
Department of Human Services
Division of Social Services: Adoption Services
P.O. Box 1437 Slot 808
Little Rock, AR 72203
(501) 682-1882

3. ADOPTION RECORDS: Closed

4. YEAR CLOSED: 1935

5. DEGREE OF AVAILABILITY: All court papers and records pertaining to the process of adoption are closed upon finalization, and a court order is required to release any information from them. Most agencies are reluctant to release even nonidentifying information, so use care when making contact.

6. AGE OF MAJORITY: 21 years old

7. ADOPTION LAWS: Sect. 56-141: (identifying information) In exceptional circumstances, specific papers and records may be inspected by adoptee, adoptive parents, or birth parents by court order.
Sect. 56-145: (medical information) Written health, genetic, and social histories are available to adoptive parents. Above information is also available to adoptee upon reaching age of majority—and to adoptee's spouse and/or children over age 2, upon death of adoptee.
Sect. 9-9-505-506: Provides for a passive reunion registry.

8. COURT OF JURISDICTION: Probate Court

9. STATE REUNION REGISTRY: Yes; see #20

10. STATE ARCHIVES/RECORDS DEPT.:
Arkansas Library of Archives & Records
One Capitol Mall
Little Rock, AR 72201
(501) 682-1527
Hist. Comm. Archives: (501) 682-6900

11. HOSPITAL RECORDS AVAILABLE: Possibly, through a doctor

12. LEGAL NOTICES REQUIRED: Unknown

13. LAND RECORDS: Available from circuit clerk or county recorder

14. DEPARTMENT OF MOTOR VEHICLES: Must be 14 years old to get a driver's license. At the current time, transcripts are $7.00. In order to receive a transcript, you must have written permission from the driver, due to the Privacy Act. The fee for this type of service depends on the amount of involvement. Payment must be in the form of a money order or cashier's check made out to the Arkansas Department of Public Safety. Mail requests to:
Office of Motor Vehicle Registration
Department of Driver Services
P.O. Box 1272
Little Rock, AR 72203
(501) 682-7213

15. LAWS REGARDING INHERITANCE: Sect. 15: The finalization of adoption proceedings severs all legal rights and responsibilities—including inheritance.

16. LAWS REGARDING TELEPHONE RECORDINGS: 18 U.S.C. 2511 (2) (d): Under federal guidelines, Arkansas residents can legally record their own conversations without obtaining consent from the opposite party.

17. PHYSICIAN LICENSING BOARD:
Arkansas State Medical Board
2100 Riverfront Drive
Suite 200
Little Rock, AR 72202-1793
(501) 296-1802

18. ATTORNEY LICENSING BOARD:
Clerk of the Supreme Court; Licensing Dept.
625 Marshall
Little Rock, AR 72201
(501) 682-6849

19. VITAL STATISTICS AGENCY:
Division of Vital Records
Arkansas Department of Health
4815 W. Markham St.-Slot #44
Little Rock, AR 72205
(501) 661-2134
(501) 661-2726 (credit card orders)*

* Additional $5 fee for credit card service. "Emergency requests" can cost up to $20 more.

RECORD	COST	AVAILABILITY	SOURCE
A. Birth	$5.00	Kept since 1914 Public information	STATE: Above COUNTY: County clerk
B. Marriage	$5.00	Kept since 1917 Public information	STATE: Above COUNTY: County clerk
C. Divorce	$5.00	Kept since 1923 Public information	STATE: Above COUNTY: Circuit court clerk
D. Death	$4.00	Kept since 1914 Public information	STATE: Above COUNTY: County clerk

20. STATE REUNION REGISTRY:

Dallas Parks
Department of Human Services
Division of Social Services
Adoption Services
P.O. Box 1437 Slot 808
Little Rock, AR 72203
(501) 682-8456

COST: $20.00—one-time fee
$5.00—for adoptees to receive nonidentifying information
SUMMARY: You need to write and request that forms for registration be sent to you.

California

1. CENTRAL INFORMATION AGENCY:

State Capitol
10th & L St.
Sacramento, CA 95814
(916) 445-4711

2. STATE ADOPTION DEPARTMENT:

Department of Social Services
Adoption Branch
744 P St., MS 19-31
Sacramento, CA 95814
(916) 322-3778 (policy office)
(916) 657-9900

3. ADOPTION RECORDS: Closed

4. YEAR CLOSED: 1935

5. DEGREE OF AVAILABILITY: Information regarding the identity of birth parents or adoptee may be released with prior consent of the opposite party once the adoptee reaches 21 years of age. Adoption decrees are available from the court of jurisdiction. Many agencies will release nonidentifying information to an adult involved party but may charge a fee for this service.

6. AGE OF MAJORITY: 18 years old

7. ADOPTION LAWS: Sect. 10439: "All records and the information specified in this article, other than the newly issued birth certificate, shall be available only upon the order of the superior court of the county of residence of the adopted child or the superior court of the county granting the order of adoption. No such order shall be granted by the superior court unless a verified petition setting forth facts showing the necessity of such an order has been presented to the court and good and compelling cause is shown for the granting of the order." Nonidentifying information is available to birth parents and adoptees.
Sect. 224: (medical information) A written report of adoptee's health and medical background is available to adoptive parents and adoptee upon reaching age 18 and/or getting married. The court can release this information sooner for reasons of medical necessity.

8. COURT OF JURISDICTION: Superior Court

9. STATE REUNION REGISTRY: No formal registry. Birth parents and adoptees should file waivers of confidentiality with their agency and/or the State Adoption Dept. If the file has a waiver from both the adoptee and birth parent, then both will be notified by the state.

10. STATE ARCHIVES/RECORDS DEPT:

California State Library
P.O. Box 942837
Sacramento, CA 94237-0001
(916) 654-0176

11. HOSPITAL RECORDS AVAILABLE: Yes

12. LEGAL NOTICES REQUIRED: Typically

13. LAND RECORDS: Available through the county recorder

14. DEPARTMENT OF MOTOR VEHICLES: Must be 16 years old to get a driver's license. At the current time, transcripts are $5.00. Payment must be in the form of a money order or cashier's check made out to the California Department of Public Safety. Mail requests to:

Division of Motor Vehicles
P.O. Box 942869
Sacramento, CA 94269
(916) 657-7669

15. LAWS REGARDING INHERITANCE: Sect. 229: Adoption proceedings sever all parental rights and responsibilities (inheritance not specified).

16. LAWS REGARDING TELEPHONE RECORDINGS: CA Penal Code Sec. 632: California has one of the strictest eavesdropping and wiretapping statutes in the country. All parties to a conversation must be aware that it is being recorded.

17. PHYSICIAN LICENSING BOARD:

Medical Board of California
1426 Howe Ave.
Sacramento, CA 95825
(916) 263-2635

18. ATTORNEY LICENSING BOARD:
State Bar of California
Membership Records
555 Franklin St.
San Francisco, CA 94102
(415) 561-8200

19. VITAL STATISTICS AGENCY:
Office of Vital Records
P.O. Box 730241
Sacramento, CA 94244
(916) 445-2684

RECORD	COST	AVAILABILITY	SOURCE
A. Birth	$13.00	Kept since 1905 Restricted access	STATE: Above COUNTY: County recorder
B. Marriage	$13.00	Kept since 1905* Public information	STATE: Above COUNTY: County recorder
C. Divorce	$9.00	Kept since 1962** Public information	COUNTY: County recorder
D. Death	$13.00	Kept since 1905 Public information	STATE: Above COUNTY: County recorder

* Some marriage records are confidential, call for more details.
** Final decrees. Initial complaints since 1966.

Emergency credit card service available (additional $5.00 fee): (800) 858-5553

Colorado

1. CENTRAL INFORMATION AGENCY:
State Capitol
200 East Colfax Avenue
Denver, CO 80203
(303) 866-5000

2. STATE ADOPTION DEPARTMENT:
Department of Human Services
Adoption Unit
1575 Sherman Street
Denver, CO 80203
(303) 866-3228

3. ADOPTION RECORDS: Closed

4. YEAR CLOSED: 1942

5. DEGREE OF AVAILABILITY: All adoption records are closed upon finalization. To release information, a court order stipulating good cause is needed. Some agencies will furnish nonidentifying information to an adoptee, although a court order may be necessary. Legislation passed in 7/93 allows release of medical and nonidentifying information.

6. AGE OF MAJORITY: 18 years old

7. ADOPTION LAWS: Sect. 19-5-301, 4: Records and papers in relinquishment and adoption proceedings from and after the filing of a petition are confidential and open to inspection only upon order of the court for good cause shown. Colorado has set a voluntary adoption registry in place to relay information between adoptive parents, biological parents, and adult adoptees.

8. COURT OF JURISDICTION: In Denver: Juvenile Court
All others: District Court

9. STATE REUNION REGISTRY: Yes; see #20

10. STATE ARCHIVES/RECORDS DEPT.:
Colorado Historical Society
1300 Broadway
Denver, CO 80203
(303) 866-3682

11. HOSPITAL RECORDS AVAILABLE: Possibly, through a doctor

12. LEGAL NOTICES REQUIRED: Typically

13. LAND RECORDS: Available through the county recorder

14. DEPARTMENT OF MOTOR VEHICLES: Must be 16 years old to get a driver's license. At the current time, transcripts are $2.20. Must have birth date and driver's license number. Payment must be in the form of a money order or certified check made out to the Colorado Department of Public Safety. Mail requests to:
Motor Vehicle Division
1881 Pier Street
Lakewood, CO 80214
(303) 205-5600

15. LAWS REGARDING INHERITANCE: Art. 4 19-4-113: Adoption decree severs all rights and responsibilities (inheritance not specified).

16. LAWS REGARDING TELEPHONE RECORDINGS: Sect. 18-9-303: At the present time, private parties may legally record their own conversations without obtaining the other party's consent.

17. PHYSICIAN LICENSING BOARD:
Colorado Board of Medical Examiners
1560 Broadway, #1300
Denver, CO 80202
(303) 894-7690

18. ATTORNEY LICENSING BOARD:
Office of the Supreme Court of Colorado
Attorney Registration
600 17th St. Suite #910 South
Denver, CO 80202
(303) 534-7841

19. VITAL STATISTICS AGENCY:

Colorado Department of Health
Vital Records
4300 Cherry Creek Dr. South
Denver, CO 80222-1530
(303) 756-4464 (service menu and recording)
(303) 692-2234

RECORD	COST	AVAILABILITY	SOURCE
A. Birth	$15.00	Kept since 1910* Restricted access***	STATE: Above COUNTY: County clerk
B. Marriage	$15.00	All years except 1940–1974** Public access	STATE: Above COUNTY: County clerk
C. Divorce	$15.00	All years except 1940–1967** Public access	STATE: Above COUNTY: District Court clerk
D. Death	$15.00	Kept since 1900 Restricted access***	STATE: Above COUNTY: County clerk

* Some counties prior to this date.
** Inquiries will be forwarded to the appropriate county office.
*** Own or immediate family.

Emergency credit card service available: 303-692-2224 (total fee for document is $19.50)

20. STATE REUNION REGISTRY:

Colorado Voluntary Adoption Registry
Colorado Dept. of Health
4300 Cherry Creek Dr. South
Denver, CO 80222
(303) 692-2227

COST: $15.00
Call: Colorado Confidential Mediator Program
Call for program information: (303) 237-6919
SUMMARY: This registry is open to adoptees 21 years of age or older, who were born in Colorado. It is also open to their birth parents, siblings, and relatives (if the birth parents are deceased). Relatives must submit a certified copy of the subject's death certificate and proof of their relationship to the deceased (i.e., marriage license, birth certificate, etc.) Once you register, you can withdraw at any time.

Connecticut

1. CENTRAL INFORMATION AGENCY:

State Capitol
300 Capitol Avenue
Hartford, CT 06106-1591
(860) 240-0555

2. STATE ADOPTION DEPARTMENT:

Department of Children and Families
Adoption Services
505 Hudson Street
Hartford, CT 06106
(860) 550-6450

3. ADOPTION RECORDS: Closed

4. YEAR CLOSED: 1974

5. DEGREE OF AVAILABILITY: Nonidentifying information is available to adoptive parents. It is also available to adoptee upon reaching age of majority. Identifying information can be released by the placing agency with the permission of birth parents. All agencies are required to release nonidentifying information to an adult adoptee. Birth parents can search through placing agency (as of October 1, 1995).

6. AGE OF MAJORITY: 18 years old

7. ADOPTION LAWS: Sect 45-68e: Nonidentifying information is available to adoptive parents and adoptee upon reaching age of majority.
Sect 45-68e: (medical information) Medical information is available to adoptive parents and adoptee upon reaching age of majority.
Sect 45-68 i-j (a): Identifying information is available to adult adoptee through placing agency. Agency, upon adoptee's request, must conduct a search and obtain necessary consent from birth parent before his/her identity can be released to adoptee.
Sect 45-68j(b): Provides for court appeal process in the event that the agency is unable to locate birth parent(s) to obtain the required consent for release of information to adult adoptee.
Sect 45-68o: Provides for each agency to establish and maintain a reunion registry.

8. COURT OF JURISDICTION: Probate Court

9. STATE REUNION REGISTRY: Yes. Adoption must be done through the state to register with the registry. Private or agency adoptions are not in registry. See also #20.

10. STATE ARCHIVES/RECORDS DEPT.:

Connecticut State Library
Department of History and Genealogy
231 Capitol Avenue
Hartford, CT 06106
(860) 566-3690

11. HOSPITAL RECORDS AVAILABLE: Possibly; contact a local search and support group first

12. LEGAL NOTICES REQUIRED: Typically

13. LAND RECORDS: Available through the town clerk

14. DEPARTMENT OF MOTOR VEHICLES: Must be 16 years old to get a driver's license. At the current time, transcripts are $10.00. Must have birth date, driver's license number, and complete address. Payment must be in the form of a money

order or certified check made out to the Connecticut Department of Public Safety. Mail requests to:

Department of Motor Vehicles
60 State Street Rm. #329
Wethersfield, CT 06161
(860) 566-3197

15. LAWS REGARDING INHERITANCE: Sect 45-64a: Final adoption decree severs all rights and responsibilities, including inheritance.

16. LAWS REGARDING TELEPHONE RECORDINGS: Sect 53a-188: At the present time, private parties may legally record their own conversations without obtaining the other party's consent.

17. PHYSICIAN LICENSING BOARD:

State Department of Public Health
Licensing and Registration
P.O. Box 340308, MS # 12APP
Hartford, CT 06154-0308
(860) 509-8000

18. ATTORNEY LICENSING BOARD:

Connecticut Bar Association
101 Corporate Place
Rocky Hill, CT 06067-1894
(860) 721-0025

19. VITAL STATISTICS AGENCY:

Public Health Statistics Section
Department of Health Services
P.O. Box 340308, MS # 11VRSn St.
Hartford, CT 06134-0308
(860) 509-7897

RECORD	COST	AVAILABILITY	SOURCE
A. Birth	$15.00	Kept since 1897 Restricted access	STATE: Above COUNTY: Registrar of vital statistics*
B. Marriage	$5.00	Kept since 1897 Public information	STATE: Above COUNTY: Registrar of vital statistics*
C. Divorce	$5.00	Kept since 1947 Public information	COUNTY: Superior Court clerk
D. Death	$5.00	Kept since 1897 Public information	STATE: Above COUNTY: Registrar of vital statistics*

* May have records prior to 1897. Birth records may be available for $5.00 at county level

20. STATE REUNION REGISTRY:

Department of Children and Families
Attn: Director, Post Adoption Services
505 Hudson Street
Hartford, CT 06106

COST: None

SUMMARY: This is only for adoptions that were handled through the state agency. Persons who may register on such a registry are: birth parents who were parties to the adoption process; adopted persons over 18 years old; adoptive parents on behalf of their child for purposes of obtaining medical information only; adult siblings of adopted persons with the birth parents' consent if they were not adopted themselves; grandparents; and alleged fathers who were not a party to the legal proceedings (provided birth mother consents, or provided that proof of her death is shown to the agency); and two or more adult adopted persons who were reared apart without consent of the birth parents.
Allow four weeks for nonidentifying information. For identifying information, you will be contacted and an interview with a staff member will be set up.
Send notarized registration form to the above address.

Delaware

1. CENTRAL INFORMATION AGENCY:

State Capitol
Dover, DE 19901
(302) 739-4000

2. STATE ADOPTION DEPARTMENT:

Dept. of Services for Children, Youth, and Their Families
Division of Family Protective Services
Attention: Adoption Coordinator
1825 Faulkland Road
Wilmington, DE 19805-1195
(302) 633-2655 (recording) or (302) 633-2670

3. ADOPTION RECORDS: Closed

4. YEAR CLOSED: 1913

5. DEGREE OF AVAILABILITY: Records are sealed upon finalization, and can be opened by petitioning the superior court, giving good cause. Many agencies will release nonidentifying information to an adult involved party.

6. AGE OF MAJORITY: 18 years old

7. ADOPTION LAWS: Title 13, Sect. 925: "Anyone wishing to inspect any of the papers filed in connection with any adoption shall petition the Judge of the Superior Court concerning setting forth the reasons for the inspection."
Sect. 924: Department of Services for Children, Youth, and Their Families, or an authorized agency may release nonidentifying information to any party to adoption.
Sect. 924: (medical information) These records are available to the adoptee or on behalf of the adoptee by a blood relative when information is needed for health reasons.

8. COURT OF JURISDICTION: Family Court

9. STATE REUNION REGISTRY: Yes; see #20. Adoptees and birth parents can file a waiver of confidentiality with their agency and/or the state adoption department

10. STATE ARCHIVES/RECORDS DEPT.:

Delaware Public Archives
Hall of Records
P.O. Box 1401
Dover, DE 19901
(302) 739-5318

11. HOSPITAL RECORDS AVAILABLE: Yes; usually kept on microfilm

12. LEGAL NOTICES REQUIRED: Unknown

13. LAND RECORDS: Available from county recorder of deeds

14. DEPARTMENT OF MOTOR VEHICLES: Must be 15 years and 10 months old to get a driving permit. At the current time, transcripts are $4.00. Must have birth date, driver's license number, and written permission if search is other than your own. Payment must be in the form of a money order or certified check made out to the Delaware Department of Public Safety. Mail requests to:

Division of Motor Vehicles
Department of Public Safety
P.O. Box 698, 303 Transportation Circle
Dover, DE 19903
(302) 739-2500

15. LAWS REGARDING INHERITANCE: Section 920: Issuance of the adoption decree severs all inheritance rights.

16. LAWS REGARDING TELEPHONE RECORDINGS: All parties to a conversation must be aware that it is being recorded.

17. PHYSICIAN LICENSING BOARD:

Delaware Board of Medical Practices
Cannon Bldg., Suite 203
Dover, DE 19904
(302) 739-4522 (ext. 203)

18. ATTORNEY LICENSING BOARD:

Delaware Bar Association
1201 Orange Street, Suite 1100
Wilmington, DE 19801
(302) 658-5279

19. VITAL STATISTICS AGENCY:

Dept. of Public Health
Office of Vital Statistics
P.O. Box 637
Dover, DE 19903-0637
(302) 739-4721

RECORD	COST	AVAILABILITY	SOURCE
A. Birth	$6.00	Kept since 1923 Restricted access	STATE: Above COUNTY: No records
B. Marriage	$6.00	Kept since 1954 Restricted access	STATE: Above COUNTY: No records
C. Divorce	$6.00*	Kept since 1944** Restricted access	COUNTY: No records
D. Death	$6.00	Kept since 1954 Restricted access	STATE: Above COUNTY: No records

* Must be obtained in county where divorce is granted.
** Office of the Prothonotary: 1020 North King St./Wilmington, DE 19801-3347/(302) 577-6470

20. STATE REUNION REGISTRY: To file an affidavit, contact the above, giving consent or denial to release identifying information and contact, or release of information without contact.

Family Court of the State of Delaware
Reunion Registry
P.O. Box 2359
Wilmington, DE 19899
(320) 577-2200
(302) 577-2302 (Adoption Unit)

District of Columbia

1. CENTRAL INFORMATION AGENCY:

District of Columbia Building
1350 Pennsylvania Avenue NW
Washington, DC 20004
(202) 727-1000

2. STATE ADOPTION DEPARTMENT:

Department of Human Services
Adoption & Placement Resources
609 H Street, NE, 3rd Floor
Washington, DC 20002
(202) 724-3990
(202) 724-8602

3. ADOPTION RECORDS: Closed

4. YEAR CLOSED: 1935

5. DEGREE OF AVAILABILITY: All adoption records are sealed upon finalization, and a court order is required to release any information from them. Most agencies will release non-identifying information to an adult involved party.

6. AGE OF MAJORITY: 18 years old

7. ADOPTION LAWS: Sect. 16-311: "Sealing and inspection of records and papers: From and after the filing of the petition, records and papers in adoption proceeding shall be

sealed. They may not be inspected by any person, including the parties to the proceedings, except upon order of the court, and only then when the court is satisfied that the welfare of the child will thereby be promoted or protected. The clerk of the court shall keep a separate docket for adoption proceedings."

8. COURT OF JURISDICTION: 1956 to present: U.S. Superior Court for Dist. of Columbia
Before 1956: U.S. District Court for Dist. of Columbia

9. STATE REUNION REGISTRY: None. However, adoptees and birth parents can file a waiver of confidentiality with their agency and/or the state adoption department.

10. STATE ARCHIVES/RECORDS DEPT.:
Library of Congress
James Madison Bldg.
101 Independence Ave. S.E.
Washington, DC 20540
(202) 707-5000 (alternate source)

Martin L. King Jr. Library
901 G Street NW
Washington, DC 20005
(202) 727-1126
(202) 727-2079 (Genealogy Dept.)

11. HOSPITAL RECORDS AVAILABLE: Usually; doctor's request may be required

12. LEGAL NOTICES REQUIRED: Rarely

13. LAND RECORDS AVAILABLE FROM:
The Recorder of Deeds
515 D Street, NW
Washington, DC 20001

14. DEPARTMENT OF MOTOR VEHICLES: Must be 16 years old to get a driver's license. At the current time, transcripts are $5.00. You should also send a copy of your own driver's license or identification. The social security number may be the same as the driver's license number. Payment must be in the form of a money order or certified check made out to the District of Columbia Department of Public Safety. Mail requests to:
Bureau of Motor Vehicle Services
Department of Motor Vehicles
301 C St. NW Room 1157 Window #5
Washington, DC 20001
(202) 727-6761

15. LAWS REGARDING INHERITANCE: Unknown

16. LAWS REGARDING TELEPHONE RECORDINGS: Sect. 23-542(b): At the present time, private parties may legally record their own conversations without obtaining the consent of the opposite party.

17. PHYSICIAN LICENSING BOARD:
Occupational & Professional Licensing
614 H. St. N.W. Rm. 100
Washington, DC 20001
(202) 727-7826 (main line)
(202) 727-5365 (records)

18. ATTORNEY LICENSING BOARD:
District of Columbia Bar
250 H. St. N.W., 6th Floor
Washington, DC 20005
(202) 626-3475

19. VITAL STATISTICS AGENCY:
Vital Records
800 9th Street SW
Washington, DC 20024
(202) 645-5962 (automated system)
(202) 783-1809 (credit card orders)

RECORD	COST	AVAILABILITY	SOURCE
A. Birth	$12.00 short form $18.00 long form†	Since 1874 Immediate family	STATE: Above COUNTY: ****
B. Marriage	$10.00*	Kept since 1811 Restricted access	STATE: **** COUNTY: ****
C. Divorce	No Fee**	Kept since 1956 Restricted access	STATE: **** COUNTY: ****
D. Death	$12.00	Kept since 1874*** Restricted access	STATE: Above

* Marriages & Divorces: Pre-1956: Clerk
U.S. Dist. Court for D.C.
Constitution Avenue & John Marshall Place, NW
Washington, DC 20001

** Since September 16, 1956: Divorce records may cost more if lengthy. Money orders only, payable to D.C. Superior Court.

*** No records kept during Civil War.

**** Birth & Marriage Records: D.C. Superior Court
Marriage License Bureau
500 Indiana Ave. NW
Room #4485
Washington, DC 20001
(202) 879-4850

Divorce: D.C. Superior Court
Domestic Relations Branch
500 Indiana Ave. NW
Room #4230
Washington, DC 20001
(202) 879-1410

† Long form of birth record is $18.00.

Florida

1. CENTRAL INFORMATION AGENCY:
State Capitol
Tallahassee, FL 32304
(904) 488-1234

2. STATE ADOPTION DEPARTMENT: (Also see #20 of this section)

Department of Health and Rehabilitative Services
Family and Child Services
1317 Winewood Blvd,
Tallahassee, FL 32301
(904) 353-0679

3. ADOPTION RECORDS: Closed

4. YEAR CLOSED: 1945

5. DEGREE OF AVAILABILITY: Juvenile records are always confidential. Adoption files are closed after finalization. A court order is required to release any identifying information. Adoption agencies will release nonidentifying information to adult adoptees, birth parents, and adoptive parents. HRS will release limited information to birth mothers. The state agency does not charge a fee for this service, although some private agencies do.

6. AGE OF MAJORITY: 18 years old

7. ADOPTION LAWS: Sect. 63.162: Identifying information regarding birth parents will be released with their consent to adoptee providing adoptee has reached the age of majority. Adoptive parents may receive same if adoptee is a minor. Identifying information can be released by court order. Petitions may be an informal letter to the court of jurisdiction.

8. COURT OF JURISDICTION: Circuit Court

9. STATE REUNION REGISTRY: Yes; see #20

10. STATE ARCHIVES:

State Library of Florida
Florida State Archives
R.A. Gray Building
Tallahassee, FL 32399-0250
(904) 487-2073

11. HOSPITAL RECORDS AVAILABLE: Yes, to the person whose name is on the file

12. LEGAL NOTICES REQUIRED: Yes. Be sure to check private legal notices in large towns. Most counties in Florida have a law bulletin.

13. LAND RECORDS: Available in tax assessor's office

14. DEPARTMENT OF MOTOR VEHICLES: Must be 14 years old to get a driver's license. At the present time, current transcripts cost $2 and historical transcripts are $3. You must have the driver's full name, driver's license number, and a recent address. Payment must be in the form of a money order or cashier's check made out to the Florida Department of Highway Safety. Mail requests to:

Driver License Division
Bureau Records
P.O. Box 5775
Tallahassee, FL 32314-5775
(904) 487-2369

15. LAWS REGARDING INHERITANCE: Sect. 63.172: Finalization severs all rights and responsibilities, including inheritance. If requested, probate judges will check the adoption files to see if a legal adoption has taken place.

16. LAWS REGARDING TELEPHONE RECORDINGS: Sect. 934.03(2)(d): Both parties must be aware that a conversation is being recorded.

17. PHYSICIAN LICENSING BOARD:

Florida Board of Medicine
1940 N. Monroe Street
Tallahassee, FL 32399-0770
(850) 488-0595

18. ATTORNEY LICENSING BOARD:

The Florida Bar Center
Membership Records
650 Apalachee Pkwy.
Tallahassee, FL 32399-2300
(850) 561-5600

19. VITAL STATISTICS AGENCY:

HRS
Office of Vital Statistics
P.O. Box 210
Jacksonville, FL 32231
(904) 359-6900

RECORD	COST	AVAILABILITY	SOURCE
A. Birth	$13.00	Kept since 1865 Restricted**	STATE: Above COUNTY: Circuit Court clerk
B. Marriage	$5.00*	Kept since 1927 Public information***	STATE: Above**** COUNTY: Circuit Court clerk
C. Divorce	$5.00*	Kept since 1927 Public information	STATE: Above**** COUNTY: Circuit Court clerk
D. Death	$5.00*	Kept since 1877 Public information**	STATE: Above COUNTY: Circuit Court clerk

* An additional search fee of $2/year is charged.
** Birth records are available to the parent requesting the child's, not the child requesting the parents. If requesting, you'll need to know the person's name, both parents' names, and the date of birth. Death records with the cause of death available to immediate family only.
*** People seeking information from marriage records should look for the marriage license and the marriage license application both. The application contains additional information. "Emergency" credit card service available, additional $10.00, plus credit card verification fee, plus cost of document.
**** These records may not be available from the state; call for clarification.

20. STATE REUNION REGISTRY:

Daniel Memorial's Adoption Information Center
134 East Church Street
Jacksonville, FL 32202
(800) 96-ADOPT
(850) 487-2760 Ext. 103 Josette Marquess

COST: No fees are charged for their services.

SUMMARY: Adult adopted persons who are 18 or older, adoptive parents, biological parents, biological siblings, and biological grandparents may file identifying information. A minor adoptee may be registered by his or her adoptive parents. When filing information, applicants must specify to whom they wish to release information. Applicant's parents may supply information and authorize its release to any or all of the following: biological parents, biological siblings, and biological grandparents. Similarly, biological parents, siblings, or grandparents may supply information to release to the adult adopted persons and/or adoptive parent.

Before identifying information is released, the registry requires proof of identity and relationship to the adoptee (i.e., sworn statements, court decrees and judgments, copies of birth certificates, marriage licenses, driver's licenses, school records, voter registration cards, social security numbers and original application, and other evidence as required). These documents are not required at the time of registration; the registry will advise when documentation is needed.

This agency does not provide nonidentifying information. The agency that handled the adoption should be contacted for this information.

Georgia

1. CENTRAL INFORMATION AGENCY:
   State Capitol
   Capitol Square SW
   200 Washington Street
   Atlanta, GA 30334
   (404) 656-2844

2. STATE ADOPTION DEPARTMENT:
   Ga. Dept. of Human Resources
   State Adoption Unit
   Rm. 13-400, 2 Peachtree St. NW
   Atlanta, GA 30303
   (404) 657-3550

3. ADOPTION RECORDS: Closed

4. YEAR CLOSED: 1935

5. DEGREE OF AVAILABILITY: Court records are sealed upon finalization, and an order by a Superior Court judge is needed to release any information.

6. AGE OF MAJORITY: 21 years old

7. ADOPTION LAWS: The copies of the original county birth record shall then be forwarded to the Division of Vital Statistics to be sealed with the original record in the files of the Division of Vital Statistics. Such sealed records may be opened by the Division of Vital Statistics only upon order of a judge of a superior court directly to adoptees and birth parents. Effective July 1, 1991, under a new law, adoptees who have reached age 21 may request the state adoption unit or private agency to contact their birth parents. If the birth parents consent, identities are released to both parties. If birth parents do not consent, appeals may be made to the courts on the old basis.

8. COURT OF JURISDICTION: Superior Court

9. STATE REUNION REGISTRY: Yes; see #20

10. STATE ARCHIVES:
    Georgia Dept. of State Archives
    330 Capitol Avenue
    Atlanta, GA 30303
    (404) 656-2350 (reference)
    (404) 656-2393 (genealogy)

11. HOSPITAL RECORDS AVAILABLE: Possibly, through a doctor

12. LEGAL NOTICES REQUIRED: No

13. LAND RECORDS: Available from clerk of county Superior Court

14. DEPARTMENT OF MOTOR VEHICLES: Must be 16 years old to get a driver's license. At the current time, transcripts are $5.00. Must have driver's license number and written permission. Payment must be in the form of a money order or certified check made out to the Georgia Dept. of Motor Vehicles:
    Department of Motor Vehicles
    Driver's License Section
    MVR Unit P.O. Box 1456
    Atlanta, GA 30371
    (404) 624-7442

15. LAWS REGARDING INHERITANCE: 74-414-11: Upon finalization all rights between birth parent(s) and adoptee are severed (does not specify inheritance).

16. LAWS REGARDING TELEPHONE RECORDINGS: GA Code Sec, 16-11-62(1): The state code does not specifically mention this situation, but the courts have held that it does not prohibit a person from recording his/her own conversations.

17. PHYSICIAN LICENSING BOARD:
    State Board of Medical Examiners
    166 Pryor Street SW
    Atlanta, GA 30303-3465
    (404) 656-3913

18. ATTORNEY LICENSING BOARD:
    Georgia State Bar Association
    800 The Hurt Building
    50 Hurt Plaza
    Atlanta, GA 30303
    (404) 527-8700

19. VITAL STATISTICS AGENCY:

Vital Records Unit: Dept. of Human Resources
Room 217-H
47 Trinity Ave. SW
Atlanta, GA 30334
(404) 656-4904
(800) 255-2414 (Credit Card orders)

RECORD	COST	AVAILABILITY	SOURCE
A. Birth	$10.00	Kept since 1919 Only to parents	STATE: Above COUNTY: County clerk ordinary
B. Marriage	$10.00	Kept since 1952 Restricted/Public**	STATE: Above COUNTY: County clerk ordinary
C. Divorce	$10.00*	Kept since 1952 Public information	STATE: Above COUNTY: Superior Court clerk
D. Death	$10.00	Kept since 1919 Immediate family	STATE: Above COUNTY: County clerk ordinary

* Certifications of divorces are released; however, copies of the actual record are withheld.

** Marriage applications are available only to persons named on the document; marriage licenses are public information.

"Emergency" credit card service available: (404) 656-7456

20. STATE REUNION REGISTRY:

Adoption Reunion Registry
State Adoption Unit
2 Peachtree Street NW
Room 13-400
Atlanta, GA 30303
(404) 657-3555

COST: Priority Search $220.00
Non-ID $35.00

SUMMARY: When you register, you automatically initiate a search. Searches will be handled in the order they are received; currently there is a 2 to 3-year backlog. You will be contacted. Do not send any pictures or documents at this time; instead, make a note on the bottom of your form and they will discuss them with you when they start on your search.

They handle only state adoptions. If adoption was done through another agency, contact that agency.

Hawaii

1. CENTRAL INFORMATION AGENCY:

State Capitol
415 S. Beretania St.
Honolulu, HI 96813
(808) 586-2211

2. STATE ADOPTION DEPARTMENT:

Hawaii Adoption Records Unit
Family Court
P.O. Box 3498
Honolulu, HI 96811-3498
(808) 539-4424

3. ADOPTION RECORDS: Closed

4. YEAR CLOSED: 1945 (limited access effective 1/1/91)

5. DEGREE OF AVAILABILITY: Court records are sealed upon finalization, and a court order showing good cause is required to get agencies to release any information. They will release nonidentifying information to an adult involved party, but they may charge a fee for this service. Certification of adoption and surrender of parental rights papers are available. The original adoption decree is usually not available, as it may contain identifying information. Family court will supply nonidentifying information for nonagency adoptions. This includes adoptions handled by the Department of Human Services.

6. AGE OF MAJORITY: 18 years old

7. ADOPTION LAWS: Sect. 578-15: "The records in adoption proceedings, after the petition is filed and prior to the entry of the decree, shall be open to inspection only by the parties or their attorneys, the director of social services and housing or his agent, or by any proper person on a showing of good cause therefore, upon order of the court."

Sect. 578-15 (effective 1991): For adoptions which occurred prior to 1/1/91, adoptive parents and/or an adult adoptee may file a written request for inspection of all adoption records. The state will then make a good-faith effort to contact the birth parents and forward any accompanying letters or pictures. If a birth parent does not file a request for confidentiality within a specific time, all records pertaining to that person will be opened to inspection by the requesting party.

Sect. 578-14.5: (a) "The department of health shall prepare a standard form entitled 'Medical Information Form,' for the purpose of perpetuating medical information on the natural parents of the adopted minor child. This form shall include a request for any information relating to the adopted child's potential genetic or other inheritable diseases or afflictions, including but not limited to known genetic disorders, inheritable diseases, and similar medical histories" . . . (g) Any of the following may file a written application with the department of health for access to medical records relating to inheritable diseases and genetic disorders: an adopted child upon reaching the age of majority, the adoptive parent on behalf of a minor adopted child, or an authorized designee of the adult adopted child or of the minor's adoptive parent.

8. COURT OF JURISDICTION:

City and County of Honolulu: First Circuit Family Court
County of Maui: Second Circuit Court
County of Hawaii: Third Circuit Court
County of Kauai: Fifth Circuit Court

9. STATE REUNION REGISTRY: No formal registry on state level. (First Circuit Family Court maintains a registry for the first circuit only)

10. STATE ARCHIVES:

State Archives
Iolani Palace Grounds
Honolulu, HI 96813
(808) 586-0329

11. HOSPITAL RECORDS AVAILABLE: Yes; most records are available for 25 years after the event (do not mention adoption)

12. LEGAL NOTICES REQUIRED: Possibly

13. LAND RECORDS: Available from registrar of conveyances; also try:

State of Hawaii
Bureau of Conveyances
Kalanimoku Building
P.O. Box 2867 (96803)
1151 Punchbowl St. Room 120
Honolulu, HI 96813
(808) 587-0134

14. DEPARTMENT OF MOTOR VEHICLES: Must be 15 years old to get a driver's license. At the present time, current transcripts are $5.00. Driver's license number is same as social security number; if you have old driver's license number from another state you can use that too; must also supply full name and date of birth. Payment must be in the form of a money order or cashier's check. Mail request to:

District of the First Circuit Violations Bureau
111 Alekea Street
Honolulu, HI 96813
(808) 538-5500

15. LAWS REGARDING INHERITANCE: Sect. 578-16: Adoptees may not inherit from birth parents. The individual's former legal parents shall cease from the time of the adoption.

16. LAWS REGARDING TELEPHONE RECORDINGS: Sect. 803-42(b)(3): At the present time, private parties may legally record their own conversations without obtaining the other party's consent.

17. PHYSICIAN LICENSING BOARD:

DCCA Professional and Vocational Licensing Div.
Board of Medical Examiners
1010 Richards Street
P.O. Box 3469
Honolulu, HI 96801
(808) 586-2708

18. ATTORNEY LICENSING BOARD:

Hawaii State Bar Association
1136 Union Mall
Penthouse 1
Honolulu, HI 96813
(808) 537-1868

19. VITAL STATISTICS AGENCY:

Vital Records Section, State Dept. of Health
P.O. Box 3378
1250 Punchbowl Street, Room 103
Honolulu, HI 96801-3378
(808) 586-4533 or 4539 or 4542

RECORD	COST	AVAILABILITY	SOURCE
A. Birth	$10.00	Varies by island* Restricted	STATE: Above COUNTY: Circuit Court clerk
B. Marriage	$10.00	Varies by island* Restricted	STATE: Above COUNTY: Circuit Court clerk
C. Divorce	$10.00	Varies by island* Restricted	STATE: Above COUNTY: Circuit Court clerk
D. Death	$10.00	Varies by island* Restricted	STATE: Above COUNTY: Circuit Court clerk

* Hawaii vital statistics information is very complicated. Contact a local search and support group for guidance on your specific situation. The automated line (808) 586-4533 can be very helpful in clarifying how to secure a vital record you need.

Idaho

1. CENTRAL INFORMATION AGENCY:

Idaho State House
700 W. Jefferson Street
Boise, ID 83720
(208) 334-2470

2. STATE ADOPTION DEPARTMENT:

Division of Family & Community Services
Adoption Department
P.O. Box 83720
Boise, ID 83720
(208) 334-5697 (adoption dept.)
(208) 334-6700 (main)

3. ADOPTION RECORDS: Closed

4. YEAR CLOSED: Unknown

5. DEGREE OF AVAILABILITY: Court records are sealed upon finalization, and a court order is required to release any information from them. Judges vary from county to county. Some will always release an adoptee's file—some never will (especially not to birth parents). Many agencies will release

nonidentifying information to an adult involved party, but they may charge a fee for this service.

6. AGE OF MAJORITY: 18 years old

7. ADOPTION LAWS: Sect. 16-1511: "Upon the motion of petitioners, or upon its own motion, the probate court shall order that the record of its proceedings in any adoption proceeding shall be sealed. When such order has been made and entered, the court shall seal such record and thereafter the seal shall not be broken, except upon the motion of petitioners or the person adopted; provided, however, that such record may be sealed again as in this section provided."
Sect. 39-259A: The state shall provide for a registry of adult adoptees who have consented to release identifying information about themselves and a registry of birth parents who have consented to release information about themselves and adoptees' birth siblings. If a match occurs, the information will be released.

8. COURT OF JURISDICTION: Probate or Magistrate Courts

9. STATE REUNION REGISTRY: Yes; see #20

10. STATE ARCHIVES/RECORDS DEPT.:
Idaho State Historical Society
Libraries: Library and Archives
450 N. 4th Street
Boise, ID 83702
(208) 334-3356

11. HOSPITAL RECORDS AVAILABLE: Possibly, through a doctor

12. LEGAL NOTICES REQUIRED: Fathers must be notified in any public paper

13. LAND RECORDS: Available through the County Recorder

14. DEPARTMENT OF MOTOR VEHICLES: Must be 16 years old to get a driver's license. At the present time, transcripts are $4.00. Social security number is the same as driver's license number. Payment should be in the form of a money order or certified check (personal checks are okay) made out to the Idaho Motor Vehicles Division. Mail requests to:
Motor Vehicles Division
Idaho Transportation Dept.
3311 W. State Street
P.O. Box 34
Boise, ID 83731
(208) 334-8736

15. LAWS REGARDING INHERITANCE: Sect. 16-1509: Unless otherwise provided for in the adoption decree or a will, finalization severs all rights and responsibilities—including inheritance.

16. LAWS REGARDING TELEPHONE RECORDINGS: Sect. 18-6702(2)(d): At the present time, a person may legally record their own conversations without obtaining the consent of the opposite party.

17. PHYSICIAN LICENSING BOARD:
Idaho State Board of Medicine
P.O. Box 83720
Boise, ID 83720-0058
(208) 334-2822

18. ATTORNEY LICENSING BOARD:
Idaho State Bar
P.O. Box 895, 450 W. State Street
Boise, ID 83701
(208) 334-4500

19. VITAL STATISTICS AGENCY:
Bureau of Vital Statistics
P.O. Box 83720
Boise, ID 83720-0036
(208) 334-5988
(208) 334-5980 (non-touch-tone phones)
(208) 589-9096 (fax orders with a credit card)

RECORD	COST	AVAILABILITY	SOURCE
A. Birth	$10.00	Kept since 1911* Restricted	STATE: Above COUNTY: Not kept
B. Marriage	$10.00	Kept since 1947 Restricted**	STATE: Above COUNTY: County recorder
C. Divorce	$10.00	Kept since 1947 Restricted**	STATE: Above COUNTY: County recorder
D. Death	$10.00	Kept since 1911 Restricted***	STATE: Above COUNTY: Not kept

* For records from 1907-1911, contact the county recorder's office.
** Records are restricted at state level, open at county.
*** Death records over 60 years old are public information.

"Emergency" credit card service available; additional $5.00 fee.; will FedEx for $15.50.

20. STATE REUNION REGISTRY:
Voluntary Adoption Registry
Idaho Dept. of Health and Welfare
Center for Health Statistics
P.O. Box 83720
Boise, ID 83720-0036
(208) 334-5988
COST: $10.00
SUMMARY: The following may file identifying information: adoptees who were born in Idaho and are 18 years of age or older, adoptive parents, natural parents, natural siblings, and natural maternal or paternal grandparents. When filing information, applicants must specify to whom they wish to release information. Adoptees and/or adoptive parents may supply information and authorize its release to any or all of the following: natural parents, natural siblings, or natural grandparents. Similarly, natural parents, siblings, or grandparents may supply information for release to the adoptee and/or adoptive parent.

Before identifying information is released, the registry requires individuals to provide proof of identity and relationship to the adoptee. Documents that may be required include: sworn statements, court decrees and judgments, copies of birth certificates, marriage licenses, driver's licenses, school records, voter registration cards, social security cards, original applications, and other evidence as may be required by the state registrar of vital statistics. These documents are not required at the time of registration; the registry will advise you when documentation is required.

Illinois

1. CENTRAL INFORMATION AGENCY:
   Central Management Office
   120 West Jefferson, 3rd Floor
   Springfield, IL 62702
   (217) 782-2000

2. STATE ADOPTION DEPARTMENT:
   Department of Children and Family Services
   1001 Walnut Street
   Springfield, IL 62701
   (217) 786-6830
   (800) 572-2390 (in Illinois only)

3. ADOPTION RECORDS: closed

4. YEAR CLOSED: 1945

5. DEGREE OF AVAILABILITY: Court records are locked upon finalization, and a court order is required to release information. Most agencies will release nonidentifying information to an adult involved party, but they may charge a fee for this service.

6. AGE OF MAJORITY: 18 years old

7. ADOPTION LAWS: Sect. 1522.8: Records and certified copies of all papers will be impounded upon finalization, and a court order is required to release any information from them.

8. COURT OF JURISDICTION: County Circuit Court

9. STATE REUNION REGISTRY: Yes; see #20

10. STATE ARCHIVES/RECORDS DEPT.:
    Illinois State Archives
    State Archives Building, Capitol Complex
    Springfield, IL 62756
    (217) 782-4682
    (217) 524-3930 (fax)

11. HOSPITAL RECORDS AVAILABLE: Yes, to doctors

12. LEGAL NOTICES REQUIRED: Yes

13. LAND RECORDS: Available through the county recorder/clerk

14. DEPARTMENT OF MOTOR VEHICLES: Must be 16 years old to get a driver's license. At the present time, transcripts are $4.00, noncertified copies are $2.00. Need driver's license number, name, and date of birth to run search. Payment must be in the form of a money order or certified check made out to the Illinois Vehicle Services Department. Mail request to:
    Office of the Secretary of State
    Attn.: Records
    2701 South Dirksen Pkwy.
    Springfield, IL 62723
    (217) 782-6992 (main)
    (217) 782-2721 (records)

15. LAWS REGARDING INHERITANCE: Sect. 521.17: Upon finalization, all legal rights and responsibilities are severed (inheritance not specified).

16. LAWS REGARDING TELEPHONE RECORDINGS: Chapter 38, paragraph 14-2(a): Both parties must be aware that a conversation is being recorded to be legal.

17. PHYSICIAN LICENSING BOARD:
    Department of Professional Regulation
    320 West Washington, 3rd Floor
    Springfield, IL 62786
    (217) 785-0800

18. ATTORNEY LICENSING BOARD:
    Attorney Registration and Disciplinary Commission
    Hilton Offices
    700 E. Adams Street, Suite 201
    Springfield, IL 62701-1625
    (217) 522-6838

19. VITAL STATISTICS AGENCY:
    State Department of Health
    Bureau of Vital Statistics
    605 West Jefferson Street
    Springfield, IL 62702-5097
    (217) 782-6553

RECORD	COST	AVAILABILITY	SOURCE
A. Birth	$15.00***	Kept since 1916* Restricted	STATE: Above COUNTY: County clerk**
B. Marriage	$5.00	Kept since 1962 Genealogical reasons	COUNTY: County clerk
C. Divorce	$5.00	Kept since 1962 Genealogical reasons	COUNTY: Circuit Court**
D. Death	$15.00	Kept since 1916* Genealogical reasons	STATE: Above COUNTY: County clerk**

* For records prior to this time, contact the county recorder's office.
** Costs for county records vary between $5 and $10.
*** Short form of birth record is $10.00; citing "genealogical purposes" may allow you access.

20. STATE REUNION REGISTRY:

Mail to: Illinois Dept. of Public Health
Division of Vital Records
Adoption Registry
605 W. Jefferson Street
Springfield, IL 62702
(217) 782-6553

COST: $40.00

SUMMARY: Birth parents may register at any time. Adoptees who are 21 years old or older may register. Adoptees between 18 and 21 may register with: 1) Written consent of both adoptive parents; 2) Written consent of a single adoptive parent with a certified copy of the adoption decree; 3) Proof of death of one adoptive parent and written consent of the guardian of the adoptee with a certified copy of the order of the guardian.

Eligible adoptees and birth parents may provide identifying information, current name and address, and authorize its release to the other parties in the adoption (birth parent[s] name released to adoptee; adoptee name released to birth parent[s].) The registry will match individuals who have authorized release of information to one another and disclose the information accordingly. The registry also will notify individuals who match if the other party does not want their identifying information released.

The information may be updated or changed at any time by the person who has previously registered by written notice to the registry. Consent or denial may also be withdrawn at any time. There is no additional fee for this information.

There is a postadoption search and/or reunion service available to individuals party to an adoption in which the child was a ward of the DCFS at the time of adoption. For information write:

IDCFS Post Adoption Program/Confidential Intermediary Service
3166 Des Plaines River Road, #23
Des Plaines, IL 60018
(847) 298-9096

Indiana

1. CENTRAL INFORMATION AGENCY:

Central Info. Agency, IN Gov't. Center
100 N. Senate, 5th Floor, Room 551
Indianapolis, IN 46204
(317) 232-3140

2. STATE ADOPTION DEPARTMENT:

State Department of Public Welfare
Social Services Div., Attn.: Div of Family and Children
402 West Washington Street, Room W.364
Indianapolis, IN 46204
(317) 232-4440

3. ADOPTION RECORDS: Closed

4. YEAR CLOSED: 1941

5. DEGREE OF AVAILABILITY: Court records are closed upon finalization, and cannot be opened except as provided in the Indiana Adoption History Program (IC 31-3-4).

6. AGE OF MAJORITY: 21 years old

7. ADOPTION LAWS: Sect. 31-3-1-2: Report of health status and report of medical history (of both adoptee and natural parents) shall be filed with adoption petition. A copy shall be sent to the adoptive parents.

Sect. 31-3-4: The Indiana Adoption History Registry allows the release of nonidentifying information relating to any adoption and nonidentifying information relating to adoptions finalized prior to July 1, 1988, to adult adoptees (21 or older), birth parents, and adoptive parents, providing that all parties sign a consent to release information form.

Sect. 31-3-4-21: Any interested person who has a need to obtain or share medical information not contained in the medical history may file a petition with any court of competent jurisdiction in the state.

8. COURT OF JURISDICTION: Circuit, Probate, and Superior Courts

9. STATE REUNION REGISTRY: Yes

10. STATE ARCHIVES/RECORDS DEPT.:

Indiana State Library
Archives Division
140 N. Senate Ave., Room 117
Indianapolis, IN 46204-2296
(317) 232-3675 (state library); (317) 232-3660 (archives)

11. HOSPITAL RECORDS AVAILABLE: Yes, to adoptees at most hospitals with birth name and maiden name of birth mother

12. LEGAL NOTICES REQUIRED: No

13. LAND RECORDS: Available through the county recorder

14. DEPARTMENT OF MOTOR VEHICLES: Must be 16 years old to get a driver's license. At the present time, transcripts are $4.00. Must have birth date, name, and social security number. Payment must be in the form of a money order made out to Indiana Bureau of Motor Vehicles. Mail requests to:

Bureau of Motor Vehicles
100 N. Senate Ave. Rm. N405
Indianapolis, IN 46204
(317) 232-2798

15. LAWS REGARDING INHERITANCE: Sect. 31-3-1-9: All legal rights and responsibilities are severed upon finalization (does not specify inheritance).

16. LAWS REGARDING TELEPHONE RECORDINGS: Sect. 35-33.5-1-5: At the present time, private parties may record their own conversations without obtaining the other party's consent.

17. PHYSICIAN LICENSING BOARD:

Medical Licensing Board, Health Professions Bureau
402 W. Washington, Room 041
Indianapolis, IN 46204
(317) 232-2960
(317) 233-4397 (records)

18. ATTORNEY LICENSING BOARD:

Indiana Bar Association
230 E. Ohio Street, 4th Floor
Indianapolis, IN 46204
(317) 639-5465

19. VITAL STATISTICS AGENCY:

State Dept. of Health
Division of Vital Records
P.O. Box 7125
Indianapolis, IN 46206-7125
(317) 233-2700

RECORD	COST	AVAILABILITY	SOURCE
A. Birth	$6.00	Kept since 1907* Genealogical reasons	STATE: Above COUNTY: Health officer
B. Marriage	No Charge	Index since 1958 Genealogical reasons	STATE: None COUNTY: County clerk
C. Divorce	Unknown	Kept since 1958 Public information	COUNTY: County clerk
D. Death	$4.00	Kept since 1900* Genealogical reasons	STATE: Above COUNTY: Health officer

* For records prior to this time, contact the county health officer.

"Emergency" credit card service available for additional $5.00; FedEx additional $10.85.

20. STATE REUNION REGISTRY:

Indiana Adoption Medical History Registry
(or Indiana Adoption History Registry)
P.O. Box 1964
Indianapolis, IN 46206-1964
(317) 233-7442

COST: None for adoption history registry
$25.00 for adoption medical history registry

SUMMARY: The consent of one or both adoptive parents may be waived if they are deceased. If one adoptive parent has consented to the release of information the consent of the other adoptive parent may be waived if he/she is an individual whose whereabouts are still unknown after diligent efforts have been made to locate the individual. The waiver also applies if the other adoptive parent is a mentally disabled person or if there is one parent in a single-parent adoption.

No fee is charged to file an adoption history registration form. The only charge that is allowed is a reasonable fee made by a child-placing agency or health care provider for the expenses incurred in the preparation of information to be released.

Medical history information is available in accordance with the changes made by Public Law 282-1985. The Indiana adoption medical history registry was established in January 1, 1986. This registry is the central depository for the storage and release of medical information.

Individuals adopted in Indiana in the past may have information in the registry; however, this depends upon someone having knowledge of the facts filing a Voluntary Medical Report. The forms for Voluntary Medical Reports are distributed to requesting individuals and Indiana licensed child placement agencies.

Indiana law provides that an adoptee, a birth parent, an adoptive parent, and a relative of a birth or adoptive parent (grandparent, sibling, or a child) may request a search of the registry file. The state or county department of public welfare, an adoption agency, or a court may also request a search.

There is no charge for this service.

Iowa

1. CENTRAL INFORMATION AGENCY:

Iowa Capitol Building
1007 East Grand Avenue
Des Moines, IA 50319-0001
(515) 281-5011

2. STATE ADOPTION DEPARTMENT:

Iowa Department of Human Services
Division of Adult, Children & Family Services
Hoover State Office Bldg.
Des Moines, IA 50319
(515) 281-6216

3. ADOPTION RECORDS: Closed*

* Records kept on the county level are public information.

4. YEAR CLOSED: 1945

5. DEGREE OF AVAILABILITY: Court records are sealed upon finalization, and a court order is required to release any information from them. Some agencies will release nonidentifying information to an adult involved party, but they are not required to do so.

A new law has recently been enacted in Iowa that opens records to all adoptees born in Iowa before July 1, 1941. A summary follows:

Adult adoptees whose adoption took place prior to July 1, 1941, may request their sealed record be opened, without showing good cause. It seems that when the sealed record law went into effect, it became retroactive, sealing all adoption records. The legislature amended the Iowa code to make access of sealed adoption records easier for adult adoptees who were adopted prior to July 1, 1941. Indicate on your affidavit that Iowa law does not require you to provide good cause. This is an amendment of Chapter 600, Termination of the Parental Rights of Adoption.

6. AGE OF MAJORITY: 18 years old

7. ADOPTION LAWS: Sect. 600.16.2: Identifying information may be disclosed to an adult adoptee by order of the court for good cause. An affidavit from a natural parent requesting that the court reveal or not reveal the parent's name is considered in determining whether there is good cause. Sect. 600.24: Access to nonidentifying information compiled before January 1, 1977, is allowed for legitimate research or medical treatment purposes.

8. COURT OF JURISDICTION: District Court

9. STATE REUNION REGISTRY: None

10. STATE ARCHIVES:
State Historical Society of Iowa
600 East Locust Ave.
Des Moines, IA 50319
(515) 281-5111

11. HOSPITAL RECORDS AVAILABLE: Possibly, through a doctor

12. LEGAL NOTICES REQUIRED: No

13. LAND RECORDS: Available through county recorder of deeds

14. DEPARTMENT OF MOTOR VEHICLES: Must be 16 years old to get a driver's license. At the present time, transcripts are $5.00. You need driver's license number to run a search; social security numbers are often the same as driver's license numbers in this state. Payment must be in the form of a money order or cashier's check made out to the Iowa Department of Transportation. Mail request to:
Iowa Department of Transportation
Motor Vehicles Division
Department of Driver Services
Park Fair Mall, P.O. Box 9204
100 Euclid Avenue
Des Moines, IA 50306-9204
(515) 239-1101

15. LAWS REGARDING INHERITANCE: Sect. 633.223/600.13: Adoption extinguishes the right of intestate succession of the adoptee from and through their birth parents and the right of intestate succession of a natural parent from the adoptee. Nothing in Iowa law prevents inheritance by will.

16. LAWS REGARDING TELEPHONE RECORDINGS: Sect. 727.8: At the present time, private parties may legally record their own conversations without informing the other party.

17. PHYSICIAN LICENSING BOARD:
Iowa State Board of Medical Examiners
Executive Hills West
1209 East Court Avenue
Des Moines, IA 50319-0180
(515) 281-5171

18. ATTORNEY LICENSING BOARD:
Iowa State Bar Association
521 E. Locust St., 3rd Floor
Des Moines, IA 50309-1939
(515) 243-3179

19. VITAL STATISTICS AGENCY:
State Department of Public Health
Division of Vital Records
Lucas State Office Building
321 E. 12th St., 4th Floor
Des Moines, IA 50319
(515) 281-4944
(515) 281-4955 (fax service with credit card)

RECORD	COST	AVAILABILITY	SOURCE
A. Birth	$10.00**	Kept since 1880 Relatives	STATE: Above COUNTY: District Court clerk*
B. Marriage	$10.00*	Kept since 1916 Relatives	STATE: Above COUNTY: District Court clerk*
C. Divorce	Unknown*	Kept since 1916 Relatives	COUNTY: District Court clerk*
D. Death	$10.00**	Kept since 1891 Relatives	STATE: Above COUNTY: District Court clerk*

* Records kept on the county level are public information.
** Must enclose a self-addressed stamped envelope.

Kansas

1. CENTRAL INFORMATION AGENCY:
Kansas State House
300 SW 10th Street
Topeka, KS 66612
(913) 296-0111

2. STATE ADOPTION DEPARTMENT:
Department of Social and Rehabilitative Services
Division of Children and Youth
300 S.W. Oakley, West Hall
Topeka, KS 66606
(913) 296-4820 (Youth Services)

3. ADOPTION RECORDS: Open

4. YEAR CLOSED: N/A

5. DEGREE OF AVAILABILITY: Court records are locked upon finalization, and either a court order or a demand by the adoptee is required to release any information from them. Most agencies will release nonidentifying information to an adult involved party and may charge a fee for this service. Some agencies will even forward letters between parties.

6. AGE OF MAJORITY: 18 years old

7. ADOPTION LAWS: Sect. 59-2278A: Identifying and nonidentifying information shall be filed with the adoption petition.
Sect. 59-2278A: Complete genetic, medical, and social history is filed with the petition.
Sect. 65-2423: Sealed documents can be opened only upon demand of an adult adoptee or an order of the court.
Recent changes in Kansas Law:
Senate Bill No. 431—New Section 12: "(a) The files and records of the court in adoption proceedings shall not be open to inspection or copy by persons other than the parties in interest and their attorneys, and representatives of the state department of social and rehabilitation services, except upon an order of the court expressly permitting the same." As used in this section, "parties of interest" shall not include genetic parents once a decree of adoption is entered.
"(b) The department of social and rehabilitation services may contact the adoptive parents of the minor child or the adopted adult at the request of the genetic parents in the event of a health or medical need. The department of social and rehabilitation services may contact the adopted adult at the request of the genetic parents for any reason. Identifying information shall not be shared with the genetic parents without the permission of the adoptive parents of the minor child or the adopted adult. The department of social and rehabilitation services may contact the genetic parents at the request of the adoptive parents of the minor child or the adopted adult in the event of a health or medical need." A copy of the birth certificate and driver's license must accompany the adult adoptee's request.

8. COURT OF JURISDICTION: District Court

9. STATE REUNION REGISTRY: None

10. STATE ARCHIVES:
Kansas History Center
6425 SW 6th Avenue
Topeka, KS. 66615-1099
(913) 272-8681

11. HOSPITAL RECORDS AVAILABLE: Possibly, through a doctor

12. LEGAL NOTICES REQUIRED: No

13. LAND RECORDS: Available from county clerk/registrar of deeds

14. DEPARTMENT OF MOTOR VEHICLES: Must be 16 years old to get a driver's license. At the present time, current transcripts are $3.50. Need driver's name and driver's license number. Payment must be in the form of a money order or cashier's check made out to the Kansas Department of Revenue. Mail request to:
Driver Control
P.O. Box 12021
Topeka, KS 66612-2021
(913) 296-3671

15. LAWS REGARDING INHERITANCE: Sect. 59-2103: All parental rights and responsibilities, including the right to inherit from adoptee, shall be severed upon finalization (does not mention adoptee inheriting from birth parents).

16. LAWS REGARDING TELEPHONE RECORDINGS: KS Criminal Code Section 21-4001: At the present time, private parties may legally record their own conversations without obtaining the other party's consent.

17. PHYSICIAN LICENSING BOARD:
Kansas State Board of Healing Arts
235 S. Topeka Blvd.
Topeka, KS 66603
(913) 296-7413

18. ATTORNEY LICENSING BOARD:
Kansas State Bar
1200 Harrison
P.O. Box 1037
Topeka, KS 66601
(913) 234-5696

19. VITAL STATISTICS AGENCY:
Office of Vital Statistics
900 SW Jackson Street, Room 151
Topeka, KS 66612-2221
(913) 296-1400

RECORD	COST	AVAILABILITY	SOURCE
A. Birth	$10.00	Kept since 1911* Relatives	STATE: Above COUNTY: Circuit Court clerk
B. Marriage	$10.00	Kept since 1913 Relatives	STATE: Above COUNTY: Probate judge
C. Divorce	$10.00	Kept since 1951 Relatives	STATE: Above COUNTY: Circuit Court clerk
D. Death	$10.00	Kept since 1911* Relatives	STATE: Above COUNTY: Circuit Court clerk

* County records may date further back.

Vital Records are open to immediate family unless you can prove an interest allowed under the law (inheritance purposes, you own property with the person, etc.). Enclose a business-sized SASE with your request.

Kentucky

1. CENTRAL INFORMATION AGENCY:
State Government Information
100 Fair Oaks
Frankfort, KY 40601
(502) 564-3130

2. STATE ADOPTION DEPARTMENT:
Department for Social Services
Cabinet for Families and Children
275 East Main Street, 6th floor West
Frankfort, KY 40621
(502) 564-2147

3. ADOPTION RECORDS: Closed

4. YEAR CLOSED: 1940* (If finalization occurred prior to 1940, case records are normally available.)

*At the state level.

5. DEGREE OF AVAILABILITY: Court records are sealed upon finalization. A court order is required to release any information from them. Almost all agencies will release nonidentifying information to an adult involved party.

6. AGE OF MAJORITY: 21 years old

7. ADOPTION LAWS: Sect. 199.572(1-6): If the birth parent(s) sign an "Identifying Information and Consent to Release Information" form, it will be kept on file; and all records shall be released to the adult adoptee. If a consent is not on file, the adult adoptee may petition the circuit court to search for the birth parent(s) listed on the original birth certificate. If they are found and consent, the adoptee may inspect the file. If the birth parents do not consent, no information will be released. If the birth parents cannot be located or are dead, the court may order all records opened. The adoptee must pay the CF&C a $150 fee to conduct the court-ordered search, which may take up to six months. The state has a better than 50 percent success rate in locating birth parents.
Sect. 199.572(4): Medical information about biological parents and blood relatives shall be given to adoptive parents before adoption is finalized; and same shall be provided to adoptee upon their request and reaching age of majority.

8. COURT OF JURISDICTION: Circuit Court

9. STATE REUNION REGISTRY: None

10. STATE ARCHIVES:
Kentucky Dept. for Libraries and Archives
P.O. Box 537
Frankfort, KY 40602-0537
(502) 564-8300 (main)
(502) 564-8704 (archives)

11. HOSPITAL RECORDS AVAILABLE: Yes, to doctors

12. LEGAL NOTICES REQUIRED: Yes, but not published

13. LAND RECORDS: Available through county court clerk

14. DEPARTMENT OF MOTOR VEHICLES: Must be 16 years old to get a driver's license. At the present time, current transcripts are $3.00. You must have name and date of birth. Payment must be in the form of a money order or cashier's check made out to Kentucky Transportation Cabinet. Mail requests to:
Transportation Cabinet
Division of Driver's Licensing-MVRS
Attn.: Fee Accounting
501 High Street, 2nd floor
Frankfort, KY 40622
(502) 564-6800

15. LAWS REGARDING INHERITANCE: Sect. 199.520(2): If adoptee is placed under the guardianship of a person or agency awaiting formal adoption, the adoptee is entitled to inheritance until such adoption is finalized.

16. LAWS REGARDING TELEPHONE RECORDINGS: Sect. 526.010: At the present time, private parties may legally record their own conversations without obtaining the other party's consent.

17. PHYSICIAN LICENSING BOARD:
Kentucky State Medical Board
310 Whitting Pkwy., Suite 1B
Louisville, KY 40222
(502) 429-8046

18. ATTORNEY LICENSING BOARD:
Kentucky Bar Association
Kentucky Bar Center
514 West Main Street
Frankfort, KY 40601-1883
(502) 564-3795

19. VITAL STATISTICS AGENCY:
Dept. for Human Resources
Office of Vital Statistics
275 East Main Street
Frankfort, KY 40621-0001
(502) 564-4212

RECORD	COST	AVAILABILITY	SOURCE
A. Birth	$9.00	Kept since 1911 Genealogical Reasons	STATE: Above COUNTY: Local health dept.
B. Marriage	$6.00	Kept since 1958* Genealogical reasons	STATE: Above COUNTY: Clerk of County Court
C. Divorce	$6.00	Kept since 1958* Genealogical reasons	STATE: Above COUNTY: Circuit Court clerk
D. Death	$6.00	Kept since 1911 Genealogical reasons	STATE: Above COUNTY: Local health dept.

* At the state level.

Louisiana

1. CENTRAL INFORMATION AGENCY:
State Information Agency
P.O. Box 94280
Baton Rouge, LA 70804
(504) 342-6600

2. STATE ADOPTION DEPARTMENT:
Dept. of Children, Youth, & Family Services
Adoption Program
P.O. Box 3318
333 Laurel Street
Baton Rouge, LA 70821
(504) 342-4040
(800) 259-2456

3. ADOPTION RECORDS: Closed

4. YEAR CLOSED: 1977

5. DEGREE OF AVAILABILITY: Court records and proceedings filed in juvenile court are not open to inspection except upon written authorization by the court. Those filed in district court are open to the public. Agencies must release nonidentifying information to an adult involved party, but they may charge a fee for this service.

6. AGE OF MAJORITY: 18 years old

7. ADOPTION LAWS: Sect. 437A: "Records of the proceedings shall not be open to inspection except on written authorization by the court, and there shall be no publication thereof."
Sect. 422.13: Parents who surrender child for adoption must provide written statement of medical history. Copies are made for the records, adoptive parents, and adoptee upon reaching age of majority.
Sect. 422.9: The formal act of voluntary surrender need not name the persons who are to become the adoptive parent or parents of the child surrendered. An attorney at law may be named in the act of surrender as the representative of the prospective adoptive parent or parents.

8. COURT OF JURISDICTION: District or Juvenile Courts

9. STATE REUNION REGISTRY: Yes

10. STATE ARCHIVES/RECORDS DEPT.:
Louisiana State Library
Secretary of State Archives & Records Division
P.O. Box 94125 (70804-9125)
3851 Essen Lane
Baton Rouge, LA 70804
(504) 922-1206

11. HOSPITAL RECORDS AVAILABLE: Yes, to doctors and/or patient

12. LEGAL NOTICES REQUIRED: No

13. LAND RECORDS: Available from Parish Clerk of Court or Parish Tax Assessor

14. DEPARTMENT OF MOTOR VEHICLES: Must be 15 years old to get a driver's license. At the current time, transcripts are $15.00. Must have name, birth date, driver's license number, and social security number; can request own or family member's records. Payment must be in the form of a money order or certified check made out to the Office of Motor Vehicles. Mail requests to:
Office of Motor Vehicles
P.O. Box 64886
Baton Rouge, LA 70896
(504) 925-6009

15. LAWS REGARDING INHERITANCE: Article 214: "The adopted person and his lawful descendants are relieved of all of their legal duties and divested of all of their legal rights with regard to the blood parent or parents and other blood relatives, except the right to inheritance from them."
Larned v. Parker, App. 1978, 360 So 2d 906: "Right of adopted person to inherit from blood parents and other blood relatives can constitute compelling reason for opening of sealed records of adoption."
Department of Public Health and Safety: "Adopted person's desire to determine his legal right of inheritance from his natural parents, as recognized by LSA-CC Article 214 is a "compelling reason," within meaning of provision of this section providing that sealed package containing original certificate of birth shall be opened only on order of competent court for compelling reason and only to extent necessary. Massey v. Parker, App. 1978, 362 So 2d 1195."

16. LAWS REGARDING TELEPHONE RECORDINGS: All parties to a conversation must be aware that it is being recorded.

17. PHYSICIAN LICENSING BOARD:
Louisiana State Board of Medical Examiners
630 Camp Street
New Orleans, LA 70130
(504) 524-6763

18. ATTORNEY LICENSING BOARD:
Louisiana State Bar Association
601 St. Charles Street
New Orleans, LA 70130
(504) 566-1600

19. VITAL STATISTICS AGENCY:
Dept. of Vital Records
Office of Health Services
325 Loyola Ave.
P.O. Box 60630
New Orleans, LA 70160
(504) 568-5152

RECORD	COST	AVAILABILITY	SOURCE
A. Birth	$15.00	Kept since 1914** Genealogical reasons	STATE: Above
B. Marriage	$5.00	Kept since 1946* Genealogical reasons	PARISH: Court clerk**
C. Divorce	$5.00	Kept since 1946* Genealogical reasons	PARISH: Court clerk**
D. Death	$5.00	Kept since 1914** Genealogical reasons	STATE: Above

* Inquiries will be forwarded to the proper office.
** In the parish where the event took place (Orleans Parish: write to state office). State has birth records less than 100 years old, deaths less than 50 years old.

20. STATE REUNION REGISTRY:
DSS/OCS
Adoption Unit
P.O. Box 3318
Baton Rouge, LA 70821

COST: $25.00

SUMMARY: The Voluntary Registry is limited to adoptions that occurred in the state of Louisiana only. The adopted person must be 18 years of age or older in order to be eligible. If the adopted person has any biological siblings adopted by the same adoptive parents, the siblings must be 18 years old or older.

The biological mother of the adopted child is eligible to register. Both the adopted child and the biological mother must meet all the mandatory requirements. The biological father is also eligible only if he formally acknowledged or legitimated the child, or signed a voluntary release for adoption. The registrant must complete the affidavit and have it notarized. The affidavit must be accompanied by a check or money order payable to Department of Social Services, Office of Community Services.

Within 30 days of registration, the registrant shall be required to participate in not less than one hour of counseling with a board certified search worker or a social worker employed by a licensed adoption agency. A list of the names and addresses of participating agencies in the state of Louisiana will be provided. Registrants who do not reside in the state of Louisiana are encouraged to contact their local Health and Human Services office for licensed adoption agencies or licensed social workers who can provide the mandatory counseling requirements and services as intermediary in case of a match. The social worker must complete the counseling form and submit it to the Louisiana Voluntary Registry after services are completed.

If there appears to be a match between an adoptee and birth parent, notification will be made to the appropriate adoption agency to contact the registered and matched parties in a confidential manner, and give the information necessary to contact each other.

If one or both birth parents of an adopted person are deceased and if this fact is known by the agency that originally placed the adopted person, this information shall be disclosed. Information will be disclosed to the birth parent if it is known that the adopted person is deceased.

There is no expiration time revealed.

Maine

1. CENTRAL INFORMATION AGENCY:
Maine State House
State House number 138
Augusta, ME 04336
(207) 582-9500

2. STATE ADOPTION DEPARTMENT:
Bureau of Child & Family Services
Maine Department of Human Services
221 State Street
State House, Station 11
Augusta, ME 04333-0011
(207) 287-5060 (Adoption Unit)

3. ADOPTION RECORDS: Closed

4. YEAR CLOSED: 1953; records are open at the Probate Court where finalized if done before August 8, 1953

5. DEGREE OF AVAILABILITY: As previously mentioned, records are open at the probate court prior to August 8, 1953. After this date, you must see the probate judge where the adoption took place and it is up to them whether they will release the information. A person also needs a court order to get the original birth certificate from the Department of Vital Statistics. It is up to the judge whether they will give you that court order to release the original birth certificate. Each county (there are sixteen) is different, and each judge may respond differently. Most agencies will release nonidentifying information and some will assist with the search for a fee.

6. AGE OF MAJORITY: 18 years old

7. ADOPTION LAWS: Title 22, Section 207A: A passive adoption registry is available to adult adoptees, birth parents and adoptive parents of minor adoptees. This has recently been expanded to include siblings, those whose adoptions were annulled, whose adoptive parents may no longer have parental rights and those freed for adoption but never adopted.

Those who have been determined by the court to be incapacitated may have their custodian or legal guardian register for them. If an adoptee or birth parent is deceased then another close relative may register.

8. COURT OF JURISDICTION: County Probate Court

9. STATE REUNION REGISTRY: Yes, see #20

10. STATE ARCHIVES/RECORDS DEPT.:
Maine State Archives
State House, Station 84
Cultural Building
Augusta, ME 04333
(207) 287-5790

11. HOSPITAL RECORDS AVAILABLE: Yes. Use a doctor, and quote your state rights under the Freedom of Information privacy acts.

12. LEGAL NOTICES REQUIRED: Yes

13. LAND RECORDS: Available from County Registry of Deeds (contact local search and support group)

14. DEPARTMENT OF MOTOR VEHICLES: Must be 16 years old to get a driver's license. At the current time, transcripts are $5.00. Must supply driver's name and date of birth. Payment must be in the form of a money order or certified check made out to the Secretary of State. Mail requests to:
Bureau of Motor Vehicles
Driver License and Control, Attn.: Driving Records
State House, Station 29
Augusta, ME 04333-0029
(207) 287-2576

15. LAWS REGARDING INHERITANCE: Sect. 4056: Termination order severs all legal rights between adoptee and birth parents, except for inheritance rights. There are many laws regarding inheritance, and this one may be revised in the future.

16. LAWS REGARDING TELEPHONE RECORDINGS: Title 15, Section 709(4): At the present time, private parties may legally record their own conversations without obtaining the other party's consent.

17. PHYSICIAN LICENSING BOARD:
Maine Board of Licensure in Medicine
State House Station 137
Augusta, ME 04333-0137
(207) 287-3601

18. ATTORNEY LICENSING BOARD:
Maine State Bar
124 State Street
P.O. Box 788
Augusta, ME 04332
(207) 622-7523

19. VITAL STATISTICS AGENCY:
Office of Vital Statistics
State House Station 11
Augusta, ME 04333-0011
(207) 287-3184 or 3181
(207) 287-8496 (fax with credit card)

RECORD	COST	AVAILABILITY	SOURCE
A. Birth	$10.00*	Kept since 1923** Public information	STATE: Above COUNTY: Town clerk
B. Marriage	$10.00*	Kept since 1892** Public information	STATE: Above COUNTY: Town clerk
C. Divorce	$10.00*	Kept since 1892** Public information	STATE: Above COUNTY: Judicial District Court clerk
D. Death	$10.00*	Kept since 1892** Public information	STATE: Above COUNTY: Town clerk

* Fees stated are for certified copies; noncertified copies are $6.00. Information can be copied for lesser charges.
**Records prior to 1923 are in the State Archives.

20. STATE REUNION REGISTRY:
Office of Vital Statistics
State House, Station 11
221 State Street
Augusta, ME 04333

COST: $20.00

SUMMARY: You need to call the Office of Vital Statistics at (202) 287-3181 and ask for a form to be sent to you. When you call, they will ask for your date of birth and your name. After verifying you were born in Maine, they will send forms to you.
The vital statistics office maintains a registry for all Maine births, regardless of the agency the adoption went through.

Maryland

1. CENTRAL INFORMATION AGENCY:
Maryland State House
State Circle
Annapolis, MD 21404
(410) 841-3000

2. STATE ADOPTION DEPARTMENT:
Department of Human Resources, Adoption Dept.
311 West Saratoga Street
Baltimore, MD 21201
(410) 767-7423

3. ADOPTION RECORDS: Closed

4. YEAR CLOSED: 1948 (Most adoption records are open and available from the State Archives if the case was finalized before July 1, 1947.)

5. DEGREE OF AVAILABILITY: Court records are closed upon finalization, and a court order is required to release any information from them. Almost all agencies will release nonidentifying information to an adult involved party, although they may charge a fee for this service. Publicly funded agencies are required under the Maryland Code

"D" rules to provide nonidentifying information. Policies regarding release of information vary among private agencies, but most are cooperative. Sometimes the searching party must be very persistent to obtain this information.

6. AGE OF MAJORITY: 18 years old (21 for enrollment in registry)

7. ADOPTION LAWS: Sect. 5-4A-01: Identifying information can be released through the state's Mutual Consent Voluntary Adoption Registry for birth parents, adoptees, and birth siblings who meet certain criteria.
Sect. 5-329: Medical information shall be released with court order if needed for health of individual or blood relative of adoptee. (Such court orders are extremely difficult to obtain in Maryland.)

8. COURT OF JURISDICTION: Circuit or Probate Courts (usually equity division)

9. STATE REUNION REGISTRY: Yes

10. STATE ARCHIVES/RECORDS DEPT.:

Maryland State Archives
Maryland Hall of Records
350 Rowe Boulevard
Annapolis, MD 21401
(410) 974-2525

11. HOSPITAL RECORDS AVAILABLE: Often through a doctor

12. LEGAL NOTICES REQUIRED: Rarely: Some cases prior to mid-1960s

13. LAND RECORDS: Available from Circuit Court (Land or Property Division)

14. DEPARTMENT OF MOTOR VEHICLES: Must be 16 years old to get a driver's license. At the present time, transcripts are $10.00; noncertified copies are $5.00. Must have birth date, driver's license number and address. Payment must be in the form of a money order or certified check made out to the Maryland Department of Transportation. Mail requests to:

Motor Vehicle Administration
6601 Ritchie Highway NE, Courier 212
Glen Burnie, MD 21062
(410) 768-7034 (main line)
(410) 787-7034 (transcripts department)

15. LAWS REGARDING INHERITANCE: Section 78: "Upon the entry of a decree of adoption, all rights of inheritance between the child and the natural relative shall be governed by the Estates Article of the Code."

16. LAWS REGARDING TELEPHONE RECORDINGS: Sect. 10-402(c)(3): At the present time, both parties to a conversation must be aware that it is being recorded.

17. PHYSICIAN LICENSING BOARD:

Maryland Board of Physicians Quality Assurance
4201 Patterson Ave.
Baltimore, MD 21215
(410) 764-4777

18. ATTORNEY LICENSING BOARD:

Maryland State Bar Association
520 West Fayette Street
Baltimore, MD 21201
(410) 685-7878

19. VITAL STATISTICS AGENCY:

Division of Vital Records
P.O. Box 68760
Baltimore, MD 21215-0020
(800) 832-3277 (recording)
(410) 764-3145 or 3038

RECORD	COST	AVAILABILITY	SOURCE
A. Birth	$6.00	Kept since 1898*	STATE: Above COUNTY: No records
B. Marriage	$6.00	Kept since 1951**	STATE: Above COUNTY: Circuit Court clerk
C. Divorce	$6.00	Kept since 1961***	STATE: Above COUNTY: Circuit Court clerk
D. Death	$6.00	Kept since 1898****	STATE: Above COUNTY: No records

* Self, parents and/or representatives authorized by a court order or notarized statement.
** Parties on certificate and/or representatives authorized by a court order or notarized statement.
*** Parties in divorce and/or representatives authorized by a court order or a notarized statement.
**** Immediate family (relationship must be given).

20. STATE REUNION REGISTRY:

MD Mutual Consent Registry
311 West Saratoga St.
Baltimore, MD 21201
(410) 767-7423

COST: $25.00

SUMMARY: In order to obtain a form to register, you need to call (301) 333-0237 and request one be sent to you.

Massachusetts

1. CENTRAL INFORMATION AGENCY:

Citizens Information Service
1 Ashbuton Place, 16th Floor
Boston, MA 02108
(617) 727-7030

2. STATE ADOPTION DEPARTMENT:
Dept. of Social Services
Dept. for Children Adoption Division
24 Farnsworth Street
Boston, MA 02210
(617) 727-0900
(800) 835-0838

3. ADOPTION RECORDS: Open* (see #7)

* Must enclose a self-addressed stamped envelope, and also provide ID.

4. YEAR CLOSED: 1972

5. DEGREE OF AVAILABILITY: Court records are closed upon finalization and a court order showing good cause is required to release any information from them. Almost all agencies will release nonidentifying information to an adult involved party.

6. AGE OF MAJORITY: 18 years old

7. ADOPTION LAWS: Sect. 210-5D: Identifying and nonidentifying information about adoptee, birth parents, or adoptive parents shall be released to adopted person over age 18, birth parents, or adoptive parents with written consent of the opposite parties.
Sect. 210-5D–(b): "If a placement agency, as defined in section 9 of chapter 28A, has received written permission from a biological parent of an adopted person to release the identity of the biological parent to the adopted person and the said agency has received written permission from the adopted person, or written permission from the adoptive parents if the adoptive person is under the age of 21, to release the identity after adoption of the adopted person to the biological parent, and the identity of the biological parent to the adopted person; provided, however, that if the biological parent is surviving, that he or she has given written consent at least 30 days before the release of said identifying information."

8. COURT OF JURISDICTION: Probate Court

9. STATE REUNION REGISTRY: none

10. STATE ARCHIVES:
Massachusetts Archives Division
Secretary of the Commonwealth
220 Morrissey Blvd.
Boston, MA 02125
(617) 727-2816

11. HOSPITAL RECORDS AVAILABLE: Yes, to doctors

12. LEGAL NOTICES REQUIRED: Yes

13. LAND RECORDS: Varies; usually available from the registrar of deeds (contact local search and support group)

14. DEPARTMENT OF MOTOR VEHICLES: Must be 16 years old to get a driver's license. At the present time, current transcripts are $10.00. May not be available. Social security number may be same as driver's license number. Payment must be in the form of a money order or cashier's check made out to the Massachusetts Department of Public Safety. Mail request to:
Department of Public Safety
Registry of Motor Vehicles
100 Nashua Street, 6th floor
Boston, MA 02114-1197
(617) 351-4500

15. LAWS REGARDING INHERITANCE: Sect. 210.7: Finalization of the adoption proceedings will sever all adoptee's rights to inheritance from birth parents.

16. LAWS REGARDING TELEPHONE RECORDINGS: Chapter 272, Section 99(b)(4): Both parties to a conversation must be aware that it is being recorded.

17. PHYSICIAN LICENSING BOARD:
Board of Registration in Medicine
10 West Street, 3rd floor
Boston, MA 02111
(617) 727-3086

18. ATTORNEY LICENSING BOARD:
Board of Bar Overseers
77 Federal Street
Boston, MA 02110
(617) 357-1860

19. VITAL STATISTICS AGENCY:
Registry of Vital Statistics
470 Atlantic Avenue, 2nd Floor
Boston, MA 02110-2224
(617) 753-8600

RECORD	COST	AVAILABILITY	SOURCE
A. Birth	$11.00*	Kept since 1841** All relatives	STATE: Above COUNTY: No records
B. Marriage	$11.00*	Kept since 1841 All relatives	STATE: Above COUNTY: No records
C. Divorce	Index Is Free***	Kept since 1952 All relatives	STATE: Index Only COUNTY: Probate Court registrar
D. Death	$11.00*	Kept since 1841** All relatives	STATE: Above COUNTY: No records

* Must enclose a self-addressed stamped envelope, and also provide ID.
** Boston records begin in 1848; state is maintaining at above address from 1901 (for all records) to present; contact State Archives for prior.
*** State will look up county where event took place at no charge.

Michigan

1. CENTRAL INFORMATION AGENCY:
Capitol Building
Lansing, MI 48933
(517) 373-1837

2. STATE ADOPTION DEPARTMENT:
Department of Social Services
P.O. Box 30037, 235 S. Grand Ave.
Lansing, MI 48909
(517) 373-3513

3. ADOPTION RECORDS: Closed

4. YEAR CLOSED: 1925

5. DEGREE OF AVAILABILITY: All court records are locked, and require a court order showing good cause for the release of any information from them. Almost all agencies will release nonidentifying information to an adult involved party, although some may charge a fee for this service. Confidential intermediary program is available through court of jurisdiction. Birth parents and/or adoptees may file a "Consent to Release of Information Form" with the placing agency at any time.

6. AGE OF MAJORITY: 18 years old

7. ADOPTION LAWS: Sect. 710.27.68: Identifying information can be released to birth parents or adult adoptees if a consent to release of information is filed.
Sect. 710.68: (2) "Within 63 days after a request for information is received, a child placing agency, court, or the department shall provide in writing to the biological parent or adult biological sibling requesting the information all of the nonidentifying information described in section 27(1) and (2) of this chapter."
(4): "If the department or a child placing agency receives a request for adoption record information in their possession from an adult adoptee, biological parent, or adult biological sibling, the department or child placing agency shall provide the person requesting the information with the identity of the court that confirmed the adoption within 28 days after receipt of the request. If a court receives such a request, the court shall provide the person requesting the information with the identity of the child placing agency, the court, and the department may waive a part or all of the fee in case of indigence or hardship." As of 1995 a Confidential Intermediary Program is available. Contact the court of jurisdiction for information.

8. COURT OF JURISDICTION: Probate or Juvenile Courts

9. STATE REUNION REGISTRY: Yes, see #20

10. STATE ARCHIVES/RECORDS DEPT.:
Michigan State Archives
717 West Allegan Street
Lansing, MI 48918-1837
(517) 373-1408

11. HOSPITAL RECORDS AVAILABLE: Yes, to doctors

12. LEGAL NOTICES REQUIRED: No

13. LAND RECORDS: Available from the county registrar of deeds

14. DEPARTMENT OF MOTOR VEHICLES: Must be 16 years old to get a driver's license. At the current time, transcripts are $6.55. Must have birth date and driver's license number and brief written reason for obtaining. Payment must be in the form of a money order or certified check made out to the Michigan Bureau of Automotive Registrations. Mail requests to:
Michigan Department of State
Record Lookup Unit
7064 Crowner Dr.
Lansing, MI 48918
(517) 322-1624

15. LAWS REGARDING INHERITANCE: Section 1.9: Unless otherwise provided for in the adoption proceedings, all rights and responsibilities between adoptee and birth parents shall be severed, including inheritance.

16. LAWS REGARDING TELEPHONE RECORDINGS: Michigan Comp. Laws Ann. Sect. 750.539 (west): Both parties must be aware that a conversation is being recorded to be legal. However, a court has held that this statute requires only third parties to obtain consent, but does not prohibit a participant from recording his/her own conversation. Sullivan v. Gray, 324 N.W.2d 58 Mich. App. 1982.

17. PHYSICIAN LICENSING BOARD:
Dept. of Commerce, Office of Health Services
State Board of Medicine
611 W. Ottawa
P.O. Box 30018
Lansing, MI 48909
(517) 373-4070

18. ATTORNEY LICENSING BOARD:
State Bar of Michigan
306 Townsend
Lansing, MI 48933
(517) 332-9030

19. VITAL STATISTICS AGENCY:
Department of Public Health
Office of Vital Health Statistics
3423 N. Logan Street
P.O. Box 30195
Lansing, MI 48909
(517) 335-8655

RECORD	COST	AVAILABILITY	SOURCE
A. Birth	$13.00*	Kept since 1867 Restricted	STATE: Above COUNTY: County clerk
B. Marriage	$13.00*	Kept since 1867	STATE: Above COUNTY: County clerk
C. Divorce	$13.00*	Kept since 1897 Restricted	STATE: Above COUNTY: County clerk
D. Death	$13.00*	Kept since 1867 Restricted	STATE: Above COUNTY: County clerk

* If age 65, fees are $5 at county level/$2.00 at state level.

20. STATE REUNION REGISTRY:
Michigan Department of Social Services
Adoption Central Registry
P.O. Box 30037
Lansing, MI 48909
(517) 336-3634

SUMMARY: Adult adoptees who wish to consent to the release of their name and address to a birth parent or brother or sister must file their consent with the placing agency and court that finalized their adoption. Birth parents who wish to consent or deny access to information about themselves must file a statement with the Adoption Central Registry. You may consent to or deny release of your name and address to your child when he or she becomes 18 by submitting a statement to the registry.

Minnesota

1. CENTRAL INFORMATION AGENCY:
State Capitol
72 Constitution Avenue
St. Paul, MN 55155
(651) 296-6013

2. STATE ADOPTION DEPARTMENT:
Dept. of Human Services
444 Lafayette Road
St. Paul, MN 55155-3831
(651) 296-3250 (adoption department)

3. ADOPTION RECORDS: Closed

4. YEAR CLOSED: 1941

5. DEGREE OF AVAILABILITY: Records are closed upon finalization, and a petition showing good cause must be submitted and a court order issued before any information will be released from them. Almost all agencies will release nonidentifying information to an adult involved party, although most charge a fee for this service. State also has an intermediary service.

6. AGE OF MAJORITY: 19 years old

7. ADOPTION LAWS: Sect. 259.47: If an adult adoptee, birth parent, or adoptive parent requests from the agency current information, the agency must contact the other parties to gather such information or to determine if the contact is desired.
Sect. 259.47: For agency placements on or after August 1, 1982, an adult adoptee may request the agency to release the names, last known addresses, birth dates, and birth places of birth parents. If the birth parent has filed an affidavit of nondisclosure, however, the adoptee must petition the court.
Sect. 259.47 (medical information): Health information that may affect physical or mental health of genetically related persons shall be released.
Sect. 259.49: If an adult adoptee requests the commissioner of health to disclose information on the original birth certificate, the commissioner has 6 months to contact the birth parents. The information will be released if, within 31 days of the commissioner's contact, the birth parents file an affidavit of disclosure.
Sect. 259.253: Parties will be informed when parent or child dies or has terminal illness, if the agency is informed of the death or illness.

8. COURT OF JURISDICTION: Probate or Juvenile Courts

9. STATE REUNION REGISTRY: None

10. STATE ARCHIVES:
Minnesota Historical Society
Library and Archives
345 Kellogg Blvd. W.
St. Paul, MN 55102-1906
(651) 296-6126
(651) 296-2143 (research information desk)

11. HOSPITAL RECORDS AVAILABLE: Possibly, through a doctor

12. LEGAL NOTICES REQUIRED: No

13. LAND RECORDS: Available from the county registrar of deeds; tract books are available at the historical society and the courthouse.

14. DEPARTMENT OF MOTOR VEHICLES: Must be 16 years old to get a driver's license. At the present time, transcripts are $4.50. You must have the driver's full name, driver's license number, birth date, and address; provide your daytime phone number. Payment must be in the form of a money order or cashier's check made out to the Driver and Vehicle Services of Minnesota. Mail request to:
Driver and Vehicle Services
Record Requests
Room 108, Transportation Bldg.
395 John Ireland
St. Paul, MN 55155
(651) 296-2023
(651) 296-6911 (automated system)

15. LAWS REGARDING INHERITANCE: Sect. 259.29: "An adoptee shall not inherit from his natural parents or kindred." How-

ever, birth parents or relatives may specifically mention the adoptee in their wills.

16. LAWS REGARDING TELEPHONE RECORDINGS: Sect. 626A.02: A telephone conversation may be recorded by one of the parties to the conversation without the consent of the other party—unless the recording is being made for the purpose of violating a law.

17. PHYSICIAN LICENSING BOARD:

Minnesota Board of Medical Practice
2829 University Avenue SE, Suite 400
St. Paul, MN 55114-1080
(651) 642-0538

18. ATTORNEY LICENSING BOARD:

Minnesota State Bar
514 Nicollete Mall #300
Minneapolis, MN 55402
(612) 333-1183

19. VITAL STATISTICS AGENCY:

Minnesota Department of Health
Birth and Death Records
717 Delaware Street SE
P.O. Box 9441
Minneapolis, MN 55414
(612) 623-5121

RECORD	COST	AVAILABILITY	SOURCE
A. Birth	$14.00	Kept since 1908* Public information	STATE: Above COUNTY: Clerk of District Court
B. Marriage	Index Is Free	Kept since 1853 Public information	STATE: Index only COUNTY: Clerk of District Court***
C. Divorce	Index Is Free	Kept since 1970 Public information	STATE: Index only COUNTY: Clerk of District Court****
D. Death	$11.00	Kept since 1908* Public information	STATE: Above COUNTY: Clerk of District Court

* Earlier records are available from the Clerk of District Court.
*** In county where license was obtained.
**** In county where divorce was filed.

Mississippi

1. CENTRAL INFORMATION AGENCY:

New Capitol Building
P.O. Box 1018
Jackson, MS 39215
(601) 359-1000

2. STATE ADOPTION DEPARTMENT:

Department of Human Services
P.O. Box 352
Jackson, MS 39205
(601) 359-4500
(601) 359-4496 (adoption exchange)

3. ADOPTION RECORDS: Closed

4. YEAR CLOSED: Not known

5. DEGREE OF AVAILABILITY: Court records regarding adoptions are closed upon finalization, and a court order showing good cause must be issued before any information will be released from them. Some agencies will release nonidentifying information to an adult involved party.

6. AGE OF MAJORITY: 21 years old

7. ADOPTION LAWS: Sect. 93-17-25: All proceedings under this chapter shall be confidential and shall be held in closed court without admittance of any person other than the interested parties, except upon order of the court . . . however, officers of the court, including attorneys, shall be given access to such records upon request.
Sect. 93-17-27: Reference to the marital status of birth parents is prohibited.
Sect. 93-17-29: Docket entries shall not contain the names of the birth parents or birth name of the adoptee.
Sect. 93-17-31: "Several chancery clerks shall keep and maintain a docket and minute book of convenient size . . . in which from July 1, 1955, all entries concerning adoptions shall be made." This provision has been interpreted to mean that county adoption records before July 1, 1955, are open. In practice, only some counties have open records.

8. COURT OF JURISDICTION: Chancery Court

9. STATE REUNION REGISTRY: None

10. STATE ARCHIVES:

Department of Archives and History
Archives and History Building
P.O. Box 571
Jackson, MS 39205
(601) 359-6850

11. HOSPITAL RECORDS AVAILABLE: Possibly, through a doctor

12. LEGAL NOTICES REQUIRED: No

13. LAND RECORDS: Available from district or clerk of chancery court

14. DEPARTMENT OF MOTOR VEHICLES: Must be 15 years old to get a driver's license. At the present time, transcripts are $7.00. You must have the driver's full name, and driver's license number and social security number are same. Payment must be in the form of a money order or cashier's check made out to the Mississippi Highway Patrol. Send an SASE.

Mail requests to:

Department of Public Safety
Attn.: Driver's Records
P.O. Box 958
Jackson, MS 39205
(601) 987-1274

15. LAWS REGARDING INHERITANCE: Sect. 93-17-13: Nothing in this chapter shall restrict the right of any person to dispose of property under a last will and testament.

16. LAWS REGARDING TELEPHONE RECORDINGS: 18 U.S.C. 2511 (2)(d): Under federal guidelines, Mississippi residents may legally record their own conversations without obtaining consent from the opposite party.

17. PHYSICIAN LICENSING BOARD:

Mississippi Board of Medicine
2688-D Insurance Center Drive
Jackson, MS 39216
(601) 354-6645

18. ATTORNEY LICENSING BOARD:

Mississippi State Bar
Licensing Dept.
P.O. Box 2168
Jackson, MS 39215-2168
(601) 354-6055; (601) 948-4471

19. VITAL STATISTICS AGENCY:

State Board of Health
Vital Records Registration Unit
P.O. Box 1700
Jackson, MS 39215
(601) 576-7981
(601) 576-7450 (automated system)

RECORD	COST	AVAILABILITY	SOURCE
A. Birth	$12.00	Kept since 1912 Restricted	STATE: Above COUNTY: Circuit Court clerk
B. Marriage	$10.00	Kept since 1926 Restricted	STATE: Above COUNTY: Circuit Court clerk
C. Divorce	$10.00	Kept since 1926 Restricted	STATE: Above COUNTY: Chancery Court
D. Death	$10.00	Kept since 1912 Restricted	STATE: Above COUNTY: Circuit Court clerk

Missouri

1. CENTRAL INFORMATION AGENCY:

State Capitol
Harry S Truman Building
Jefferson City, MO 65101
(573) 751-2000

2. STATE ADOPTION DEPARTMENT:

Division of Family Services
Department of Social Services
P.O. Box 88
Jefferson City, MO 65103
(573) 751-8981; in Missouri: 800-554-2222

3. ADOPTION RECORDS: Closed

4. YEAR CLOSED: 1917

5. DEGREE OF AVAILABILITY: Court records are closed upon finalization, and a court order is required to release any information from them. The child-placing agency or the juvenile court will usually release nonidentifying information to the adoptive parents, legal guardians, and adult adoptees upon written request.
Missouri provides a reunion registry between birth parents and adoptees who have reached age of majority. The registry has made many matches since 1986.

6. AGE OF MAJORITY: 21 years old

7. ADOPTION LAWS: Sect. 453.120: Records of adoption proceedings are not open to inspection except upon order of the court.
Sect. 453.121: Provides for a reunion registry between birth parents and adoptees who have reached the age of majority.

8. COURT OF JURISDICTION: County Circuit Court, Juvenile Division

9. STATE REUNION REGISTRY: Yes; see #20

10. STATE ARCHIVES/RECORDS DEPT.:

Missouri State Archives
600 West Main Street
P.O. Box 778
Jefferson City, MO 65102
(573) 751-3280

11. HOSPITAL RECORDS AVAILABLE: Possibly, through a doctor

12. LEGAL NOTICES REQUIRED: Possibly; Sect. 511.410, 420.

13. LAND RECORDS: Available through the county recorder of deeds

14. DEPARTMENT OF MOTOR VEHICLES: Must be 16 years old to get a driver's license. At the current time, transcripts are $1.50. Must have name, birth date, and social security number. Payment must be in the form of a money order or certified check made out to the Missouri Driver's License Bureau. Mail requests to:

Driver's License Bureau
P.O. Box 200
Jefferson City, MO 65105-0200
(573) 751-4600

15. LAWS REGARDING INHERITANCE: Sect. 453.090: Upon finalization, all legal rights and responsibilities between birth parents and adoptee are severed (does not specify inheritance).

16. LAWS REGARDING TELEPHONE RECORDINGS: Falls under Federal Law 18 U.S.C. 2511 (2)(d): Recording one's own conversation without the consent of the other participant is permissible when it is not done for the purpose of committing a criminal or torturous act.

17. PHYSICIAN LICENSING BOARD:
Missouri Board of Healing Arts
3605 Missouri Blvd.
P.O. Box 4
Jefferson City, MO 65102
(573) 751-0098

18. ATTORNEY LICENSING BOARD:
The Missouri Bar Association
326 Monroe
P.O. Box 119
Jefferson City, MO 65102
(573) 635-4128

19. VITAL STATISTICS AGENCY:
Missouri Department of Public Health
Bureau of Vital Records
P.O. Box 570
930 Wildwood
Jefferson City, MO 65102-0570
Birth: (573) 751-6387
Death: (573) 751-6376
Marriage/Divorce: (573) 751-6400

RECORD	COST	AVAILABILITY	SOURCE
A. Birth	$10.00	Kept since 1910* Restricted	STATE: Above COUNTY: Health department*
B. Marriage	Free**	Kept since 1948 Restricted	STATE: No Records COUNTY: County judge
C. Divorce	Free**	Kept since 1949 Restricted	STATE: Above COUNTY: Circuit Court clerk
D. Death	$10.00	Kept since 1910 Restricted	STATE: Above COUNTY: Health department*

* County records may date back to 1874.
** For a certified statement.

20. STATE REUNION REGISTRY:
Missouri Division of Family Services
Adoption Information Registry
P.O. Box 88
Jefferson City, MO 65103

SUMMARY: The registry accepts applications from adult adoptees age 21 years and over, who were adopted in Missouri, or whose biological parents had their parental rights terminated in Missouri. The registry also processes applications from those biological parents who relinquished a child for adoption in Missouri.
The registration form must be accompanied by a copy of a document confirming the adoptee or biological parents' identity, i.e., birth certificate, marriage certificate, adoption decree.

Montana

1. CENTRAL INFORMATION AGENCY:
Capitol Building
Helena, MT 59601
(406) 444-2511

2. STATE ADOPTION DEPARTMENT:
Department of Family Services
Social Services Bureau-Adoption Division
48 Last Chance Gulch
Helena, MT 59601
(406) 444-5900

3. ADOPTION RECORDS: Closed

4. YEAR CLOSED: 1973

5. DEGREE OF AVAILABILITY: All court records are closed upon finalization, and a court order showing good cause is required to release any information from them. Some agencies will release nonidentifying information to an adult involved party.

6. AGE OF MAJORITY: 18 years old

7. ADOPTION LAWS: Sect. 40-8-126: All court records held on any level are closed and can be opened only with a court order.
Sect. 40-8-122: The medical and social history of the birth parents shall be provided to the adoptive parents.
Sect. 50-15-304: The amended birth certificate must contain the true date and place of birth. Effective 10/97: Adoptees born prior to 1997 (and after 1997) can receive a copy of their original birth certificate without a court order.

8. COURT OF JURISDICTION: District or Tribal Courts

9. STATE REUNION REGISTRY: Yes; see #20

10. STATE ARCHIVES/RECORDS DEPT.:
Montana State Historical Society
Archives Division
225 N. Roberts Street
Helena, MT 59620
(406) 444-2694

11. HOSPITAL RECORDS AVAILABLE: Possibly, through a doctor

12. LEGAL NOTICES REQUIRED: Unknown

13. LAND RECORDS: Available through the county clerk/recorder

14. DEPARTMENT OF MOTOR VEHICLES: Must be 15 years old to get a driver's license. At the current time, transcripts are $4.00. Must have birth date and driver's license number, which will be the same as the person's social security number. Payment must be in the form of a money order or certified check made out to the Driver Services Bureau. Mail requests to:
Motor Vehicles Division, Driver Services
303 North Roberts
Helena, MT 59620-1419
(406) 444-4590

15. LAWS REGARDING INHERITANCE: Sect. 40-8-125: Birth parents shall have no rights over adoptee's property by descent and distribution (no mention of the reverse).

16. LAWS REGARDING TELEPHONE RECORDINGS: Sect. 45-8-213: Telephone recordings are illegal in Montana except to the extent with permission and knowledge of all parties concerned.

17. PHYSICIAN LICENSING BOARD:
Professional and Occupational Licensing Boards
Attn.: Board of Medical Examiners
111 N. Jackson
P.O. Box 200513
Helena, MT 59620-0513
(406) 444-4284
Verbal information is free; there is a $15 fee for written info.

18. ATTORNEY LICENSING BOARD:
State Bar of Montana
Suite 2A, P.O. Box 577
46 Last Chance Gulch
Helena, MT 59624-0577
(406) 442-7660

19. VITAL STATISTICS AGENCY:
Montana Dept. of Public Health and Human Services
Vital Records and Statistics
1400 Broadway
Cogswell Building, Rm. #C118
P.O. Box 4210
Helena, MT 59604
(406) 444-4228

RECORD	COST	AVAILABILITY	SOURCE
A. Birth	$10.00	Kept since 1907 Restricted	STATE: Above COUNTY: County clerk
B. Marriage	$10.00	Kept since 1943* Restricted	STATE: Index Only COUNTY: District Court clerk
C. Divorce	$10.00	Kept since 1943* Restricted	STATE: Index Only COUNTY: District Court clerk
D. Death	$10.00	Kept since 1907 Restricted	STATE: Above COUNTY: County clerk

* For search fee, will tell you county where event took place. Documents are considered "public records with limited conditions."

20. STATE REUNION REGISTRY:
Montana Adoption Resource Center
P.O. Box 634
Helena, MT 59624

COST: $50.00

SUMMARY: The following will be provided to you for your $50.00 fee: a reunion registry form and information regarding this service; affidavit and instructions for obtaining original birth certificate; a list of nationally based adoption search resources (including International Soundex's "Adoption: A Lifelong Process"); a reading materials list; referral to Montana search representatives.

When a match is made between two people from the information in the registry, a staff member reviews the data to confirm a match, and both parties are notified in writing. Contact will then be up to them. Upon request, the agency will provide a list of mental health professionals who attended adoption specific training sponsored by Montana Post-Adoption Center.

This registry does not conduct searches. You must be 18 years old to register.

Nebraska

1. CENTRAL INFORMATION AGENCY:
State Capitol
1445 "K" Street
Lincoln, NE 68509
(402) 471-2311

2. STATE ADOPTION DEPARTMENT:
Dept. of Social Services
Human Service Div.
Adoption Unit
P.O. Box 95044
Lincoln, NE 68509-5026
(402) 471-3121

3. ADOPTION RECORDS: Closed

4. YEAR CLOSED: 1941

5. DEGREE OF AVAILABILITY: Many agencies will release nonidentifying information to an adult involved party. Adoptees 19 to 24 years can request nonidentifying information.

6. AGE OF MAJORITY: 19 years old

7. ADOPTION LAWS: Sect. 43-113: All papers held by the court are sealed upon finalization, and a court order showing good cause is required to open them.
Sect. 43-124: The State Bureau of Vital Statistics provides relative consent forms for the purpose of matching consenting birth parents and adult adoptees over the age of 25.

8. COURT OF JURISDICTION: County Court

9. STATE REUNION REGISTRY: Yes; see #20

10. STATE ARCHIVES/RECORDS DEPT.:
State Historical Society Library
Archives Division
P.O. Box 82554
Lincoln, NE 68501-2554
(402) 471-4751

11. HOSPITAL RECORDS AVAILABLE: Possibly, through a doctor

12. LEGAL NOTICES REQUIRED: No

13. LAND RECORDS: Available through the county registrar of deeds or county clerk

14. DEPARTMENT OF MOTOR VEHICLES: Must be 15 years old to get a driver's license. At the current time, transcripts are $2.00. You will need two of the following three things: name, driver's birth date, and driver's license number. Payment must be in the form of a money order or certified check made out to the Nebraska Department of Motor Vehicles. Mail requests to:
Department of Motor Vehicles
Driver Records Section
P.O. Box 94789
Lincoln, NE 68509
(402) 471-4343

15. LAWS REGARDING INHERITANCE: Sect. 43-106.01: Finalization shall terminate all birth parents' rights upon the child . . . and "nothing contained in this section shall impair the right of such child to inherit."

16. LAWS REGARDING TELEPHONE RECORDINGS: Sect. 86-702(2)(c): At the present time, private parties may legally record their own conversations without obtaining the other party's consent.

17. PHYSICIAN LICENSING BOARD:
Professional and Occupations Licensure Division
301 Centennial Mall S
P.O. Box 95007
Lincoln, NE 68509
(402) 471-2115

18. ATTORNEY LICENSING BOARD:
Nebraska State Bar Association
635 South 14th Street
Lincoln, NE 68508
(402) 475-7091

19. VITAL STATISTICS AGENCY:
State Department of Health
Bureau of Vital Statistics
P.O. Box 95065
Lincoln, NE 68509
(402) 471-2871

RECORD	COST	AVAILABILITY	SOURCE
A. Birth	$10.00	Kept since 1904* Restricted	STATE: Above COUNTY: Unknown
B. Marriage	$9.00	Kept since 1909 Restricted	STATE: Above COUNTY: County Court clerk
C. Divorce	$9.00	Kept since 1909 Restricted	STATE: Above COUNTY: District Court clerk
D. Death	$9.00	Kept since 1904 Restricted	STATE: Above COUNTY: Unknown

* For records prior to 1904, contact the central information agency. Send an SASE with your request.

20. STATE REUNION REGISTRY:
Department of Public Welfare
Division of Social Services
P.O. Box 95044
Lincoln, NE 68509
Attn.: Jerry Dominguez
(402) 471-3121
(402) 471-9254

SUMMARY: Send a letter giving all the information pertaining to your birth and adoption to the above address in care of Jerry Dominguez. In the letter, also give your permission to release information on you for the purpose of reuniting. Upon receipt of your letter they will send you information on their registry.

Nevada

1. CENTRAL INFORMATION AGENCY:
State Capitol
Carson City, NV 89710
(702) 687-5000

2. STATE ADOPTION DEPARTMENT:
Department of Human Resources
Division of Child and Family Services
711 East 5th Street
Capitol Complex
Carson City, NV 89710-1002
(702) 684-4400

3. ADOPTION RECORDS: Closed

4. YEAR CLOSED: Unknown

5. DEGREE OF AVAILABILITY: Court records are closed upon finalization, and a court order is required to release information from them. Nonidentifying information is available to an adult involved party.

6. AGE OF MAJORITY: 18 years old

7. ADOPTION LAWS: Sect. 127.140: No information will be released from the court records except by order of the court.

8. COURT OF JURISDICTION: District Court

9. STATE REUNION REGISTRY: Yes; see #20

10. STATE ARCHIVES/RECORDS DEPT.:
Nevada State Library and Archives
100 Stewart Street
Carson City, NV 89710
(702) 687-5210

11. HOSPITAL RECORDS AVAILABLE: Possibly, through a doctor

12. LEGAL NOTICES REQUIRED: No (contact a local support group)

13. LAND RECORDS: Available through the county recorder

14. DEPARTMENT OF MOTOR VEHICLES: Must be 16 years old to get a driver's license. At the current time, transcripts are $5.00. Must have birth date and driver's license number, which will often be the same as the person's social security number. Payment must be in the form of a money order or certified check made out to the Nevada Department of Motor Vehicles. Mail requests to:
Department of Motor Vehicles
Records Section
555 Wright Way
Carson City, NV 89711-0250
(702) 687-5370

15. LAWS REGARDING INHERITANCE: Sect. 127.160: "The child shall not owe his natural parents, or their relatives any legal duty nor shall he inherit from his natural parent or kindred."

16. LAWS REGARDING TELEPHONE RECORDINGS: Sect. 200-620 (1): At the present time, private parties may legally record their own conversations without obtaining the other party's consent.

17. PHYSICIAN LICENSING BOARD:
Nevada Board of Medical Examiners
P.O. Box 7238
Reno, NV 89510
(702) 688-2559

18. ATTORNEY LICENSING BOARD:
State Bar of Nevada
1325 Airmotive Way, Suite 140
Reno, NV 89502
(702) 329-4100

19. VITAL STATISTICS AGENCY:
Nevada Office of Vital Statistics
505 East King Street,
Carson City, NV 89710
(702) 684-4280
In state: (800) 992-0900

RECORD	COST	AVAILABILITY	SOURCE
A. Birth	$11.00	Kept since 1911 Immediate family	STATE: Above
B. Marriage	$5.00	Kept since 1968 Immediate family	COUNTY: County clerk/recorder Where licensed
C. Divorce	$1/Page	Kept since 1968 Immediate family	COUNTY: County recorder/clerk Where granted
D. Death	$8.00	Kept since 1911 Immediate family	STATE: Above

20. STATE REUNION REGISTRY:
Department of Human Resources
Division of Child and Family Services
711 E. Fifth Street-Capitol Complex
Carson City, NV 89710-1002
(702) 684-4415

COST: No Charge

SUMMARY: You must be 18 years of age or older to register. The state adoption registry will contain the following information about adoptions handled in the state of Nevada: birth parents, or parents who have relinquished their child in Nevada, either to Nevada State Welfare or to a private adoption agency in Nevada; if the adoptive home study was conducted in Nevada; if the adoption was finalized in Nevada.

Complete confidentiality is ensured to those people who do not wish to be contacted by either their birth parents or by the adopted child. Nevada State Welfare will not be involved in the direct contacts unless requested to do so.

The application form must be filled out and notarized to be accepted.

New Hampshire

1. CENTRAL INFORMATION AGENCY:
New Hampshire State House
107 North Main Street
Concord, NH 03301
(603) 271-1110

2. STATE ADOPTION DEPARTMENT:
Dept. of Health and Human Services
Division for Children, Youth & Families
6 Hazen Drive
Concord, NH 03301
(603) 271-4451

3. ADOPTION RECORDS: Closed

4. YEAR CLOSED: 1938

5. DEGREE OF AVAILABILITY: Records are closed upon finalization, and a court order showing good cause is required to release any information from them. Many agencies will release nonidentifying information to an adult involved party. If birth parents sign a release, agencies can then release information without a court order.

6. AGE OF MAJORITY: 18 years old

7. ADOPTION LAWS: Sect. 170-B.19: "All papers and records, including birth certificates, pertaining to the adoption . . . are subject to inspection only upon written consent of the court for good cause shown."
Sect. 170-B.19: Identifying information may be obtained by an adult adoptee over 21 with the consent of the birth parents.

8. COURT OF JURISDICTION: Probate Court

9. STATE REUNION REGISTRY: None

10. STATE ARCHIVES:
New Hampshire State Library
Archives
71 South Fruit Street
Concord, NH 03301
(603) 271-2236

11. HOSPITAL RECORDS AVAILABLE: Possibly, through a doctor

12. LEGAL NOTICES REQUIRED: No

13. LAND RECORDS: Available from the town clerk/registry of deeds

14. DEPARTMENT OF MOTOR VEHICLES: Must be 16 years old to get a driver's license. At the present time, transcripts are $10.00 (noncertified $7.00). Need driver's name and birth date. Payment must be in the form of a money order or cashier's check made out to the State of New Hampshire DMV.

Mail request to:
Department of Motor Vehicles
Attn.: Driving Records
10 Hazen Drive
Concord, NH 03305
(603) 271-2371

15. LAWS REGARDING INHERITANCE: Sect. 20.3: "Upon issuance of the final decree of adoption, the adopted child shall lose all rights of inheritance from his natural parent or parents. . . ."

16. LAWS REGARDING TELEPHONE RECORDINGS: At the present time, New Hampshire residents must inform all parties to a conversation that is being recorded.

17. PHYSICIAN LICENSING BOARD:
New Hampshire Board of Reg. in Medicine
2 Industrial Park Drive, Suite 8
Concord, NH 03301-8520
(603) 273-1203

18. ATTORNEY LICENSING BOARD:
New Hampshire Bar Association
112 Pleasant Street
Concord, NH 03301
(603) 224-6942

19. VITAL STATISTICS AGENCY:
Bureau of Vital Records
6 Hazen Drive
Concord, NH 03301-6527
(603) 271-4654

RECORD	COST	AVAILABILITY	SOURCE
A. Birth	$10.00*	Kept since 1640 Immediate family	STATE: Above COUNTY: Town clerk
B. Marriage	$10.00**	Kept since 1640 Immediate family	STATE: Above COUNTY: Town clerk
C. Divorce	$10.00**	Kept since 1880 Immediate family	STATE: Above COUNTY: Superior County clerk
D. Death	$10.00**	Kept since 1640 Immediate family	STATE: Above COUNTY: Town clerk

* Births before 1900, contact State Archives.
** Marriages, deaths, and divorces before 1900, contact State Archives.

New Jersey

1. CENTRAL INFORMATION AGENCY:
New Jersey State House
Trenton, NJ 08625
(609) 292-2121

2. STATE ADOPTION DEPARTMENT:
State of New Jersey
Division of Youth and Family Services
Adoption Registry
CN 717
Trenton, NJ 08625
(609) 292-8816

3. ADOPTION RECORDS: Closed

4. YEAR CLOSED: 1941: (Adoption records are open if finalized prior to 1940-41.)

5. DEGREE OF AVAILABILITY: Records are sealed upon finalization, and a court order is required to release any information from them. Many agencies will release nonidentifying information to an adult involved party. Depending upon agency policy, some agencies will help with searches and serve as an intermediary when concerned parties are located.

6. AGE OF MAJORITY: 18 years old

7. ADOPTION LAWS: Chapter 367, Section 9:3-52: "All records of proceedings relating to adoption . . . shall be filed under seal by the clerk of the court and shall at no time be open to inspection . . . unless the court is shown 'good cause' and then at that time the records will be made available to the petitioner."
Section 9:3-41-1: Adoptive parents shall be provided with all available information relevant to the adoptee's development, personality, temperament, and birth parents' complete medical histories.

8. COURT OF JURISDICTION: County Surrogate, Superior, or Juvenile Courts

9. STATE REUNION REGISTRY: Yes; see #20

10. STATE ARCHIVES/RECORDS DEPT.:
New Jersey State Library & Archives
2300 Stuyvesant Ave. (Library)
185 W. State Street (Archives)
CN 307
Trenton, NJ 08625
(609) 530-3200

11. HOSPITAL RECORDS AVAILABLE: Yes, through a doctor (contact a local search and support group)

12. LEGAL NOTICES REQUIRED: No

13. LAND RECORDS: Available from the county registrar or county clerk

14. DEPARTMENT OF MOTOR VEHICLES: Must be 17 years old to get a driver's license. A the current time, transcripts are $10.00. Need name, birth date, driver's license number or old address. Payment must be in the form of a money order or certified check made out to the New Jersey Division of Motor Vehicles. Mail requests to:
New Jersey Division of Motor Vehicles
Abstract Request/Data Output
CN 142
Trenton, NJ 08666
(609) 292-6500

15. LAWS REGARDING INHERITANCE: Chapter 367, Section 9:3-50: Unless otherwise provided for in the adoption proceedings, all legal rights and responsibilities are severed upon finalization, including inheritance.

16. LAWS REGARDING TELEPHONE RECORDINGS: Section 2A:156-4(West): At the present time, private parties may legally record their own conversations without obtaining the other party's consent.

17. PHYSICIAN LICENSING BOARD:
New Jersey Board of Medical Examiners
140 E. Front Street
Trenton, NJ 08625
(609) 826-7100

18. ATTORNEY LICENSING BOARD:
New Jersey Board of Bar Examiners
CN 973
Trenton, NJ 08625
(609) 984-7783

19. VITAL STATISTICS AGENCY:
State Department of Health
Bureau of Vital Statistics*
CN 370
Trenton, NJ 08625-0370
(609) 292-4087

RECORD	COST	AVAILABILITY	SOURCE
A. Birth	$4.00	Kept since 1878 Restricted	STATE: Above COUNTY:**
B. Marriage	$4.00	Kept since 1878 Restricted	STATE: Above COUNTY:**
C. Divorce	$10.00	Kept since 1878 Restricted	STATE: Above COUNTY:***
D. Death	$4.00	Kept since 1878 Restricted	STATE: Above COUNTY:**

* Speedy Vital Check, MasterCard, or Visa, $5.00 extra, exact information (609) 633-2860.
** For records between 1848–78, contact: Archives and History Bureau, State Library Div., State Dept. of Education, Trenton, NJ 08625.
*** For divorce records, contact Superior Court: Chancery Div., State House Annex, Rm. 320, Trenton, NJ 08625.

20. STATE REUNION REGISTRY:

State of New Jersey
Adoption Registry
Division of Youth and Family Services
P.O. Box 717
Trenton, NJ 08625
(609) 292-8816

SUMMARY: You have to call (609) 292-8816 and request a form be mailed to you. They will take your name and number and call you back.

Due to a limited staff, they have a four-week backlog to determine if you are on their registry, and a 90-day wait for nonidentifying information.

New Mexico

1. CENTRAL INFORMATION AGENCY:

State Capitol
Santa Fe, NM 87504
(505) 827-4011

2. STATE ADOPTION DEPARTMENT:

Human Services Department
Social Services Division
Adoption Services
Drawer 5160
Santa Fe, NM 87502-5160
(505) 827-8456

3. ADOPTION RECORDS: Closed

4. YEAR CLOSED: 1950

5. DEGREE OF AVAILABILITY: Adoption records are locked upon finalization, and a court order is required to release any information from them. The state adoption department will release nonidentifying information to an adult involved party. Also has confidential intermediary program.

6. AGE OF MAJORITY: 18 years old

7. ADOPTION LAWS: Section 40-7-53: Identifying information may be made available to an adult adoptee or birth parent with the consent of the opposite party. (Contact State Adoption Department.)

8. COURT OF JURISDICTION: District Court

9. STATE REUNION REGISTRY: None

10. STATE ARCHIVES:

New Mexico State Library
Archives Division
4004 Montezuma
Santa Fe, NM 87503
(505) 827-7332

11. HOSPITAL RECORDS AVAILABLE: Possibly, through a doctor

12. LEGAL NOTICES REQUIRED: Yes, but may be in Spanish or in a newspaper in another city

13. LAND RECORDS: Available from county recorder

14. DEPARTMENT OF MOTOR VEHICLES: Must be 15 years old to get a driver's license. At the present time, transcripts are free. You must have the driver's full name and driver's license number. Payment must be in the form of a money order or cashier's check made out to the New Mexico Department of Motor Vehicles. Mail request to:

Department of Motor Vehicles
Joseph Montoya Building
Driver Services
P.O. Box 1028
Santa Fe, NM 87504-1028
(505) 827-2294

15. LAWS REGARDING INHERITANCE: Section 40-7-15: A judgment of adoption severs all legal rights and responsibilities between birth parent(s) and adoptee, including inheritance.

16. LAWS REGARDING TELEPHONE RECORDINGS: Section 30-12-1: At the present time, private parties may legally record their own conversations without obtaining the other party's consent.

17. PHYSICIAN LICENSING BOARD:

N.M. Board of Medical Examiners
491 Old Santa Fe Trail
Lamy Bldg., 2nd Floor
Santa Fe, NM 87501
(505) 827-7317

18. ATTORNEY LICENSING BOARD:

State Bar of New Mexico
121 Tijeras NE, Suite 100
Albuquerque, NM 87125
(505) 842-6132

19. VITAL STATISTICS AGENCY:

Department of Health
Office of Vital Records
P.O. Box 26110
Santa Fe, NM 87502
(505) 827-0121

RECORD	COST	AVAILABILITY	SOURCE
A. Birth	$10.00	Kept since 1920 Immediate family	STATE: Above COUNTY: County health department
B. Marriage	$1.50	Public information	STATE: No records COUNTY: County clerk
C. Divorce	$0.35/page	Public information	STATE: No records COUNTY: District Court clerk
D. Death	$5.00	Kept since 1920 Immediate family	STATE: Above COUNTY: Will request from state

New York (including New York City)

1. CENTRAL INFORMATION AGENCY:

State Capitol
Albany, NY 12224
(518) 474-2121

2. STATE ADOPTION DEPARTMENT:

Department of Social Services
New York State Adoption Services
40 N. Pearl Street
Albany, NY 12243-0001
(518) 474-9600

3. ADOPTION RECORDS: Closed

4. YEAR CLOSED: 1938

5. DEGREE OF AVAILABILITY: The (a) order of adoption, (b) record of all proceedings upon which it is based, and (c) adoption index are kept in the office of the court granting the adoption. Such records are kept under seal and are indexed by the name of the adoptive parents and by the full original name of the child.

In order to obtain access to the sealed records, order of adoption, or index thereof, an order of a judge or surrogate of the court in which the order was made, or of a justice of the supreme court must be obtained. Such orders may be granted only upon a showing of good cause and on due notice to the adoptive parents and birth parents, or a person designated by the court to preserve their rights. Medical information is more freely disclosed than any other information. Court orders opening full records are rarely granted; more often, that portion of the records necessary to the well-being of the adopted person is released, with identifying information concerning the birth parents deleted.

Additionally, nonidentifying information is available from the state in cases in which an adoptee has attained the age of 21. Registration with the Adoption Information Registry is ordinarily required. However, some agencies maintain their own registries and will give such information to adoptive parents upon request, and adoptees who have attained the age of 21, and will charge a fee for searching their records.

For adoptees, the fee for registration with the Adoption Information Registry is $75.00. Agencies ostensibly are permitted to charge an additional $50.00 to search their records, but often they charge more.

6. AGE OF MAJORITY: 18 years old

7. ADOPTION LAWS: New York Domestic Relations Law Section 114: Requires the sealing of the order of adoption, all records of the proceedings and the index of adoptions.

New York Social Services Law Section 373-a: Permits agencies to release to adoptive parents medical and psychological information about the birth parents on behalf of their adoptive child.

Note 1: In private placement adoptions, to obtain medical information about birth parents which may or may not be included in the adoption petition, a court order is required and will be freely given.

Note 2: Hospitals will often release medical information about the birth of the adoptee directly to the adoptee. However, medical records concerning the birth mother are considered confidential and will not be released to the adoptee unless there is an authorization to do so in the birth mother's medical records.

Adoptees are entitled to nonidentifying information about their birth families upon attaining the age of 21. Pursuant to Public Health Law Section 4138-b-d, registries and data collection processes are in place to provide searching adoptees with this information. A verified application must be made in order to secure such data. The state will then communicate with the agency (if any), and the court in which the adoption took place. If it was an agency adoption, nonidentifying information will usually be forwarded by the agency directly to the adoptee. If the adoptee requests that the information come from the state, or if the adoption was a private-placement adoption, the information on file will be forwarded by the state to the adoptee. If there is no nonidentifying information, the state will send none.

In the case of agency adoptions, some agencies may release this information directly to the adoptee without first registering with the Adoption Information Registry. They often charge a fee and/or require the adoptee to come in for counseling first.

New York Public Health Law Section 4138(d): If all required parties have registered with the New York State Adoption Information Registry, identifying information will be given to the adoptee.

8. COURT OF JURISDICTION: Family, Surrogate, or Supreme Courts

9. STATE REUNION REGISTRY: Yes; see #20

10. STATE ARCHIVES/RECORDS DEPT.:

New York State Historical Association
State Archives Division
10D-45 Cultural Education Center
Albany, NY 12230
(518) 237-8643

11. HOSPITAL RECORDS AVAILABLE: Possibly, through a doctor

12. LEGAL NOTICES REQUIRED: Possibly

13. LAND RECORDS: Available from the county clerk
(New York City: through the registrar)

14. DEPARTMENT OF MOTOR VEHICLES: Must be 16 years old to get a driver's license, (in New York City, 17 years old). At the current time, transcripts are $5.00. You must have birth date or driver's license number, and last known address. Payment must be in the form of a money order or certified

check made out to the Commissioner of Motor Vehicles. Mail requests to:

Department of Motor Vehicles
Certified Document Center
Empire State Plaza
Albany, NY 12228
(518) 473-5595

15. LAWS REGARDING INHERITANCE: Domestic Relations Law, Section 117: Adoptees may not inherit from an intestate natural relative.

16. LAWS REGARDING TELEPHONE RECORDINGS: Penal Law, Section 250.00: At the present time, private parties can legally record their own conversations without obtaining the other party's consent.

17. PHYSICIAN LICENSING BOARD:

New York State Department of Education
Division of Professional Licensing Services
3021 Cultural Education Center
Albany, NY 12230
(800) 342-3729
(518) 474-3817

18. ATTORNEY LICENSING BOARD:

New York Bar Association
One Elk Street
Albany, NY 12207
(518) 463-3200

19a. VITAL STATISTICS AGENCY:

State Department of Health
Vital Records Section
Albany, NY 12237-0023
(518) 474-3075
(518) 474-1105 (index assistance)

NEW YORK STATE

RECORD	COST	AVAILABILITY	SOURCE
A. Birth	$15.00*	Kept since 1880 Immediate family	STATE: Above COUNTY: Albany office
B. Marriage	$5.00	Kept since 1880 Immediate family	STATE: Above COUNTY: Albany office
C. Divorce	$15.00	Kept since 1963 Immediate family	STATE: Above COUNTY: Albany office
D. Death	$15.00	Kept since 1880 Immediate family	STATE: Above COUNTY: Albany office

Genealogical copies of records are $11.00

* The state has an "emergency" service. If you have a Visa or MasterCard, the state will forward a certified copy of a record in its possession for $30.50. The record will be mailed FedEx. There are special telephone numbers: (518) 474-3038 or (518) 474-3077 to call for this service.

19b. VITAL STATISTICS AGENCY:

Department of Health of New York
Bureau of Vital Records & Statistics
125 Worth St.
Room 133
New York, NY 10013
(212) 788-4500 (birth records)

NEW YORK CITY

RECORD	COST	AVAILABILITY	SOURCE
A. Birth	$15.00***	Kept since 1898 Immediate family	STATE: * CITY: City clerk's office in borough
B. Marriage	$10.00**	Kept since 1866 Immediate family	STATE: * CITY: City clerk's office in borough of occurrence
C. Divorce	$15.00	Kept since 1963 Immediate family	STATE: * CITY: City clerk's office in borough of occurrence
D. Death	$15.00***	Kept since 1920** Immediate family	STATE: * CITY: City clerk's office in borough of occurrence

* Dept. of Health of New York City
Bureau of Records & Statistics
125 Worth Street
New York, NY 10013

** Death records for 1865-1919
Marriage records for 1847-65:
Dept. of Records and Inf. Svcs.
Archives Div.,
31 Chambers St.
New York, NY 10007
(212) 566-5292

*** For Visa/MC service:
(212) 962-6105.
An additional $5 will be charged.
Inf. about death records: (212) 566-8197; marriages: (212) 669-8090

20. STATE REUNION REGISTRY:

New York State Health Department
Adoption Information Registry, 2nd Floor
733 Broadway
Albany, NY 12237-0023

COST: Adopted Person $75
Adoptive Parents $20 each
Biological Parents $20 each

Authorized agencies may require an additional fee up to $50 to search their records for the registry (you will be notified if an agency fee is needed).

SUMMARY: It must be clear whether the individual filing is an adopted person, an adoptive parent, or a biological parent. No registration may be accepted from anyone unless the adopted person is at least 21 years of age.

If identifying information is requested about an adoption that took place before 4/1/84, and one or both of the adop-

tive parents is dead, the adopted person must submit a certified copy of the death certificate. The form must be signed in the presence of a notary public. Print "CONFIDENTIAL" on the envelope in which the form is returned.
The time needed to process each application varies according to what has happened since the adoption. Several agencies, including vital records offices, the court of adoption, and one or more adoption agencies, must search their records. It will take about six months to obtain nonidentifying information. Identifying information cannot be released until all necessary parties to the adoption have registered and consented to the release of the information. This can take years, or may never take place at all.

North Carolina

1. CENTRAL INFORMATION AGENCY:
   State Capitol
   Raleigh, NC 27611
   (919) 733-4240

2. STATE ADOPTION DEPARTMENT:
   Dept. of Human Resources
   Adoption Department
   Division of Social Services
   325 North Salisbury
   Raleigh, NC 27603
   (919) 733-3801

3. ADOPTION RECORDS: Closed

4. YEAR CLOSED: 1938

5. DEGREE OF AVAILABILITY: Court records are closed upon finalization, and a court order is required to release any information from them. All agencies will release nonidentifying information to an adult adoptee. Birth parents are not entitled to any nonidentifying information.

6. AGE OF MAJORITY: 18 years old; however, must be 21 to receive nonidentifying information

7. ADOPTION LAWS: Section 48-26: "Any necessary information . . . of an adoption proceeding may be disclosed upon written motion in cause before the clerk of original jurisdiction . . . when good cause is shown."
   Section 48-25: "Nonidentifying information about birth family may be released to an adoptee over the age of 21."

8. COURT OF JURISDICTION: Superior Court

9. STATE REUNION REGISTRY: None

10. STATE ARCHIVES:
    Department of Cultural Resources
    Archives and Records Section
    109 East Jones Street
    Raleigh, NC 27601-2807
    (919) 733-3952

11. HOSPITAL RECORDS AVAILABLE: Possibly, through a doctor

12. LEGAL NOTICES REQUIRED: Unknown

13. LAND RECORDS: Available from county registrar of deeds

14. DEPARTMENT OF MOTOR VEHICLES: Must be 16 years old to get a driver's license. At the present time, transcripts are $7.00. You must have the driver's full name and birth date; having the driver's license number will help, but is not necessary. Payment must be in the form of a money order or cashier's check made out to the North Carolina Department of Transportation. To receive information on accidents, you must have driver's written permission. Mail request to:
    Department of Transportation
    Division of Motor Vehicles
    Motor Vehicle Building
    1100 New Bern Avenue
    Raleigh, NC 27697
    (919) 733-2403

15. LAWS REGARDING INHERITANCE: Section 48-23: "The natural parents of the person adopted, if living, shall, from and after the entry of the final order of adoption, be relieved of all legal duties and obligations due from them to the person adopted. . . ." (Does not specify inheritance.)

16. LAWS REGARDING TELEPHONE RECORDINGS: Falls under Federal Law 18 U.S.C. 2511 (2)(d): Recording one's own conversation without the consent of the other participant is permissible when it is not done for the purpose of committing a criminal or tortuous act.

17. PHYSICIAN LICENSING BOARD:
    North Carolina Board of Medical Examiners
    P.O. Box 20007
    Raleigh, NC 27619
    (919) 828-1212

18. ATTORNEY LICENSING BOARD:
    North Carolina State Bar
    208 Fayetteville St. Mall
    P.O. Box 27601
    Raleigh, NC 25908
    (919) 828-4620

19. VITAL STATISTICS AGENCY:
    Department of Human Resources
    Division of Health Services—Vital Records Section
    P.O. Box 29537
    225 N. McDowell Street
    Raleigh, NC 27626-0537
    (919) 733-3526

RECORD	COST	AVAILABILITY	SOURCE
A. Birth	$10.00	Kept since 1913 Public information	STATE: Above COUNTY: *
B. Marriage	$10.00	Kept since 1962 Public information	STATE: No records COUNTY: Deeds registrar
C. Divorce	$10.00	Kept since 1958 Public information	STATE: No records COUNTY: Superior Court clerk
D. Death	$10.00	Kept since 1930 Public information	STATE: Above COUNTY: Deeds registrar

* Amended certificates kept only

Registrar on state level after 1948

North Dakota

1. CENTRAL INFORMATION AGENCY:
   State Capitol
   Bismarck, ND 58505
   (701) 328-2000

2. STATE ADOPTION DEPARTMENT:
   Children and Family Services
   Judicial Wing
   600 East Boulevard
   Bismarck, ND 58505-0250
   (701) 328-2316 (main line);
   in state (800) 245-3736

3. ADOPTION RECORDS: Closed

4. YEAR CLOSED: unknown

5. DEGREE OF AVAILABILITY: Court records are closed upon finalization, but special provisions exist for disclosing information (see adoption laws). Almost all agencies will release nonidentifying information to an adult involved party, although some may charge a fee for this service.

6. AGE OF MAJORITY: 21 years old

7. ADOPTION LAWS: Sect. 14,15,16: Nonidentifying information about the birth parents shall be provided to the adoptive parents and adoptees who are 21 or older.

8. COURT OF JURISDICTION: District or Probate Courts

9. STATE REUNION REGISTRY: No

10. STATE ARCHIVES/RECORDS DEPT.:
    State Historical Society of North Dakota
    Archives Division
    612 East Boulevard Ave.
    Bismarck, ND 58505
    (701) 328-2666

11. HOSPITAL RECORDS AVAILABLE: Possibly, through a doctor

12. LEGAL NOTICES REQUIRED: Unknown

13. LAND RECORDS: Available from county registrar of deeds

14. DEPARTMENT OF MOTOR VEHICLES: Must be 16 years old to get a driver's license. At the current time, transcripts are $3.00. You must have driver's full name and birth date. It helps to have the driver's license number also (but isn't necessary). Payment must be in the form of a money order or certified check made out to the North Dakota Driver's License Division. Mail requests to:
    Driver's License Division
    608 E. Blvd. Ave.
    Bismarck, ND 58505-0700
    (701) 328-2603

15. LAWS REGARDING INHERITANCE: Section 14-15-14: The petition and adoption decree terminate all legal rights and responsibilities between the adoptee and birth parents, including inheritance.

16. LAWS REGARDING TELEPHONE RECORDINGS: Section 12.1-15-02(3)(c): At the present time, private parties may legally record their own conversations without obtaining the other party's consent.

17. PHYSICIAN LICENSING BOARD:
    North Dakota Board of Medical Examiners
    418 East Broadway Avenue, Suite 12
    Bismarck, ND 58501
    (701) 328-6500

18. ATTORNEY LICENSING BOARD:
    North Dakota State Bar Association
    Judicial Wing
    600 E. Blvd., 1st floor
    Bismarck, ND 58505-0530
    (701) 224-4201

19. VITAL STATISTICS AGENCY:
    State Capitol
    Division of Vital Records
    600 East Boulevard Avenue
    Bismarck, ND 58505-0200
    (701) 328-2360

RECORD	COST	AVAILABILITY	SOURCE
A. Birth	$7.00	Kept since 1899 Public information*	STATE: Above COUNTY: Unknown
B. Marriage	$5.00	Kept since 1925 Public information	STATE: Above COUNTY: County judge
C. Divorce	Unknown	Kept since 1949 Restricted	STATE: None COUNTY: District Court clerk
D. Death	$5.00	Kept since 1893 Public information*	STATE: Above COUNTY: Unknown

* Birth records are public information as long as birth was legitimate; death records are public, but copies showing cause of death are available to immediate family only.

Ohio

1. CENTRAL INFORMATION AGENCY:
   Ohio State House
   Broad and High Streets
   Columbus, OH 43215
   (614) 466-2000

2. STATE ADOPTION DEPARTMENT:
   Ohio Department of Human Services
   Bureau of Family Services—Adoptions
   65 East State Street, 5th floor
   Columbus, OH 43215
   (614) 466-9274

3. ADOPTION RECORDS: Closed

4. YEAR CLOSED: 1964

5. DEGREE OF AVAILABILITY: Court records are closed upon finalization, and a court order is required to release any information from them. Most agencies will release nonidentifying information to an adult involved party, although some may charge a fee for this service. Court permission is required under Ohio Administration Code 5101; 2-48-29.

6. AGE OF MAJORITY: 18 years old

7. ADOPTION LAWS: Section 3107.12-17: The history of the birth family can be inspected by the adoptive parents or an adult adoptee as the court so orders. Adoptive parents may request that the birth parents undergo a physical examination (only for adoptions finalized after August 1978).
   Section 3107.39: Identifying information about birth parents and siblings will be released to an adult adoptee with their consent. An adoptee must petition the probate court for access to the registry. Fee $50.00.

8. COURT OF JURISDICTION: Probate Court

9. STATE REUNION REGISTRY: Yes; see #20

10. STATE ARCHIVES/RECORDS DEPT.:
    Ohio Historical Society
    Archives Division
    1982 Velma Avenue
    Columbus, OH 43211-2497
    (614) 297-2500

11. HOSPITAL RECORDS AVAILABLE: Possibly; tax-supported hospitals must supply admission records—O.R.C.—149)

12. LEGAL NOTICES REQUIRED: Possibly; contact local search and support group for more information

13. LAND RECORDS: Available from the county recorder or Ohio State auditor's office

14. DEPARTMENT OF MOTOR VEHICLES: Must be 16 years old to get a driver's license. At the current time, transcripts are $2.00. Must have name, birth date, and driver's license and social security numbers. Payment must be in the form of a money order or certified check made out to the Treasurer, State of Ohio. Mail requests to:
    Bureau of Motor Vehicles
    4300 Kimberly Pkwy.
    P.O. Box 16520
    Columbus, OH 43232
    (614) 752-7600

15. LAWS REGARDING INHERITANCE: Section 3107.15: Upon finalization, the adoptee "is a stranger to his former relatives for all purposes including inheritance. . . ."

16. LAWS REGARDING TELEPHONE RECORDINGS: Section 2933.52(b)(4): At the present time, private parties may legally record their own conversations without obtaining the other party's consent.

17. PHYSICIAN LICENSING BOARD:
    State Medical Board of Ohio, Records Division
    77 South High Street, 17th floor
    Columbus, OH 43266-0315
    (614) 466-2932

18. ATTORNEY LICENSING BOARD:
    Supreme Court of Ohio
    Office of Attorney Reg.
    30 East Broad Street
    Columbus, OH 43266-0419
    (614) 466-1553

19. VITAL STATISTICS AGENCY:
    Ohio Department of Health Division of Vital Statistics
    P.O. Box 15098
    Columbus, OH 43215-0098
    (614) 466-2531

RECORD	COST	AVAILABILITY	SOURCE
A. Birth	$7.00**	Kept since 1908*** Public information	STATE: Above COUNTY: Probate Court
B. Marriage	Unknown	Kept since 1949*** Public information	STATE: None COUNTY: Probate judge
C. Divorce	Unknown*	Kept since 1949*** Public information	STATE: None COUNTY: Probate judge
D. Death	$7.00**	Kept since 1908*** Public information	STATE: Above COUNTY: Probate Court

* Index only. Will refer to county for actual record.
** For certified copies. Noncertified copies cost $1.10
*** State has births only from 1945; marriages from 1949; divorces from 1949; and deaths from 1945. Any event prior to these dates is now in the State Archives.

20. STATE REUNION REGISTRY:
Ohio Department of Health
Division of Vital Statistics
P.O. Box 15098
Columbus, OH 43215-0098
(614) 466-2531
(614) 466-5635

COST: $50.00

SUMMARY: You must write a letter requesting a form be sent to you for the purpose of registering. In the letter, state all the information you have concerning the birth and adoption. Upon receipt of your letter, you will receive the proper form and information about the registry.

Oklahoma

1. CENTRAL INFORMATION AGENCY:
Oklahoma State Capitol
2302 Lincoln Blvd.
Oklahoma City, OK 73105
(405) 521-2011

2. STATE ADOPTION DEPARTMENT:
Department of Human Services
Division of Child Welfare
P.O. Box 25352
Oklahoma City, OK 73125
(405) 521-2475

3. ADOPTION RECORDS: Closed

4. YEAR CLOSED: 1953

5. DEGREE OF AVAILABILITY: Court records are closed upon finalization. A court order is required to release any information from them. Almost all agencies will release non-identifying information to an adult involved party.

6. AGE OF MAJORITY: 18 years old

7. ADOPTION LAWS: Section 60.17: All papers and records pertaining to the adoption process are withheld from public inspection except upon an order from the court showing good cause.
Section 60.5A: The court may order a complete medical history of the adoptee, birth parents, and birth grandparents to be filed with the adoption petition.
Section 60.18: Persons searching in this state should be aware that the name of the attending physician and the hospital can be altered on the amended birth certificate.

8. COURT OF JURISDICTION: District Court where the adoptive family resides

9. STATE REUNION REGISTRY: Yes; see #20

10. STATE ARCHIVES/RECORDS DEPT.:
Oklahoma Historical Society
Attn.: Archives Division
200 N.E. 18th Street
Oklahoma City, OK 73105
(405) 521-2502

11. HOSPITAL RECORDS AVAILABLE: Possibly, through a doctor

12. LEGAL NOTICES REQUIRED: Yes

13. LAND RECORDS: Available from the county recorder of deeds

14. DEPARTMENT OF MOTOR VEHICLES: Must be 16 years old to get a driver's license. At the current time, transcripts are $10.00. Must have name and birth date, or must have driver's license number, which is the same as the person's social security number. Payment must be in the form of a money order or certified check made out to the Oklahoma Department of Public Safety. Mail requests to:
Department of Public Safety
Driver Records Service
P.O. Box 11415
Oklahoma City, OK 73136
(405) 425-2026

15. LAWS REGARDING INHERITANCE: Section 60.16: "Upon finalization, the birth parent shall be relieved of all parental responsibilities for such child and have no rights over such adopted child or to his property by descent and distribution. . . ." However, the adoptee retains the right to inheritance.

16. LAWS REGARDING TELEPHONE RECORDINGS: Section 176.4(5): At the present time, private parties may legally record their own conversations without obtaining the other party's consent.

17. PHYSICIAN LICENSING BOARD:
Oklahoma Board of Medical Licensing and Supervision
P.O. Box 18256
Oklahoma City, OK 73154
(405) 848-6841

18. ATTORNEY LICENSING BOARD:
Oklahoma Bar Association
P.O. Box 53036
Oklahoma City, OK 73152
(405) 524-2365

19. VITAL STATISTICS AGENCY:
Oklahoma Department of Health
Vital Records Section
P.O. Box 53551
Oklahoma City, OK 73152
(405) 271-4040

RECORD	COST	AVAILABILITY	SOURCE
A. Birth	$5.00	Kept since 1908 Immediate family	STATE: Above COUNTY: Court clerk
B. Marriage	$5.00	Unknown Genealogical reasons	STATE: No records COUNTY: Court clerk
C. Divorce	$5.00	Unknown Genealogical reasons	STATE: No records COUNTY: Court clerk
D. Death	$10.00	Kept since 1908 Genealogical reasons*	STATE: Above COUNTY: Court clerk

* A death certificate will be made available to anyone who can provide the facts about the death correctly.

20. STATE REUNION REGISTRY:

Department of Human Services
Adoption Section
P.O. Box 25352
Oklahoma City, OK 73125
(405) 521-2475

COST: None

SUMMARY: The registry is only for adoptions handled by the Department of Human Services. It is open to adult adoptees 18 years of age or older, or birth parents, siblings, aunts, uncles, and grandparents of adoptees.

The registry does not conduct searches if family members have not registered.

To register, write a letter to the Department of Human Services stating your wish to be on the Voluntary Adoption Reunion Registry. Include your name, address, phone number, and birth data. If you are an adoptee, you need the first and last names of your adoptive parents and the date your adoption was finalized. Please specify the persons you wish to contact. If you move, it is essential that you notify the registry of your new address and phone number so that you can be notified if a relative contacts the Department of Human Services.

Oregon

1. CENTRAL INFORMATION AGENCY:

Oregon State Capitol
Salem, OR 97310

2. STATE ADOPTION DEPARTMENT:

Department of Human Resources
Children Services Division
Adoption Services
500 Summer Street NE, 2nd Floor
Salem, OR 97310-1017
(503) 945-5914

3. ADOPTION RECORDS: Closed

4. YEAR CLOSED: 1957

5. DEGREE OF AVAILABILITY: Court records are sealed upon finalization, and a court order is required to release any information from them. Many agencies will release nonidentifying information to an adult involved party, although some may charge a fee for this service.

Searchers should be aware of ORS code 109.340 Section 3, which states: "Nothing herein contained shall prevent the clerk from certifying copies of the decree of adoption to the petitioners in such proceeding or their attorney."

6. AGE OF MAJORITY: 18 years old

7. ADOPTION LAWS: Section 109.430: Nonidentifying and identifying information shall be made available in a Voluntary Adoption Registry for birth parents, adult adoptees, adult birth siblings, and adoptive parents of a deceased adoptee.

Section 109.340, Sect. 3: Upon finalization, all records, papers, and files relating to the adoption shall be sealed. These documents shall not be inspected by anyone except under order of a court of competent jurisdiction.

8. COURT OF JURISDICTION: Circuit or District Courts

9. STATE REUNION REGISTRY: Yes; see #20

10. STATE ARCHIVES/RECORDS DEPT.:

Oregon State Library
Archives Division
800 Summer Street NE
Salem, OR 97310
(503) 373-0701

11. HOSPITAL RECORDS AVAILABLE: Possibly, through a doctor

12. LEGAL NOTICES REQUIRED: Yes; check with local search and support group

13. LAND RECORDS: Available from the county clerk

14. DEPARTMENT OF MOTOR VEHICLES: Must be 16 years old to get a driver's license. At the current time, transcripts are $2.00. Must have birth date and driver's license number. Payment must be in the form of a money order or certified check made out to the Oregon Department of Transportation. Mail requests to:

Department of Transportation
Motor Vehicles Division
1905 Lana Avenue NE
Salem, OR 97314
(503) 945-5000

15. LAWS REGARDING INHERITANCE: Section 109.041: The adoptee's "natural parents, their descendants and kindred shall be the same to all legal intents and purposes after the entry of such decree as if the adopted person had been born in lawful wedlock to his adoptive parents and had not been born to his natural parents." (Does not specify inheritance)

16. LAWS REGARDING TELEPHONE RECORDINGS: Section 165.540(1)(c): Both parties to a conversation must be aware that it is being recorded to be legal.

17. PHYSICIAN LICENSING BOARD:
Oregon Medical Examiner Board
620 Crown Plaza
1500 SW 1st Ave.
Portland, OR 97201
(503) 229-5770

18. ATTORNEY LICENSING BOARD:
Oregon State Bar Association
5200 SW Meadows Road
P.O. Box 1689
Lake Oswego, OR 97035-0889
(503) 620-0222

19. VITAL STATISTICS AGENCY:
Department of Vital Statistics
Oregon Health Division
P.O. Box 14050
Portland, OR 97214
(503) 731-4108 (for additional information)*
(503) 731-4095 (recording)

* For a $10.00 fee, telephone orders will be charged to Visa or MasterCard.

RECORD	COST	AVAILABILITY	SOURCE
A. Birth	$15.00**	Kept since 1903 Immediate family	STATE: Above COUNTY: County clerk
B. Marriage	$15.00	Kept since 1907 Immediate family	STATE: Above COUNTY: County clerk
C. Divorce	$15.00	Kept since 1925 Immediate family	STATE: Above COUNTY: District Court clerk
D. Death	$15.00	Kept since 1903 Immediate family	STATE: Above COUNTY: County clerk

** You must have the name, date of birth, mother and father's names, and mother's maiden name. Credit card and fax service available at (503) 234-8417.

20. STATE REUNION REGISTRY:
Children's Services Division
Attn: Adoption Registry
500 Summer Street NE, 2nd Floor
Salem, OR 97310-1017
(503) 945-5914

COST: $25.00 for identifying information
$45.00 for nonidentifying information
$400.00 for search

SUMMARY: Agency provides identifying information and nonidentifying information. People who qualify for identifying information: birth parents; adult adoptee 18 or over; adult genetic sibling of adoptee; adoptive parents of a deceased adoptee; adult sibling of deceased birth parent of adoptee. If adoptee of deceased birth parents is deceased, a copy of the death certificate must be provided. In approximately six weeks you will be notified of your qualification to receive identifying information and whether or not a match has occurred.

When there is a match, you will be notified by the Children's Services Division. Counseling may be necessary prior to the release of information.

To register to receive identifying information, return the Affidavit for Identifying Information form, completed and notarized, a copy of your birth certificate, and a check or money order payable to Children's Services Division.

To register to receive nonidentifying information, you must be: a birth parent of the adoptee; adoptee over age 18; adoptive parents or guardians of adoptee; and if adoptee is deceased, the adoptee's spouse, if the spouse is birth parent to the adoptee's children or the guardian of any child of the adoptee or any child of the adoptee who is over age 18. (Siblings are not eligible for nonidentifying information.)

To register to receive nonidentifying information, return the request form completed and signed with a check or money order payable to Children's Services Division in the amount of $45.00.

Due to the number of requests, it may take up to two months to process the affidavits for identifying information and nonidentifying information forms.

Pennsylvania

1. CENTRAL INFORMATION AGENCY:
Main Capitol Building
Harrisburg, PA 17125
(717) 787-2121

2. STATE ADOPTION DEPARTMENT:
Office of Children, Youth and Families
Pennsylvania Adoption Exchange
P.O. Box 2675
Lanco Lodge, 2nd floor
Harrisburg, PA 17105-2675
(717) 257-7015
1-(800) 227-0225

3. ADOPTION RECORDS: Closed

4. YEAR CLOSED: Not known

5. DEGREE OF AVAILABILITY: Court records are closed upon finalization, and a court order is required to release any information from them. Many agencies will release nonidentifying information to an adult involved party. If no agency was involved, a court order must be obtained for nonidentifying information. The court will then turn this information over to a designated agent (adoption department).

6. AGE OF MAJORITY: 18 years old

7. ADOPTION LAWS: Section 2905: (identifying information) The court may contact birth parents and inform them of an adult adoptee's or adoptive parent's petition to gain access

to identity of birth parents. If they consent, this information will be released.
Section 2533: Birth parent's and adoptee's medical histories must be obtained for the adoption petition.
Section 2909: The medical histories shall be delivered by the attending physician or birth parents to an intermediary for adoption records. Any identifying information shall be removed.
Section 21-1-50: Agencies have the right to destroy all records 50 years from the date of placement.

8. COURT OF JURISDICTION: Court of Common Pleas

9. STATE REUNION REGISTRY: Yes; see #20

10. STATE ARCHIVES/RECORDS DEPT.:
Pennsylvania State Library
P.O. Box 1026
Harrisburg, PA 17108-1026
(717) 787-8007

11. HOSPITAL RECORDS AVAILABLE: Possibly, through doctor if original name is known

12. LEGAL NOTICES REQUIRED: Yes

13. LAND RECORDS: Available from the county recorder of deeds

14. DEPARTMENT OF MOTOR VEHICLES: Must be 16 years old to get a driver's license. At the current time, transcripts are $5.00. Must have name and birth date and driver's license numbers. Need driver's written permission to run records. Payment must be in the form of a money order or certified check made out to the Pennsylvania Department of Transportation. Mail requests to:
Department of Transportation
Bureau of Accident Analysis
Operations Information Section
Transportation and Safety Building
P.O. Box 68691
Harrisburg, PA 17106-8691
(717) 391-6190

15. LAWS REGARDING INHERITANCE: Section 23.321: "A decree terminating all rights and duties of a parent entered by a court of competent jurisdiction shall extinguish the power or the right of such parent to receive notice of adoption proceedings." When the adoption is finalized, all birth parents' rights are terminated.

16. LAWS REGARDING TELEPHONE RECORDINGS: Title 18, Section 5704(4): All parties to a conversation must be aware that it is being recorded.

17. PHYSICIAN LICENSING BOARD:
Pennsylvania State Board of Medicine
P.O. Box 2649
Harrisburg, PA 17105
(717) 783-1400

18. ATTORNEY LICENSING BOARD:
Pennsylvania Bar Association
P.O. Box 186
100 South Street
Harrisburg, PA 17108
(717) 238-6715

19. VITAL STATISTICS AGENCY:
State Department of Health
Division of Vital Statistics

For non-USPS mailings:
101 South Mercer
New Castle, PA 16101

For USPS:
P.O. Box 1528
New Castle, PA 16103
(412) 656-3126

RECORD	COST	AVAILABILITY	SOURCE
A. Birth	$4.00	Kept since 1893–1906* Immediate family	STATE: Above COUNTY: Unknown
B. Marriage	$3.00	Kept since 1885 Public information	STATE: Above COUNTY: Marriage license clerk
C. Divorce	$3.00	Kept since 1946 Public information	STATE: Above COUNTY: Prothonotary at the courthouse
D. Death	$3.00	Kept since 1906** Immediate family	STATE: Above COUNTY: Unknown

* After 1906, information is restricted.
** Must have exact date of death; multiyear death procedure additional $20 for each decade. Enclose SASE with request.

"Emergency" credit card service available.

20. STATE REUNION REGISTRY:
State Department of Vital Statistics
P.O. Box 1528
New Castle, PA 16103
(412) 656-3126
Attn.: Adoption Registry
Medical History Registry
(800) 227-0225

COST: There is no fee.
SUMMARY: Adult adoptees at least 18 years of age or older must write a letter giving their address, phone number, date of birth, adoptive parents' first and last names, and any other information they feel would be beneficial. In the letter, also inquire if the birth parents have registered.
Birth parents: Write a letter giving all vital information, i.e., name, address, phone number, date of birth, and name at time of birth. In the letter, also inquire if the adoptee has registered. Technically, only the birth parent can register with the state.

The registry handles only adoptions that took place through the Department of Public Welfare Office of Children, Youth, and Families.

Puerto Rico

1. ADDRESS REQUESTS FOR VITAL RECORDS TO:
   Puerto Rico Dept. of Health
   Demographic Registry
   P.O. Box 9342
   San Juan, Puerto Rico 00908
   (809) 728-7980

2. COST:
   Certified Birth Certificate $4
   Certified Marriage Certificate $4
   Certified Death Certificate $4

3. COMMENTS: Records date back as far as June 1931.

Rhode Island

1. CENTRAL INFORMATION AGENCY:
   Rhode Island State House
   82 Smith Street
   Providence, RI 02903
   (401) 277-2080

2. STATE ADOPTION DEPARTMENT:
   Dept. of Children, Youth and Families
   610 Mt. Pleasant Avenue
   Providence, RI 02908-1935
   (401) 457-5306
   (401) 277-3352 (adoption registry)
   Registry Address: 1 Dorrance Plaza
   Providence, RI 02903

3. ADOPTION RECORDS: Closed

4. YEAR CLOSED: Prior to 1930

5. DEGREE OF AVAILABILITY: Court records regarding any adoption proceeding are closed unless upon court order. Many agencies will release nonidentifying information to an adult involved party.

6. AGE OF MAJORITY: 18 years old

7. ADOPTION LAWS: Section 14-1-5: All records "concerning the adoption of children, together with stenographic notes and transcripts of said hearings, shall not be available for public inspection unless the court shall otherwise order."

8. COURT OF JURISDICTION: Family Court

9. STATE REUNION REGISTRY: Yes; see #20

10. STATE ARCHIVES:
    Rhode Island State Library
    Archives Division: State House
    337 Westminster
    Providence, RI 02903
    (401) 277-2353

11. HOSPITAL RECORDS AVAILABLE: Possibly, through a doctor

12. LEGAL NOTICES REQUIRED: No

13. LAND RECORDS: Available from town or city clerks
In Providence: recorder of deeds

14. DEPARTMENT OF MOTOR VEHICLES: Must be 16 years old to get a driver's license. At the present time, transcripts are $16.00. You must have the driver's full name, birth date, and address. Include driver's license number (if you have it). Payment must be in the form of a money order or cashier's check made out to Operator Control. Mail request to:
    Department of Transportation
    Division of Motor Vehicles
    345 Harris Avenue
    Providence, RI 02909
    (401) 277-2994

15. LAWS REGARDING INHERITANCE: Section 15-7-17: "The petition for adoption will not deprive an adopted child of the right to inherit from and through his natural parents in the same manner as all other natural children; provided, however, that the right to inherit from and through natural parents of an adopted child born out of wedlock shall be provided in ss. 33-1-8. . . ."

16. LAWS REGARDING TELEPHONE RECORDINGS: Section 11-35-21(c)(2): At the present time, private parties may legally record their own conversations without obtaining the other party's consent.

17. PHYSICIAN LICENSING BOARD:
    Division of Professional Regulation
    3 Capitol Hill, Room 104
    Providence, RI 02908-5097
    (401) 277-2827

18. ATTORNEY LICENSING BOARD:
    Rhode Island State Bar Association
    115 Cedar Street
    Providence, RI 02903
    (401) 421-5740

19. VITAL STATISTICS AGENCY:
    State Department of Health
    Division of Vital Statistics
    Canon Bldg. 3, Room 101
    Capitol Hill
    Providence, RI 02908-5097
    (401) 277-2812

RECORD	COST	AVAILABILITY	SOURCE
A. Birth	$15.00*	Kept since 1853 Genealogical reasons	STATE: Above COUNTY: Town clerk
B. Marriage	$15.00*	Kept since 1853 Genealogical reasons	STATE: Above COUNTY: Town clerk
C. Divorce	$15.00*	Kept since 1962 Genealogical reasons	STATE: None COUNTY: Family Court clerk
D. Death	$15.00*	Kept since 1853** Genealogical reasons	STATE: Above COUNTY: Town clerk

* $10.00 fee first two years, $0.25 for additional years.
** Death records available from this office from 1945 to present.
Add a $5.00 fee for priority service; make checks or money orders payable to General Treasury.

20. STATE REUNION REGISTRY:
Rhode Island Adoption Registry
c/o R.I. Family Court
J. J. Garrihy Complex
1 Durrance Place
Providence, RI 02908
(401) 277-3352
COST: $25.00 registration fee
SUMMARY: This is a passive registry (adoptive parents cannot file a denial but can have their objections heard).

South Carolina

1. CENTRAL INFORMATION AGENCY:
South Carolina State House
Columbia, SC 29211
(803) 898-7561

2. STATE ADOPTION DEPARTMENT:
South Carolina Department of Social Services
Adoption and Birth Parents Services
P.O. Box 1520
Columbia, SC 29202-1520
(803) 734-6095

3. ADOPTION RECORDS: Closed

4. YEAR CLOSED: 1963

5. DEGREE OF AVAILABILITY: Records are sealed upon finalization, and a court order is required to release information from them. Many agencies will release nonidentifying information to an adult involved party.

6. AGE OF MAJORITY: 18 years old

7. ADOPTION LAWS: Section 20-7-1780: Nonidentifying information shall be made available to adoptive parents, biological parents, and adult adoptees about each other, at the discretion of the chief executive officer of the agency. Identifying information shall be made available to adoptees 21 and over and their birth siblings through the filing of correspondence affidavits of consent.
Section 20-7-1740: Birth parents shall provide medical history of the biological family of the adoptee.

8. COURT OF JURISDICTION: In Denver: Juvenile Court
All others: District Court

9. STATE REUNION REGISTRY: Yes; see #20

10. STATE ARCHIVES/RECORDS DEPT.:
South Carolina State Library
Department of Archives and History
1430 Senate Street
P.O. Box 11669
Columbia, SC 29211
(803) 734-8596

11. HOSPITAL RECORDS AVAILABLE: Yes

12. LEGAL NOTICES REQUIRED: Yes

13. LAND RECORDS: Available from registrar of Mense Conveyances

14. DEPARTMENT OF MOTOR VEHICLES: Must be 16 years old to get a driver's license. At the current time, transcripts are $2.00. Must have name, birth date, and driver's license number. Payment must be in the form of a money order or certified check made out to the South Carolina Department of Public Safety. Mail requests to:
Department of Public Safety
Driver Records
P.O. Box 100178
Columbia, SC 29202-3178
(803) 251-2940

15. LAWS REGARDING INHERITANCE: Section 15-45-130: "From the date the final decree of adoption is entered, the adopted child shall be considered a natural child of the adopting parents for all inheritance purposes, both by and from such child, to the exclusion of the natural or blood parents or kin of such child."

16. LAWS REGARDING TELEPHONE RECORDINGS: Fall under Federal Law 18 U.S.C. 2511 (2)(d): Recording one's own conversation without the consent of the other participant is permissible when it is not done for the purpose of committing a criminal or torturous act.

17. PHYSICIAN LICENSING BOARD:
Medical Examiner's State Board
3700 Forest Drive (29204)
P.O. Box 11289
Columbia, SC 29201
(803) 734-8901

18. ATTORNEY LICENSING BOARD:

South Carolina Bar
950 Taylor Street
P.O. Box 608
Columbia, SC 29202
(803) 799-6653

19. VITAL STATISTICS AGENCY:

SC Department of Health & Environmental Control
Division of Vital Records
2600 Bull Street
Columbia, SC 29201
(803) 898-3630

RECORD	COST	AVAILABILITY	SOURCE
A. Birth	$12.00	Kept since 1915 Restricted**	STATE: Above COUNTY: Health department
B. Marriage	$12.00	Kept since 1950 Restricted**	STATE: Above COUNTY: Probate judge
C. Divorce	$12.00	Kept since 1962 Restricted**	STATE: Above COUNTY: County Court clerk
D. Death	$12.00	Kept since 1915* Immediate family	STATE: Above COUNTY: Probate judge

* Also for 1915-40, contact State Archives.
** Call for clarification, or to see if this affects your request.
Priority fee of $5.00 to have document mailed within 3 working days; credit card service available: total fee is $18.00.

20. STATE REUNION REGISTRY:

South Carolina Department of Social Services
Adoption and Birth Parents Services
P.O. Box 1520
Columbia, SC 29202-1520
(803) 734-6095

COST: $10.00

SUMMARY: To obtain a registration form, you must first call (803) 734-6095 and give your name, address, date of birth, and adoptive parents' names and address. After they verify this information, a form will be sent to you.

South Dakota

1. CENTRAL INFORMATION AGENCY:

South Dakota Capitol Building
Pierre, SD 57501
(605) 224-3011

2. STATE ADOPTION DEPARTMENT:

Department of Social Services
Child Protection Services
Richard F. Kneip Building
700 Governor's Drive
Pierre, SD 57501-2291
(605) 773-3227

3. ADOPTION RECORDS: Closed

4. YEAR CLOSED: Unknown

5. DEGREE OF AVAILABILITY: All adoption records are closed upon finalization. A court order is required to release any information from them. Most agencies will furnish nonidentifying information to adult concerned parties.

6. AGE OF MAJORITY: 18 years old

7. ADOPTION LAWS: Section 25-6-15.1: All adoption records are confidential.
Section 25-6-15.2: Nonidentifying information shall be released to adoptive parents or adult adoptees.
Section 25-6-15.3: The Department of Social Services shall maintain a voluntary registry for adoptees and birth parents who consent to the release of information. Any consent shall indicate to whom the information may be released and whether the adoptee desires release of this identifying information after their death. A person who uses this voluntary registry may revoke their consent at any time.

8. COURT OF JURISDICTION: Circuit Court

9. STATE REUNION REGISTRY: Yes; see #20

10. STATE ARCHIVES/RECORDS DEPT.:

South Dakota State Historical Society, State Archives
900 Governor's Drive
Pierre, SD 57501-2217
(605) 773-3804

11. HOSPITAL RECORDS AVAILABLE: No

12. LEGAL NOTICES REQUIRED: No

13. LAND RECORDS: Available from county registrar of deeds

14. DEPARTMENT OF MOTOR VEHICLES: Must be 16 years old to get a driver's license. At the current time, transcripts are $2.20. Must have birth date and driver's license number. Payment must be in the form of a money order or certified check made out to the South Dakota Department of Public Safety. Mail requests to:

Division of Commerce
Driver's License Program
118 West Capitol Avenue
Pierre, SD 57501
(605) 773-3546

15. LAWS REGARDING INHERITANCE: Section 25-6-17: "The natural parents of an adopted child are from the time of the adoption relieved of all parental duties towards and of all responsibility for the child so adopted, and have no right

over it . . ." (no specific mention of inheritance) Note: In the 1976 case of Harrell vs. McDonald—SD-242,NW,2d 148: "A child born out of wedlock and subsequently adopted, did not, by virtue of her adoption, lose her right to inherit from her natural mother."

16. LAWS REGARDING TELEPHONE RECORDINGS: Sect. 18-9-303: At the present time, private parties may legally record their own conversations without obtaining the other party's consent.

17. PHYSICIAN LICENSING BOARD:
South Dakota Board of Medical Examiners
1323 South Minnesota Avenue
Sioux Falls, SD 57105
(605) 336-1965

18. ATTORNEY LICENSING BOARD:
South Dakota State Bar Association
222 East Capitol
Pierre, SD 57501
(605) 224-7554

19. VITAL STATISTICS AGENCY:
Department of Health
Vital Records
445 East Capitol Avenue
Pierre, SD 57501-3182
(605) 773-3355

RECORD	COST	AVAILABILITY	SOURCE
A. Birth	$7.00	Kept since 1905 Restricted	STATE: Above COUNTY: County treasurer
B. Marriage	$7.00	Kept since 1905 Restricted	STATE: Above COUNTY: County treasurer
C. Divorce	$7.00	Kept since 1905 Restricted	STATE: Above COUNTY: Court clerk
D. Death	$7.00	Kept since 1905 Restricted	STATE: Above COUNTY: County treasurer

"Emergency" credit card service available: (605) 773-4961.

20. STATE REUNION REGISTRY:
Adoption Unit
Department of Social Services
Kneip Building
700 Governor's Drive
Pierre, SD 57501
(605) 773-3227
COST: None
SUMMARY: You must be 18 years of age or older to register. The registry is for adult adoptees who were born or whose adoption was finalized in the state of South Dakota and their birth parents. Siblings 18 years of age or older may also register.
A birth parent shall not be matched with the adult adopted person without the consent of the other birth parents unless: (a) There is only one birth parent listed on the birth certificate; or (b) The other birth parent is deceased.
In the event a match occurs, the State Department of Social Services will notify you by mail, prior to releasing the identifying information.
Should any information on your registration change, or you wish to withdraw your consent, notify the Department of Social Services.

Tennessee

1. CENTRAL INFORMATION AGENCY:
State Capitol
Nashville, TN 37219
(615) 741-3011

2. STATE ADOPTION DEPARTMENT:
Department of Children's Services
Post Adoption Branch
436 6th Avenue North
Nashville, TN 37243
(615) 532-5637

3. ADOPTION RECORDS: Open (Adoptions prior to March 16, 1951, and others with limited conditions, see note in #20.)

4. YEAR CLOSED: 1951; opened to adoptee and certain others, 1995

5. DEGREE OF AVAILABILITY: Court records are closed upon finalization, and a court order is required to release information from them. Upon finalization, all agency records of adoption are sent to the Tennessee Department of Human Services in Nashville. Upon written request from an adult adoptee, DHS will release specific nonidentifying information.

6. AGE OF MAJORITY:
18 years old for nonidentifying information
21 years old for search

7. ADOPTION LAWS: Section 36-1-139: Procedures exist for reuniting preadoptive siblings when they reach age 18 or older.
Section 36-1-40: Adoptees over age 18 may request information about their biological family.
Section 36-1-131: Defines which courts may issue orders to open records: Court of original jurisdiction or Chancery Court.
Section 36-1-141: Authorized DHS to conduct search for birth parents upon written request from adult adoptee. Also authorized release of original birth certificate if birth parents cannot be found.

8. COURT OF JURISDICTION:

Before 1950: Probate or County Courts
After 1950: Chancery or Circuit Courts

9. STATE REUNION REGISTRY: Yes; see #20

10. STATE ARCHIVES/RECORDS DEPT.:

State Library and Archives
403 7th Avenue North
Nashville, TN 37243
(615) 741-7996

11. HOSPITAL RECORDS AVAILABLE: Possibly, through a doctor

12. LEGAL NOTICES REQUIRED: No

13. LAND RECORDS: Available from county registrar of deeds

14. DEPARTMENT OF MOTOR VEHICLES: Must be 16 years old to get a driver's license. At the current time, transcripts are $5.00. Must have birth date and driver's license number. Payment must be in the form of a money order or certified check made out to the Tennessee Department of Safety. Mail requests to:

Department of Revenue
Motor Vehicles Division
1150 Foster Avenue
Nashville, TN 37249-4000
(615) 251-5251

15. LAWS REGARDING INHERITANCE: Section 36-126: "An adopted child shall not inherit real or personal property from a natural parent or relative thereof when the relationship between them has been terminated by adoption . . ."

16. LAWS REGARDING TELEPHONE RECORDINGS: Falls under Federal Law U.S.C.2511(2)(d): Recording one's own conversation without the consent of the other participant is permissible when it is not done for the purpose of committing a criminal or torturous act.

17. PHYSICIAN LICENSING BOARD:

Tennessee Board of Medical Examiners
425 5th Avenue North, First Floor
Cordell Hull Building
Nashville, Tennessee 37247
(615) 532-4384

18. ATTORNEY LICENSING BOARD:

Tennessee Bar Association
706 Church Street, Suite 100
Nashville, TN 37243-0740
(615) 741-3234

19. VITAL STATISTICS AGENCY:

State Department of Public Health
Division of Vital Statistics
421 5th Avenue North
Cordell Hull Building, C-3-324
Nashville, TN 37247-0350
(615) 741-1763
For vital records prior to 1949, contact:
TN Vital Records, TN Tower, 3rd Floor
Nashville, TN 37247-0350

RECORD	COST	AVAILABILITY	SOURCE
A. Birth	$10.00	Kept since 1914 Immediate family	STATE: Above COUNTY: County Court clerk
B. Marriage	$10.00	Kept since 1945 Immediate family	STATE: Above COUNTY: County Court clerk
C. Divorce	$10.00	Kept since 1945 Immediate family	STATE: Above COUNTY: Circuit Court
D. Death	$5.00	Kept since 1914 Immediate family	STATE: Above COUNTY: County Court clerk

"Emergency" credit card service available.

20. STATE REUNION REGISTRY:

Department of Children's Services
Post Adoption Branch
436 6th Avenue North
Nashville, TN 37243
(615) 532-5637

COST: Nonidentifying information: $45.00
Identifying information: $135.00
Determination of record availability $150.00

SUMMARY: You must send a letter to the state agency requesting you be put on file. In the letter, state your full name, first and last names of both adopted parents, and what service you want. You can ask if there have been any inquiries, ask for identifying information, and you can search for siblings. The state maintains a postadoption file, and all inquiries are kept on file. Note: T.C.A. 36-1-127, which went into effect in 1995, opened all adoption records prior to March 16, 1951. Also opened were any Tennessee Children's Home Society (any branch) adoptions, due to concerns about practices at some of the branches. For adoptions after the 1951 date, the adoptee has a "right to know equal to the right of privacy," meaning the adoptee can access identifying information; but if the parent doesn't want contact, and the adoptee subsequently contacts the birth parent, the adoptee could face criminal and/or civil charges. Contact the state for a copy of this law, and for clarification of its impact on your search.
Persons adopted through Tennessee Children's Home Society should contact them for assistance at:

Tennessee Children's Home Society
P.O. Box 34334
Memphis, TN 38134
(901) 386-2197

Texas

1. CENTRAL INFORMATION AGENCY:
State Capitol
Austin, TX 78711
(512) 463-4630

2. STATE ADOPTION DEPARTMENT:
Department of Human Resources
Attn.: Adoption Registry, Y-943
P.O. Box 149030
Austin, TX 78714-9030
(512) 834-4485 (adoption records)
(512) 438-4800 (main)

3. ADOPTION RECORDS: Closed

4. YEAR CLOSED: 1935

5. DEGREE OF AVAILABILITY: Court records are closed upon finalization and a court order is required to release information from them. Many agencies will release nonidentifying information to an adult involved party.

6. AGE OF MAJORITY: 18 years old

7. ADOPTION LAWS: Section 49.001: Provides for a voluntary registry of adoptees, birth siblings, and birth parents over age 21.
Section 16.032: Birth parents and/or the child-placing agency will compile the health, social, educational, and genetic histories of the adoptee. This will be provided to the adoptive parents at or before placement of the adoptee, and to the adoptee at age of majority, and to surviving spouse or progeny upon death of adoptee.

8. COURT OF JURISDICTION: District Courts

9. STATE REUNION REGISTRY: Yes; see #20

10. STATE ARCHIVES/RECORDS DEPT.:
Texas State Library
Archives and Library Building
1201 Brazos
P.O. Box 12927
Austin, TX 78711-2927
(512) 463-5480

11. HOSPITAL RECORDS AVAILABLE: Possibly, through a doctor

12. LEGAL NOTICES REQUIRED: Possibly

13. LAND RECORDS: Available from county clerk

14. DEPARTMENT OF MOTOR VEHICLES: Must be 16 years old to get a driver's license. At the current time, transcripts are $4.00. Must have birth date and driver's license number. Payment must be in the form of a money order or certified check made out to the Texas Department of Public Safety. Mail requests to:
Department of Highways and Public Transportation
Motor Vehicles Dept.
Driver's Record Section
P.O. Box 15999
40th Street and Jackson Ave.
Austin, TX 78761-5999
(512) 424-2000

15. LAWS REGARDING INHERITANCE: Section 15.07: "A decree terminating the parent-child relationship divests the parent and the child of all legal rights, privileges, duties, and powers, with respect to each other, except the child retains the right to inherit from and through the divested parent unless the court otherwise provides."

16. LAWS REGARDING TELEPHONE RECORDINGS: Section 16.02(c)(4): At the present time, private parties may legally record their own conversations without obtaining the other party's consent.

17. PHYSICIAN LICENSING BOARD:
Board of Examiners for the State of Texas
Attn.: Verifications
P.O. Box 149134
Austin, TX 78714-9134
(512) 305-7010

18. ATTORNEY LICENSING BOARD:
State Bar of Texas
Membership Department
P.O. Box 12487
Austin, TX 78711
(512) 463-1463

19. VITAL STATISTICS AGENCY:
Texas Department of Health
Bureau of Vital Statistics
P.O. Box 12040
Austin, TX 78711-2040
(512) 458-7111

RECORD	COST	AVAILABILITY	SOURCE
A. Birth*	$11.00	Kept since 1903 Immediate family	STATE: Above COUNTY: County clerk
B. Marriage*	$9.00	Kept since 1966 Immediate family	STATE: Above COUNTY: County clerk
C. Divorce*	$9.00	Kept since 1966 Immediate family	STATE: Above COUNTY: District Court clerk
D. Death*	$9.00	Kept since 1903 Immediate family	STATE: Above COUNTY: County clerk

"Emergency" service available for an additional $5.00 fee.

* The genealogy department of the Texas State Library has indexes to many of these vital records. Before requesting vital records through Vital Statistics, contact the Texas State Library. (See #10.)

20. STATE REUNION REGISTRY:

Department of Human Resources
Attn.: Adoption Registry, Y-943
P.O. Box 149030
Austin, TX 78714-9030
(512) 450-3282

COST: $5.00 Inquiry stage
$15.00 Registry fee

SUMMARY: You need to send a letter requesting your name be put on the registry, accompanied by a check for $5.00. In the letter, give your name, address, phone number, name of adoptive parents, and county the adoption took place in. After determining that you are eligible (adopted through state agency), you will be notified by mail and sent a form to be completed and returned with a check for $15.00 to register. You also need proof of one hour of counseling upon registering.

Utah

1. CENTRAL INFORMATION AGENCY:

State Capitol of Utah
Salt Lake City, UT 84114
(801) 538-3000

2. STATE ADOPTION DEPARTMENT:

Dept. of Social Services, Division of Social Services
120 North 200 West
Salt Lake City, UT 84103
(801) 538-4100; (801) 281-5100

3. ADOPTION RECORDS: Closed

4. YEAR CLOSED: Always

5. DEGREE OF AVAILABILITY: Court records are closed upon finalization. A court order is required to release information from them. Most agencies will furnish nonidentifying information to an adult involved party.

6. AGE OF MAJORITY: 21 years old

7. ADOPTION LAWS: Section 78-30-15: "The court shall order that the petition . . . or any other documents filed in connection with the hearing, shall be sealed and shall not be open to inspection or copy except upon order of the court. . . ."
Section 78-30-17: The health, genetic, and social histories of the adoptee shall be made available to the adoptive parents, adoptee's guardian, children or spouse of the adoptee, and the adoptee's adult siblings.
Section 78-30-18: Provides for mutual consent voluntary adoption registry.

8. COURT OF JURISDICTION: District Court

9. STATE REUNION REGISTRY: Yes; see #20

10. STATE ARCHIVES/RECORDS DEPT.:

Utah State Archives
Archives Division
State Capitol, Archives Bldg.
Salt Lake City, UT 84114-1021
(801) 538-3012

11. HOSPITAL RECORDS AVAILABLE: Yes, through a doctor

12. LEGAL NOTICES REQUIRED: No

13. LAND RECORDS: Available through the county recorder and

Bureau of Land Management:
Salt Lake City District
P.O. Box 45155 (84145-0155)
2370 South 2300 West
Salt Lake City, UT 84116
(801) 539-4141

14. DEPARTMENT OF MOTOR VEHICLES: Must be 16 years old to get a driver's license. At the current time, transcripts are $4.00. Must have birth date and driver's license number. Payment must be in the form of a money order or certified check made out to the Utah Driver's License Services. Mail requests to:

Driver's License Services
P.O. Box 30560
Salt Lake City, UT 84130-0560
(801) 965-4437

15. LAWS REGARDING INHERITANCE: Section 78-30-11: Expressly provides for the adoptee to inherit from both their adoptive parents and birth parents. (Keep in mind that searches should be done for reasons of the heart—not the pocketbook.)

16. LAWS REGARDING TELEPHONE RECORDINGS: Section 77-23a-4(7)(b): At the present time, private parties may legally record their own conversations without obtaining the other party's consent.

17. PHYSICIAN LICENSING BOARD:

Division of Occupational and Professional Licensing
160 East 300 South
P.O. Box 146741
Salt Lake City, UT 84114
(801) 530-6628

18. ATTORNEY LICENSING BOARD:

Utah State Bar
645 South 200 East
Salt Lake City, UT 84111
(801) 531-9077

19. VITAL STATISTICS AGENCY:

Utah State Department of Health
Bureau of Vital Statistics
288 North 1460 West
Salt Lake City, UT 84114
(801) 538-6105

RECORD	COST	AVAILABILITY	SOURCE
A. Birth	$12.00	Kept since 1905 Immediate family	STATE: Above COUNTY: County clerk
B. Marriage	$9.00	Kept since 1887 Public information**	STATE: No records COUNTY: *
C. Divorce	$9.00	Kept since 1887 Public information	STATE: No records COUNTY: District Court
D. Death	$9.00	Kept since 1905 Public information	STATE: Above COUNTY: County clerk

* Salt Lake County Marriage License Department
2001 South State Street, Salt Lake City, UT 84190
** (801) 468-3439

20. STATE REUNION REGISTRY:
Bureau of Vital Statistics
288 North 1460 West
P.O. Box 142855
Salt Lake City, UT 84114-2855
(801) 538-6363
COST: $25.00 (lifetime fee)
SUMMARY: You need to contact the adoption clerk at the above phone number and ask for the information form to be sent to you. They will send out an information sheet with the requirements for eligibility. If you meet all of the requirements, you will need a certified copy of your birth certificate to send in with the completed, notarized form. This is a mutual consent registry.

Vermont

1. CENTRAL INFORMATION AGENCY:
Vermont State House
State Street
Montpelier, VT 05633
(802) 828-1110

2. STATE ADOPTION DEPARTMENT:
Social Services Div., Adoption Coordinator
103 South Main
Waterbury, VT 05671
(802) 241-2131

3. ADOPTION RECORDS: Closed

4. YEAR CLOSED: 1946

5. DEGREE OF AVAILABILITY: Court records are closed upon finalization. A court order is required to release information from them. Almost all agencies will furnish nonidentifying information to an adult involved party. As of 1996, legislation was pending for increased openness.

6. AGE OF MAJORITY: 18 years old

7. ADOPTION LAWS: Section 451: All court records are sealed, and such "seals shall not be broken and those records and papers shall not be exhibited except by order of a superior court, or probate court."
Section 461: The court shall release nonidentifying information to an adoptee or adoptive parent upon written request.
Section 462: A consent to disclose identifying information form may be filed with the court by an adoptee who has attained the age of 18 or by a birth parent of the adoptee.

8. COURT OF JURISDICTION: Probate Court

9. STATE REUNION REGISTRY: Yes; see #20

10. STATE ARCHIVES/RECORDS DEPT.:
Vermont Historical Society Library
Pavilion Office Building—Archives Division
109 State Street
Montpelier, VT 05609-1103
(802) 828-2369
(802) 828-2291 (historical)

11. HOSPITAL RECORDS AVAILABLE: Possibly, through a doctor

12. LEGAL NOTICES REQUIRED: No

13. LAND RECORDS: Available from town and city clerks

14. DEPARTMENT OF MOTOR VEHICLES: Must be 16 years old to get a driver's license. At the current time, transcripts are $4.00 (for a transcript of the most recent 3 years); the complete record is $8.00. Must have birth date and driver's license number. Payment must be in the form of a money order or certified check made out to the Vermont Department of Motor Vehicles. Mail requests to:
Department of Motor Vehicles
State Office Building
120 State Street
Montpelier, VT 05603-0001
(802) 828-2050

15. LAWS REGARDING INHERITANCE: Section 448: "A person adopted shall have the same right of inheritance from and through his natural parents as though the adoption had not occurred. . . ."

16. LAWS REGARDING TELEPHONE RECORDINGS: Falls under Federal Law 18 U.S.C. 2511(2)(d)a: Recording one's own conversation without the consent of the other participant is permissible when it is not done for the purpose of committing a criminal or torturous act.

17. PHYSICIAN LICENSING BOARD:
Vermont State Board of Medicine
109 State Street
Montpelier, VT 05609-1106
(802) 828-2673

18. ATTORNEY LICENSING BOARD:
Office of the Court Administration, Att'y. Licensing
109 State Street
Montpelier, VT 05609-0702
(802) 828-3281

19. VITAL STATISTICS AGENCY:
State Department of Health
Vermont Vital Records
P.O. Box 70
Burlington, VT 05402
(802) 863-7275

RECORD	COST	AVAILABILITY	SOURCE
A. Birth	$7.00	Kept since 1857* Public information	STATE: Above COUNTY: City clerk
B. Marriage	$7.00	Kept since 1857* Public information	STATE: Above COUNTY: City clerk
C. Divorce	$7.00	Kept since 1860* Public information	STATE: Above COUNTY: County Court clerk
D. Death	$7.00	Kept since 1857* Public information	STATE: Above COUNTY: City clerk

* Records from 1980 to the present available from address above. Anything prior to 1980:
Vermont Public Records
Reference and Research
US Rt. 2 Middlesex, Drawer 33
Montpelier, VT 05633-7601

20. STATE REUNION REGISTRY:
Vermont Adoption Registry
103 South Main
Waterbury, VT 05671
(802) 241-2131

COST: No fee

SUMMARY: This registry is available for all state, agency, and private adoptions.

Virginia

1. CENTRAL INFORMATION AGENCY:
State Capitol
Capitol Square
Richmond, VA 23219
(804) 786-0000

2. STATE ADOPTION DEPARTMENT:
Division of Social Services
Adoption Reports Unit
730 E. Broad Street
Richmond, VA 23219-1849
(804) 692-1275
(804) 692-1286

3. ADOPTION RECORDS: Closed

4. YEAR CLOSED: Not known

5. DEGREE OF AVAILABILITY: Nonidentifying information is available to the adoptee (18 years or older) upon request from the state adoption unit or the agency who originally handled the adoption. This information can be somewhat informative concerning the birth family's circumstances at the time of the adoptee's placement, even though names and places will be removed. Obtaining these records should be the first step in the search process. The information from the state is likely to be comprehensive—a photostatic copy of the file, with the names and identifying information cut out with scissors.

Adoptees who reside in the commonwealth will be asked to attend a meeting in Richmond to receive their report of nonidentifying information in person. Those who reside in other areas will be asked to provide the name of a social worker or mental health professional to whom this report can be released. The professional, in turn, would release the information to the adoptee.

Birth parents are not permitted access to any records or information. However, most local agencies and the state adoption unit will accept a waiver of confidentiality letter from the birth parents to the adoptee. The biological parent should update this letter every time an address or phone number change occurs. Original birth certificates are not available to anyone.

6. AGE OF MAJORITY: 18 years old

7. ADOPTION LAWS: Section 63.1-236: Adult adoptees (18 or older) may petition the courts for a search to be done by the placing agency or appropriate county department of social services for the birth parents. The adoptee (petitioner) must show good cause. Generally, the judge wants to hear a request for medical history as good cause. The adoptee should also request contact with the birth parents if so desired. The cost is $15.00 and the adoptee does not need to make a personal appearance or be represented by legal counsel. Everything can be done by letter or by petitions (forms available from the circuit court), and the state attorney general's office represents the adoptee. Often the judge grants the petition and appoints an agency to conduct a six-month search. The adoptee is not given any information until the search is completed. If the search is successful and all parties agree to meet—a reunion happens. Birth parents may not petition the court. The commonwealth has set no standards for the comprehensiveness of any search efforts made by agencies or their appointed search person.

8. COURT OF JURISDICTION: Circuit Court or Chancery division

9. STATE REUNION REGISTRY: None. However, adoptees can write for application for disclosure (see #2).

10. STATE ARCHIVES:
State Library Building
Archives Division
800 E. Broad Street
Richmond, VA 23219
(804) 692-3888

11. HOSPITAL RECORDS AVAILABLE: Typically, these will be available if a doctor writes the letter

12. LEGAL NOTICES REQUIRED: Possibly

13. LAND RECORDS: Available from Circuit, County Corporation, Chancery, or Hustings Courts

14. DEPARTMENT OF MOTOR VEHICLES: Must be 16 years old to get a driver's license. At the present time, transcripts are $5.00 and are available to the driver only. Payment must be in the form of a money order or cashier's check made out to the Virginia Division of Motor Vehicles. Mail request to:
Division of Motor Vehicles
Driver's License Information
P.O. Box 27412
Richmond, VA 23269
(804) 367-0538

15. LAWS REGARDING INHERITANCE: Section 63.1-2-34: "For the purpose of descent and distribution, a legally adopted child . . . shall not inherit from the natural parents. . . ."

16. LAWS REGARDING TELEPHONE RECORDINGS: Section 19.2-62(B)(2): At the present time, private parties may legally record their own conversations without obtaining the other party's consent.

17. PHYSICIAN LICENSING BOARD:
Virginia State Board of Medicine
6606 West Broad Street
4th Floor
Richmond, VA 23230-1717
(804) 662-9908

18. ATTORNEY LICENSING BOARD:
Virginia State Bar Association
Membership Department
707 E. Main Street, Suite 1500
Richmond, VA 23219-2803
(804) 775-0500

19. VITAL STATISTICS AGENCY:
Virginia Department of Health
Division of Vital Records
109 Governor Street
P.O. Box 1000
Richmond, VA 23208-1000
(804) 225-5000

RECORD	COST	AVAILABILITY	SOURCE
A. Birth	$8.00	Kept since 1853* Immediate family	STATE: Above COUNTY: Health department
B. Marriage	$8.00	Kept since 1853 Immediate family	STATE: Above COUNTY: Court clerk
C. Divorce	$8.00	Kept since 1918 Immediate family	STATE: Above COUNTY: Court clerk
D. Death	$8.00	Kept since 1912 Immediate family	STATE: Above COUNTY: Health department

* Birth records from 1853-96 are in State Archives (see #10).

Washington

1. CENTRAL INFORMATION AGENCY:
State Capitol
Olympia, WA 98504
(360) 753-5000

2. STATE ADOPTION DEPARTMENT:
Dept. of Social and Health Services
Bureau of Children's Services
P.O. Box 45710
Olympia, WA 98504-5713
(360) 902-7968
(800) 562-5682 (adoption unit)

3. ADOPTION RECORDS: Closed

4. YEAR CLOSED: 1953

5. DEGREE OF AVAILABILITY: Court records are sealed upon finalization, and a court order is required to release any information from them. Many agencies will release nonidentifying information to an adult involved party. Birth parents are now entitled to a noncertified copy of the original birth certificate of their child upon request—SSB #6493-4

6. AGE OF MAJORITY: 21 years old

7. ADOPTION LAWS: Section 26.33.340: Nonidentifying information may be disclosed for medical reasons.
Section 26.33.350: Birth family medical information, including mental, physical, and sensory handicaps must be provided to the adoptive parents prior to adoption.

8. COURT OF JURISDICTION: Superior or Family Courts

9. STATE REUNION REGISTRY: None. Does have a confidential intermediary program

10. STATE ARCHIVES:
Washington State Library
Archives Division
State Library Building
P.O. Box 40238
Olympia, WA 98504-0238
(360) 753-5485

11. HOSPITAL RECORDS AVAILABLE: Possibly, through doctor and/or court order

12. LEGAL NOTICES REQUIRED: Yes, must be published in the state newspaper

13. LAND RECORDS: Available from county auditor

14. DEPARTMENT OF MOTOR VEHICLES: Must be 16 years old to get a driver's license. At the present time, transcripts are $4.50. You must have the driver's full name and driver's license number. Payment must be in the form of a money order or cashier's check made out to the Washington State Treasurer. Mail request to:
Dept. of Motor Vehicles
Highway/Licenses Building
P.O. Box 9030
Olympia, WA 98507-9030
(360) 902-3900

15. LAWS REGARDING INHERITANCE: Section 26.32.140: "By a decree of adoption . . . the child shall be . . . to all intents and purposes, and for all legal incidents, the child, legal heir, and lawful issue of his/her adopter or adopters. . . ."

16. LAWS REGARDING TELEPHONE RECORDINGS: Section 9.73.030(1)(b): All parties engaged in a recorded conversation must be announced, and the announcement to record must be recorded.

17. PHYSICIAN LICENSING BOARD:
Washington Board of Medical Examiners
1300 Quincy Street, P.O. Box 47866
Olympia, WA 98504
(360) 753-2287

18. ATTORNEY LICENSING BOARD:
Washington State Bar Association
2101 4th Avenue
Seattle, WA 98121
(206) 727-8200

19. VITAL STATISTICS AGENCY:
Center for Health Statistics
1112 SE Quince Street ET-14
P.O. Box 9709
Olympia, WA 98507-9709
(360) 753-5936

RECORD	COST	AVAILABILITY*	SOURCE
A. Birth	$13.00	Kept since 1907 Public information	STATE: Above COUNTY: County auditor
B. Marriage	$13.00	Kept since 1968 Public information	STATE: Above COUNTY: County auditor
C. Divorce	$13.00	Kept since 1968 Public information	STATE: Above COUNTY: County clerk
D. Death	$13.00	Kept since 1907 Public information	STATE: Above COUNTY: County auditor

* Some records may be restricted
For dates prior to the state's availability, contact the county where the event occurred. They provide "emergency" credit card service, but you must call between 9 A.M. and noon, or 1 and 4 P.M.; fees start at $21.00 for service.

West Virginia

1. CENTRAL INFORMATION AGENCY:
State Capitol
1900 Kanawha Boulevard E
Charleston, WV 25305
(304) 558-3456

2. STATE ADOPTION DEPARTMENT:
Department of Health & Human Services
State Capitol Complex, Bldg. 6, Rm. 850
Charleston, WV 25305
(304) 558-7980

3. ADOPTION RECORDS: Closed

4. YEAR CLOSED: Not known

5. DEGREE OF AVAILABILITY: Court records are closed upon finalization. A court order is required to release information from them. Many agencies will furnish nonidentifying information to an adult involved party.

6. AGE OF MAJORITY: 18 years old

7. ADOPTION LAWS: Section 48-4-4: Court records can be opened only with a order showing "good cause."

8. COURT OF JURISDICTION: Juvenile or Circuit Courts

9. STATE REUNION REGISTRY: Yes, see #20

10. STATE ARCHIVES/RECORDS DEPT.:
West Virginia Historical Society
1900 Kanawha Blvd.
Cultural Center: Capitol Complex
Charleston, WV 25305-0300
(304) 558-0220

11. HOSPITAL RECORDS AVAILABLE: Yes, through doctor

12. LEGAL NOTICES REQUIRED: Varies

13. LAND RECORDS: Available through clerk of County Court

14. DEPARTMENT OF MOTOR VEHICLES: Must be 16 years old to get a driver's license. At the current time, transcripts are $5.00. Must have name, birth date, and driver's license and social security numbers. Payment must be in the form of a money order or certified check made out to the West Virginia Division of Motor Vehicles. Mail requests to:

Motor Vehicle Division
State Office Building #3
1800 Kanawha Blvd. E
Charleston, WV 25317
(304) 558-3900

15. LAWS REGARDING INHERITANCE: Art. 4 19-4-113: Adoption decree severs all rights and responsibilities—inheritance not specified.

16. LAWS REGARDING TELEPHONE RECORDINGS: Section 48-4-5: At the present time, private parties may legally record their own conversations without obtaining the other party's consent.

17. PHYSICIAN LICENSING BOARD:

West Virginia Board of Medicine
101 Dee Drive
Charleston, WV 25311
(304) 558-2921

18. ATTORNEY LICENSING BOARD:

West Virginia State Bar
2006 Kanawha Boulevard East
Charleston, WV 25311
(304) 558-2456

19. VITAL STATISTICS AGENCY:

State Department of Health
Division of Vital Statistics
State Office Building #3 - Room 516
Charleston, WV 25305
(304) 558-2931

RECORD	COST	AVAILABILITY	SOURCE
A. Birth	$5.00	Kept since 1917 Immediate family	STATE: Above COUNTY: County Court clerk
B. Marriage	$5.00	Kept since 1921 Immediate family	STATE: Above COUNTY: County Court clerk
C. Divorce	$5.00	Kept since 1968 Immediate family	STATE: Above COUNTY: Circuit Court clerk
D. Death	$5.00	Kept since 1917 Immediate family	STATE: Above COUNTY: County Court clerk

20. STATE REUNION REGISTRY:

Mutual Consent Registry, T. Goodman, Coordinator
Dept. of Health and Human Services
State Capitol Complex, Bldg. 6, Room 850
Charleston, WV 25305
(304) 558-2891

COST: No fee at present time

SUMMARY: West Virginia has a reunion registry. The registry will provide a system for adult adoptees, birth parents, and siblings to mutually consent to the release of identifying information, i.e., names and addresses. Complete and return the Affidavit of Interest form so that you can be provided information when the registry is formally established. This mutual consent registry is for state adoptions only.

Wisconsin

1. CENTRAL INFORMATION AGENCY:

Adoption Information Center
1212 South 70th
West Allis, WI 53214
(800) 522-6882

2. STATE ADOPTION DEPARTMENT:

Department of Health and Social Services
Division of Community Services
Attn.: Adoption Search Coordinator
P.O. Box 8916
Madison, WI 53708-8916
(608) 266-7163

3. ADOPTION RECORDS: Closed

4. YEAR CLOSED: 1929

5. DEGREE OF AVAILABILITY: Court records are sealed upon finalization, and a court order is required to release any information from them. Every agency will release nonidentifying information to an adult involved party. The state will search for birth parent or adoptee but not other relatives.

6. AGE OF MAJORITY: 21 years old

7. ADOPTION LAWS: Section 48.93: All court records are locked, and can be opened only through a court order showing good cause.
Section 48.93: Nonidentifying information shall be given to the adoptive parents at time of adoption. It shall also be made available to adoptee upon reaching age 18 for a fee.
Section 48.93: Copies of the adoptee's medical records shall be given to the adoptive parents at the time the decree is granted. It shall also be made available to the adoptee upon reaching age 18 for a fee.

8. COURT OF JURISDICTION: Probate or Circuit Court

9. STATE REUNION REGISTRY: None

10. STATE ARCHIVES:

Wisconsin State Historical Society
University of Wisconsin—Archives Department
816 State Street
Madison, WI 53706
(608) 264-6400

11. HOSPITAL RECORDS AVAILABLE: Yes, through a doctor

12. LEGAL NOTICES REQUIRED: Yes, since 1973

13. LAND RECORDS: Available from county registrar of deeds

14. DEPARTMENT OF MOTOR VEHICLES: Must be 16 years old to get a driver's license. At the present time, transcripts are $3.00. You must have the driver's full name and driver's license number. Will search records for additional $3.00 fee if you have incomplete information. Payment must be in the form of a money order or cashier's check made out to the Registration Fee Trust. Mail request to:

Department of Motor Vehicles
Driver Records File
P.O. Box 7995
Madison, WI 53707-7995
(608) 266-2353

15. LAWS REGARDING INHERITANCE: Section 851.51: Adoptees cannot inherit from or through their birth parents. However, wills can alter the effect of this statute, so adoptees and birth parents should check with an attorney in the state in which they are located to determine their rights.

16. LAWS REGARDING TELEPHONE RECORDINGS: Section 968.32(2)(c): At the present time, private parties may legally record their own conversations without obtaining the other party's consent.

17. PHYSICIAN LICENSING BOARD:

Physician Licensing Board
Department of Regulations and Licensing
P.O. Box 8935
Madison, WI 53708-8935
(608) 266-2112

18. ATTORNEY LICENSING BOARD:

State Bar of Wisconsin
402 West Wilson Street (53703)
P.O. Box 7158
Madison, WI 53707
(608) 257-3838

19. VITAL STATISTICS AGENCY:

Wisconsin Division of Health
Vital Records
P.O. Box 309
Madison, WI 53701-0309
(608) 266-1371 (births); (608) 266-1372 (other records)

RECORD	COST	AVAILABILITY	SOURCE
A. Birth	$12.00	Kept since 1814 Public information*	STATE: Above COUNTY: Courthouse
B. Marriage	$7.00	Kept since 1935 Public information*	STATE: Above COUNTY: Courthouse
C. Divorce	$7.00	Kept since 1907 Public information*	STATE: Above COUNTY: Courthouse
D. Death	$7.00	Kept since 1914 Public information*	STATE: Above COUNTY: Courthouse

* Anyone can get noncertified copies of vital records, but a birth must be legitimate to get a noncertified copy of the document.

Wyoming

1. CENTRAL INFORMATION AGENCY:

State Capitol
Capitol Avenue 200 W. 24th Street
Cheyenne, WY 82001
(307) 777-7220

2. STATE ADOPTION DEPARTMENT:

Department of Family Services
Division of Youth Services
Hathway Building, 3rd Floor, Rm. 318
2300 Capitol
Cheyenne, WY 82002
(307) 777-3570

3. ADOPTION RECORDS: Closed

4. YEAR CLOSED: Not known

5. DEGREE OF AVAILABILITY: Court records are sealed upon finalization, and a court order is required to release any information from them. Many agencies will release nonidentifying information to an adult involved party. The adult (19 years or older) adoptee petitions the court and may appoint an intermediary access to the file—if the birth parent does not want contact, no information will be given.

6. AGE OF MAJORITY: 18 years old

7. ADOPTION LAWS: Section 1-22-104(d): Upon entry of the final decree of adoption, all records in the proceedings shall be sealed and may be available for inspection only by a court order for good cause shown.
Section 1-22-116: A medical history shall be provided to adoptive parents after the adoption decree or to the child after he attains the age of majority.

8. COURT OF JURISDICTION: District Court

9. STATE REUNION REGISTRY: No

10. STATE ARCHIVES:

Wyoming State Library
Archives Division
Cheyenne, WY 82002
(307) 777-7041

11. HOSPITAL RECORDS AVAILABLE: Possibly: Through doctor

12. LEGAL NOTICES REQUIRED: Varies

13. LAND RECORDS: Available from county clerk

14. DEPARTMENT OF MOTOR VEHICLES: Must be 16 years old to get a driver's license. At the present time, transcripts are $5.00. You must have the driver's full name and driver's license number. Payment must be in the form of a money order or cashier's check made out to the Wyoming Transportation Department. Mail request to:

Wyoming Transportation Department
Attn.: Driving Records
P.O. Box 1708
Cheyenne, WY 82003-1708
(307) 777-4802

15. LAWS REGARDING INHERITANCE: Section 1.726.14: "Upon the entry of a final decree of adoption the former parent . . . shall have no right to the control or custody of the child." (Does not specify inheritance)
Section 1-22-114(b): "An adoptee is entitled to the same rights of person and property as children and heirs at law of the person who adopted him."

16. LAWS REGARDING TELEPHONE RECORDINGS: Section 7-3-602(b): At the present time, private parties may legally record their own conversations without obtaining the other party's consent.

17. PHYSICIAN LICENSING BOARD:

Board of Medical Examiners
Barrett Building
Cheyenne, WY 82001
(307) 777-6463

18. ATTORNEY LICENSING BOARD:

Board of Law Examiners
500 Randall Avenue
P.O. Box 109
Cheyenne, WY 82003
(307) 632-9061

19. VITAL STATISTICS AGENCY:

Division of Health and Medical Services
Vital Records Services
Hathway Building
Cheyenne, WY 82002
(307) 777-7591

RECORD	COST	AVAILABILITY	SOURCE
A. Birth	$12.00*	Kept since 1909 Restricted	STATE: Above COUNTY: County clerk
B. Marriage	$12.00*	Kept since 1941 Restricted	STATE: Above COUNTY: County clerk
C. Divorce	$12.00*	Kept since 1941 Restricted	STATE: Above COUNTY: District clerk
D. Death	$9.00*	Kept since 1909 Restricted	STATE: Above COUNTY: County clerk

* $8.00 for each 5 year back search

20. CONFIDENTIAL INTERMEDIARY PROGRAM:
Mail to:

Department of Family Services
Division of Youth Services
Hathway Building, 3rd Floor
2300 Capitol
Cheyenne, WY 82002
(307) 777-6346

COST: $25.00 filing fee
$100 for an intermediary search
SUMMARY: Write to above address for application

APPENDIX 3

International Directories

This international directory doesn't cover every country in the world simply because many countries lack the infrastructure that is needed for serious record-keeping. Still, you'll find here a helpful start to your searches abroad.

Albania

1. ADDRESS REQUESTS FOR VITAL RECORDS TO:
Office of Civil Registration
(name of town), Albania

2. COMMENTS: A national identity card and civil registration system have been in place since the government takeover in 1946. However, this government has been notoriously unhelpful in the past and since this area is currently experiencing a great deal of upheaval, it may be difficult to get information for a while. When requesting vital statistic information, we suggest that in addition to writing the specific town (as outlined above), you also write letters to each of the following libraries. You may find a sympathetic individual at one of them who is willing to help.

Biblioteka Kombetare
(Albania's National Library)
Tirana, Albania

Biblioteka e Shtetit
(Shkoder Public Library)
Shkoder, Albania

Biblioteka e Shtetit
(Korce Public Library)
Korce, Albania

Biblioteka e Shtetit
(Durres Public Library)
Durres, Albania

Biblioteka e Shtetit
(Elbasan Public Library)
Elbasan, Albania

Biblioteka e Shtetit
(Gramshi Public Library)
Gramshi, Albania

Biblioteka e Shtetit
(Gjirokaster Public Library)
Gjirokaster, Albania

Australia

The Australian section is subdivided into the following territories: Capital Territory, New South Wales, Northern Territory, Queensland, South Australia, Tasmania, Victoria, and Western Australia.

CAPITAL TERRITORY

1. ADDRESS REQUESTS FOR VITAL RECORDS TO:
Office of the Registrar General
National Mutual Centre, 4th Floor
Darwin Place
P.O. Box 788
Canberra City, ACT, Australia 2601
(011) (6162) 758-686

2. COST: Certified Birth Certificate $15 AU
Certified Marriage Certificate $15 AU
Certified Death Certificate $15 AU

3. COMMENTS: All records date back as far as January 1, 1930.

(The following information regarding recent legislation changes in Australia is taken from a letter from Mary Iwanek to William Gage.)

> In 1990, the states of Queensland and New South Wales, Australia, passed legislation accepting all the recommendations made in the report by the New South Wales Standing Committee on Social Issues (see "New Zealand," page 310). These Australian states now have the most open legislation giving access to identifying information to adopted people age 18 and over and their birth parents. There is no compulsory counseling, and support services are optional at a nominal fee which can be waived if the applicant is unable to pay for some reason.
>
> The Australian states have the same parliamentary system as the U.S. It is interesting to note that in 1987, Queensland passed legislation setting up a passive contact registry whereby all three parties to an adoption had to register before contact was able to be made. When passing the latest legislation, the Government admitted that passive contact registries do not work. In New South Wales, out of 154 politicians in both houses, only one voted against the legislation.
>
> Mary Iwanek
> Dept. of Sociology and Social Work
> Victoria University of Wellington
> P.O. Box 600
> Wellington, New Zealand

Search assistance currently available in Australia includes:

Adoption Jigsaw (S.A.), Inc.
20 McKenzie Road
Elizabeth Downs, South Australia 5113

Adoption Jigsaw (W.A.), Inc.
Glennis Dees
P.O. Box 252
Hillarys
Perth, Western Australia 6025

Adoption Jigsaw (Victoria) Ltd.
GPO Box 5260BB
Melbourne, Victoria 3001
Australia

NEW SOUTH WALES

1. ADDRESS REQUESTS FOR VITAL RECORDS TO:
Office of the Registrar General
P.O. Box 30 GPO
Sydney, New South Wales
Australia 2001
(011) (612) 228-8988

2. COST: Certified Birth Certificate $17 AU
Certified Marriage Certificate $17 AU
Certified Death Certificate $17 AU

3. COMMENTS: All records date back as far as March 1856. Persons wanting records from New South Wales should contact the nearest Family History Center affiliated with the Church of Jesus Christ of Latter-Day Saints. They have extensively microfilmed records from this region, although they mainly center around the turn of the century.

NORTHERN TERRITORY

1. ADDRESS REQUESTS FOR VITAL RECORDS TO:
Office of the Registrar General
GPO Box 3094
Darwin, Northern Territory
Australia, 5794
(011) (6189) 6119

2. COST: Certified Birth Certificate $10 AU
Certified Marriage Certificate $10 AU
Certified Death Certificate $10 AU

3. COMMENTS: All records date back as far as August 1870.

QUEENSLAND

1. ADDRESS REQUESTS FOR VITAL RECORDS TO:
Office of the Registrar General
P.O. Box 188
Brisbane, North Quay
Queensland, Australia 4000
(011) (617) 224-6222

2. COST: Certified Birth Certificate $17 AU
Certified Marriage Certificate $17 AU
Certified Death Certificate $17 AU

3. COMMENTS: All records date back as far as March 1856. Persons wanting records from Queensland should contact the nearest Family History Center affiliated with the Church of Jesus Christ of Latter-Day Saints. They have extensively microfilmed records from this region, although they mainly center around the turn of the century.

SOUTH AUSTRALIA

1. ADDRESS REQUESTS FOR VITAL RECORDS TO:
Office of the Principal Registrar
Dept. of Public and Consumer Affairs
GPO Box 1351
Adelaide, South Australia
Australia, 5001
(011) (618) 226-1999

2. COST: Certified Birth Certificate $16 AU
Certified Marriage Certificate $16 AU
Certified Death Certificate $16 AU

3. COMMENTS: All records date back as far as July 1842. Persons wanting records from South Australia should contact the nearest Family History Center affiliated with the Church of Jesus Christ of Latter-Day Saints. They have extensively microfilmed records from this region, although they mainly center around the turn of the century.

TASMANIA

1. ADDRESS REQUESTS FOR VITAL RECORDS TO:
Office of the Registrar General
GPO Box 875 J
Hobart, Tasmania
Australia 7001
(011) (6102) 308-011

2. COST: Certified Birth Certificate $15 AU
Certified Marriage Certificate $15 AU
Certified Death Certificate $15 AU

3. COMMENTS: All records date back as far as December 1838.

VICTORIA

1. ADDRESS REQUESTS FOR VITAL RECORDS TO:
Office of the Government Statist
295 Queen Street
P.O. Box 4332
Melbourne, Victoria
Australia 3001
(011) (613) 603-5800

2. COST: Certified Birth Certificate $25 AU
Certified Marriage Certificate $25 AU
Certified Death Certificate $25 AU

3. COMMENTS: All records date back as far as July 1853. Persons wanting records from Victoria should contact the nearest Family History Center affiliated with the Church of Jesus Christ of Latter-Day Saints. They have extensively microfilmed records from this region, although they mainly center around the turn of the century.

WESTERN AUSTRALIA

1. ADDRESS REQUESTS FOR VITAL RECORDS TO:
Office of the Registrar General
Oakleigh Bldg.
22 St. George's Terrace
Perth, Western Australia
Australia 6000
(011) (619) 425-7555

2. COST: Certified Birth Certificate $18 AU
Certified Marriage Certificate $18 AU
Certified Death Certificate $18 AU

3. COMMENTS: All records date back as far as September 1841. Persons wanting records from Western Australia should contact the nearest Family History Center affiliated with the Church of Jesus Christ of Latter-Day Saints. They have extensively microfilmed records from this region, although they mainly center around the turn of the century.

Austria

1. ADDRESS REQUESTS FOR VITAL RECORDS TO:
Standesamt
(name of town), Austria

2. COMMENTS: There is no national depository for vital records in Austria; however, most local records date back to the late 1700s. To get a copy of a birth, marriage, or death record, write to the Civil Registration District Office (Standesamt) where the event happened. Almost every large Austrian city has its own library and archives, which could be very helpful. A few of these are listed below.

Austrian National Library
Osterreichische Nationalbibliothek
Josefsplatz 1
1015 Vienna, Austria

Salzburg Landesarchiv
Postfach 527
5010 Salzburg, Austria

Steiermarkisches Landesarchiv
Burgergasse 2A
8010 Graz, Austria

Archiv der Stadt Linz
Postfach 1000
4041 Linz, Austria

Stadtarchiv und Stadtmuseum
Prandtauer Strasse 2
3100 St. Polten, Austria

Bundesstaatliche Studien Bibliothek
Kaufmanngasse 11
9020 Klagenfurt, Austria

Tiroler Landesarchiv
Herrengasse 1
6010 Innsbruck, Austria

Austrian State Archives
Osterreichisches Staatsarchiv
Nottendorfergasse 2
1030 Vienna, Austria

Steiermarkisches Landesbibliothek
Postfach 861
8011 Graz, Austria

Niederosterreiches Landesarchiv
Herrengasse 11-13
1014 Vienna, Austria

Oberosterreichisches Landesarchiv
Anzengruber Strasse 19
4020 Linz, Austria

Kartner Landesarchiv
Landhaus
A-9020 Klagenfurt, Austria

Bibliothek des Oberosterreichischen
Landesmuseums, Museum Strasse 14
4020 Linz, Austria

Stadtarchiv Innsbruck
Badgasse 2
6020 Innsbruck, Austria

Belgium

1. ADDRESS REQUESTS FOR VITAL RECORDS TO:
Registres de l'Etat Civil
(name of town), Belgium

2. COMMENTS: There is no national depository for vital records in Belgium; however, most local records date back to the late 1700s. To get a copy of a birth, marriage, or death record, write to the Civil Registration District Office where the event happened. Almost every large Belgian city has its own library and archives, which could be very helpful. A few of these are listed below.

Belgian National Library
Bibliotheque Royale Albert 1er
4 Boulevard de l'Empereur
1000 Brussels, Belgium

Antwerp State Archives
Rijksarchief te Anterpen
Door Verstraetepl 5
2018 Antwerp, Belgium

Archives de l'Archeveche
Archeveche de Malines
Wollemarkt 15
2800 Mechelen, Belgium

Archief en Stadsbibliotheek
Steenweg 1
2800 Mechelen, Belgium

Bibliotheek van de Rijksunversiteit te Gent
9 Rozier
9000 Ghent, Belgium

Archives de la Ville de Bruxelles
65 rue des Tanneurs
1000 Brussels, Belgium

Antwerp City Archives
Stadarchief
Venusstraat 11
2000 Antwerp, Belgium

Antwerp Public Library
Stadsbibliotheek
Hendrik Conscienceplein 4
2000 Antwerp, Belgium

Rijksarchief te Gent
Geraard de Duivelsteen
9000 Ghent, Belgium

Archives Geerales du Royaume
2-4 Rue de Ruysbroeck
1000 Brussels, Belgium

Bibliotheque Publique de la Ville de Liege
8 place de Carmes
4000 Leige, Belgium

Archives de l'Etat a Liege
79 Rue du Chera
4000 Liege, Belgium

Suzanna Byrne
The Old Vicarage
Stationsstraat 66
3580 Neerpelt
Belgium

Suzanna Byrne is an Irish-born adoptee who searched for and found her own birth mother. Since that time, she has let it be known that she is willing to assist other searchers who require assistance in either Belgium or Ireland.

Bulgaria

1. ADDRESS REQUESTS FOR VITAL RECORDS TO:
Executive Committee
People's Council
(name of town), Bulgaria

2. COMMENTS: Although Bulgaria has been notoriously uncooperative with our requests in the past, recent changes and upheaval in the government may increase access to records. Formal registrations did not begin until the late 1800s; however, many churches have records from before that time. At present, Bulgaria is separated into 26 districts, each of which has its own archives. Most major cities maintain separate archives and libraries, which could also be useful. Several are listed below:

Central Archives of Bulgaria
Ul. Slavjanska 4
1000 Sofia, Bulgaria

Military Historical Archives
Veliko Tarnovo
1000 Sofia, Bulgaria

Central Archives Administration
Alabin 58
1000 Sofia, Bulgaria

Sofia City Library
Ul. Gurko 1
1000 Sofia, Bulgaria

Cyril and Medodius National Library
Boul Tolbuhin 11
1504 Sofia, Bulgaria

Zentralno Statisticesko Upravlenie
Ul. Sesgi Septemvri 10
1000 Sofia, Bulgaria

Ivan Vazov National Library
N. Vapcarov 17
4000 Plovdiv, Bulgaria

Canada

The Canadian information is divided into several provinces: Alberta, British Columbia, Manitoba, New Brunswick, Newfoundland, Nova Scotia, Northwest Territories, Ontario, Prince Edward Island, Quebec, Saskatchewan, and the Yukon Territory.

ALBERTA

1. ADDRESS REQUESTS FOR VITAL RECORDS TO:
Division of Vital Statistics
P.O. Box 2023
Edmonton, Alberta
Canada T5J 4W7
(403) 427-2683

2. COST: Certified Birth Certificate $20 CAN
Certified Marriage Certificate $20 CAN
Certified Death Certificate $20 CAN

Make checks payable to the Provincial Treasurer.

3. COMMENTS: Birth records date back to 1853; marriage to 1898; death to 1893.

4. ADOPTION SEARCH:
Alberta Post Adoption Registry
9th Floor, Seventh St. Plaza
10030 107 Street
Edmonton, Alberta
Canada T5J 3E4
(403) 427-6387

Recent legislation allows adult adoptees access to their own birth name in full; however, not their original birth certificate. The 1995 legislation allows that adult adoptees can now have an active search done for them by a private agency, with a few between $250.00 to $1,000.00. Legislation in 1996 allows birth parents to search for their adult children and allows siblings to search for siblings who have been adopted.

BRITISH COLUMBIA

1. ADDRESS REQUESTS FOR VITAL RECORDS TO:
British Columbia Ministry of Health
Division of Vital Records
818 Fort Street
Victoria, British Columbia
Canada V8W 1H8
(604) 387-0041

2. COST: Certified Birth Certificate $27 CAN
Certified Marriage Certificate $27 CAN
Certified Death Certificate $27 CAN
Make checks payable to Dept. of Vital Statistics/British Columbia.

3. COMMENTS: Most vital records date back as far as 1870s.

4. ADOPTION SEARCH:
Reunion Registry operated by:
Family Services of Greater Vancouver
#202, 1600 West 6th Avenue
Vancouver, British Columbia
Canada V6J 1R3
(604) 736-7917
Will search on behalf of birth parents or adoptees, will also provide nonidentifying information to an adult involved party. Fees will be charged.

MANITOBA

1. ADDRESS REQUESTS FOR VITAL RECORDS TO:
Vital Statistics
254 Portage Avenue
Winnipeg, Manitoba
Canada R3C OB6
(204) 945-3701

2. COST: Certified Birth Certificate $18 CAN
Certified Marriage Certificate $18 CAN
Certified Death Certificate $18 CAN
Make checks payable to the Minister of Finance.

3. COMMENTS: Most records date back as far as 1882.

4. ADOPTION SEARCH:
Post Adoption Registry
Basement
270 Osborne Street North
Winnipeg, Manitoba
Canada R3C 1V7
(204) 945-8301
Will search on behalf of the adoptee. An adult involved party can register for contact and nonidentifying information. No fees apply.

NEW BRUNSWICK

1. ADDRESS REQUESTS FOR VITAL RECORDS TO:
Department of Health and Community Services
Division of Vital Statistics
Office of the Registrar General
P.O. Box 6000
Fredericton, New Brunswick
Canada E3B 5H1
(506) 453-2385

2. COST: Certified Birth Certificate $25 CAN (wallet sized, $20 CAN)
Certified Marriage Certificate $25 CAN (wallet sized, $20 CAN)
Certified Death Certificate $25 CAN (wallet sized, $20 CAN)
Make checks payable to Dept. of Vital Statistics/New Brunswick.

3. COMMENTS: Records date back as far as the 1880s. Persons wanting records from New Brunswick should contact the nearest Family History Center affiliated with the Church of Jesus Christ of Latter-Day Saints. They have extensively microfilmed records from this region.

4. ADOPTION SEARCH:
Post Adoption Services
Health and Community Services
P.O. Box 5100
Fredericton, New Brunswick
Canada E3B 5G8
(506) 453-2949

NEWFOUNDLAND

1. ADDRESS REQUESTS FOR VITAL RECORDS TO:
Vital Statistics Division
Dept. of Health
Confederation Building
St. John's, Newfoundland
Canada A1B 4J6
(709) 729-3308

2. COST: Certified Birth Certificate $10 CAN
Certified Marriage Certificate No fee
Certified Death Certificate No fee
Have records from 1892, anything prior to that year at Provincial Archives: (709) 729-3065.
Make checks payable to Dept. of Vital Statistics/Newfoundland.

3. COMMENTS: Records date back as far as the 1890s.

4. ADOPTION SEARCH:
Post Adoption Registry
Dept. of Social Services
3rd Floor, Confederations Bldg.
P.O. Box 8000
St. John's, Newfoundland
Canada A1B 4J6
(709) 729-2662

NOVA SCOTIA

1. ADDRESS REQUESTS FOR VITAL RECORDS TO:
Nova Scotia Department of Health
Deputy Registrar General
1723 Hollis Street
P.O. Box 157
Halifax, Nova Scotia
Canada B3J 2M9
(902) 424-8381

2. COST: Certified Birth Certificate $20 CAN
Certified Marriage Certificate $20 CAN
Certified Death Certificate $20 CAN
Make checks payable to Dept. of Vital Statistics/Nova Scotia.

3. COMMENTS: Records date back as far as 1907, depending on county. Persons wanting records from Nova Scotian cities should contact the nearest Family History Center affiliated with the Church of Jesus Christ of Latter-Day Saints. They have extensively microfilmed records from this region.

4. ADOPTION SEARCH:
Adoption Disclosure
Family and Children's Services
Dept. of Community Services
P.O. Box 696
Halifax, Nova Scotia
Canada B3J 2T7
(903) 424-3205

NORTHWEST TERRITORIES

1. ADDRESS REQUESTS FOR VITAL RECORDS TO:
Dept. of Safety and Public Service
Government Offices of the Northwest Territories
P.O. Box 1320
Yellowknife, Northwest Territories
Canada X1A 2L9
(403) 873-7404

2. COST: Certified Birth Certificate $10 CAN
Certified Marriage Certificate $10 CAN
Certified Death Certificate $10 CAN
Make checks payable to Government Offices of the Northwest Territories.

3. COMMENTS: Records date back as far as 1925.

4. ADOPTION SEARCH:
Family and Children's Services
Dept. of Social Services
Post Adoption Unit
Precambrian Bldg.
500,4920-52 Street
Yellowknife, Northwest Territories
Canada X1A 3T1
(403) 920-8920

ONTARIO

1. ADDRESS REQUESTS FOR VITAL RECORDS TO:
Office of the Registrar General
Parliament Building
Toronto, Ontario
Canada M7A 1Y5
(416) 965-1687

2. COST: Certified Birth Certificate $13 CAN
Certified Marriage Certificate $13 CAN
Certified Death Certificate $13 CAN
Make checks payable to Dept. of Vital Statistics/Ontario.

3. COMMENTS: Records date back as far as the 1860s. Use "genealogical research" as your reason for making a request. Persons wanting records from Ontario should contact the nearest Family History Center affiliated with the Church of Jesus Christ of Latter-Day Saints. They have extensively microfilmed records from this region.

4. ADOPTION SEARCH:
Management and Support Branch
Adoptions and Operational Services
Ministry of Community and Social Services
24th Floor, 2 Bloor Street West
Toronto, Ontario
Canada M7A 1E9
(416) 327-4730

PRINCE EDWARD ISLAND

1. ADDRESS REQUESTS FOR VITAL RECORDS TO:
Department of Health and Social Services
Prince Edward Island
Director of Vital Statistics
P.O. Box 2000
Charlottetown, Prince Edward Island
Canada C1A 7N8
(902) 368-4420

2. COST: Certified Birth Certificate $20 CAN
Certified Marriage Certificate $20 CAN
Certified Death Certificate $20 CAN
Make checks payable to the Minister of Finance.

3. COMMENTS: Records date back as far as the mid-1900s.

4. ADOPTION SEARCH:
Adoption Coordinator
Child and Family Services Division
Dept. of Health and Social Services
P.O. Box 2000
Charlottetown, Prince Edward Island
Canada C1A 7N8
(902) 368-4932

QUEBEC

1. ADDRESS REQUESTS FOR VITAL RECORDS TO:
Registre de Reference*
Ministere de la Justice
300 Boulevard, RC 20
Quebec (Quebec)
Canada G1K 8K6
(418) 649-3527

*Call for clarification of exact address to request document you need.

2. COST: Certified Birth Certificate $12 CAN
Certified Marriage Certificate $12 CAN
Certified Death Certificate $12 CAN
Make checks payable to Dept. of Vital Statistics/Quebec.

3. COMMENTS: Records date back as far as the mid 1920s. Records prior to 1888 are held at the Quebec National Archives Regional Offices. Records are also kept locally by churches and individual cities. You must fill out a Service Request Form with your request for information; they will not process your request without the form.

4. ADOPTION SEARCH:
CPEJ
Montreal Adoption Service
1001 De Maisonnuve Blvd. E.
Montreal, Quebec
Canada H2L 4R5
(514) 527-7261

SASKATCHEWAN

1. ADDRESS REQUESTS FOR VITAL RECORDS TO:
Dept. of Health
Province of Saskatchewan
Division of Vital Statistics
1919 Rose Street
Regina, Saskatchewan
Canada S4P 3V7
(306) 787-3092

2. COST: Certified Birth Certificate $20 CAN
Certified Marriage Certificate $20 CAN
Certified Death Certificate $20 CAN
Make checks payable to Department of Health.

3. COMMENTS: Records date back as far as the 1880s.

4. ADOPTION SEARCH:
Post Adoption Registry
Saskatchewan Social Services
#207, 2240 Albert Street
Regina, Saskatchewan
Canada S4P 3V7
(306) 787-3654

YUKON

1. ADDRESS REQUESTS FOR VITAL RECORDS TO:
Division of Vital Statistics
Yukon Health and Human Resources
P.O. Box 2703
Whitehorse, Yukon
Canada Y1A 2C6
(403) 667-5207; (403) 668-3786(fax service)

2. COST: Certified Birth Certificate $10 CAN
Certified Marriage Certificate $10 CAN
Certified Death Certificate $10 CAN
Make checks payable to Dept. of Vital Statistics/Yukon.

3. COMMENTS: Records date back as far as the late 1890s.

4. ADOPTION SEARCH:
Dept. of Health and Social Services
Family and Children's Services
P.O. Box 2703
Whitehorse, Yukon
Canada Y1A 2C6

Denmark

1. ADDRESS REQUESTS FOR VITAL RECORDS TO:
Reverend
Lutheran Church
(name of town), Denmark

2. COMMENTS: The vast majority of vital records are held by local Lutheran churches, libraries, and archives throughout Denmark. There is no national records center. An alternative that may be faster for most Americans will be the Church of Jesus Christ of Latter-Day Saints and their Family History Centers. Many of Denmark's vital records have been microfilmed by this organization and are available for viewing upon request. Persons interested in following this route should contact the closest LDS church and inquire about the nearest Family History Center.
Major sources of information for Denmark are:
Lutheran parish registers (Kirkeboger)
Census returns (Folketallinger)
Probate records (Skifteprotokoller)
Military service records (Stamboger) at Haerens Archives, Copenhagen, Denmark

Court records (Tingboger Eller Retsprotokoller) at provincial and local archives
Deeds and mortgage records (Skode and Panteprotokoller) at provincial and local archives
Emigration records (Udvandringsjournaler) at provincial archive for Sjaelland
Passport records (Pasprotokoller) at provincial archives
Land registration records (land Matrikler) at national, provincial, and local archives
Death certificates (Dodeblade) at provincial archives, and in Copenhagen
Records of domestics (Tyendeprotokoller) at provincial archives
School records (Skoleprotokoller) at provincial archives and schools
Trade licenses (Raadstue og Borgerskabsprotokoller) at city archives

Vital records (Civile Registre):
Civil marriages (Borgerlige Vielser) at city and provincial archives
Death certificates (Dodsattester) at provincial archives
Civil registration (Personregistre) at provincial archives in Aabenraa
General registration (Folkregister) at local registration offices

The best source of information (the most complete) is the general registration (Folkregister) at local registration offices.

Most large cities in Denmark also maintain libraries and archives which may be of additional assistance. A few are listed below:

Danish National Archives
Rigsarkivets Bibliotek
9 Rigsdagsgarden
1218 Copenhagen K, Denmark

Copenhagen Archives
Kobenhavns Stadsarkiv
Radhuset
DK-1599 Copenhagen V, Denmark

Frederiksberg Komunes Biblioteker
Solbjergvej 21-25
2000 Frederiksberg, Denmark

Landsarkivet for de sonderjyske Landsdele
45 Harderslevvej
DK 6200 Abenra, Denmark

Landsarkivet for Fyn
Jernbanegade 35
DK 5000 Odense C, Denmark

Danish World Archives
Ved Vor Frue Kirke
P.O. Box 1731
9100 Aalborg, Denmark

Danish National Library
Det Kongelige Bibliotek
P.O. Box 2149
1016 Copenhagen K, Denmark

Nordjyske Landsbibliotek
P.O. Box 839
9100 Aalborg, Denmark

Copenhagen Public Library
Kobenhavns Komunes Biblioteker
Kultorvet 2
DK-1175 Copenhagen K, Denmark

Esbjerg Kommunes Hovedbibliotek
P.O. Box 69
6701 Esbjerg, Denmark

Finland

1. ADDRESS REQUESTS FOR VITAL RECORDS TO:

Nationally: Population Register Center
PL-7
SF-00521 Helsinki, Finland
(011) (358) (0) 189-3909

Locally: Reverend
Lutheran Church
(name of town), Finland

2. COMMENTS: People searching for vital records in Finland have three things going for them. The first is that Finland maintains very good records of its citizens, emigrants, and immigrants—oftentimes dating back to the late 1600s. The second is that the vast majority of vital records registered since the turn of the century are with the Lutheran Church. Even though most local churches will have these records, copies have also been forwarded on to the Population Register Center in Helsinki. Records can be requested on both levels if necessary.

The Church of Jesus Christ of Latter-Day Saints here in the United States has microfilmed most of the vital records and religious registries. You should contact your closest LDS church and inquire about the location of the nearest Family History Center.

Many of Finland's larger cities also maintain their own libraries and archives. A few are listed below:

Genealogical Society of Finland
Suomen Sukututkimussenuran Kirjasto
Mariank 7C
00170 Helsinki, Finland

National Library
Helsingin Yliopisto Kirjasto
Unioninkatu 36
P.O. Box 36
00171 Helsinki, Finland

Oulun Maakunta—Arkisto
P.O. Box 31
90101 Oulu, Finland

Helsingin Kaupunginarkiston
Toinen Linja 4F
00530 Helsinki, Finland

National Archives
Valtionarkiston Kirjasto
P.O. Box 258
00171 Helsinki, Finland

Vassan Maakunta-Arkisto
Raastuvank 1A
PL 240
65101 Vassa, Finland

France

1. ADDRESS REQUESTS FOR VITAL RECORDS TO:
Le Mairie
(name of town), France

2. COMMENTS: Persons wanting to obtain vital records from France will need to write to the mayor of the town where the event happened; no central national registry exists. Most records date back to the late 1700s, and some religious records date back even further. The most helpful sources of information is the Civil Registration (comparable to Vital Records in the U.S.). However, in order to protect the privacy of living persons, records for the last hundred years are considered to be confidential and have restrictions on use and access.

The Church of Jesus Christ of Latter-Day Saints' Family History Library has many telephone directories of France, from about 1980 to the present. Each directory covers a specific area, with each town listed separately, showing people's names in alphabetical order. In addition, it is important to note that the Family History Library has more than 100,000 microfilms/microfiche files, which contain records of people who have lived in France. These records include birth, marriage, and death records from churches and civil officials, passport applications, border crossings, passenger lists, notarial records, and private and genealogical collections.

Minitel is a French online computer network service connected by telephone lines. Minitel includes several databases and services including telephone directories. For more information contact:

Minitel Services Company
888 Seventh Ave., 28th Floor
New York, NY 10106-1301
(212) 399-0080

In addition, France maintains a national archives and library that can be useful. Both are listed below. Most cities and towns in France also have their own local libraries and archives which are each controlled centrally. The fastest way to narrow down your search is to contact them directly, to determine which libraries/archives will be the most helpful in your particular case.

French National Library
Bibliotheque Nationale
58 rue Richelieu
75084 Paris, France

French National Archives
Archives Nationales
60 rue des Frances-Bourgeois
75141 Paris, France

Central Archival Authority
Direction des Archives de France
60 rue des Frances-Bourgeois
75141 Paris, France

Central Library Authority
Direction des Bibliotheques
3-5 Blvd Pasteur
75015 Paris, France

Germany

1. ADDRESS REQUESTS FOR VITAL RECORDS TO:
Standesamt
(name of town), Germany

2. COMMENTS: Germany opened adoption records to adoptees age 16 or older in 1977. The social structure of Germany makes searching easy since the population tends to be less mobile than that of the U.S. The following are German branches of the Red Cross and International Social Services. Since adoption records are open, they will be able to provide assistance.

Frau Ingrid Baer, Direktorin
Internationaler Sozialdienst Deutscher Zweig e.V.
Am Stockborn 5-7
D-6000 Frankfurt/Main 50
Germany

Deutsches Rotes Kreuz
Generalsekretariat
Suchdienst Muenchen
Zentrale Auskunfts-und Dokumentationsstelle
Infanteriestrasse 7A
D-8000 Muenchen 40
Germany

As an adoptee born in Germany looking for a birth parent, your records in Germany are open to your inspection. These records are normally complete and give a great deal of information about the birth parents and their families. Since there was no central vital records agency in either of the Germanys before reunification, you will have to write to the town where you were born to request these records.

Your birth certificate and/or immigration papers should point you in the right direction.

Modern telephone directories, with over 32 million addresses and telephone numbers, are now available for all of Germany on CD-ROM. For more information, contact:

IBS America, Inc
Re: "Tel-info"
P.O. Box 684
Marblehead, MA 01945-0648

German-born adoptees and/or German or American birth parents with German-born children will find great assistance by contacting:

Leonie D. Boehmer
805 Alvarado, N.E.
Albuquerque, NM 87108
(505) 268-1310

Both Germanys have adhered to a system of personal identity cards since the early 1900s. Most of these records can be obtained from local churches and from the system of libraries and archives that exist throughout the country listed below:

Historic Emigration Office
Museum fur Hamburgische Geschichte
Holstenwall 24
2000 Hamburg 36, Federal Republic of Germany

National Library
Deutsche Staatsbibliothek
Postfach 1312
1086 Berlin, German Democratic Republic

Stadtarchiv Dresden
Archivstr. 14
Dresden, German Democratic Republic

Archenhold Sternwarte
Alt-Treptow 1
1193 Berlin, German Democratic Republic

Staatsbibliothek Preussischer Kulturbesitz
Postfach 1407
1000 Berlin 30, Federal Republic of Germany

Stadtarchiv Berlin
Postfach 660
Berlin, German Democratic Republic

Deutsch Staatsbibliothek
Postfach 1312
1086 Berlin, German Democratic Republic

Stadtarchiv und Wissenschalftliche Stadbibliothek
Stadtverwaltung
5300 Bonn, Federal Republic of Germany

Greece

1. ADDRESS REQUESTS FOR VITAL RECORDS TO:

Civil Registration Office—Registrar
(name of town), Greece

2. COMMENTS: Most local civil registry offices keep records back to the 1920s, and churches usually even further. In addition to writing locally, you can also contact the Greek National Library at the following address:

National Library
Odos El Venizelu 32
1106-79 Athens, Greece

Hungary

1. ADDRESS REQUESTS FOR VITAL RECORDS TO:

Locally: Civil Registration Office
(name of town), Hungary

Nationally: National Office of Personal Registration
H-Budapest PF 81
1450 Hungary

2. COMMENTS: A national identity card system is maintained by the National Office of Personal Registration. Since there is no central office for vital records, you must write to the Civil Registration District Office in the town where you wish to obtain copies of birth, marriage, or death certificates. Files with vital records date back to the late 1800s, and are available from the local parish church. Every large city in Hungary has many archives and libraries that prove to be of great value to researchers. Listed below are just a few of the main archives and libraries:

National Board of Archives
Muvelodesi Miniszterium Leveltari
Uri u. 54-56
1014 Budapest, Hungary

National Library
PF 10
1525 Budapest, Hungary

Hungarian National Archives
Magyar Orszagos Leveltar
Becsikapu-ter 4
PF 8
1250 Budapest, Hungary

Orszagos Szechenyi Konyvtar
Budavari Palota F-epult
1827 Budapest, Hungary

Central Statistical Office
Kozponti Statisztikai Hivatal
Kelenti Kaoly u 5

Budapest City Archives
Budapest Fovaros Leveltar
Varshaz u. 9/11
1052 Budapest, Hungary

Gorky Stat Library
Allami Gorkij KonyvtarMolnar u. 11
1056 Budapest, Hungary

You may also find help by contacting the following:

American Hungarian Library and Historical Society
215 East 82 St.
New York, NY 10028
(212) 744-5298

Hungarian Reformed Federation of America
2001 Massachusetts Avenue NW
Washington, DC 20036-1011

Hungarian Research Library, Kossuth Foundation
Butler University
Indianapolis, IN 46208
(317) 283-9225

Iceland

1. ADDRESS REQUESTS FOR VITAL RECORDS TO:
The Statistical Bureau of Iceland
Althyduhusid
Hverfisgata 8-10
101 Reykjavik, Iceland
(011) (354) (1) 266-99

2. COMMENTS: A national card identity system is maintained by the Statistical Bureau of Iceland on all residents dating from 1953. Records prior to this date were kept by the local church, usually Lutheran. Most of the church records will date as far back as the late 1700s. There is no charge for obtaining a copy of birth, marriage, or death certificates. Listed below are addresses for a few of the key libraries and archives in Iceland:

National Library of Iceland Landsbokasafin Islands
P.O. Box 210
121 Reykjavik, Iceland

National Archives of Iceland
Thjodskjalasafu Islands
P.O. Box 313
121 Reykjavik, Iceland

Reykjavik City Archives
Borgarbokasafn Reykjavikur
Thingholtsstraeti 29-A
101 Reykjavik, Iceland

Ireland

1. ADDRESS REQUESTS FOR VITAL RECORDS TO:
Office of the General Registrar
Joyce House
8-11 Lombard Street East
Dublin 2, Ireland
(011) (353) 1-711-000

2. COST: Certified Birth Certificate $6.50 IRE
Certified Marriage Certificate $6.50 IRE
Certified Death Certificate $6.50 IRE

3. COMMENTS: Records date back as far as the 1840s. When requesting records that originated in Dublin, address your letter to the Superintendent Registrar at the above address. Persons wanting records from Ireland should contact the nearest Family History Center (here in the U.S.) affiliated with the Church of Jesus Christ of Latter-Day Saints. They have extensively microfilmed records from this region. Of special interest is the Register of Ireland General Registry Office Birth, Marriages and Deaths, 1845–1959.

NORCAP, the National Organization for the Counseling of Adoptees and Birth Parents, is a registered charitable group, and as such, they offer search advice and assistance to persons seeking to be reunited in the United Kingdom, including Northern Ireland and Ireland.

Among the services NORCAP offers are: (1) Recordscan—a service available to members who cannot conduct records research themselves, (2) a quarterly newsletter, and (3) a professional, not-for-profit intermediary service. Membership in NORCAP is required to obtain assistance. Annual membership costs vary depending on each individual's needs. For further information, contact:

England and Ireland Search Help
M. Catherine O'Dea
P.O. Box 360074
Cleveland, OH 44136

Other helpful resource persons are:

Conor MacHale (excellent researcher with easy access to the General Registry in Dublin)
Tireragh
30 Lakelands Drive
Stillorgan
Co. Dublin
Republic of Ireland

Dick Spring (of special interest to Irish-U.S. adoptees)
TD Minister/Tanaiste
Dept. of Foreign Affairs
80 St Stephen's Green
Dublin 2, Republic of Ireland

Sister Santo (of special interest to Sacred Heart Adoption Society persons)
Sacred Heart Convent
Balckrock
County Cork
Republic of Ireland

Italy

1. ADDRESS REQUESTS FOR VITAL RECORDS TO:
Ufficio di Stato Civile
(name of town)

2. COMMENTS: Italy has no central office for vital records. You must contact the town where the event occurred in order to obtain copies of birth, marriage, or death certificates. Most of the towns kept records from the early 1800s, but more generally available are those from the mid-1800s to the present. Every large city and state in Italy has many libraries and archives that have valuable information for the researcher in them. Listed below are just a few of the main libraries and archives:

Archivio di Stato di Genova
Via Tommaso Reggio 14
16123 Genoa, Italy

Biblioteca Nazionale Centrale
Vittorio Emanuele II
National Central Library
Viale Castro Pretorio 105
00185 Rome, Italy

Archivio di Stato di Macerata
Piazza Guidiccioni 2
55100 Lucca, Italy

Archivio di Stato di Verona
Via Franceschine 2
37100 Verona, Italy

Archivio di Stato di Salerno
Piazza Abate Conforti 7
84100 Salerno, Italy

Archivio Centrale dello Stato
Italian Central Archives
Piazzale degle Archiv
00144 Rome, Italy

The Netherlands

1. ADDRESS REQUESTS FOR VITAL RECORDS TO:
Office of Civil Registration
(name of town), The Netherlands

2. COMMENTS: While there is no central vital statistics agency for The Netherlands, most local Civil Registration Offices have records extending back to the early 1800s. You may also want to write the National Archives and Provincial Libraries listed below:

National Library
Koninklijke Bibliotheek
Postbus 90407
The Hague, The Netherlands

Provinciale Bibliotheek Central Limburg
Godweerdersingel 34
6041 CX Roermond, The Netherlands

Provinciale Bibliotheek
Centrale Groningen
Postbus 2503
9704 CM Groningen, The Netherlands

Provinciale Bibliotheek Centrale
Overijssel Oost.
Postbus 72
7620 AB Borne, The Netherlands

Provinciale Bibliotheek van Friesland
Postbus 464
8901 BG Leeuwarden, The Netherlands

Rijkarchief in de Provincie Noord Brabant
Zuid Willemsvaart 2
5211 NW's Hertogenbosch, The Netherlands

National Archives
Algemeen Rijksarchief
Prins Willem Alexanderhof 20
The Hague, The Netherlands

Provinciale Bibliotheek Centrale
Zuid Holland
Westfrankelandsedijk 1
3115 HG Schiedam, The Netherlands

Provinciale Bibliotheek Centrale
Noord Holland
Hofplein 1
1811 LE Alkmaar, The Netherlands

Stichting Provinciale Bibliotheek
Centrale Gelderland
Zeelandsingel 40
Postbus 9052
6800 GR Assen, The Netherlands

Provinciale Bibliotheek Centrale Drenthe
Postbus 78
9400 AB Assen, The Netherlands

New Zealand

1. ADDRESS REQUESTS FOR VITAL RECORDS TO:

Registrar General's Office
Levin House
330 High Street
P.O. Box 3115
Lower Hutt, Wellington, New Zealand

2. COST: Certified Birth Record $16NZ
Certified Marriage Record $16NZ
Certified Death Record $16 NZ

3. COMMENTS: If the records being searched date from the mid-1800s up to 1920, a faster way to search is to contact your closest Church of Jesus Christ of Latter-Day Saints here in the U.S., and inquire as to the nearest Family History Center. They have almost all birth and death records between these times on microfilm and are always expanding their collection.

In 1985, the New Zealand Parliament passed the Adult Adoption Information Act of 1985. This legislation opened previously closed adoption records of the New Zealand Department of Social Welfare to adult adoptees and their birth parents. A report written for the New South Wales Standing Committee on Social Issues by Mary Iwanek, a locally renowned and well-regarded social work professional in the field of adoption/reunions, summarized the Act.

Ms. Iwanek observed:

> In passing the Adult Adoption Information Act of 1985, Parliament has accepted the view that adoption practice in the past had been premised on false assumptions, particularly relating to the myth of rebirth and birth mothers being able to forget and make a new start.
>
> It accepted that society has a responsibility to adopted people and birth parents to provide identifying information which would enable all parties involved to find peace of mind and resolution of internal conflicts.

The act provides that any adoptee aged 20 years or older, or any birth parents of such an adult adoptee, may make an application to the New Zealand Department of Social Welfare for any identifying information kept in their files.

In order to protect the privacy of those affected by passage of this act, a "veto" system was also implemented. Either party can request that no identifying information be released. A veto can be filed at any time and remains in effect for ten years. It can also be rescinded at will.

If no veto has been filed, the act directs the department to locate the adoptee, make the birth parent's request known to them, and obtain their permission to release information. It also specifies that the adoptee, and not the adoptive parents, should be contacted.

Furthermore, this legislation mandates that all adoptee applicants be counseled by an authorized social worker. This compulsory counseling may be in person, over the telephone, or by written correspondence—at the adoptee's option.

Specific vital record request forms have been provided. It is recommended that anyone wishing to open their records first contact:

Mary Iwanek
Dept. of Sociology and Social Work
Victoria University of Wellington
P.O. Box 600
Wellington, New Zealand

Norway

1. ADDRESS REQUESTS FOR VITAL RECORDS TO:

Locally: Reverend
Lutheran Church
(name of town)

Local Office of the Population Register
(name of town)

Nationally: The Central Office of the Population Register
P.O. Box 8131
0033 Oslo, Norway

2. COMMENTS: The local churches carry out a civil registration of members of their church. For those who are not members of the state church, civil registration is done by the local Office of Population Register. Church registers may be traced as far back as the late 1600s, while civil registration for births and deaths date only as far back as 1915, marriages from 1918. Churches and local registers send information to the Central Office of the Population Register for statistical purposes. You may also obtain information from the National Archives, and the National Library, both listed below:

The National Library:

Universitetsbiblioteket
og Nasjonalbiblioteket
Drammensvn 42
0255 Oslo, 8 Norway

The National Archives:

Riksarkivet
Folke Bernadottes vei 21
Postboks 10 Kringsja
N-0807 Oslo, 8 Norway

Poland

1. ADDRESS REQUESTS FOR VITAL RECORDS TO:

Office of Civil Registration
(name of town), Poland

2. COMMENTS: While there is no central vital statistics agency, most local civil registration offices have records extending back to the mid-1900s. Individual church records usually go back even further. You may also want to write the Polish National Archives and provincial libraries listed below:

National Library
Biblioteka Narodowa
Hankiewicza 1
00 973 Warsaw, Poland

National Archives
Naczelna Dyrekcja
Archiwow Panstowowych
U1 Dluga 6
SKR Poczt 1005
00 950 Warsaw, Poland

Biblioteka Slaska
U1 Francuska 12, 529
40-956 Katowice, Poland

Central Statistical Office
A1 Niepodleglosci 208
00-925 Warsaw, Poland

Portugal

1. ADDRESS REQUESTS FOR VITAL RECORDS TO:

Los Registros Civiles
(name of town), Portugal

2. COMMENTS: You'll have to write to the town where the event took place to get a copy of a vital record, since no national agency exists. Most records date back to the turn of the century, although you should be aware that these records are not one hundred percent complete. Here are some additional sources that may be of assistance:

Portuguese National Library
Biblioteca Nacional
Ocidental do Campo Grande, 83
1751 Lisbon, Portugal

Arquivo Distrital de Porto
Praca da Republica, 38
4000 Porto, Portugal

Biblioteca Publica e Arquivo Distrital
Largo Conde de Vila Flor
7000 Evora, Portugal

Biblioteca Publica e Arquivo Distrital
Governo Regional dos Acores
Rua Ernesto de Canto
9500 Ponta Delgada,
Acores Portugal

Arquivo Distrital de Viseu
Largo de Santa Cristina
3500 Viseu, Portugal

Biblioteca Publica e Arquivo Distrital
Largo da Republica
2400 Leiria, Portugal

Biblioteca Publica e Arquivo de
Angra do Heroismo
Rua da Rosa 49
9700 Angra do Heroismo
Acores, Portugal

Arquivo Distrital de Guarda
Rua de Batalha Reis
6300 Guarda, Portugal

Arquivo Distrital de Setubal
Rua de Dama Braga 15
2900 Setubal, Portugal

Arquivo Distrital de Aveiro
Praca da Republica
3800 Aveiro, Portugal

Romania

1. ADDRESS REQUESTS FOR VITAL RECORDS TO:

Office of Civil Registration
(name of town), Romania

2. COMMENTS: Unfortunately Romania has no central vital statistics agency; however, most district civil registration offices have records back to the 1860s. As in many European countries, individual church records may extend further back. You may also want to try the Romanian National Archives and Library listed below:

National Archives
Arhivele Statululi
b-dul Gheorghe Gheorghiu-Dej 29
Bucharest, Romania

National Library
Biblioteca Centrala de Stat
Str lon Ghica 4
Bucharest, Romania

South Africa

1. ADDRESS REQUESTS FOR VITAL RECORDS TO:

Registration Office
Department of Home Affairs
Cape Town, Republic of South Africa
(011) (2721) 211-000

2. COMMENTS: The above office has most records since the mid-1920s. At the present time, there is no charge for this service. However, since they can and often do refuse these kinds of requests, the following is recommended.

The Church of Jesus Christ of Latter-Day Saints has extensively microfilmed birth, marriage, and death records for many parts of South Africa. It is recommended that people searching there should contact their nearest LDS church here in the U.S. and inquire as to the nearest Family History Center. They may be able to provide you with the information you need on a local basis.

Spain

1. ADDRESS REQUESTS FOR VITAL RECORDS TO:

Registros Civiles
(name of town), Spain

2. COMMENTS: Fortunately, Spanish records are fairly extensive and complete. While there is no central vital statistics agency, most local Civil Registration Offices have records extending back to the late 1800s. Also, there is a national identity card system that all residents are required to use beginning at the age of 14. You may also want to write the Spanish National Archives and Provincial Libraries listed below.

National Library
Bibliotec Nacional
Paseo de Recoletos—20
28001 Madrid, Spain

Barcelona Provincial Library
Archivo General de la Diputacion
Pza Sant Jaume
08002 Barcelona, Spain

Seville City Archives
Archivo Municipal de Sevilla
Pza. Nueva 1
41001 Seville, Spain

National Archives
Archivo Historico Nacional
Serrno 115
28006 Madrid, Spain

Cordoba Provincial Archives
Archivo Historico Provincial
Pompeyos 6
14003 Cordoba, Spain

Salamanca Provincial Archives
Archivo Historio Provincial de Salamanca
Patio Escuelas 1
37008 Salamanca, Spain

Victoria City Archive
Archivo Bibliotec Municipal de Victoria
Ayuntamiento de Victoria General Alna 26
01005 Victoria—Gasteiz Alna
Spain

Pamplon Provincial Archives
Archivo Realy General de Navarra Av.
San Ignacio 1
31002 Pamplona, Spain

Sweden

ADDRESS REQUESTS FOR VITAL RECORDS TO:

County Registrar
County Administration
(county seat, county), Sweden

This form of record-keeping came into being only in 1947. Before that, all records were kept by the church. In Sweden, an overwhelming percentage of the population is Lutheran, and so the Lutheran churches should have records for just about everyone who has ever lived in Sweden or is Swedish.

If the person you're looking for was in Sweden before 1947, you'll need to go to the appropriate church. And even if the person was in Sweden after 1947, the church will still be a good place to turn—despite the introduction of county registrars, the Lutheran church is still keeping accurate and comprehensive parish records. Most churches have records dating back as far as the late 1600s.

To write to a Lutheran church in Sweden for local vital statistic records, you should address your request to the reverend of the local church in the town where the event took place. Sweden is broken up into 227 towns in 24 counties. A "pastorate" is made of two or three parishes. Where the vicar resides is called the *moderforsamling* (mother parish) and the other parishes in the pastorate are called the *annexforsamling* (annes parishes). Occasionally the records are kept together for the whole pastorate, so check the main parish first. You may want to contact the Swedish embassy or consulate for assistance in locating parishes, or contact the National Library:

National Library
Kungliga Biblioteket
Box 5039
102-41 Stockholm, Sweden

Parish records contain a wealth of information and will most prove helpful in your search. They include dates of birth and christenings, marriage records, death and burial records, arrivals and removals, catechism dates, communion dates, confirmation dates, household examination rolls (in other words, a census for the county), and church accounts. Parish records should provide you with a full legal name, a date of birth, the names of the person's parents, a place of residence, occupation, listings of legitimate and illegitimate births, names of witnesses to marriages, and other valuable information.

Without leaving the States, you can visit your local Family History Center and inquire about Swedish records. Most FHCs will have microfilm containing Swedish records—

there are over 80,000 rolls of microfilm available! It is recommended that people searching Swedish records contact their nearest Church of Jesus Christ of the Latter-Day Saints here in the U.S. and inquire as to the nearest Family History Center. They may be able to provide you with the information you need on a local basis.

Switzerland

ADDRESS REQUESTS FOR VITAL RECORDS TO:

Office of Civil Registration
(name of town), Switzerland

While there is no central vital statistics agency in Switzerland, most local civil registration offices have records extending back to the late 1800s. Individual church records usually go back even further. You may also want to write to the Swiss National Archives and provincial libraries listed below:

National Library
Schweizerische Landesbibliothek
Hallwylstr. 15
3003 Bern, Switzerland

Zurich Archives
Staatsarchiv des Kantons Zurich
Winterhurestr. 170
8057 Zurich, Switzerland

Zurich Central Library
Zentralbibliothek Zurich
Zahringerplatz 6
8025 Zurich, Switzerland

National Archives
Schweizerisches Bundesarchiv
Archivstr. 4
3012 Bern, Switzerland

Geneva Archives
Archives de l'Etat
1 rue de l'Hotel de Ville
1211 Geneva 3, Switzerland

Bern City Archives
Staatsarchiv des Kantons Bern
Falkenplatz 4
3012 Bern, Switzerland

United Kingdom

Information on the U.K. varies, from England and Wales, to Northern Ireland, to Scotland.

ENGLAND AND WALES

1. ADDRESS REQUESTS FOR VITAL RECORDS TO:

Office of the General Registrar
Smedley Hydro
Southport
Merseyside PR8 2HH, England

2. COST: Certified Birth Certificate 15 pounds
Certified Marriage Certificate 15 pounds
Certified Death Certificate 15 pounds

3. COMMENTS: Records date back as far as the 1830s. Persons wanting records from England or Wales should contact the nearest Family History Center affiliated with the Church of Jesus Christ of Latter-Day Saints. They have extensively microfilmed records from this region.

Adoption records in the U.K. were opened to adult adoptees in the 1970s. The National Organization for the Counseling of Adoptees and Birth Parents (NORCAP) is a registered charitable group in Great Britain. As such, they offer search advice and assistance to persons seeking to be reunited in the U.K.

Among the services NORCAP offers: (1) Recordscan—a service available to members who cannot conduct records research themselves (2) a quarterly newsletter and (3) a professional, not-for-profit intermediary service.

Membership in NORCAP is required to obtain assistance. Annual membership costs vary depending on each individual's needs. Those wishing assistance should contact:

(In the U.S.)

England and Ireland Search Help
M. Catherine O'Dea
P.O. Box 360074
Cleveland, OH 44136

(In the U.K.)

Pamela Hodgkins
3 New High St.
Headington, Oxford
OX35AJ England

NORTHERN IRELAND

1. ADDRESS REQUESTS FOR VITAL RECORDS TO:

Department of Health and Social Services
Office of the General Registrar
Oxford House
49-55 Chichester Street
Belfast, BT1 4HL
Northern Ireland
(011) (44) 232-235211

2. COST: Certified Birth Certificate 4.50 pounds
Certified Marriage Certificate 4.50 pounds
Certified Death Certificate 4.50 pounds

3. COMMENTS: Records date back as far as the 1860s. Persons wanting records from Northern Ireland should contact the nearest Family History Center affiliated with the

Church of Jesus Christ of Latter-Day Saints. They have extensively microfilmed records from this region.

SCOTLAND

1. ADDRESS REQUESTS FOR VITAL RECORDS TO:
Scotland Office of General Registrar
New Register House
Edinburgh, EH1 3YT
Scotland

2. COST: Certified Birth Certificate 10 pounds
Certified Marriage Certificate 10 pounds
Certified Death Certificate 10 pounds

3. COMMENTS: Records date back as far as the 1850s. Persons wanting records from Scotland should contact the nearest Family History Center affiliated with the Church of Jesus Christ of Latter-Day Saints. They have extensively microfilmed records from this region.
War Babes is another group that helps searchers in the U.K. In November 1990, a lawsuit was brought in the U.S. by this group against the National Personnel Records Center in St. Louis, Missouri. The terms of this settlement now permit the son or daughter of an American serviceman (whether the offspring was British or American) to try to locate his or her father using records kept at the NPRC under the provisions of the Freedom of Information Act. Persons wishing assistance should contact:
War Babes
15 Plough Avenue
South Woodgate
Birmingham, B323TQ
England

Virgin Islands

The records are broken down by island:

ST. CROIX

1. ADDRESS REQUESTS FOR VITAL RECORDS TO:
Birth and Death Records
Dept. of Health—Virgin Islands
Office of the Registrar of Vital Statistics
P.O. Box 520
Christiansted, St. Croix
Virgin Islands 00820
(809) 773-4050

Marriage Records
Territorial Court of the Virgin Islands
Chief Deputy Clerk
P.O. Box 929
St. Croix, Virgin Islands 00820
(809) 778-3350

2. COST: Certified Birth Certificate $7
Certified Marriage Certificate $7
Certified Death Certificate $7

3. COMMENTS: Records date back as far as 1919.

ST. THOMAS AND ST. JOHN

1. ADDRESS REQUESTS FOR VITAL RECORDS TO:
Birth and Death Records
Dept. of Health—Virgin Islands
Office of the Registrar of Vital Statistics
St. Thomas, Virgin Islands 00802
(809) 774-1734

Marriage Records
Territorial Court of the Virgin Islands
Court Clerk
P.O. Box 70
Charlotte Amalie, St. Thomas
Virgin Islands 00801
(809) 774-6680

2. COST: Certified Birth Certificate $7
Certified Marriage Certificate $5
Certified Death Certificate $7

3. COMMENTS: Records date back as far as 1906.

A P P E N D I X 4

Missing and Abducted Children

There is nothing more tragic than having your child missing, and fearing that he or she has been abducted. If this has happened to you, you have our deepest sympathies.

There is an excellent resource for locating missing and abducted children:

National Center for Missing and Exploited Children
National Headquarters
2101 Wilson Blvd., Suite 550
Arlington, VA 22201
1-800-843-5678
1-800-THE LOST

The National Center for Missing and Exploited Children is a large resource center that fights child abduction in a variety of ways. Mandated by Congress, the NCMEC works closely with the U.S. Department of Justice (specifically, with the justice department's Office of Juvenile Justice and Delinquency Prevention). The NCMEC makes information about missing children public, and tries to raise the country's awareness of the ongoing problem of child abduction. The organization has created a hotline for missing children, which is available nationally. They train police officers and other professionals, teaching them how to be effective in this sensitive area.

What can they do for you? The National Center for Missing and Exploited Children will give you the names of local agencies that can help you, as well as local support groups. They can also supply you with a wealth of helpful publications on the subject, and if you give them a photo of the child they will disseminate it.

If the child was abducted by a stranger, or if the child is a runaway, you must file a missing child report with the local police department. If your child was abducted by a family member, you still have to file a missing child report with the local police department, but you will also need to provide proof of legal custody.

The Internet can be helpful when a child is missing or abducted. We've provided a lot of information on the Web sites available, which you'll find on page 196 "Searching for Abducted Children and Missing Persons."

The majority of abducted children are taken by their noncustodial parent. You may find that all you need to do is contact the powerful databases listed elsewhere in this book (in Chapter Eleven, "Registries and Databases," and Chapter Twelve), and do a search for the name of the noncustodial parent. When you find that parent, often you will have found your child.

Index